The Effective Republic

The Effective Republic

Administration and Constitution

in the Thought of Alexander Hamilton

Harvey Flaumenhaft

Duke University Press   *Durham and London 1992*

*This book is dedicated
to my mother,
Fay Flaumenhaft,
and to the memory
of my father,
Louis Flaumenhaft,
and of my teacher,
Herbert J. Storing*

Contents

Acknowledgments

A generous grant from the National Endowment for the Humanities supported my completion of the final version of this book.

Adaptations of parts of an earlier version appeared in the following publications:

Review of Gerald Stourzh's *Alexander Hamilton and the Idea of Republican Government*, in *The American Political Science Review* 67 (June 1973): 637–39;

"Alexander Hamilton on the Foundation of Good Government," *The Political Science Reviewer* 6 (Bicentennial Issue: Fall 1976): 143–214;

"Hamilton's Administrative Republic and the American Presidency," in *The Presidency in the Constitutional Order*, edited by Joseph M. Bessette and Jeffrey Tulis (Baton Rouge: Louisiana State University Press, 1981), pp. 65–112;

"Americanism Abroad," in *Constitutionalism in Perspective*, edited by Sarah Baumgartner Thurow (Lanham, Md.: University Press of America, 1988), pp. 240–51.

I am grateful for permission to reprint from those publications. The following papers also presented earlier versions of parts of this book:

"Alexander Hamilton on the Administration of Liberty," presented to a panel on "American Liberty: The Problematic Character of a Founding Concept," at the Annual Meeting of the Northeastern Political Science Association, Mount Pocono, Pennsylvania, 10–12 November 1977;

"The Administrative Republic of Alexander Hamilton," presented to a conference on "Alexander Hamilton's Contribution to the American Presidency: A Model for Our Time?" at the White Burkett Miller Center of Public Affairs, University of Virginia, 4–5 April 1978;

"A Place for Duration in the Republic: Hamilton on the Senate," presented to a panel of the Claremont Institute for the Study of Statesmanship and Political Philosophy, at the Annual Meeting of the American Political Science Association, Washington, D.C., 30 August 1984.

I am most obliged to those to whom this book is dedicated—my parents, Fay Flaumenhaft and the late Louis Flaumenhaft, to both of whom I owe more than I can say, and the late Herbert J. Storing, whose delightful classes at the University of Chicago introduced me to the study of the American founding. I am also much obliged, for instruction and assistance at various times in my career, to Joseph Cropsey, Robert A. Goldwin, and the late Morton Grodzins. Jeffrey D. Wallin was helpful in his capacity as an officer at the National Endowment for the Humanities. Kathryn Kinzer has been very helpful as Librarian of St. John's College in Annapolis. The editors at Duke University Press, as well as the reviewers to whom they sent the manuscript, have been helpful and pleasant to work with. I owe much to the generosity of my late parents-in-law, Joseph Oxenhorn and Ruth Oxenhorn. The encouragement, support, and conversation of Leon Kass and Amy Kass have played a large part in the genesis of this book over the years. The good advice of Kathleen Blits and the generous editorial suggestions of Jan Blits have greatly helped me in making final revisions for publication. My wife, Mera Flaumenhaft, in addition to providing encouragement and delight, has pored over various versions of this book and has much improved it by her counsel.

The Effective Republic

Introduction

At Washington, if anywhere, are to be found those who preside over the fortunes of free government in our day. The form of government whose home is in that place is distinguished among free governments by the name of "presidential" government. Presiding over its birth and its first days was that monumental man named Washington. Indeed, without the splendid solidity of Washington's character, there would have been no such government to speak of. But that character would have been less effective without the brilliant operation of the mind of another man—Alexander Hamilton— who spoke of Washington as "an Aegis very essential to me." The exploits for which that aegis was essential were informed by the master writings from which Hamilton learned that "the science of politics . . . like most other sciences has received great improvement . . . in modern times." According to a writer who taught Hamilton much of that improved political science, "in the birth of societies, it is the chiefs of republics who make the institution; and it is afterward the institution which forms the chiefs of republics." Unlike Hamilton, we are not among the chiefs who have instituted republics; our republic was made by our predecessors. Those who made it formed those who modified it, and we in turn have been formed by this institutional inheritance, so that we cannot be fully free unless we inform ourselves about the minds of its original makers. Hamilton was among those who laid the foundation of the constitutional edifice within which we dwell, subject to constraint yet able to be free; but Hamilton was not merely one among many. He was the chief minister of the first chief magistrate of the American republic, as well as the chief proponent in America of chiefdom in a republic. To understand the institution of the American presidency, to understand ourselves as the posterity for whom it was to have a central place in securing the blessings of liberty, we must rethink the thoughts of Alexander Hamilton.[1]

As a contribution to our doing so, this book will present Hamilton's thinking about the parts of government and their work. In order that the reader may enter as directly as possible into that thinking, the words of Hamilton himself are used as much as possible, though I often omit quotation marks—conflating, compressing, and rearranging Hamilton's phrases and sentences without constantly repeating "Hamilton says." In presenting Hamilton's words, I interpret them, as well as link and arrange them and add some emphasis. I try to make available to readers the material that they need in order to understand Hamilton's thought, and to judge it also, but it is not my aim to facilitate a judgment on the correctness of Hamilton's judgment about the *particulars* of the political controversies and the policy decisions in which he took so large a part. My aim is, rather, by carefully examining what he said in his discussion of particular affairs, to consider Hamilton's *principles*.

Though I do sometimes speak about the course of events that occasioned or resulted from what Hamilton wrote, and though I do stay close to the very words in which Hamilton treated those particulars, this book is a study not so much in history as in political science. It does not tell the story of Hamilton's deeds in the American founding. It lays out his analysis of the republican problem and its possible solution—an analysis that has a claim on the attention of all thoughtful students of politics.

Though Hamilton denied that general principles alone suffice for handling particulars, he insisted that abiding principles are needed to guide deliberation and decision. And not only did he assert that principles are required for good political practice—he in fact intended to preside over the production of a multivolume treatise in political science, with himself as the author of a volume in which conclusions would be drawn from the historical research of his collaborators. He died before that treatise could come into being, but we do have many thousands of pages from his pen which explicate the politics of his day, with extraordinary thoroughness and clarity, in statements which relate his judgments on particulars to fundamental principles.

These discussions of political principle do, however, lie scattered among more than two dozen thick volumes of papers on occasional topics that arose amid the urgencies of action. Many of his most pertinent remarks are not in those of his writings which are read most frequently, and even the ones which are read most frequently are only fragments of his thinking. Wide as their relevance may be, and deep as their arguments may go, they

were as much the occasional products of urgency as were his lesser-known
newspaper articles and his letters to other men of affairs. Whatever comprehensive thinking about principles informed the statesmanship of Hamilton
must be pieced together, therefore, from his fragmentary remarks about the
affairs of his time. It is the aim of this book to set forth those political principles constitutive of Hamilton's thought, in the words he employed for the
purpose of discussing political particulars.

This book is not the first attempt to deal with the thought of Alexander
Hamilton. It has been treated in narrations of his life and career, the most
notable of these being Broadus Mitchell, *Alexander Hamilton* (New York,
2 vols., 1957, 1962), John C. Miller, *Alexander Hamilton and the Growth of the
New Nation* (New York, 1959), and Forrest McDonald, *Alexander Hamilton:
A Biography* (New York, 1979). McDonald's book is an especially interesting treatment of Hamilton's achievements and intentions, particularly in
political economy, where it has no peer, but it does not adequately treat
administration as a constitutional theme. Another historian whose work is
especially suggestive is Douglass Adair, whose essays have been collected
as *Fame and the Founding Fathers* (New York, 1974). But an account of
Hamilton's deeds in their sequence and their context is not a systematic
and analytic account of the principles that governed them. Histories cannot be disregarded, but histories alone cannot supply an adequate view of
Hamilton's political science.

In that political science, administration becomes a constitutional
theme. But previous studies of Hamilton's political thought neglect the
administrative thought located at its center, while studies of his administrative thought inadequately locate it within the political thought surrounding
it. This book seeks to avoid both deficiencies.

There are several studies which treat Hamilton's thought topically
rather than narratively. Some of the most interesting of these, however,
treat it too sketchily. Outstanding examples are Paul Eidelberg's "Reinter-
pretation of the Intentions of the Founding Fathers," *The Philosophy of
the American Constitution* (New York, 1968), and Leonard D. White's *The
Federalists*, "A Study in Administrative History" (New York, 1959).

There are studies which not only treat Hamilton's thought topically
(rather than narratively) but also treat it at some length (rather than dealing
briefly with him as one of "the Founding Fathers" or as one of "the Federalists"). Like Eidelberg's book and White's, however, these studies do not
adequately bring together Hamilton's political and administrative themes.
Outstanding examples are Lynton K. Caldwell's *The Administrative Theories
of Hamilton and Jefferson* (Chicago, 1944), which is too narrow an account

to convey an understanding of Hamilton, and Clinton Rossiter's *Alexander Hamilton and the Constitution* (New York, 1964), which is too sweeping in its remarks.

David F. Epstein's *The Political Theory of* The Federalist (Chicago, 1984) is a study not of Hamilton but of "Publius." While it has interesting things to say about an important portion of what Hamilton wrote, it does not range over the whole body of Hamilton's writings, and a large part of what is treated in it was the product of another pen than Hamilton's. The same is true of Martin Diamond's "Democracy and The Federalist: A Reconsideration of the Framers' Intent," *The American Political Science Review* 53 (1959): 52–68, and "The Federalist," in Leo Strauss and Joseph Cropsey, eds., *History of Political Philosophy* (Chicago, 1963).

The best treatment of Hamilton's thought at some length is Gerald Stourzh's *Alexander Hamilton and the Idea of Republican Government* (Stanford, 1970), which appeared during the writing of the preliminary version of this book. My review of it for *The American Political Science Review* 67 (1973): 637–39, notes that Stourzh makes clear important parts of Hamilton's work but not its principle of energy; I indicate there why I think that Stourzh's account of Hamilton's thought does not adequately articulate what Stourzh correctly calls "the core of his lifework."

"The test of good government," according to Hamilton, "is its aptitude and tendency to produce a good administration." And while "administration of government, in its largest sense, comprehends all the operations of the body politic, whether legislative, executive, or judiciary," yet "in its most usual and perhaps its most precise signification, it falls peculiarly within the province of the executive department." There is, however, "an idea, which is not without its advocates, that a vigorous executive is inconsistent with the genius of republican government"—even though "energy in the executive is a leading character in the definition of good government." Energy in the executive is not, according to Hamilton, the only characteristic of good government, but it is a leading one, and it was the one most in need of Hamilton's efforts on its behalf. He sought, he said, to "blend the advantages of a monarchy and republic in our constitution." He repeatedly affirmed his attachment to republican government, but though he had "strong hopes" for the success of the republican theory, he was "far from being without doubts." "I consider its success," he said, "as yet a problem." Successful republican government was not an accomplished fact but a project to be accomplished: "It is yet to be determined by experience whether it be consistent with that *stability* and *order* in Government which are essential to public strength & private security and happiness." The republican form of government needed improvements that would give to its administration the advantages of the monarchical form. Hamilton's political thought was concerned with completing the arrangements required by the enlightened modern commitment to popular representation as the foundation of good government. Upon that foundation of popular representation, Hamilton sought to erect a structure of effective administration. Demanding that Americans either accept the consequences of their commitment or else embrace an alternative, Hamilton sought to enlighten the heirs of the Enlightenment about the harsh necessity of decisive choice.

In seeking to discern the broad outlines of what Hamilton tried to teach his countrymen, readers may find it helpful to have the following brief synopsis of the argument of this book.

After an opening chapter on principles in the study of Hamilton's thought, this book has three parts. The *first* part shows Hamilton's views on popular representation as the distinctive foundation of government according to enlightened modern principles. The book's *central* part shows Hamilton's views on efficacious administration as an unpopular but necessary completion for the principles that require popular representation as the foundation of good government. This part discusses the problem of adequately arranging for efficacy of government in a government amply arranged with a view to safety against government. The solution involves apportioning the powers of government so as to provide a place for both of the ingredients of efficacy—unity and duration. That is to say, government must be organized both to concentrate power sufficiently for many wills to act as one at one time and to stabilize power sufficiently for many actions to be in concert for constant purposes during a long time. This part of the book shows how Hamilton presents himself as a great friend of republican government, one who seeks to give it that efficacy without which it cannot avoid being soon destroyed and afterward discredited—an efficacy which requires the establishment of properly differentiated parts within organizational machinery founded upon popular representation. The book's *final* part, on constitutional integrity, shows Hamilton's view of the judiciary as that part of the government which has especially to do with the wholeness of the body politic. The book closes with a return to first principles.

I

Principles

We Americans dwell together in a building long admired as commodious and even noble. But its inconveniences obtrude upon us, and its very safety has been questioned. Shall we prop it up or pull it down, make small repairs or thorough renovations? Or shall we just leave well enough alone? Our wish to reexamine the founding of our constitution springs not from an antiquarian love of lingering in museums; it arises neither from a pious longing to perform the rites of civic reverence, nor from a petulant delight in mocking heroes or battling authorities. We must make plans about the house that we've inherited; and in making plans for maintenance or renovation, a prudent heir examines plans and records left by those who built the house.

The American founders, not worshiping the work of human hands, nor disregarding wantonly what already was laid down, fearlessly pulled down connecting walls that made their habitation an apartment in a dangerous old castle; coolly they surveyed the edifice hastily erected afterward to enclose and join their several rooms; and they deliberately proceeded with a fundamental renovation. They found they had to show in full that the evils which Americans experienced proceeded not from minute or partial imperfections, but from "fundamental errors in the structure of the building," which could only be amended by "an alteration in the first principles and main pillars of the fabric." The "frail and tottering edifice," it seemed to them, was "ready to fall upon our heads and to crush us beneath its ruins." The "renovated edifice" was something very new.[1]

Among the builders of the new edifice, Alexander Hamilton was regarded as a master. In "Character Sketches of Delegates to the Federal Convention" another delegate wrote of him: "There is no skimming over the

surface of a subject with him, he must sink to the bottom to see what foundation it rests on." Among his professional colleagues also, Hamilton stood
supreme. According to a chief justice of New York's supreme court, one who
had been assemblyman, state senator, and Hamilton's opponent as counsel
in various cases: "Hamilton . . . more than any other man, did the thinking of the time." And another chief justice of New York's supreme court,
Chancellor James Kent, professor of law and writer of an authoritative set
of commentaries on American law, looking back in 1836 on the members of
the New York bar "who took a leading share in business for some years after
the close of the American War," said that then, when everything was new,
great talent was needed, and "among all his brethren, Colonel Hamilton
was indisputably pre-eminent."[2] To his domestic party opponents, Hamilton seemed a "colossus." More than once, Jefferson would plead thus with
Madison: "We have had only middling performances to oppose him . . .
when he comes forward, there is nobody but yourself who can meet him. . . .
For God's sake take up your pen, and give a fundamental reply."[3] A distinguished foreign observer, Talleyrand, said that he considered Napoleon,
Pitt, and Hamilton to be the three greatest men of the age, and that without
hesitation he would give first place to Hamilton.[4]

It might be argued that Hamilton's thought is not worth much consideration apart from an historical account of what he did, for he was not
a theoretical writer but a statesman—a man who had to make decisions
and engage in advocacy concerning particulars. Hamilton himself was well
aware that the business of decision and advocacy differ from theorizing.
Criticizing Adams as chief executive, he wrote about how widely the "business" of government differs from the "speculation" of it, and "the energy
of the imagination dealing in general propositions" from "that of *execution in detail*."[5] What is choiceworthy in the circumstances, he pointed out,
depends on what is feasible in the circumstances: "what may be good at
Philadelphia may be bad at Paris, and ridiculous at Petersburgh."[6] Moreover, speech that urges the choice of a particular action must be adapted to
its audience. Not only must one emphasize or single out minor points that
are likely to have effect,[7] one must sometimes adopt some of the prejudices
of those one addresses, and even "a little of their nonsense."[8] Much of what
Hamilton accomplished was done by others through whom he acted. Such
influence requires sometimes drafting papers based on premises which the
author may reject but is willing nonetheless to suppose authoritative.[9]

Though differing from theory, decision and advocacy may have a
grounding in thoughtfully articulated principle. When asked for his advice
on one occasion, Hamilton replied that he regretted troubling the Presi-

dent with "the perusal of so voluminous a discussion"; but because "the judgments formed, in particular cases, are almost always connected with a general train of ideas, in respect to some more comprehensive principles or relations," he therefore "thought it advisable to lay that train before you, for the better explanation of the grounds of the opinions, I now give, or may hereafter have occasion to give on the like subjects, in obedience to your commands."[10] When departing in a particular case from what he thought to be sound general principle, Hamilton was inclined to indicate that he was doing so.[11] To avoid pedantry, he said, one must admit exceptions to any general rule, but such avoidance is not the same as an easy inconsistency: "a wise and good man may, on proper grounds, relinquish an opinion which he has once entertained, and the change may even serve as a proof of candor and integrity. But with such a man, changes of this sort, especially in matters of high public importance, must be rare. The contrary is always a mark, either of a weak and versatile mind, or of an artificial and designing character; which, accommodating its creed to circumstances, takes up or lays down an article of faith, just as may suit a present convenience."[12]

It was belief that principles are indispensable in politics which led Hamilton to stake his life in opposition to the career of Aaron Burr. Hamilton lamented the plan of some New Yorkers to run Burr against Adams for vice president in the second national election, Burr being a man with "no other principles than to mount"—"unprincipled"—"for or against nothing, but as it suits his interest or ambition"—"determined . . . to make his way to be the head of the popular party, and to climb *per fas aut nefas* to the highest honors of the State, and as much higher as circumstances will permit"—"bold, enterprising, and intriguing"—"his object to play the game of confusion." For Hamilton to say this, thus taking part in elections while Secretary of the Treasury, was a departure from a principle which hitherto had been his rule, and thus it needed to be justified. He said that though he had hitherto scrupulously avoided interference in elections, the occasion was, in his opinion, sufficiently important to warrant in this instance a departure from that rule. "It is incumbent upon every good man to resist the present design," he wrote; "I feel it to be a religious duty to oppose his career." Calling Burr "an embryo-Caesar" who "cares nothing about the means of effecting his purpose," Hamilton again justified his departure from that rule which deems it most proper for someone in his situation to avoid interference in any matter relating to the elections for members of the government. A decade later Hamilton's associates had to choose between Burr and Jefferson for the chief magistracy. To the argument that Burr was preferable because "he holds no pernicious theories, but is a mere *matter-of-fact* man,"

Hamilton replied that "If Burr's conversation is to be credited, he is not far from being a visionary." But while admitting that Burr "has no fixed theory," and that "his peculiar notions will easily give way to his interest," Hamilton asked: "Is it a recommendation to have no theory? Can that man be a systematic or able statesman who has none?" His answer was: "I believe not. No general principles will hardly work much better than erroneous ones."[13]

Unless there are true principles in politics, it would be folly to make an attempt at "establishing good government from reflection and choice" rather than to acquiesce in being "forever destined to depend, for . . . political constitutions, on accident and force." It would be deceitful to proclaim that "My motives must remain in the depository of my own breast: my arguments will be open to all, and may be judged of by all. They shall at least be offered in a spirit, which will not disgrace the cause of truth."[14]

Hamilton's principles, however, lie scattered about through many volumes of official reports, newspaper essays, speeches, letters, and miscellaneous papers. His collected writings require selection and arrangement to yield the principles that guided his handling of particulars. "Judiciously collected," said Fisher Ames about Hamilton's writings, "they will be a public treasure."[15]

When Hamilton was approached by Hopkins, the man who was to republish *The Federalist* in 1802, Hamilton "hesitated his consent to republication"; he gave Hopkins the impression that "he did not regard the work with much partiality"; "but, nevertheless," said Hopkins, Hamilton "consented to republication" of the collected *Federalist* papers, insisting however that the edition include the *Pacificus* letters, which, he remarked to Hopkins, "some of his friends had pronounced . . . his best performance"; the hesitant Hamilton told Hopkins that "*Heretofore* I have given the people *milk; hereafter* I will give them *meat*," words indicating to Hopkins "his formed purpose—to write a treatise on government."[16]

According to Chancellor Kent, Hamilton contemplated "a full investigation of the history and science of civil government and the various modifications of it upon the freedom and happiness of mankind." He wished "to have the subject treated in reference to past experience and upon the principles of Lord Bacon's inductive philosophy, and to engage the assistance of others in the enterprise."[17]

At the age of forty-nine, however, Hamilton was killed, "religiously" opposing the career of "an embryo-Caesar," before he could write that treatise—leaving us the work of discovering for ourselves what animated his work.

For the appropriate attitude in which to examine the arguments of

Hamilton, we might get light from Francis Bacon, Hamilton's scientific source. In the Second Book of his *Advancement of Learning*, Bacon writes: "for the more public part of government, which is Laws, I think good to note only one deficience; which is, that all those which have written of laws, have written either as philosophers or as lawyers, and none as statesmen. As for the philosophers, they make imaginary laws for imaginary common-wealths, and their discourses are as the stars, which give little light because they are so high. For the lawyers, they write according to the states where they live, what is received law, and not what ought to be law: for the wisdom of a lawmaker is one, and of a lawyer another."

Part One
Popular Representation

II

The Characteristic Spirit
of Society

We begin with the end by which governing itself is governed. The prime end of all laws, said Hamilton in the controversy with which his public career began, is "utility." But, it might be asked, utility for what? If we had to put his politics into a word, that word would be *security*: good government secures for the people safety and prosperity. Good governing, he said, is "productive of solid and durable advantages" for the people—advantages which he identified as "their union, safety, and prosperity." But their union is itself only for the sake of their safety and prosperity. In a resolution he intended to submit to Congress in 1783, but abandoned for lack of support, he wrote that it would be unwise to "continue this extensive empire under a government unequal to its protection and prosperity." Hamilton abandoned this resolution, but not his resolute effort to produce a government equal to the work of governing. As the Convention adjourned in 1787, having done its work of proposing a workable government, Hamilton wrote for himself some "Conjectures about the New Constitution," in which he spoke about the people's belief in "the necessity of the union to their safety and prosperity." Subsequently urging the ratification of the proposed Constitution, Hamilton as "Publius" seemed to equate vindicating it with showing it to be "necessary to the public safety and prosperity." [1]

The preservation of liberty, it is true, was often listed by Hamilton alongside safety and prosperity as governing aims. Sometimes it even replaced safety [2] or prosperity. [3] However, he treated popular liberty not as a stage or an arena for displaying popular action, but rather as a protective device, which, moreover, properly established might help the people it protected to become yet more productive. As America moved toward independence, he asked: "will you give up your freedom"—"or, which is the same thing, will you resign all security for your life and property?" And he called the checks and controls on government which are provided by representation "that *moral* security which is the very essence of civil liberty."[4]

Sweet as liberty may be, what secures it must give way when it becomes an impediment to the protection which it is to serve. Writing of standing armies, and the corresponding appendages of military establishments, Hamilton called safety from external danger the most powerful director of national conduct. Even the ardent love of liberty, he said, will after a time give way to its dictates. The violent destruction of life and property incident to war, the continual effort and alarm attendant on a state of continual danger, will compel nations the most attached to liberty to resort, for repose and security, to institutions which have a tendency to destroy their civil and political rights. To be more safe they at length become willing to run the risk of being less free. Liberty secures one's safety against one's own government; but in order to obtain the means of security against overwhelming danger from foreign governments, one may have to forego means of security against one's own.[5]

Although Hamilton recognized that government must submit to necessity, his judgment of measures often referred to their effects upon the nation's "honor," "character," "dignity," "reputation," or "respectability."[6] But when Hamilton appealed to honor, he did not mean that political men should soar in quest of glory. He meant that men who cannot take care of themselves unless they cheat cannot respect themselves, and that men will have contempt for and put no trust in other men who cannot take care of themselves, whose words are not reliable and whose deeds are not sober.[7]

National honor is an affair of durable solidity, not of lofty splendor: in matters of state we ask about utility. Political society is a means of coping with men's insecurity, an insecurity preceding political society, though political society may complicate that insecurity. Political society is machinery for organizing swords and purses. Fear and desire are the beginnings of government; its ends are safety and prosperity.

Not that amid such beginnings and ends a merely petty interest attaches to the means. Men need shelter, so they build, and they try to make their houses safe and also comfortable; but a stately house is not merely a shelter: it is a noble and magnificent shelter, a delight to the overseeing eyes of its builders, its supervisors, and its resident owners. And so, while the Union was yet a congeries of shacks hastily thrown together on a great estate, Hamilton called for its rebuilding on proper foundations into a more stately dwelling. Writing on the sixth anniversary of the independence of the United States, in the very last paragraph of his series "The Continentalist," he said that there is "something noble and magnificent" in the spectacle of a great federal republic, closely linked in the pursuit of a common interest, tranquil and prosperous at home, respectable abroad.[8] And writing of the need for funding to make the public debt solid and stable, one important effect being to make it "useful as Capital," Hamilton showed how even an "edifice" of "business," a structure of interested enterprise that one would not think to call noble, may present a "spectacle" so "wonderful" as to evoke, by its vast liveliness, a kind of disinterested delight.[9]

ii   Hamilton wrote for men who mostly accepted as self-evidently true the ends of political society as he stated them. What was not self-evident to them, and what he found it repeatedly necessary to argue, was that, having accepted the ends, they had to abandon beliefs which did not well consist with achieving those ends. He sought to liberate them from opinions having their source in antiquity, for the animating spirit of earlier society was different from and inferior to that of modern society.

During the War for Independence, Hamilton treated antiquity as antiquated. Writing against "visionary" expectations, he listed as one required item of expense a numerous magistracy, for whom competent provision must be made, or we may be certain our affairs will always be committed to improper hands, and experience will teach us that no government costs so much as a bad one. Preach, he said, till tired of the theme, the necessity of disinterestedness in republics—nevertheless, the virtuous declaimer will neither persuade himself nor any other person to be content with a double mess of porridge, instead of a reasonable stipend for his services. (It was the custom with the Lacedæmonians, Hamilton notes, that when any new senator was elected, he was presented at their public tables with a double allowance as a mark of distinction.) We might as soon reconcile ourselves to the Spartan community of goods and wives, or to their iron coin, their long beards, or their black broth. In the circumstances as well as in the manners of society among us, there is a dissimilarity that is "total," and it is "as ridiculous to seek for models in the simple ages of Greece and Rome, as it would be to go in quest of them among the Hottentots and Laplanders." Civic office, no longer the "simple" activity of honor-loving virtue, is a paid employment. Self-government is not taking part oneself in the work of governing: it is the right to a voice in the hiring and firing of deputies who serve the public by freeing the populace for private business.[10]

Simplicity, however, does not adequately characterize what makes the ancients unfit models for emulation: it would be better to speak of their spiritedness. During discussion of an act acknowledging the independence of Vermont from New York, a speaker in the New York Assembly asked what the Romans would have done if an inconsiderable part of their citizens had presumed to declare themselves a separate and independent state—and he urged that the Americans should prove themselves as valiant as the Romans. In answer to those observations drawn from the examples of Roman magnanimity, Hamilton said that neither the manners nor the genius of Rome are suited to the republic or the age in which we live: all her maxims and habits were military, and her government was constituted for war; while ours is unfit for it, and our situation still less than our constitution invites us to emulate the conduct of Rome, or to attempt a display of unprofitable heroism.[11]

Shortly afterward, donning his toga as "Publius,"[12] Hamilton returned to the contrast between ancient society and modern. Defending the proposed new Constitution against opponents who feared a standing army, he argued that standing armies were likely to arise not so much from government under the Constitution (if it were adopted) as from the disunion that would follow a rejection of the Constitution; and in this argument, anticipating the question why standing armies did not spring up out of the contentions which so distracted the ancient republics of Greece, he characterized modern society. Hamilton wrote that the concurrence of two factors has produced an entire revolution in the system of war, distinguishing the ancient republics of Greece (in which "the true condition of the people" was "the condition of a nation of soldiers") from "the present day" or "modern times" (in which "disciplined armies, distinct from the body of the citizens" have been rendered the inseparable companion of frequent hostility). In the first place, "the industrious habits of the people of the present day" are "incompatible with the condition of a nation of soldiers"; instead of being warlike, modern men are "absorbed in the pursuits of gain, and devoted to the improvements of agriculture and commerce." And, secondly, the means of revenue have been greatly multiplied in several ways: gold and silver have increased, the arts of industry have grown, and the science of finance has been the offspring of modern times.

A little later, defending the absence of a constitutional interdiction of a standing army in time of peace, Hamilton called attention to the need for garrisons on the western frontier, and his arguments against furnishing these by occasional detachments from the militia were similar to the arguments he made in reply to those who objected to select corps as dangerous. Only in extremities, he said, should modern men be "dragged from their occupations and families to perform that most disagreeable duty." Even to achieve a merely tolerable exactness in military movements is a business that requires time and practice. If the great body of the yeomanry and of the other classes of the citizens were obliged to be under arms for the purpose of going through military exercises and evolutions as often as might be necessary for acquiring the degree of perfection which would entitle them to be called a well regulated militia, this would be a real grievance to the people and a serious public inconvenience and loss. The public loss would be the deduction from the productive labor of the country, and to attempt something which would so considerably abridge the mass of labor and industry would be unwise; but the popular grievance would guarantee that the experiment, if made, could not succeed, because it would not be long endured.

Later still, writing of finance in the modern system of war, Hamilton called it the signal merit of a vigorous system of national credit that it enables a government to support war without violating property, destroying industry, or interfering unreasonably with individual enjoyments. The citizens retain their capital to carry on their several businesses and a due proportion of its produce for obtaining their usual comforts. Agriculture, commerce, and manufactures may receive some check, but they receive no serious wound. Thus war by the use of credit becomes less a scourge.[13]

Nonetheless, although what distinguishes the ancient citizens from the industrious moderns is more adequately characterized as spiritedness than simplicity, the more adequate characterization does not yet go quite far enough. It would be better to speak of ancient ferocity. This may be seen in Hamilton's denial of the claim that one country has the right to confiscate debts owed to aliens of another country against which it is at war. He opposed the appeal to Roman law, which permitted the practice: "nothing but the barbarism of times in which war was the principal business of man could ever have tolerated" such a practice "contrary to what is so plainly dictated by original principles of justice and good faith." The "ferocious maxims of antiquity"—"the ferocious maxims of the times, when war was the chief occupation of man"—might coincide with "some precedents of modern rapacity," but "the rigor of the ancient rule" has been relaxed by "the humane innovations of later times," according to the pronouncements of "enlighted reason." The usages of war must change amidst "the conflict between respect for ancient maxims and the impressions of juster views, seconded by the more enlightened policy of modern times." In ancient times "the world was yet too young—moral science too much in its cradle—to render the Roman jurisprudence a proper model for explicit imitation." The history of Rome shows that "war and conquest were the great business of that people" and that "for the most part, commerce was little cultivated"; "hence it was natural that the rights of war should be carried to an extreme, unmitigated by the softening and humanizing influence of commerce." Against the pretended right there had been by Hamilton's time the negative usage of nearly a century and a half—"a period the most enlightened as well as the most commercial in the annals of the world." The "reason or motive" of the present customary law of nations, that there is no right to confiscate or sequester private debts in time of war, is "the advantage and safety of commerce."[14]

iii The American interest in prosperity and safety would be well served by American observance of the modern maxims that mitigate "the rigor of the ancient maxims of war." The United States cannot better show its wisdom than by showing moderation in this respect—that is, by adhering strictly to all the maxims which favor the rights of creditors. Credit, public and private, is of the greatest consequence to every country; of this, it might "emphatically" be called "the invigorating principle." Credit, as a substitute for capital, is "among the principal engines of useful enterprise and internal improvement": the United States owe, in a great degree, to the fostering influence of credit, their present mature growth; they continue to possess "an immense mass of improvable matter"—and to a country so situated, credit is peculiarly useful. The intelligent merchant in need of credit is freed from the illusions of ferocity by his dependence on potential creditors. Potential creditors also have "the usual sharp-sightedness of avarice": the national government's credit depends on the national government's being given authority to tax, because for anyone to depend upon the engagements of a government that must itself depend upon thirteen other governments for the means of fulfilling its contracts would require a degree of credulity not often to be met with in the pecuniary transactions of mankind.[15]

More urgently, credit is "one of the main pillars of public safety." In the modern system of war, even the wealthiest nations must have recourse to large loans, so that one who would imagine the expense of a single campaign in a war with a great European power would see that war, without credit, would be more than a great calamity—it would be ruin. Modern states, like ancient ones, are far from pacific. The modern commercial system has not eliminated war, but only changed its objects. Hamilton went so far as to call it a "novel and absurd experiment in politics" to try "tying up the hands of Government from offensive war, founded upon reason of state."[16]

But this is far from wars of glory as the stage or the arena for displaying virtue viewed as valor. There are causes, he pointed out, which render war in this country more expensive, and consequently "more difficult to be carried on than in any other"; "the theories of the speculative and the feelings of all" are opposed to it. "The support of public opinion (perhaps more essential to our government than to any other) could only be looked for in a war evidently resulting from necessity." Hamilton spoke of no natural right to make war for glory, but he did speak of a "natural right to trade"; and, defending agreement to "a liberal plan of intercourse with the British territories in our neighborhood," he went on to call "legalized commerce" between the inhabitants of bordering territory "the natural course of things": in every case where territory is contiguous, he said, the alternative is freedom of intercourse, or violent hatred and enmity.[17]

Indeed, the Constitutional Convention itself grew out of seeds that had been sown in expectation that, with changes in the power to regulate trade, the veins of commerce in every part would be replenished and would acquire additional motion and vigor from a free circulation in the commodities of every part. Hamilton drafted the Address of the Annapolis Convention, a document declaring that the idea of "extending the powers of their Deputies, to other objects, than those of Commerce, which has been adopted by the State of New Jersey, was an improvement on the original plan, and will deserve to be incorporated into that of a future Convention," and that the "power of regulating trade is of such comprehensive extent, and will enter so far into the general System of the foederal government, that to give it efficacy, and to obviate questions and doubts concerning its precise nature and limits, may require a correspondent adjustment of other parts of the Foederal System."

The graceful animosity of valor was the animating principle of the body politic in ancient times; but "in the present state of things the health of a state particularly a commercial one depends on a due quantity and regular circulation of cash, as much as the health of an animal body depends on the due quantity and regular circulation of the blood." Money is "the vital principle of the body politic"; money is "that which sustains its life and motion and enables it to perform its most essential functions." This is why a complete power to procure a regular and adequate supply of money, as far as the resources of the community will permit, is an indispensable ingredient in a constitution. Commerce, by increasing the quantity of money in circulation and the celerity with which it circulates, must render the payment of taxes easier and facilitate the requisite supplies to the treasury. The flow of cash not only helps to fill the treasury, but also increases the people's wealth by activating their industrious habits. "The prosperity of commerce" has become "the primary object of their political cares" for "all enlightened statesmen," who "now" perceive and acknowledge it to be "the most useful as well as the most productive source of national wealth." By multiplying the means of gratification and by promoting the introduction and circulation of the precious metals, those darling objects of human avarice and enterprise, the prosperity of commerce serves to vivify and invigorate the channels of industry and to make them flow with greater activity and copiousness. Thus it makes the assiduous merchant, the laborious husbandman, the active mechanic, and the industrious manufacturer—indeed, all orders of men—look forward with eager expectation and growing alacrity to this pleasing reward of their toils.[18]

iv   From the argument that commercial prosperity facilitates taxation, Hamilton wished his readers to conclude that since the union of states fostered commercial prosperity it should therefore be preserved as useful for facilitating the raising of governmental revenue. This was a relatively small part of the argument for the utility of union; but in discussing it, Hamilton touched, in passing, upon a very big question, which he treated as a very small one. Noting that "the often-agitated question, between agriculture and commerce" had "from indubitable experience received a decision, which has silenced the rivalships, that once subsisted between them, and has proved . . . that their interests are intimately blended," he remarked that it is "astonishing, that so simple a truth should ever have had an adversary." Earlier, he had accounted for the persistence of the question by noting that the avarice of many of the landholders will be opposed to a perpetual tax upon land, however moderate: they will ignorantly hope to shift the burdens of the national expense from themselves to others—a disposition "as iniquitous as it is fruitless." It is from a fundamentally commercial point of view that agriculture and commerce are allies rather than rivals.[19]

Of old, however, the question of agriculture versus commerce had not been about the relative profitability of two lines of business, but about whether traders seeking profits or farmers cultivating the earth made better citizens. Since then, Hobbes, seeking to reconstitute politics on a basis that rejected the illusions and obfuscations of pride, had taught that "the office of the sovereign, be it monarch or assembly, consisteth in the end, for which he was trusted with the sovereign power, namely the procuration of the *safety of the people*. . . . But by safety here, is meant not a bare preservation, but also all other contentments of life, which every man by lawful industry, without danger or hurt to the commonwealth, shall acquire to himself." And Locke, building on the base, had taught the politics of increase: "the increase of lands and the right imploying of them is the great art of government. And that Prince who shall be so wise and godlike as by established laws of liberty to secure protection and encouragement to the honest industry of Mankind against the oppression of power and narrowness of Party will quickly be too hard for his neighbors."[20]

The prevalence of the principle that the business of politics is business provoked a radical reaction, the echoes of which were heard in America. Much of Hamilton's work was a struggle against those who would not give up an innovating modernity but had not freed themselves from the vestigial influence of antiquated views. He thought that the practice of modern society, imbued with the spirit of business, tended to merge agriculture into commerce; landowning was but one form of gainful enterprise. A "considerable time" after the public stock had "reached the desirable point and put an end to the excessive spirit of speculation," which had then "for some time" been "far more active, even to intemperateness in other pursuits, in trading adventures and in lands," Hamilton found it "curious to observe how little clamor there is against the spirit of speculation in its present direction; though it were not difficult to demonstrate that it is no less extravagant or pernicious in the shape of land-jobbing than in that of Stock-jobbing." But "virtuous sensible men lamenting the partialities of all over-driven speculation, know at the same time that they are inseparable from the spirit and freedom of commerce and that the cure must result from the disease." However, "many of the noisy patriots who were not in condition to be stock-jobbers are land-jobbers, and have a becoming tenderness for this species of extravagance."[21]

The chief of the partisans of agrarian society was Jefferson, whose "visionary theory" of "as little government as possible" was a combination of "pernicious dreams." These went so far in rejecting the savagery of warrior society as to abandon the means of defense, while they blocked development beyond the primitive level of an almost exclusively agricultural society by offering no encouragement to active commercial enterprise and its accompaniment, the arts of manufacture. Jefferson went so far as to be "distressed at the codfish having latterly emigrated to the southern coast, lest the people there should be tempted to catch them, and commerce, of which we have already too much, receive an accession."[22]

Jefferson rejected the arguments for manufactures, which were derived from European political economists, as referring not to what is choice-worthy in itself but rather to what happened to be necessary in circumstances which, fortunately, were not America's. Asking which kind of society conduces to the long life and vigorous health of republican government, Jefferson answered that republican health and a certain kind of moral virtue go together, and the soil from which they grow is the cultivation of the soil, for the man who labors in the earth depends for his livelihood not on other men but on nature and himself; both salesmen and slaves take orders from those whom they depend upon and serve.[23]

            Hamilton's minimal argument on behalf of encouraging manufac-
V   tures had to do with war.[24] But his Report on Manufactures went far beyond the minimal argument that it is safer to be "independent of other nations for essential, particularly for military supplies." The report presented the arguments of those unfriendly to the encouragement of manufactures as if the objections were almost exclusively economic: the standard was "productiveness." Although Hamilton "readily" conceded that the cultivation of the earth has "intrinsically a strong claim to preeminence over every other kind of industry," giving among the reasons its "including a state most favorable to the freedom and independence of the human mind," nevertheless, this reason was not emphasized and was next-to-last in a list of five, all the others of which did not consider what kind of man is formed by the economic activity. He observed that manufacturing cooperates with nature as much as agriculture does; the latter differs from the former not in kind, but only in being simpler. Moreover, manufacturing labor is "more constant, more uniform, more ingenious" than agricultural labor. In advocating manufacturing establishments, Hamilton discussed each of the principal circumstances why they not only increase "the produce and revenue of the society" or "the total mass of industrious effort in a community" beyond what they could possibly be without such establishments, but together even add to it "a degree of energy and effect which is not easily conceived." Among these circumstances he listed: "the division of labor. . . . An extension of the use of machinery. . . . Additional employment to classes of the community not ordinarily engaged in the business. . . . The furnishing greater scope for the diversity of talents and dispositions, which discriminate men from each other. . . . The affording a more ample and various field for enterprise."

    Hamilton said in paraphrase what Adam Smith had said in *The Wealth of Nations* about the productivity of division of labor. But Hamilton did not present what Smith had also said in that same book about the evil consequences which attend this increased productivity and about the remedies necessary for mitigating these evil consequences. Attention was diverted toward the prospect of stimulating the capacity to produce and away from the stunting of other human capacities as a by-product of the process of production. The measurement of productivity does not take into account the character produced in the producer by the process of production, except insofar as this character has further effect in producing things of utility. Hamilton approved of manufacturing as productive of men who are producers of more. Because a manufacturing commercial society is a very diverse society, it employs a great variety of talents and greatly stimulates ingenuity; there is thus more productive exertion of the human mind in such a society. Mechanical ingenuity and the spirit of enterprise were the human products of manufacturing that Hamilton considered. Whether the multitude of the people in such a society would be masses lacking a citizen's intelligence and spirit was not Hamilton's question in considering the American economy; his question, rather, concerned national productivity as the means to secure national "strength" and "prosperity" at a time when "a spirit of manufacturing prevails . . . in a greater degree than it has done at any antecedent period."[25]

vi   Hamilton was aware that the goods of modernity could not be secured without suffering evils that came with them, but he thought that the evils of modern society are no reason to forego it as a means of securing the goods it does provide. Defending the funding system against the objection that "*Paper Speculation* . . . nourishes in our citizens vice and idleness, instead of industry and morality," Hamilton wrote that although "Jobbing in funds has some bad effects among those engaged in it"—"fosters a spirit of gambling, and diverts a certain number of individuals from other pursuits"—nonetheless the effect upon the citizens at large is different: stock operates as capital and thus "promotes among them industry, by furnishing a larger fund of employment." He treated the theme more fully as Secretary of the Treasury, reporting on public credit, and he treated it most fully in retirement from office, drafting an unfinished defense of his policy in office.

The substance of the argument against funding systems, he says, is that by facilitating credit they occasion a tendency to run in debt, and consequently a progressive accumulation of debt and its perpetuation—at least till it is crushed beneath the load of its own enormous weight. But analysis shows that this argument "turns upon the abuses of a thing intrinsically good"—and in this analysis Hamilton set forth "the principles which have regulated every part of my conduct in my late office."

Giving reasons of safety and prosperity, he asserts that "every State" ought to aim at rendering its ability to borrow—its credit—commensurate with the utmost extent of the lending faculties of the community and of all others who can have access to its loans. This is questioned only by "an ignorance which benights the political world and disputes the first principles of Administration." The "principle" on which this questioning is "founded" would "equally combat every institution that promotes the perfection of the Social organization, for this perfection in all its shapes by giving a consciousness of strength and resource and inspiring pride tends to ambitious pursuits to war expence and debt."

This questioning is countered by the true principle, the principle that "Tis the portion of man assigned to him by the eternal allotment of Providence that every good he enjoys shall be alloyed with ills, that every source of his bliss shall be a source of his affliction—except Virtue alone, the only unmixed good which is permitted to his temporal Condition." The true principle raises counterquestions: "shall we on this account forego every advantage which we are fitted to enjoy? Shall we put in practice the horrid system of the detestable Robespierre? Shall we make war upon Science and its professors? Shall we destroy the arts useful as well as pleasurable? Shall we make knowledge a crime, ignorance a qualification? Shall we lay in ruins our towns and deform the face of our fields? Shall we enchain the human mind and blunt all its energies under the withering influences of privation and the benumbing strokes of Terror? Shall we substitute the unmingled misery of a gloomy and destructive depotism to the alternate sunshine and storms of Liberty?"

A case can be made against improvements in agriculture, commerce, and manufactures—and against science, learning, and knowledge as their source. "Science, learning, and knowledge promote those inventions, discoveries and improvements which accelerate the progress of labour and industry and with it the accumulation of that opulence which is the parent of so many pleasures and pains, so many blessings and calamities." Putting aside the progress of the mind, we see how perilous is prosperity itself: "A prosperous state of agriculture, commerce and manufactures nourishes and begets opulence, resource, and strength. These by inspiring a consciousness of power never fail to beget in the councils of nations under whatever form of Government a sentiment of superiority, pride, ambition, insolence. These dispositions lead directly to War and consequently to expences and to all the calamities which march in the train of War." And "the same causes leading to opulence, increasing the means of enjoyment naturally sharpen the appetite for it, and so promote luxury, extravagance, dissipation, effeminacy, disorders in the moral and political system, convulsions, revolutions, the overthrow of nations and empires." Indeed, a case can be made on these grounds against liberty itself: "True liberty by protecting the exertions of talents and industry and securing to them their justly acquired fruits, tends more powerfully than any other cause to augment the mass of national wealth and to produce the mischiefs of opulence."

Behind "the horrid system of the detestable Robespierre" are "speculative men"; although funding systems, by giving the greatest possible energy to public credit, are "a source of national security, strength, and prosperity," men nevertheless make objections to them "very similar to those which speculative men urge against national and individual opulence, drawn from its abuse."

Robespierre's speculative predecessor was Rousseau. Rousseau had spoken of the "paradoxes anglois en faveur de luxe," and he had expanded on the singular maxims of "notre Philosophie" and the paradoxes so worthy of "nos jours," in his *Discours sur les Sciences et les Arts*. Luxury, he said, goes together with arts. Our philosophy claims, contrary to the experience of all ages, that luxury makes the splendor of states. Having forgotten the necessity for sumptuary laws, it would even deny that luxury is diametrically opposed to good mores, which are essential to the duration of empires. Even if luxury be a sign, indeed a multiplier of riches—what will become of virtue, Rousseau asked, when one needs to enrich oneself whatever the price? The politically minded among the ancients spoke unceasingly of mores and virtue; ours speak but of commerce and money. If these modern men suspended their calculations, they might learn that one has everything with money but good mores and citizens—that as the commodities of life multiply, as the arts are perfected and luxury is extended, true courage is enervated, military virtues vanish. Elsewhere, a few sentences after saying that something bad to the eyes of avarice is not bad to the eyes of reason, Rousseau calls himself a man of paradoxes: paradoxes, he says, are necessary when one reflects, and he'd rather be a man of paradoxes than a man of prejudices.

The distinction made by Hamilton in such questions was not between the "homme à paradoxes" and the "homme à préjugés." Rather, in all questions about the advantages or disadvantages of national credit, "as in similar questions with respect to all the sources of social happiness and national prosperity," Hamilton says he distinguishes between "the true politician" and "the political-empiric."

Political-empirics (that is, political quacks) are of two sorts. The sort most usual, because theirs is the easiest course, includes all those "hunters after popularity" who, knowing better, make a traffic of the weak sides of the human understanding and passions: "without proposing or attempting any substitute, they content themselves with exposing and declaiming against the ill sides of things and with puzzling and embarrassing every practicable scheme of administration which is adopted." The other sort "attempt to travel out of human nature and introduce institutions and projects for which man is not fitted and which perish in the imbecility of their own conception and structure."

The "true politician," by contrast, acts from a "view of human nature" as "a compound of good and ill tendencies—endued with powers and actuated by passions and propensities which blend enjoyment with suffering and make the causes of welfare the causes of misfortune." Hence, "he will not attempt to warp or distort it from its natural direction," but, rather, in dealing with man "he will seek to promote his action according to the byass of his nature, to lead him to the development of his energies according to the scope of his passions." Finding "human society" to be the "aggregate" of this human nature, and hence "erecting the social organization on this basis," he will neither "attempt to promote its happiness by means to which it is not suited" nor "reject the employment of the means which constitute its bliss because they necessarily involve alloy and danger"; but "he will favour all those institutions and plans which tend to make men happy according to their natural bent, which multiply the sources of individual enjoyment and increase those of national resource and strength," while "taking care to infuse in each case all the ingredients which can be devised as preventives or correctives of the evil which is the eternal concomitant of temporal blessing."

Thus, Hamilton wrote, "I proposed the *funding* of the public debt"—"as a first step to this great result." He did, with respect to credit, what a true politician will do. A true politician, observing the immense importance of credit to the strength and security of nations, will "endeavour to obtain it for his own country in its highest perfection by the most efficient means"; "yet not overlooking the abuses to which like all other good things it is liable," he will "seek to guard against them," by "promoting a spirit of true national economy," by "pursuing steadily, especially in a country which has no need of external acquisition, the maxims of justice, moderation and peace," and by "endeavoring to establish as far as human inconstancy allows" certain "fixed principles in the administration of the finances calculated to secure efficaciously the extinguishment of debt as fast at least as the probable exigencies of the nation is likely to occasion the contracting of it." This last is the chief thing. Although credit is a great and very useful power, it is "a new power in the mechanism of national affairs," and, "as is the case with every new and great contrivance," the "art of regulating it properly" has been "till lately imperfectly understood." But now "the desideratum" has been found;

it is the rule that makes "contemporary provision for the extinguishment of principal as well as for the payment of interest in the act of contracting new debt"—this is "the true panacea."[26]

If, of all the goods enjoyed by man, virtue alone is unalloyed with ills, why not forego some of those advantages which we are fitted to enjoy, in order to foster virtue, that "only unmixed good?" Might not some suppression of arts and sciences be a necessary preservative for "the alternate sunshine and storm of liberty," rather than being "the unmingled misery of a gloomy and destructive despotism?" Hamilton's words suggest an answer: the portion assigned to man "by the eternal allotment of Providence" does not permit bliss in man's "temporal condition." To govern men as if it were possible to overcome affliction is an act of tyrannical pride. Virtue may be an "unmixed" good, but it is part of a life in which men are compelled to trade off one good-mixed-with-ill for another good-mixed-with-ill. Hamilton's phrases, echoing of theology, point back to the source of the principle of commercial society, of enlightened society devoted to commerce on principle, as distinguished from a society merely containing men who engage in commerce. His phrases thus point to the source of the principles of government appropriate to enlightened, commercial society.

vii   When Hamilton contemplated certain harsh features of antiquity, he recoiled in horror. Concerning the Spartan practice of exposing infants who were deformed, sickly, or weak, his notes on Plutarch remark: "A horrid practice, mentioned with no mark of disapprobation." As remarkable to Hamilton as the horrid practice of infanticide was the lack of disapproval of this Spartan practice by the ancient non-Spartan who wrote about it.[27]

Elsewhere, Hamilton called the foundation of the Roman law of war "inhuman." As we learn from Cicero, he says, the right of capturing the property and of making slaves of the persons of enemies is referred to the right of killing them, which was regarded as absolute and unqualified, extending even to women and children; and thus it would seem that, on the principle of the Roman law, we might rightfully kill a foreigner who had come into our country during peace, and was there at the outbreak of war with his country. Considering this tradition which is taught to us by Cicero, Hamilton then asks: "Can there be a position more horrible, more detestable?"—and he contrasts with the Roman law "the improvement of moral science in modern times," which restrains the right of killing an enemy to the time of battle or resistance, except by way of punishment for some enormous breach of the law of nations, or for self-preservation, in case of immediate and urgent danger—and rejects altogether the right of imposing slavery on captives.[28]

The rejection of ancient ferocity restricts plunder as well as killing. Commercial interest itself requires that a country except from capture any property under the protection of its laws which belongs to subjects of an enemy country. It is not, however, only the clever calculation of commercial society which teaches men the exception. Involving "no refinement," it depends on "obvious considerations" and is "agreeable to common sense and to nature"; "the spontaneous feelings of equity" accord with it. The contrary conduct would be condemned as plunder by "natural reason, unwarped by particular dogmas"; we will condemn it "if we abstract ourselves from extraneous impressions and consult a moral feeling." Hamilton goes so far as to call it "indeed, astonishing that a contrary rule should ever have been countenanced by the opinion of any jurist, or by the practice of any civilized nation."[29]

The teachers of antiquity who did not speak with such horror of infanticide or of the plunder, the enslavement, and the slaughter of defeated human beings would seem to have been deficient in "natural reason" and "spontaneous moral feeling." Since there was much commerce in the ancient world, simple commerce would seem to be an insufficient nurturer of human nature. Something else was needed to bring human society to that state of maturity in which the natural reason and the spontaneous moral feeling might be "unwarped." Between the harsh barbarism of antiquity and the enlightened commercial society of modernity, mankind underwent some tutelage.

Politic use of pagan religion could somewhat mitigate ancient ferocity. The "wise Prince" Numa Pompilius "went a great way in civilizing the Romans": "The chief engine he employed for this purpose" was "religion, which could alone have sufficient empire over the minds of a barbarous and warlike people to engage them to cultivate the arts of peace."[30]

But humane civilization in the West was the outcome of Christian religion: "the praise of a civilized world is justly due to Christianity—war, by the influence of the humane principles of that religion, has been stripped of half its horrors." And so it happens that when the French at the end of the eighteenth century are "influenced by the same spirit of domination which governed the ancient Romans," they "renounce Christianity, and . . . relapse into barbarism"; and then "war resumes the same hideous and savage form which it wore in the ages of Gothic and Roman violence."[31]

Christianity, however, while making savage men gentle, also led to a new kind of ferocity, the ferocity of a religious zeal which, seeking to form society with a view to the highest things, made life here on earth hellish in the name of a heavenly hereafter. Over politic men then came a yearning for government whose ends were limited to the basic goods upon which men could more easily agree. The liberal state, indifferent about attitudes toward the highest things, seemed to provide the machinery needed for securing safety and prosperity. The pacification of warlike men was earlier the work of Christian charity, but was ultimately the work of men reacting to a world of bigotry produced by Christian zeal. The spirit of bigotry, born from a meeting between the spirit of spiritedness and the spirit of spirituality, could be overcome by the spirit that informed commerce: the tolerant spirit of enlightened interest.

It was a long time, said Hamilton, before the kingdoms of Europe were convinced of the folly of persecution, with respect to those who were schismatics from the established church: while some kingdoms were impoverishing and depopulating themselves, by their severities to the nonconformists, their wiser neighbors were reaping the fruits of their folly—augmenting their own numbers, industry, and wealth, by receiving with open arms the persecuted fugitives. "Bigotry in politics as well as in religions" is "equally pernicious." The "zealots" of either description are "ignorant of the advantage of a spirit of toleration." But "now" every "enlightened" nation acknowledges "the force of this truth"—that "whatever speculative notions of religion may be entertained, men will not on that account, be enemies to a government, that affords them protection and security." And "in politics, and for the same reasons" the "same spirit of toleration . . . has made great progress among mankind." Persecution is folly; the choice, Hamilton argues, is between extirpation and toleration. The number of malcontents in the state is either small or great. If small, there can be no room for apprehensions; if great, then opposition to the government is only to be overcome by making it their interest to be its friends or by extirpating them from the community. A middle line which will betray a spirit of persecution in the government, but will only extend its operation to a small number, will answer to no other purpose than to disable a few and inflame and rivet the prejudices of the rest. But the impracticability of such a general extirpation suggests the opposite conduct as the only proper one. The lesson of advantageous toleration is not that attitudes do not matter, but rather that tolerance properly employed can subvert intolerance, so as to produce civil behavior and, eventually, attitudes of civility.[32]

Not that the danger of fanatical religion had utterly vanished: the fire of fanaticism had subsided, but men of malice might fan the embers for their own use. Less than ten years before making these remarks, Hamilton had seen in the Quebec Bill an attempt by which "arbitrary power, and its great engine the Popish religion," were "to all intents and purposes, established in that province"—"instead of being tolerated as stipulated by the treaty." Moreover, "No protestant Englishman would consent to let the free exercise of his religion depend on the mere pleasure of any man," for "the privilege of worshipping the deity in the manner his conscience dictates, which is one of the dearest he enjoys, must in that case be rendered insecure"—"Yet this is the unhappy situation, to which the protestant inhabitants of Canada are reduced." The bill "more fully than anything they have done" shows "the dark designs of the ministry." They have "formed a systematic project of absolute power": "By giving a legal sanction to the accustomed dues of the priests, it was intended to interest them in behalf of administration; and by means of the dominion they possess over the minds of the laity, together with the appearance of good will towards their religion, to prevent any dissatisfaction, which might arise from the loss of their civil rights, and to propitiate them to the . . . subjugation of the colonies and afterwards that of Britain itself." Thus, "should it ever comport with the designs of an ambitious and wicked minister, we may see an inquisition erected in Canada, and priestly tyranny may hereafter find as propitious a soil in America as it ever has in Spain or Portugal."[33]

After American independence removed the danger, however, salutary vigilance became excessive zeal; the fighters against fanaticism became an impediment to fostering a liberal society. The naturalization section of New York's state constitution required all foreigners who became citizens of New York to "take an oath of allegiance to this State, and abjure and renounce all allegiance and subjection to all and every foreign King, Prince, Potentate and State, in all matters ecclesiastical as well as civil." When the New York Assembly debated a clause in a bill for regulating elections which authorized election officials to require voters to take an oath, Hamilton argued for omitting the words "both in matters ecclesiastical as well as civil." In those who then were bringing forward oaths like this, Hamilton saw the vigilance of those who would bring engines to extinguish fires which had subsided many days before. He questioned whether it was proper to propose this test at all, but he was decidedly against going so far as to extend it to ecclesiastical matters. Why give to those not led astray by bigotry, he asks, any occasion to be dissatisfied with you—why wound the tender conscience of any man? The dangers that have been alleged, he says, do not exist on the part of the person born and educated here: Americans are unincumbered with that dangerous fanaticism which terrified the world some centuries back, but which is now dissipated by the light of philosophy. The dangers now are only imaginary—at least with respect to us.[34]

"Liberality" was urged by Hamilton in discussing foreign relations as well as domestic concerns: he commended America for making it a policy to bottom our system with regard to foreign nations upon "those grounds of moderation and equity, by which reason, religion, and philosophy had tempered the harsh maxims of more early times"—"these salutary advances toward improvement in true civilization and humanity."[35]

Hamilton hailed the humane effects of Christianity in liberating men from a harsh society characterized by killing and plunder. But he hailed as well the liberal teaching that when civil society busied itself about men's souls, it did not thereby make them virtuous, but rather so distracted and divided them that the world became a wretched scene of dearth and danger. He joined with those humane men of enlightenment who, looking away from Christian zeal as the public bond among men, had worked for a society imbued with the spirit of commerce and governed in accordance with the natural rights of mankind.[36]

III

The Natural Rights
of Mankind

Ignorance of "the natural rights of mankind," said Hamilton, cannot be admitted in "this enlightened age." To understand government one must know that "in a state of nature" a man may have *physical* power but he has no "*moral* power to deprive another of his life, limbs, property or liberty; nor the least authority to command, or exact obedience from him; except that which arose from the ties of consanguinity." One must also know that "the deity, from the relations we stand in, to himself and to each other, has constituted an eternal and immutable law, obligatory upon all mankind, prior to any human institution whatever." This is "what is called the law of nature, 'which, being coeval with mankind, and dictated by God himself is, of course, superior in obligation to any other. It is binding over all the globe, in all countries, and at all times. No human laws are of any validity, if contrary to this; and such of them as are valid, derive all their authority mediately, or immediately, from this original.'" Identifying Blackstone as the source of this quotation, Hamilton recommends the following teachers for the study of the law of nature: Grotius, Puffendorf, Locke, Montesquieu, and Burlemaqui. He says that he might mention other excellent writers on this subject; but he does not do so, for the reader who diligently attends to these, he says, will not require any others.

The opinion that man in a state of nature is perfectly free from all restraint of law and government, Hamilton points out, was also held by Hobbes: but according to Hobbes, "Moral obligation . . . is derived from the introduction of civil society; and there is no virtue, but what is purely artificial, the mere contrivance of politicians for the maintenance of social intercourse." Hobbes came to "this absurd and impious doctrine" because "he disbelieved the existence of an intelligent, superintending principle, who is the governor, and will be the final judge of the universe." Hamilton believes, by contrast, that the natural rights of mankind depend upon that law upon which "the supreme being gave existence to man, together with the means of preserving and beatifying that existence. He endowed him with rational faculties, by the help of which to discern and pursue such things, as were consistent with his duty and interest, and invested him with an inviolable right to personal liberty, and personal safety."[1]

Although the natural law established by God teaches a duty not to violate the rights of others, and even to help others to pursue their rightful interests, nonetheless one has a right to look out first for one's own greatest interests. It is a dictate of humanity to contribute to the support and happiness of our fellow creatures and more especially those who are allied to us by the ties of blood, interest, and mutual protection—but humanity does not require us to sacrifice our own security and welfare to the convenience or advantage of others. Self-preservation is the first principle of our nature. When our lives and properties are at stake, it would be foolish and unnatural to refrain from such measures as might preserve them because they would be detrimental to others.[2]

The natural law establishes "rules of morality and justice" which are "applicable to nations as well as to individuals": "Without this there is an end of all distinct ideas of right or wrong, justice or injustice, in relation to society or government. There can be no such thing as rights, no such thing as property or liberty; all the boasted advantages of a constitution of government vanish into air. Every thing must float on the variable and vague opinions of the governing party, of whomsoever composed."

Yet, Hamilton admits, the rules established by the law of nature are binding only in general—there are certain great cases which operate as exceptions. He warns, however, that the admission of exceptions to these rules is one of the most common as well as one of the most fruitful sources of error and abuse. Hence, just ideas should be formed of their true nature, foundation, and extent. To minds which are either depraved or feeble, or under the influence of any particular passion or prejudice, it is enough that cases are merely attended with some extraordinary circumstances to induce their being considered as among the exceptions. With such minds, convenience is a substitute for necessity—and some temporary, partial advantage is an equivalent for a fundamental and permanent interest of society.

He characterizes two kinds of exceptions. The first is necessity: a nation may find itself in circumstances such that it is involuntarily unable to observe a right or perform a duty or is unable to do so without some manifest and great national calamity that threatens the existence or at least the permanent welfare of the nation. The second kind of exception is exemplified by "certain feudal rights, which once oppressed all Europe and still oppress too great a part of it"—"rights which made absolute slaves of a great part of the community, and rendered the condition of the greatest proportion of the remainder not much more eligible." These rights—"though involving that of property"—nonetheless, being "contrary to the social order, and to the permanent welfare of society, were justifiably abolished in the instances in which abolitions have taken place, and may be abolished in all the remaining vestiges." It is true, said Hamilton, that wherever a right of property is infringed for the general good, compensation ought to be made if the nature of the case admits, but the impracticability of compensation ought not to be an obstacle to a "clearly essential reform."[3]

Hamilton might have given an example closer to home, for when he said that "all men are . . . by nature, entitled to a parity of privileges,"[4] he included the black slaves of America. During the War for Independence, his friend Colonel John Laurens of South Carolina hoped to induce the government of that state to arm blacks to fight the British. Of this plan Hamilton wrote that some great military judges make it a maxim that with sensible officers soldiers can hardly be too stupid; he mentions this, he says, "because I frequently hear it objected to the scheme of embodying negroes that they are too stupid to make soldiers." So far was this from appearing to Hamilton a valid objection, that he thought "their want of cultivation (for their natural faculties are probably[5] as good as ours)" joined to "that habit of subordination which they acquire from a life of servitude" would "make them sooner become soldiers than our White inhabitants." Hamilton foresaw that "this project will have to combat much opposition from prejudice and self-interest": "The contempt we have been taught to entertain for the blacks, makes us fancy many things that are founded neither in reason nor experience"; and "an unwillingness to part with property of so valuable a kind will furnish a thousand arguments to show the impracticability or pernicious tendency of a scheme which requires such a sacrifice." But "if we do not make use of them in this way, the enemy probably will"; and "the best way to counteract the temptations they will hold out will be to offer them ourselves." It was "an essential part of the plan" to "give them their freedom with their muskets." This would "secure their fidelity, animate their courage, and I believe . . . have a good influence upon those who remain, by opening a door to their emancipation." This, "I confess, has no small weight in inducing me to wish the success of the project; for the dictates of humanity and true policy equally interest me in favour of this unfortunate class of men."[6]

Not long after the war, attending a meeting to organize the Society for Promoting the Manumission of Slaves, Hamilton became a member of the committee formed for further action. A year later he signed a petition to the New York legislature urging the end of the slave trade as a commerce "repugnant to humanity" and "inconsistent with the liberality and justice which should distinguish a free and enlightened people."

Later, during the controversy over the Jay Treaty, when opponents of this treaty charged Great Britain with breaches of the treaty of peace which concluded the War for Independence, one of the allegations was that the British had breached the peace treaty when they carried off captured black slaves to whom they had promised liberty during the war. Hamilton argued against the American construction of the disputed clause—and for the "less exceptionable" British construction which considered the clause to have been inserted, for greater caution, to secure evacuations without depredation. In case of any ambiguity, said Hamilton, the odiousness of the effect inclines the scale against the American interpretation. In the interpretation of treaties, things odious or immoral are not to be presumed; but the abandonment of those who had been induced to quit their masters on the faith of official proclamations promising them liberty, causing them to fall again into slavery under the yoke of their masters, is "as *odious* and *immoral* a thing as can be conceived." Hamilton acknowledges here that the rights of men do not simply harmonize. Securing one man's right might require another man to suffer a lesser wrong. Two wrongs do not make a right, he says; one immoral thing does not obviate the immorality of a prior immoral thing. To have withdrawn slaves from their masters as a public enemy and to have employed them against those masters was an act, though odious, far less odious than would have been the abandonment of those persons to the bondage of their former masters after they had been so used on the promise of liberty. Because the feelings of every real friend to liberty must be in unison with this assertion, Americans must agree to the British construction of the disputed article in the treaty: for if we consider the first act as improper and suppose that there was an intention to make reparation, the true and the only way consistent with justice and morality was to stipulate compensation for the former slaves—but this the article does not do. It might promise to abstain from new acts of depredation, but it may not revoke the liberation affected by the previous depredations. The blacks *already* withdrawn from their masters, "being men," were "by the laws of God and nature . . . capable of acquiring liberty," the giving of which was "irrevocable," the revoking of which would have been "the extreme of treachery, perfidy, and baseness." [7]

ii   Although every man has equally from God a natural right to life and property, this life and property are insecure in the state of natural liberty. Without constraint the passions of men will not conform to the dictates of reason and justice, says Hamilton, and men have therefore instituted government. It is the primary end of society to bestow upon men in their natural insecurity that moral security for their lives and property to which they are entitled. The ultimate ends do not progress beyond the original inducements: civil society is natural society modified to secure ends present in natural society. Civil society is a compact for collective security, and to be "justly established," it "must be a voluntary compact, between the rulers and the ruled . . . liable to such limitations as are necessary for the security of the *absolute rights* of the latter." Civil liberty is the secure condition of being governed by laws to which one has given consent, either in person or by a representative.

When positive law ceases to give security to life and property, men may exercise their original right to defend themselves. They may seek to restore their fundamental positive law, which lays down who shall say what the laws are; or they may "betake themselves to the law of nature," which is beyond the fundamental positive law.[8]

The "resort to first principles" ought, however, to be the beginning of better government: hence, "commotion" needs "prudent and moderate" management. To avoid anarchy, the passion that moves the multitude against tyranny and oppression must be guided by the reason and knowledge of leadership; there is need for regular authority in opposing and overthrowing authorities. And solemn authorization must be given by the people in order to alter the constitutional authority of their representatives.[9]

Prudent men will not only be cautious about resorting to first principles; they will also insure that government acquires the means of forcefully suppressing sedition and insurrection. The lessons taught by the examples of other nations have been corroborated by our own experience: "seditions and insurrections are unhappily maladies as inseparable from the body politic, as tumors and eruptions from the natural body." Hence "the idea of governing at all times by the simple force of law (which we have been told is the only admissible principle of republican government)" has no place but in "reveries": "In all societies, however constituted," rather, "emergencies . . . will sometimes arise" in which "the national government may be necessitated to resort to force." Since "human nature" is what it is "throughout the globe, and in all ages," there must exist "in a large proportion" of every nation "germs of the profoundest discontent, ready to burst into vegetation the moment there should appear an efficacious prospect of protection and shade." Even republics governing at most times "by the simple force of law" sometimes need to suppress revolt, thus maintaining their rule of law at some times by force of organized force.[10]

Although in very extraordinary cases it might be necessary to relinquish authority over a part for the safety of the whole,[11] it is the ordinary necessity of government for its authority first to be vindicated and then for its clemency to be displayed. When government has had to make a spectacular show of force so as to secure respect for the authority necessary to secure the rights of individuals, the multitude will be very apt to conclude that an affair of trifling consequence vanished under its own insignificance and that the government took up the matter in too high a tone of authority, with a prudish nicety and irritability about their own dignity. This is because of the human mind's propensity for leaning to the speciousness of professed humanity rather than to the necessary harshness of authority and because of vague, imperfect notions of what is due to public authority in an infant popular government, where the great danger is that public authority will not be sufficiently respected.[12]

iii   Authority must be vindicated, but it can be built solidly only upon the universal principles of liberty, said Hamilton. "The nations of Turkey, Russia, France, Spain, and all the other despotic kingdoms, in the world, have an inherent right, when ever they please, to shake off the yoke of servitude (though sanctified by the immemorial usage of their ancestors); and to model their government upon the principles of civil liberty."[13]

The American people "descrying tyranny at a distance, and guided only by the light of just principles, before they had yet felt the scourge of oppression, could nobly hazard all in defense of their rights."[14]

Hence "the world has its eye upon America. The noble struggle we have made in the cause of liberty, has occasioned a kind of revolution in human sentiment. The influence of our example has penetrated the gloomy regions of despotism, and has pointed the way to inquiries which may shake it to its deepest foundations. Men begin to ask every where: who is this tyrant, that dares to build his greatness on our misery and degradation?" However, Hamilton warned, unless "the consequences prove, that we really have asserted the cause of human happiness," it will turn out that "with the greatest advantages for promoting it, that a people ever had, we shall have betrayed the cause of human nature."[15]

Among America's advantages, said Hamilton, was a circumstance which enabled government to raise an equal proportion of revenue without burdening the lower classes of the people in the same degree as in Europe. The

favorable circumstance, he said, was this: the much greater equality of fortunes. By means of it, men in this country may be made to contribute to the
public exigencies in a much juster proportion to their property. In France,
he said, the rich have gained so entire an ascendant that there is a constant
sacrifice of the ease and happiness of the people to their avarice and luxury.
Their burdens are not in proportion to those of the middle order, and still
less to those of the poor (and even in England and Holland, he said, where
the case is not altogether the same, it is nonetheless so in great measure).[16]

A few years after Hamilton had thus favorably compared America's circumstances to those of Europe, and especially to those of France, he spoke
of France's prospects in a letter to his friend Lafayette. The United States
had recently begun its administration of the new Constitution and France
its struggle to find a replacement for the ancien régime. Hamilton wrote that
he had seen "with a mixture of pleasure and apprehension" the progress of
the events which had lately taken place in Lafayette's country: "As a friend
to mankind and to liberty," he said, "I rejoice in the efforts which you are
making to establish it while I fear much for the final success of the attempts,"
as well as "for the fate of those I esteem who are engaged in it," and "for
the danger in case of success of innovations greater than will consist with
the real felicity of your Nation." He explained "why this foreboding of ill,
when all the appearances have been so much in your favor": "I dread disagreements among those who are now united (which will be likely to be
improved by the adverse party) about the nature of your constitution"; "I
dread the vehement character of your people, whom I fear you may find
it more easy to bring on, than to keep within proper bounds, after you
have put them in motion" and "I dread the interested refractoriness of your
nobles, who cannot all be gratified and who may be unwilling to submit to
the requisite sacrifices"; "And I dread the reveries of your philosophic politicians who appear in the moment to have great influence and who being
mere speculatists may aim at more refinement than suits either with human
nature or the composition of your Nation."[17]

The way of life whose animating spirit is enlightened interest, and the
civil society which derives from mankind's natural rights, need to be embodied in a proper structure of government. Such a structure needs a proper
foundation; and in this also, Hamilton thought modernity an improvement
on antiquity.

IV

The Structural Foundation
of Government

Opponents of the new Constitution argued from the premise that powers as ample as those to be established could not safely be reposed in a government over a country so extensive as the United States. Hamilton replied that it is absurd to confide to any government the direction of the most essential national interests while not daring to trust it with the authorities indispensable for managing that direction properly and effectively. This is not to deny, he says, that it will deserve the most vigilant and careful attention of the people, to see that it be modeled in such a manner as to admit of its being safely vested with the requisite powers. A government whose constitution renders it unfit to be trusted with all the powers which a free people ought to delegate to any government would be an unsafe and improper depository of the national interests. But the adversaries of the Convention's plan have wandered from the question. They ought to have confined themselves to showing that the internal structure of the proposed government was such as to render it unworthy of the confidence of the people. They ought not to have wandered into inflammatory declamations and unmeaning cavils about the extent of the powers. The powers are not too extensive for the objects of federal administration, or in other words for the management of our national interests. Any amendments which might, upon mature consideration, be thought useful would apply to the organization of the government, not to the mass of its powers.

The only serious republican alternative is the petty republic. The opponents of the plan, he said, have with great assiduity cited and circulated the observations of Montesquieu on the necessity of a contracted territory for a republican government. They subscribe with ready acquiescence to this principle; to its consequences, however, they seem not to have adverted.

The opponents do not note that when Montesquieu recommends a small extent for republics, the standards which he had in view were of dimensions far short of the limits of almost every one of the American states. Virginia, Massachusetts, Pennsylvania, New York, North Carolina, Georgia—none of them can by any means be compared with the models from which he reasoned and to which the terms of his descriptions apply. If such presumptions as the plan's opponents make are fair—which are, in sum, that the liberties of the United States would probably be easily subverted under a government having the powers proposed—then there ought to be at once an end of all delegated authority. The people should resolve to recall all the powers which they have heretofore let go out of their own hands; and, in order that they may be able to manage their own concerns in person, they should divide themselves into as many states as there are counties.

The opponents of the power of the proposed national government object, for example, to making it possible in extraordinary cases for the national government to recur to a force different from the militia. Yet this necessity applies to the state governments themselves. The opponents thus urge as an objection what, as far as it has any foundation in truth, is an inevitable consequence of civil society upon an enlarged scale, a scale beyond that of petty republics.

The true alternatives to something like the proposed constitution are thus extreme. If we adopt Montesquieu's teaching that a government cannot be republican unless its territory is very small, then we must either at once take refuge in the arms of a monarchy or else split ourselves into innumerable little commonwealths.[1]

In principle these were the alternatives—one large monarchy or very many very little republics—if Americans refused to grant the government of the Union those extensive powers needed to maintain an extensive republic. Americans generally did not like monarchy: it concentrates power to the highest degree. But if they could not establish effective government of a republican form, they would eventually get, at best, limited monarchy, or more likely what they'd get is despotism; and America's best hope for effective government of a republican form was the proposed Constitution.

Hamilton sought to disarm those who opposed the increase in powers essential to that plan by showing that the increase in the powers of the government of the United States would not introduce a completely new foundation, but rather would more effectively complete the foundation already chosen. The foundation of American governmental structure was the large republic. Only a rejection of the large republic could justify the refusal to generate an effective national government, which might become ever more completely *the* government of the nation. Hamilton therefore had to discuss why the large republic is better in principle than the small.[2]

The arguments of the adversaries rested upon a premise which would prove, if true, that we ought to resort to the expedient of separate confederacies, moving within more practicable spheres. The adversaries wished to have the Union, which essentially involved what they did not wish to have: effective government of the Union. "Let us not attempt to reconcile contradictions," insisted Hamilton, "but firmly embrace a rational alternative." The question of the extent of the Union's governmental powers is not truly a question because the alternative to the Union is not truly an alternative for choice. It would become such an alternative only by reconsidering the spirit of modern life and the modern view that derives civil society from natural rights. From the principles of modern government comes the foundation that supports the structure of modern government. Modern government is, fundamentally, representative popular government. And the representative republic perfected is extensive.

The argument against reposing extensive powers in the Union must go further than the adversaries wish. Without the powers proposed to make it a more perfect union, the very incompletely united and therefore incompetent union would fall apart. The extent of the country is the strongest argument in favor of an energetic government, for any other government can certainly never preserve the union of so large an empire. Yet the states, if unconnected, would be unacceptably small. The entire separation of the states into thirteen unconnected sovereignties, says Hamilton, is a project too extravagant and too replete with danger to have many advocates. Hence, the ideas of men who speculate upon the dismemberment of the empire seem generally turned toward three confederacies; there is little probability that there would be a greater number. But the likely fragments of the former Union, though not as useful as the Union for the ends of government, would nevertheless each require a government like the one proposed for the Union, but now being opposed. Each confederacy, says Hamilton, would comprise an extent of territory larger than that of the kingdom of Great Britain. No well-informed man will suppose that the affairs of such a confederacy can be properly regulated by a government less comprehensive in its organs or institutions than that which has been proposed by the Convention. When the dimensions of a state attain to a certain magnitude, it requires the same energy of government and the same forms of administration which are requisite in one of much greater extent. When civil power is properly organized and exerted, it is capable of diffusing its force to a very great extent; and it can, in a manner, reproduce itself in every part of a great empire by a judicious arrangement of subordinate institutions.

ii One reason for rejecting the small republic, in which the people themselves govern, follows from the preference for commercial society over warlike society. Those industrious habits of the people of the present day, who are absorbed in the pursuits of gain and devoted to the improvements of agriculture and commerce, are not only incompatible with the condition of a nation of soldiers, but are incompatible as well with the condition of a nation of citizens in the fullest sense. Discussing the power of appointing officers of government, Hamilton wrote that "The exercise of it by the people at large, will be readily admitted to be impracticable: as, waiving every other consideration it would leave them little time to do anything else." If that little time left to the people at large, after they had exercised the power of appointing officers of government, were then used by the people at large to exercise other powers of governing, they then presumably would be left with no time at all for gainful pursuits and improvements of agriculture and commerce. Comfortable preservation has its price. And this in more than one sense: the modern multiplication of the means of revenue, which has concurred with modern gainful habits of industry and improvement so as to produce armies distinct from the citizens, can also support free governments which are distinct from the citizenry as a body and are better staffed—provided, that is, that the citizens remember that taxes are cheaper than personal service and are less dangerous than cheaply paid public servants.[3]

Moreover, the industrious habits of modern men require not only time but also space in which to operate—that is, they require an extensive market. But an extensive market needs an extensive territory under one government; for, with a multiplicity of governments, commercial intercourse would be fettered, interrupted, and narrowed by a multiplicity of causes. A unity of commercial interests can result only from a unity of government.[4]

The choice for the large republic rather than the small depends upon a preference for the great society of modern times. Its defenders had to struggle against confusion. Nostalgic attraction to simplicity confronted them in combination with repulsion from the sweat of poverty and the blood of ferocity. What prevailed was a superficial confusion, but beneath this there lay deep paradox. To sound the depths of the modern reaction against the modern foundation of government built upon by Hamilton, again one must consider Rousseau.

According to Rousseau's *Contrat Social*, a citizen's principal affair in a good state is public service with his person rather than support of the public with his purse. He flies to the assemblies in the public place rather than remaining at his own place totally absorbed in domestic cares. In the citizen's spirit the public affairs outweigh the private; there is even much less of private affairs, because the sum of common happiness furnishes so considerable a portion of the individual's happiness that there remains to him less of it to seek in particular cares. Paying troops to go to combat, paying deputies to go to council—this, Rousseau wrote, puts the fatherland into servitude under soldiers, puts it up for sale by representatives. From greedy interest in the gain produced by commerce and from soft love of the commodious things produced by arts, men yield part of their profit as payment for public service in order that they themselves may augment their profit by employing the ease they so gain. But those who give silver get themselves into irons: statutory labor is less contrary to liberty than are taxes. *Finance* is a slave's word: a citizen, far from paying to be exempt from civic duties, would pay to fulfill them himself. Rousseau noted his own distance from common ideas. He noted that *finance* is a word unknown in the city, and that *city* is a word whose true sense has been almost entirely effaced among the moderns: most take a town for a city, and a burgher for a citizen, not knowing that the houses make the town but the citizens the city.

In our days, Rousseau wrote, the English, though nearer to liberty than any others subject to a prince, are not citizens. The English think themselves to be free, but they are free only during the election of the members of the parliament; so soon as the members are elected, the English people is a slave, a nothing, which has shown in the short moments of its liberty that it merits losing it. At the instant that a people gives itself representatives, Rousseau declared, it is free no more; it *is* no more. The idea of representatives is modern, coming from the iniquitous and absurd feudal government, which degrades mankind. In ancient republics, and even monarchies, the people never had representatives; the word was unknown. In an ancient Greek city, everything that the people had to do, it did by itself: it ceaselessly assembled in the public square. That people may have had the advantage of a mild climate, but it also had the good character to avail itself of good fortune: it was not greedy; its great affair was its liberty. To be sure, Rousseau acknowledged, it had slaves to do its labors, and slavery is illegitimate; but there are unhappy situations where one can only preserve his liberty at the expense of that of others and where the citizen cannot be perfectly free unless the slave is extremely a slave. Modern peoples do not have slaves: they pay for the liberty of others with their own and they boast

of a preference in which there is more cowardice than humanity. Concluding with the view that for the citizenry to exercise itself rightfully the city
must be very small, Rousseau asked whether it will not then be subjugated
by external enemies. He answered that it need not be subjugated if attention
is properly paid to a totally new matter: confederations.[5]

Hamilton recognized the overwhelming urgency of safety from external danger: it overwhelms, after a time, even the ardent love of liberty.[6] He
wished to avoid the condition of the independent little republic unable to
withstand the power of a great enemy. But he also simply condemned the
condition of the independent little republic continually at war with neighbors as little as itself. Moreover, Hamilton condemned mere confederation
as no solution to the problem. And external considerations did not, for him,
conflict with internal considerations. The extensive republic is better than
the petty one not only because it is safer from external danger, but also
because it is more prosperous: the people stick to their business, which is
not principally civic. It is also safer within: its internal affairs are better
managed precisely because the people do not themselves directly govern.

iii   The men who would hold office in the extensive republic are more
likely to merit office than would those who would man the governments of the county-sized petty republics into which the American states
might be decomposed. The division of the larger states would, by the multiplication of petty offices, answer the views of men who lacked qualifications
to extend their influence beyond the narrow circles of personal intrigue,
Hamilton said, whereas the extension of the spheres of election would
present to the people a greater latitude of choice, a greater option which
promised greater knowledge and more extensive information in the national
councils. Talents for low intrigue and the little arts of popularity may alone
suffice to elevate a man to the first honors in a single state; but it will require
other talents and a different kind of merit to establish him in the esteem and
confidence of the whole Union or of so considerable a portion of it as would
be necessary to make him a successful candidate for the distinguished office
of President of the United States.[7]

However, Hamilton went further than suggesting that the affairs of
larger countries will be conducted by better men. To the observation that
a pure democracy, if it were practicable, would be the most perfect government, Hamilton replied that experience has proved that no position in
politics is more false than this. Little commonwealths are jealous, clashing,
and tumultuous—the wretched nurseries of unceasing discord and the miserable objects of universal pity or contempt. Unceasing agitations and fre-

quent revolutions are the continual scourges of petty republics. Indeed, the ancient democracies, in which the people themselves deliberated, never possessed one feature of good government. Their very character was tyranny, their figure deformity. When they assembled, the field of debate presented an ungovernable mob. These assembled mobs were incapable of deliberation. They were also prepared for every enormity: in these assemblies the enemies of the people systematically brought forward their plans of ambition; they were opposed by their enemies of another party—and it became a matter of contingency whether the people subjected themselves to be led blindly by one tyrant or by another. Thus, no friend to order or to rational liberty can read without pain and disgust the history of the commonwealths of Greece. They were a constant scene of the alternate tyranny of one part of the people over the other or of a few usurping demagogues over the whole. This, together with the lack of a solid federal union to restrain the ambition and rivalry of the different cities, ended—after a rapid succession of bloody wars—in their total loss of liberty and their subjection to foreign powers. It is impossible to read the history of the petty republics of Greece and Italy without feeling sensations of horror and disgust at the distractions with which they were continually agitated and at the rapid succession of revolutions by which they were kept in a state of perpetual vibration between the extremes of tyranny and anarchy.

But why was it that the petty republics of Greece and Italy enjoyed only occasional calms that were short-lived contrasts to the furious storms—why did they enjoy only intervals of felicity that soon were overwhelmed by the tempestuous waves of sedition and party rage? Hamilton explains that the original government of most of these republics had been monarchy, which had succumbed to its natural disease, despotism; in reaction they had established popular governments in which (Sparta excepted) the jealousy of power hindered the people from trusting out of their own hands an authority competent to maintain the repose and stability of the commonwealth. Thus, they had erected government to keep them safe from each other and from strangers; and then, finding themselves not safe from their government, they exchanged it for one which left them even less safe from each other and from strangers. It was their jealousy of power that left them to vibrate between extremes, between unsafe anarchy and unsafe tyranny.

Hamilton acknowledged that when we read the history of the petty republics of Greece and Italy, we do see rays of glory break forth from the gloom, dazzling us with brilliance. But those rays, he said, are momentary; their brilliance is transient and fleeting. While they dazzle us, they at the same time admonish us to lament that the vices of government should pervert the direction and tarnish the luster of those bright talents and exalted endowments for which the favored soils that produced them have been so justly celebrated. Hamilton did not answer those who might ask whether government so formed as to be unavoidably accompanied by those tarnishing vices was not itself a fertilizer needed for the soil to show forth those bright talents and exalted endowments. Be that as it may, the Greeks were *not* "as wise as they were courageous": their intervals of foreign war were filled up by domestic vicissitudes, convulsions, and carnage—and, inflated by glory, they ended under subjugation. To show forth glory that immediately decays is too fleeting an achievement for imitation. A statesman should try to secure a more enduring good. His work is to frame government, and to adjust the frame of government, for "durable liberty."

Arguing on behalf of more power for the authority conducting the struggle for independence, Hamilton wrote that history is full of examples where, in contests for liberty, a jealousy of power has either defeated the attempts to recover liberty or to preserve it in the first instance—or has afterward subverted it by clogging government with too great precautions for its security or by leaving too wide a door for sedition and popular licentiousness. In a government framed for durable liberty, no less regard must be paid to giving the magistrate a proper degree of authority to make and execute the laws with vigor, than to guarding against encroachments upon the rights of the community. As too much power leads to despotism, too little leads to anarchy, and both eventually to the ruin of the people. These maxims are well known but never sufficiently attended to in adjusting the frames of governments. Some momentary interest or passion is sure to give a wrong bias and pervert the most favorable opportunities.

Hence the advocates of despotism have been able to draw arguments not only against the forms of republican government, but against the very principles of civil liberty from the disorders that disfigure the annals of the petty ancient republics. Happily for mankind, Hamilton said, there are some glorious instances of stupendous fabrics reared on the basis of liberty which have flourished for ages—but these are few. America might furnish "the broad and solid foundation of other edifices no less magnificent," which will be equally permanent monuments of the errors of the advocates of despotism.[8]

iv America is the beneficiary of progress. Had it been found impracticable to devise models of a structure more perfect than that of the petty ancient republic, then "the enlightened friends to liberty" would have had to abandon the cause of republican government as indefensible. Hamilton explains why it did not have to come to this. The science of politics like most other sciences has received great improvement. The efficacy of various principles is now well understood, which either were not known at all or were imperfectly known to the ancients. These principles are means, and powerful means, by which the excellencies of republican government may be retained and its imperfections lessened or avoided. Hamilton gives a catalog of circumstances that tend to the amelioration of popular systems of civil government; these, he says, are either wholly new discoveries or have made their principal progress toward perfection in modern times. After listing the regular distribution of power into distinct departments, the introduction of legislative balances and checks, and the institution of courts composed of judges holding their offices during good behavior, he comes to the representation of the people in the legislature by deputies of their own election—and then says he will venture, however novel it may appear to some, to add one more on a principle, which has been made the foundation of an objection to the new constitution: the enlargement of the orbit within which such systems are to revolve.

The foundation of modern republicanism is seen in considering the reason why, in a comparison of our governments with those of the ancient republics, we must without hesitation give the preference to our own: we must do so because every power with us is exercised by representation and not in tumultuary assemblies of the collective body of the people, where what almost always has to govern is the art or impudence of the orator or tribune rather than the utility or justice of the measure. It is, however, only by enlarging the orbit within which popular systems are to revolve that full effect can be given to the principle which makes the American republic superior to the ancient republic—the principle of representation. And, with reciprocal action, it is only by representation that republican government can be made extensive. In the New York Ratifying Convention, Hamilton called the principle that no government but a despotism can exist in a very extensive country a melancholy consideration indeed—for if it were founded on truth, we ought to dismiss the idea of a republican government even for the state of New York. But it has been taken from a celebrated writer (Montesquieu), who, misunderstood, has been the source of frequent fallacies. It relates only to democracies, where the whole body of the people meet to transact business and where representation is unknown. Such were a number of ancient and some modern independent cities. These maxims respecting the extent of country have been applied, contrary to their proper meaning, by men who read without attention, to republics in general. But this application is wrong in respect to all representative governments.

Extensiveness is good for a republic because the public councils of a large whole are less likely to act with partiality than are the public councils of a smaller whole not containing a variety of interests. The national councils, being directed by men drawn from an extensive country, will be less apt to be tainted by the spirit of faction and will be more out of the reach of those occasional ill humors or temporary prejudices and propensities which frequently contaminate the public deliberations in smaller societies—begetting injustice and oppression of a part of the community and engendering schemes that gratify a momentary inclination or desire but terminate in general distress, dissatisfaction, and disgust. The national representation, because it will emanate from a greater variety of interests and in much more various proportions than are found in any single state, will be much less apt to espouse either agriculture or commerce with a decided partiality than will the representation of any single state. And besides presenting an obstacle to the predominance of partiality in the public councils of the whole, extensiveness also helps to repress both faction in local councils and local insurrection against public authority; for when a country is extensive, local disorders are disorders in a mere part and hence may be overcome by those parts which remain sound.[9]

Extensiveness, which helps to make a republican government safer from the strife of popular factions that tend continually to agitate and overturn petty republics, also makes the people safer from their governors. Those who conspire to subvert and destroy the liberty of a community that is large need more time to mature their schemes for execution. In a more extensive country it is also harder for the government to succeed in subduing popular resistance that is widespread—if the citizens understand their rights and are disposed to defend them. That original right of self-defense which is paramount to all positive forms of government may be exerted against the usurpations of the national rulers with much better prospect of success than against the usurpations of the rulers of an individual state. The smaller the extent of territory, the harder it will be for the people to form a regular or systematic plan of opposition, and the easier it will be to defeat their early efforts. Intelligence can be more speedily obtained of their preparations and movements, and the military force in the possession of the usurpers can be more rapidly directed against the part where the opposition has begun. In this situation there must be a peculiar coincidence of circumstances to ensure success to the popular resistance. The obstacles to usurpation and the facilities of resistance increase with the increased extent of the state. By contrast, the natural strength of the people in a large community, in proportion to the artificial strength of the government, is greater than in a small one and is more competent to a struggle against the government's attempts to establish a tyranny. This is because the advantages obtained in one place must be abandoned to subdue the opposition in others, and the moment the part which had been reduced to submission was left to itself, its efforts would be renewed and its resistance revived.[10]

V   Yet, although it is better for the people to consent to be governed in an extensive country than in a tiny one, in no government is consent safely given once for all time: a people not represented will be a people oppressed. It is a mistake to confine arbitrary government to monarchy. What makes a government arbitrary rather than free is not the placement of the supreme power in one man instead of in many. Rather, a people are in the strictest sense slaves and the government is despotic with respect to them, when that people are ruled by laws which they have no part in framing, and which are to bind them without binding, in the same manner, the legislators themselves.

Great Britain is a free country only because its inhabitants have a share in the legislature; if they were once divested of that, they would cease to be free. Because the people of Great Britain have reserved to themselves a share in the legislature, the constitution of Great Britain is a limited monarchy. Every Englishman who can be considered as a free agent has a right to participate in framing the laws which are to bind him, either as to his life or property. The use and design of this right is to preserve the subject's life and property from the encroachments of oppression and tyranny, to secure his liberty from exorbitant power. The Englishman's right to share in the legislative power is meant as a check upon the regal authority, to prevent its degenerating into despotism. But since many inconveniences would result from the exercise of this right in person, it is appointed by the constitution that the Englishman shall delegate it to another in whom he chooses to confide; his own vote is to elect his representative. The whole power and very being of the House of Commons is thus derived from the rights of the people, and its very aim and intention is to secure these rights. Even the property qualification for voting is justified, in the authoritative commentary on the British constitution, by the liberal principle of independence— not by any invidious or plutocratic principle. England is free because at its "foundation," though not in its entirety, it is "democratical." The principle of this is that no laws have any validity or binding force without the consent and approbation of the people, given in the persons of their representatives, periodically elected by themselves.[11]

The intimate connection of interest between these representatives and their constituents—the people of Great Britain—is the means of accomplishing the end of preserving the subjects' life, liberty, and property. The representative in this case is bound by every possible tie to consult the advantage of his constituent. Gratitude for the high and honorable trust reposed in him demands a return of attention and regard to the advancement of his constituent's happiness; so also does self-interest, that most powerful incentive of human actions. Moreover, the trust must expire in a few years, and if he desires the future favor of his constituents, he must not abuse the present instance of it, but must pursue the end for which he enjoys it—otherwise he forfeits it and defeats his own purpose. Besides, if he consents to any laws hurtful to his constituent, he is bound by the same laws and must partake of the disadvantage of them, as will his friends, relations, children—all whose ease and comfort are dear to him. And should he concur in any flagrant acts of injustice or oppression, he will be within the reach of popular vengeance.

With the people of America, the members of the British House of Commons have no such intimate connection of interest, Hamilton says, but the contrary—so that the authority of the British Parliament over America would probably be a more intolerable and excessive species of despotism than an absolute monarchy. (Hamilton notes that Hume, "in enumerating those political maxims which will be eternally true," says—giving "many solid reasons"—that "though free governments have been commonly the most happy, yet are they the most ruinous to their *provinces*.") The power of an absolute prince is not temporary, but perpetual. He is under no temptation to purchase the favor of one part of his dominions at the expense of another; rather, it is his interest to treat them all upon the same footing. But very different is the case with regard to the Parliament. The Lords and Commons both have a private and separate interest to pursue. They would make us bear a disproportional part of the public burdens to avoid them as much as possible themselves. The people of Britain must be an order of superior beings, not cast in the same mold with the common degenerate race of mortals, if the sacrifice of our interest and ease to theirs be not extremely welcome and alluring. They are only mere mortals, fonder of themselves than of their neighbors, and their representatives will gratify the natural propensities of their constituents in order to ingratiate themselves and enhance their popularity.[12]

In a free government the people secure their rights to life and property by participating in the legislative power, most conveniently by means of their election of representatives, who will be bound by their own interests to protect the interests of their constituents. The people's being free, their having a share in the government, does not preclude their also having a king. To exclude monarchy from the class of free governments is a mistake. Although there is no reason of the least force or plausibility for our subjection to parliamentary decrees, said Hamilton before our independence was declared, nonetheless there are the most valid reasons for our allegiance to the king of Great Britain. That king himself, being the supreme executive magistrate, is regarded by the constitution as the supreme protector of the empire. For this purpose he is the generalissimo, or first in military command; in him is vested the power of making war and peace, of raising armies, equipping fleets, and directing all their motions. Thus the law of nature and the British Constitution both continue allegiance to the person of the king and found it upon the principle of protection. It is a delusion to believe that the commotions in America originated in a plan formed by some turbulent men to erect it into a republican government; our author declares himself to be a warm advocate for limited monarchy, and an unfeigned well-wisher to the present royal family.[13]

But the ground of that advocacy of limited monarchy was a road leading beyond limited monarchy. The teaching that all men have equal natural rights, and can be rightfully governed only with their consent, views limited monarchy in the light of the fundamental maxim of republican government that all power, mediately or immediately, is derived from the consent of the people—in opposition to those doctrines of despotism which uphold the divine right of kings or lay the foundations of government in force, conquest, or necessity.[14] That all government is a delegation of power is "this republican maxim."[15] And those who delegate power, the people, are the "original fountain of all legitimate authority." Hamilton asserted that ratification by the people was necessary for laying the foundations of our national government deeper than in the mere sanction of delegated authority. The existing federal system has infirmities, he said, because of its resting on no better foundation than the consent of the several legislatures of the states— the consent, that is, of the authorities to which the people had consented. The fabric of American empire ought to rest on the solid basis of the consent of the people themselves. Not that the people need to be unanimous: the fundamental maxim of republican government requires that the sense of the majority should prevail.[16]

Less than a dozen years after the Declaration of Independence, Hamilton was writing that, independent of all other reasonings, it is a full answer to those who require a more peremptory provision against peacetime military establishments to say that the essential and after all the only efficacious security for the rights and privileges of the people which is attainable in civil society is this: that the whole of the government be in the hands of the representatives of the people.[17]

Even less than a year after the Declaration of Independence, Hamilton had taken the principle of representative government far beyond simply advocating limited monarchy. Gouverneur Morris in May 1777 had written to Hamilton about New York's new state constitution. Morris, "very happy that our Form of Government meets with your Approbation," had "apologized" for it. Hamilton replied that despite his partly agreeing about the defects, "I think your Government far the best that we have yet seen, and capable of giving long and substantial happiness to the people." To the central point, he answered thus: "that instability is inherent in the nature of popular governments, I think very disputable": "unstable democracy, is an epithet frequently in the mouth of politicians," but "the fluctuation of governments in which the popular principle has borne a considerable sway" has proceeded not from its inherent nature but from other causes: "from its being compounded with other principles" ("compound governments, though they may be harmonious in the beginning, will introduce distinct interests; and these interests will clash, throw the state into convulsions and produce change or dissolution") and "from its being made to operate in an improper channel" ("when the deliberative or judicial powers are vested wholly or partly in the collective body of the people, you must expect error, confusion or instability"). "But a representative democracy, where the right of election is well secured and regulated and the exercise of the legislative, executive, and judiciary authorities, is vested in select persons, chosen *really* and not *nominally* by the people, will in my opinion be most likely to be happy, regular and durable." [18]

Hamilton went on to become a warm advocate for what he calls here a properly constituted "representative democracy." He applied the term not only to the first Constitution of the State of New York, but also to the proposed Constitution of the United States, in notes he made for a speech in the New York Ratifying Convention. The portion of these notes that is here relevant contains three parts. In the first part Hamilton discusses the meanings of words used for forms of government. In the central part he gives as the "consequence" of his first part that "the proposed government" is "a *representative democracy*." In the final part Hamilton writes of how "this representative democracy as far as is consistent with its genius has all the features of good government." [19]

vi   Two men are named by Hamilton in these notes on forms of government. Rousseau is the example of those who contribute to confusion by defining democracy otherwise than in Hamilton's sense—the sense in which Hamilton applies that term, properly qualified, to the form proposed for the government of the United States, a form having as far as is consistent with its genius all the features of good government. In treating one of these features, separation of powers, Hamilton mentions Montesquieu.

For understanding the foundation of American government, some genealogy can be helpful. Following Hobbes, Locke's reconstitution of English views on government was developed in the comprehensive French "design" of Montesquieu and in the "elegant" English essays of Hume.[20] Hume's successors in English, Blackstone and Smith, sought to further the enlightenment of government on a foundation of commercial liberty, whereas Montesquieu's successor in French, Rousseau, wrapping himself in russet, attacked that enlightened and enlightening commercial liberty in the name of antique virtue radically modernized. The name of Rousseau is the French connection to that which Hamilton's work resists. Reading the French quite well, and rejecting Rousseau and Robespierre, Hamilton harked back to Hume.

What was accepted as human nature seemed artificial to Rousseau: according to him it is man's nature to be capable of transformation, by the unintended consequences of doing what comes naturally, into civilized man. Natural man becomes an artful transformer of his natural surroundings and a proprietor whose sense of his own is inseparable from comparing himself with his fellows. He is compelled by burgher drives to enter civil society. To be transformed from a town-dwelling burgher into a city-constituting citizen does not, however, come naturally—it requires a supremely artful act. The supreme practitioners of acting to transform the interiors of men were Moses and Mohammed. Christianity, Rousseau says, does not well consist with citizenship—but neither does the burgher spirit, or, rather, spiritlessness. Rousseau left his successors to cope with the difficulty of totally transforming man in his natural particularity into part of a totality.[21] They sought at first to emulate ancient Romans, as actors among actors, employing terror to eliminate those who did not show the virtue to be citizens. Afterward, workers upon workers sought to outdo their predecessors, seeking to transform the base metal of burgher society into radically cooperative humanity.

Hamilton's art, by contrast, does not seek to transform burghers into citizens by forming their interiors: it seeks to arrange external relations that channel rather than suppress what is internal. His art tries to turn human nature to advantage without transforming human nature as it has been given. Its emblem might be the mechanic's lever, not the crucible of the alchemist. It follows Hume: "All plans of government, which suppose great reformation in the manners of mankind, are plainly imaginary."[22] It is time, said Rousseau in his *Confessions*, to say something of this Mr. Hume: he had acquired a great reputation in France, and especially among the Encyclopedists, by his treatments of commerce and of politics, and lastly by his history of the House of Stuart; and I, Rousseau continued, having read only his history in translation, had been persuaded by what had been said to me that Mr. Hume joined a very republican soul to the English paradoxes in favor of luxury. Rousseau reported his reluctance to cross to England to satisfy his desire to meet Hume, though mutual friends had urged him to do so: I hadn't naturally any penchant for England, he said.[23] Hamilton, by contrast, was a great student of Hume's *Essays* on commerce and politics, as he was of *The Inquiry into the Nature and Causes of the Wealth of Nations*, by Hume's great student Adam Smith.[24]

vii   What the Americans learned from English-speaking and English-minded authors led them to oppose the English authorities, who seemed to exceed their authority as spokesmen for Englishmen. The fight against American taxation by English representatives became a war for American independence. The attitudes which fueled the flames of war did not disappear with victory.

The principle of an intimate connection of interest between representative and constituent, upon which rests representation as a means to secure the rights of the people, led many Americans to be afraid of giving too much power to the government of their Union. In defending the proposed Constitution against this fear, Hamilton wrote at length about the power of taxation, which he called the most important of the authorities proposed to be conferred upon the Union. With respect to an indefinite power of taxation in the Union—one not confined to duties on imports, but including a power of internal taxation in the national legislature—the objection most frequently repeated was that the House of Representatives would not be sufficiently numerous to receive all the different classes of citizens. In order to combine the interests and feelings of every part of the community, and to produce a due sympathy between the representative body and its constituents, it was said to be necessary that all classes of citizens should have some of their own number in the representative body, so that their feelings and interests might be the better understood and attended to. This argument, says Hamilton, is well calculated to lay hold of the prejudices of those to whom it is addressed. In showing why the object at which it seems to aim is in the first place impracticable and is also, in the sense in which it is contended for, unnecessary, Hamilton undertakes to clarify further the principle of representation.

The idea of an actual representation of all classes of the people by persons of each class is altogether visionary, says Hamilton. It would never happen unless the Constitution expressly provided that each different occupation should send one or more members, instead of leaving the votes of the people free. Whether the representation of the people be more or less numerous, the same effect will arise from the natural operation of the different interests and views of the various classes of the community: the representative body will consist almost entirely of proprietors of land, of merchants, and of members of the learned professions. It might be objected that besides these three we have seen other descriptions of men in the local legislatures. It is true that strong minds in every walk of life will rise superior to the disadvantages of situation and will command the tribute due to their merit. This is as it should be. The door ought to be equally open to all, says Hamilton, and he trusts, for the credit of human nature, that we shall see examples of such vigorous plants flourishing in the soil of federal as well as of state legislation. Nevertheless, these occasional instances are exceptions to the rule. They are not numerous enough to influence the general complexion, character, or spirit of the government.

Moreover, these exceptions will become even more exceptional in time. Hamilton told the New York Ratifying Convention that while property continues to be pretty equally divided, and a considerable share of information pervades the community, the tendency of the people's suffrages will be to elevate merit even from obscurity; but as riches increase and accumulate in a few hands, as luxury prevails in society, virtue will be in a greater degree considered as only a graceful appendage of wealth, and the tendency will be to depart from the republican standard. This is a disposition of human nature, Hamilton says, that neither he nor his opponents can correct: it is a common misfortune that awaits their state constitution like all others. Nonetheless, asking why there is such frequent talk of aristocracy, Hamilton calls it ridiculous to call this government an aristocracy. Where, he asks, do we find men elevated to a perpetual rank above their fellow citizens and possessing powers entirely independent of them? The arguments only go to prove that there are men who are rich, men who are poor, some who are wise, and others who are not—that indeed every distinguished man is an aristocrat. This reminds Hamilton of a description of the aristocrats in something lately published: the author of *The Federal Farmer* reckons in the aristocracy all governors of states, members of Congress, chief magistrates, and officers of the militia. But the question to be asked is whether the new government renders a rich man more eligible than a poor one—and the answer is that it requires no such qualification. It is bottomed on the broad and equal principle of the state constitution of New York.

Replying to the argument that a national power of internal taxation would result in double taxation, Hamilton in the public prints asserted that any real difficulty in the exercise of the power of internal taxation must naturally tend to make it a fixed point of policy in the national administration to go as far as may be practicable in making the luxury of the rich tributary to the public treasury, in order to diminish the necessity of those impositions which might create dissatisfaction in the poorer and most numerous classes. Happy it is, he said, when the government's interest in the preservation of its own power coincides with a proper distribution of the public burdens and tends to guard the least wealthy part of the community from oppression.

The requisite intimate connection of interest does not require that the body of representatives mirror the constituents in all their multitudinous variety. Indeed, the true and the strong chords of sympathy between the representative and the constituent are that the representative depends on the constituent for continuance in office, and that the representative and his posterity will be bound by the laws to which he assents.

In the New York Ratifying Convention, arguing that in point of number the representation would be perfectly secure, Hamilton called it fallacious to suppose that the representative will have no motive of action but either corruption or a sense of duty. He is to return to the community. He is dependent on the will of the people, and it cannot be his interest to oppose their wishes. There are certain conjunctures when it may be necessary and proper to disregard the opinions which the majority of the people have formed, but in the general course of things the popular views and even prejudices will direct the actions of the rulers. All governments, even the most despotic, depend to a great degree on opinion, but in free republics this is most peculiarly the case. It is the fortunate situation of our country, Hamilton remarked, that the minds of the people are exceedingly enlightened.

In particular, he said in print, there is no danger that the interests and feelings of the different classes of citizens will not be understood or attended to by men of those three descriptions of which the representation will almost entirely consist. They will truly represent all those different interests and views.

The learned professions need little discussion. Truly forming no distinct interest in society, they will, according to their situation and talents, be indiscriminately the objects of the confidence and choice of each other and of other parts of the community. The man of a learned profession, who will feel neutrality in the rivalries between the different branches of industry, is likely to prove an impartial arbiter between them, ready to promote either, so far as it shall appear to him conducive to the general interests of the society.

In politics, and particularly in relation to taxes, the landed interest is perfectly united from the wealthiest landlord to the poorest tenant. Every landholder will have an interest in keeping the taxes on land as low as possible, and common interest may always be reckoned upon as the surest bond of sympathy.

Merchants are the natural representatives of the various classes of practitioners of mechanical and manufacturing arts. These mechanics and manufacturers, with few exceptions, are inclined to give their votes to merchants, and to those whom merchants recommend, in preference to persons of their own professions or trades. Experience confirms that they do so; Hamilton mentions some considerations why it is discerning of them to do so. The interests of the merchant are at least as close to those of any one branch of mechanical or manufacturing arts as those of any two such branches are to each other. What greater affinity can be conceived between the carpenter and blacksmith or the linen manufacturer and stocking weaver than between the merchant and either of them? The merchant is the natural patron and friend of the mechanic and manufacturer because their arts furnish the materials of, and many of them are immediately connected with, his commercial operations. The merchant will thus understand, and be disposed to cultivate as far as may be proper, the interests of the mechanical and manufacturing arts, to which his commerce is so nearly allied. The merchant, moreover, is not merely friendly to their interests: he is abler than they to promote their interests effectually. They are aware that habits in life have not been such as to give them those acquired endowments without which, in a deliberative assembly, the greatest natural abilities are for the most part useless. They are also aware that the influence and weight and superior acquirements of the merchants render them more equal to a contest with any spirit which might happen to infuse itself into the public councils unfriendly to the manufacturing and trading interests.

To be well served, partial interests need to be served "effectually." So do general interests: a representative body could not be large enough to contain members of every branch even of mechanical and manufacturing professions and trades—unless it were far more numerous than would be consistent with any idea of regularity or wisdom in its deliberations. Generally speaking, in a system where election of representatives has established a coincidence of interest between the representatives and the people, what matters is not how closely the representative body mirrors the people at large, but how generally knowledgeable are the people's representatives. Taking into account the momentary humors or dispositions which may happen to prevail in particular parts of the society, and to which a wise administration will never be inattentive, Hamilton asks his readers whether the man whose situation leads to extensive inquiry and information is less likely to be a competent judge of their nature, extent, and foundation than is one whose observation does not travel beyond the circle of his neighbors and acquaintances. To answer, one should be aware that no part of the administration of government requires extensive information and a thorough knowledge of the principles of political economy so much as does the business of taxation. The man who understands those principles best will be least likely to resort to oppressive expedients, since the most productive system of finance will always be the least burdensome. A judicious exercise of the power of taxation requires an acquaintance with the general spirit, habits, and modes of thinking of the people at large and with the resources of the country—this is all that can be reasonably meant by a knowledge of the interests and feelings of the people.[25]

V

The Partition of Power

We have now arrived at a transition in the argument. Let us first look back and then look forward.

It was want of safety against the power of their governors that first led men to popular government, said Hamilton. The interests of the people required government intimately connected with the people. In the first crude attempts to institutionalize this connection, government *for* the people was identified with government *by* the people. Modern enlightenment, founding government on the equal right of every man to secure his safety and prosperity, had revived the ancient prejudice against establishing power far from the hands of the people who are to be affected by the exercise of that power. The modern doctrine of equality had, however, also generated a modern improvement which permitted government to be popular while freeing it from defects of government by the collective body of the people. This principle of popular representation, said Hamilton, gave to modern republics the decisive advantage over ancient republics.

The animating principle of the ancient body politic was animosity: the true condition of the people in the ancient republics was that of a nation of soldiers; in those barbarous times war was the principal business of man. Antiquity was a time of sweat and blood, of poverty and ferocity. The classical republics, those wretched nurseries of unceasing discord, were inflated with the love of glory. The virtue of their citizens was valor, but their valiant displays were vicious. The assembled people, jealous of authority, were an ungovernable mob; when not fighting against other peoples, they clashed tumultuously among themselves. Domestic carnage filled up the intervals of foreign wars. Among themselves they alternated between anarchy and despotism; with others, between despotism and servitude.

But the ferocious maxims of antiquity gave way to the humane innovations of later times, in accordance with pronouncements of enlightened reason. It came to be acknowledged that profitable business, not heroic display, is the business of government. The industrious habits of a modern people, absorbed in gainful pursuits and devoted to productive improvements, are incompatible with the condition of a nation of soldiers, where civic life centers on an assembly of warriors whose delight is domination. The industrious habits of a modern people are incompatible with the condition of a nation of citizens in the fullest sense; for if merely the power of appointing officers of government were ordinarily exercised by the people at large, the people would have little time for anything else. If those who might otherwise go about their business, with enterprise and industry, instead were busy where the action is, the citizenry would be impoverished—unless the action were that collective piracy which supported the armed splendor of antiquity. But modern humanity discountenances fierce rapacity; modern enlightenment looks not to dominion and plunder, but to commerce and production.

The common good, the good common to common men, requires that participation in government be uncommon. Government by the people cannot secure popular safety and prosperity. A people's liberty is not a stage or an arena for displaying popular action; it is rather a protective fence, which, properly erected by popular fear and desire and prudently managed by wise and energetic leadership, may become a productive force. Liberty is that moral security for life and property provided by checks and controls on government. Political society is a means of coping with men's insecurity, an insecurity preceding political society, though political society may complicate that insecurity. Swords and purses, when properly organized by political machinery, protect the lives of vulnerable men exposed to the violence of other men and energize the work of needy men laboring to ease their lives by transforming nature's rawness. Fear and desire are the governing beginnings of government: its ends are safety and prosperity. The ancient republic provided a stage or an arena for contests by sword and word; this now gives way to reliable machinery for cooperation.

ii   We must, said Hamilton, prefer our own governments to those of the ancient republics, because every power with us is exercised by representation, not in tumultary assemblies of the collective body of the people, where the art or impudence of the orator or tribune, rather than the utility or justice of the measure, could seldom fail to govern. We must prefer our own governments, not because they are our own, but because they are preferable. But that which leads us to prefer them requires us to perfect them if we can. Those who estimate the value of institutions, not from the prejudices of the moment, but from experience and reason, Hamilton went on, must be persuaded that jealousy of power has prevented our reaping all the advantages which we ought to have obtained from the example of other nations and has rendered the constitutions of the American governments in many respects feeble and imperfect.[1]

The apportioning of governmental power among several depositories of power, justifiable as an auxiliary precaution against abuse of power, was to be the means for completing the governmental innovation made by the principle of popular representation.

iii   The end of government is to secure the safety and prosperity of the people, who are its source. Government by the collective body of the people endangers and impoverishes the people. Popular representation secures the people against government, while securing the people against themselves by removing government from the hands of the collective body of the people. The body of representatives is different from the body of the people. The representative body is superior to the people in its ability to serve the people's interests. The interests of the representatives are not superior to the people's interests, but the representatives might come to think they are. Safety requires, therefore, that the members of the representative assembly be both numerous and frequently elected. But while representation is at the foundation of good government, representation is not the whole of it. Not only is government which is unchecked by popular representatives a danger to the people; the people are also endangered by an unchecked representative body.[2]

Hamilton asserted that forceful resistance against despotic attempts by government is easier in a republic that is large, even if it is not federal. To allay fears fanned by opponents of the proposed Constitution, he repeatedly argued that when a republic is not only extensive but federal, that is, when its parts are republics in their own right, then the people are even safer: the governments of the component republics stand ready to sound the alarm at the prospect of tyranny, and in the extremity they can lead the well-regulated forces of an outraged people against the usurpers who may occupy the general government of their extensive republic. But we must consider with caution such arguments from a man who warned repeatedly that the states endangered the Union far more than they were endangered by it. Ultimately, to be sure, if the representatives betray their constituents, there is no resource left but the exertion of that original right of self-defense which is paramount to all positive forms of government. But insurrection is a destructive means of keeping legislators lawful; its employment as a remedy for the abuse of power results in great inconveniences. Hence in speaking of the balance between the national and the state governments, one should not think only or even chiefly of insurgent armies led by state governments. That balance forms a double security for the people: not only may the state governments check any despotic attempts by the national government, but a more perfect federal union can check the pernicious proclivities of state governments.

In a nation of states the particular state governments may contribute to safety against the general government of the whole by their multiplying the depositories of power; from one point of view the state governments are *the* parts of the whole. But there is something problematic in a multiplicity of depositories of power that are wholes of a sort similar to the whole of which they are parts. The government of such a whole verges on being a mere league of governments or a government over governments—that is, no government at all. If the whole is not to be an anarchy, the parts must lose their similarity to the whole, thus leaving the government of the whole a great mass of power deposited in a single representative body. However urgent the question of the partition of power among the component parts of a compound republic, the central question is the question of the partition of power among the several departments in a single government.[3]

Government flowing from the people must be divided to work *for the people*. The propriety of this partition resides in the fact that some partition of governmental power is essential to free government: the very definition of despotism is—a government in which all power is concentrated in a single body. Its most obvious form is absolute monarchy. Absolute monarchy, however, is not the only form contrary to free government. No single body, not even a representative assembly, is a safe depository of ample unchecked power. Practically speaking, government must have both purse and sword, but purse and sword must not both be in the same hands.[4]

iv   There is a sense in which good government is thoroughly representative; under the proposed Constitution, said Hamilton, the President of the United States would be himself a representative of the people who would act to protect the people against an unfaithful Congress. Nonetheless, one of the several governmental branches has the proper name "The House of Representatives." The assembly has the name most properly, for it is *the* representative body. By means of representation, the people obtain public servants, whom the people hire to free themselves for business other than the public business and whom they can fire for acting as if free to neglect their tie to the people. The ends of representative government are served by government conducted according to law; legislation is the most manifestly public of acts. And legislation by a numerous assembly most represents the multitudinous people. The legislature seems to represent the immediate being of the society. There is no question that free government requires a freely elected popular assembly: the question is what else it needs.[5]

The principle of representative government is perfected by the partitioning of governmental power. But it is more difficult to hold to such partition than to representation. Insofar as the parts do not approach being whole governments themselves, the parts must be differentiated organs. But one of them, the popular legislative assembly, the part most properly called representative, tends to primacy and even hegemony; and when the part becomes partitioner, the partitioning of governmental power in its sovereign sense is destroyed. The partitioning of power, and even the intermixture of the powers of the parts, have a general explanation in the need for checks upon power and in the need for balance to preserve the system of checks. The general explanation, however, explains only partly. The whole explanation must show partitions of power as differentiations of power, each with its peculiar property.[6]

Government flowing from the people must be divided to *work* for the people. Partition, it's been often said, prevents bad deeds by multiplying the agencies which must cooperate to act. But it should be added that partition also can promote good deeds by differentiating agencies so that different sorts of work get done. The device for diminishing danger from government can be employed for promoting governmental efficacy; government can be energized by the very safeguard against governmental oppression. A modern "Publius" can hope to popularize unpopular truths by building upon popular acceptance of the rule which teaches the propriety of a partition among the various branches of power.[7]

Part Two
Efficacious Administration

VI

Administrative Efficacy

The people had to choose: government by the people, affecting democratic workings, or government from and for the people, effecting popular works. Popular representation freed the populace from continual contention and for productive industry, while safeguarding them against their governors. Americans had accepted this governing principle, Hamilton thought, but imperfectly. Representative popular government could succeed as an alternative to the discredited participatory popular government only by developing administrative efficacy. For protecting the people against turmoil and invasion, and for managing their prosperity, popular representation as such did not suffice.

The partition of power understood as a differentiation of parts enables government to effect its works. Government flowing from the people must be divided to work *for the people;* if the government is to *work* for the people, the division must be a differentiation. The proper end of government is popular, as is its source. Popular representation is the foundation relied upon to keep the ends of government popular. According to Hamilton, the chief executive is in a sense a representative, but in the most precise signification the representatives are the officials who are most numerous and have the shortest duration in office of all the men publicly elected. On the other hand, Hamilton also thought that although the administration of government (the actual business of governing) is in one sense the work of all the parts of the government, yet in the most precise signification the administration of government is the work of the executive part. The "democratical" part of government, the numerous assembly of representatives with short duration in office, cannot itself do the actual work of governing. Popular representation is of little avail without efficacious administration. The people are the beginning and the end of good government—but between the source and outcome operates that organization of means which is administration. The double meaning of *administration* is as significant for the projector of the modern republic as is the multiple meaning of *politeia* for the contemplator of the classical polis.

Practically speaking, the classical political aspiration was shown by Thucydides, who depicted Pericles reminding his fellow-citizens that they would leave behind in everlasting remembrance the splendor of their domineering spirit. The persuasion of a Pericles could concentrate and stabilize a multitude of such imperious wills; his leadership of the polis sometimes required the suspension of even the appearance of politics. But, unfortunately, Periclean leadership requires fortune to supply a Pericles; the deficiency of institutionalized authority must be supplied by extraordinary personal persuasiveness. Pericles, with the mind he had and the esteem in which he was held, was able to hold down the multitude, says Thucydides, leading them rather than being led by them, speaking harsh things rather than sweet things—and so, though the polis in word was a democracy, in work it was rule by the first man; whereas those who came after Pericles, being equal among themselves but each one straining to be first, gave in on practical affairs to what seemed sweet to the people.

At its peak, that polity preeminently spoken of as an arrangement in which the assembled people's power prevailed was in fact an arrangement in which a chief subjected affairs to his initiative: the mind of the one headman effectively prevailed over the valiant he-men because he knew how to speak to them. The first *technologia,* the know-how originally set out in speech among the Greeks, was the art that spoke about artful public speech. The term *technologia* was borrowed by the Romans to designate a systematic treatment of language.[1]

With the coming of modernity, politic men were taught to seek what is useful even if not resplendent: the factual or effectual truth. They were taught to look not to the fact of doing, but to its effect; for the vulgar, who fill the world, are taken with outcomes, with what eventuates from doing. The multitude desires liberty, the politic men were taught, not in order to command but in order to live securely—to live under government that keeps the laws unbroken.[2]

So taught, politic men reassessed the inherited wisdom. The ancients, Bacon said, were puerile: prone to prattle, but unable to generate. Their teachings were fine words barren of works. The classical wise men were adolescents, they were ostentatious and pugnacious, like the classical citizens. They merely substituted disputation for slaughter, the word for the sword.

Rhetoric was the substance of ancient wisdom.[3] Following Bacon's work, Descartes sought to grasp the principles of universal know-how. Undercover, boldly private and privately bold, with patience and with resolution, Descartes, as he turned men's minds from the contemplation of the looks of things to methodical operation, also overturned the public things.[4] In the governing of men, pacification by the spirit of modern technology was to replace the polemic art of ancient rhetoric.

According to Hobbes, democracy is the worst form of government: though the right of sovereignty be in the assembly, which is virtually the whole civil body, yet a democracy in effect is no more than an aristocracy of orators, interrupted sometimes with the temporary monarchy of one orator. Hobbes explains why what is most preferred is worst: men favor popular government over monarchy because they suppose that not to participate in public business is grievous to all men; this supposition is made because the desire of praise is natural to human beings and is most delightfully satisfied when they can show their wisdom, knowledge, and eloquence in deliberating on most momentous matters of the greatest difficulty. But this loss of an opportunity for vainglory is a grievance only if it is a grievance to be restrained from fighting; and though the valiant may delight in fighting, only the desire for applause would lead a man to mind the public rather than his own business. Moreover, Hobbes continues, large assemblies are inconvenient for deliberations: few men are skilled in public affairs; the display of alluring eloquence, which seeks victory, replaces the informing effort which seeks truth; faction arises, leading to sedition and civil war, or to instability in the laws; and secrets cannot be kept from the enemy. Hence, Hobbes concludes, aristocracy is good to the extent that it is like monarchy, and bad to the extent that it is like popular government; and democracy would be good, like monarchy, to the extent that the people in a democracy would bestow on one man or a few the power of deliberating, being content with the naming of magistrates and public ministers—being content, that is to say, with the authority without the "ministration."[5]

Subsequently, the work of the modern republican spirit, in which the polemic polity of spiritedness gave way to the productive spirit of political economy, was promoted by the publication of Montesquieu's work *De l'Esprit des Lois*. Montesquieu discussed the need to separate the legislative, executive, and judicial powers, in the chapter on the constitution of England in the book on the laws that form political liberty in relation to the constitution. There he says that political liberty in a citizen is that tranquility of mind which proceeds from each person's opinion of his own security. This requires a government such that one citizen does not fear another.

In a free state every man who is counted as having a free soul ought to be governed by himself, and so the people as a body need to have the legislative power. But this is impossible in a large state and is subject to many inconveniences in a small one. The people therefore need to do by their representatives what they cannot do by themselves. It was, however, a great vice in most of the ancient republics, says Montesquieu, that the people had a right to take active resolutions which require some execution: the people ought not to enter into the government except to choose its representatives. Moreover, the representative body also ought not to take any active resolution: it ought only to make laws or see if those which it has made have been well executed.[6]

Spiritedness, to be sure, continued to play a part in modern civil society, as may be seen from Adam Smith's discussion, in *The Wealth of Nations*, of the sources of the quarrel that developed out of taxation without representation. Bad conscience, however, overwhelmed the display of spiritedness, and the poetry of antagonism gave way to the prose of cooperation. Hume contrasts "the prudent views of modern politics," which seek not glory but security, with "the ancient Greek spirit of jealous emulation."[7]

From the point of view of modern prudence, it seemed better to be businesslike than to be rhetorical. Along with the downgrading of rhetoric, came a change in vocabulary. To judge from the earliest listing in the *Oxford English Dictionary*, the word *energy* entered English "with reference to speech or writing," having the meaning of "force or vigour of expression"—as in Sidney's *Defense of Poesie* (1581): "That same forcibleness or Energeia (as the Greeks call it) of the writer." According to the *Dictionary*, "This sense (found in Late Latin and in Romanic) is originally derived from . . . Aristotle's use of *energeia* (Rhet. III.xi.sec.2) for the species of metaphor which calls up a mental picture of something 'acting' or moving." With the progress of modernity, *energy* outgrew its primary rhetorical meaning. When Hamilton spoke of "energy," what he had in mind was not display: he meant business. The rejection of classical politics culminates in the politics of administration.

ii   Hamilton early learned and taught that the administration of government, in modern popular government at least as much as in all others, has its own requirements, which cannot be ignored: for example, expertise.

Even war, the very action whose outcome might be thought most simply to result from the spiritedness of citizens, turns out to be an affair of specialized know-how. During the War for Independence, Hamilton saw American defeat as a lesson in the necessity of changing the American military system: militia were not the best bulwark of American liberty. Before the war broke out, he had exclaimed about how soon a people possessed of natural bravery may, by disciplining their men in that order and method in which they are deficient, be brought to equal the most regular troops—especially where circumstances favor irregular warfare against superior military regularity and skill. Experience, however, had taught a harsh lesson, which Americans ought to have learned. The doctrine that the militia of the country is its natural bulwark, and would at all times be equal to the national defense, almost lost us our independence, Hamilton said, and it cost millions that might have been saved: the facts of Americans' own recent experience forbid a reliance of this kind. The steady operations of war against a regular and disciplined army can be successfully conducted only by a force of the same kind. This position is confirmed by considerations of economy as much as of stability and vigor. The American militia in the course of the War for Independence, by their valor on numerous occasions, erected eternal monuments to their fame, he said, but the bravest of them feel and know that the liberty of their country could not have been established by their efforts alone, however great and valuable they were. War, like most other things, is a science to be acquired and perfected by diligence, by perseverance, by time, and by practice.

But Americans would not learn the lesson. Next-best measures were therefore necessary. In transmitting a detailed proposal for a military academy, Hamilton wrote that insofar as the circumstances and policy of a country forbid a large military establishment, that which does exist at any time should be perfected as much as is possible. Since it is agreed that Americans are not to keep on foot numerous forces instructed and disciplined, military science in its various branches ought therefore to be cultivated with peculiar care in proper nurseries, so that there may always exist a sufficient body of such knowledge ready to be imparted and diffused and a competent number of persons qualified to act as instructors to the additional troops which events may successively require to be raised. The most pacific policy on the part of a government will not preserve it from being engaged in war more or less frequently; hence, to avoid great evils, it must either have a respectable force prepared for service or the means of preparing such a force with expedition. The latter, most agreeable to the spirit of the American government and nation, is the object of a military academy.[8]

It was not against expertise in war alone that the popular spirit in America was prejudiced. Noting that there had been no answer to his suggestion that engineers be employed to assist in forming a plan for a port that had been surveyed, Hamilton wrote that help from those with technical knowledge was necessary for the complicated task. But, he said, self-sufficiency and a contempt of the science and experience of others are traits of character too prevalent in this country.

Lack of technical knowledge had supported opposition to something of the utmost importance in governing the country: the national bank. The most incorrigible theorist among that bank's opponents would, he said, in one month's experience as head of the Treasury, be compelled to acknowledge it to be an absolutely indispensable engine in the management of the finances and would become a convert to its perfect constitutionality.

Earlier, those who objected to granting a power of internal taxation to the national legislature, when they claimed that a national legislature would lack sufficient knowledge of local circumstances, showed themselves to lack sufficient knowledge of the place of detailed technical knowledge in government. Even under governments of the more popular kind, nations usually commit the administration of their finances to single men or to boards composed of a few individuals, who first prepare the plans of taxation which afterward are passed into laws by the authority of the sovereign or legislature. Inquisitive and enlightened statesmen are deemed everywhere to be those who are best qualified to make a judicious selection of the objects proper for revenue. When the objection is applied to real property, to houses and lands, it seems better founded, but only at first sight. Whether land taxes are laid by permanent or periodical valuations or by occasional assessments according to the best judgment of officers whose duty it is to make them, the execution of the business must be devolved upon discreet persons in the character of commissioners or assessors who are elected by the people or appointed by the government for the purpose. The law can do no more than name the persons or prescribe the manner of their election or appointment, fix their numbers and qualifications, and draw the general outlines of their powers and duties; the attention of the legislature can only reach to general principles, while local details must be referred to those who are to execute the plan.

Later, after Hamilton had left the Treasury, where he himself had prepared plans of taxation for the infant republic, his successor in the post sent him a report that disquieted him, but he would not attempt to suggest anything, he said—because he did not now know details. The only exception to his refusal was this general observation: if the means previously provided were likely to prove inadequate, Congress ought to be told so explicitly; his own maxim had been that executive arrangements should not fail for lack of full disclosure to the legislature—if adequate provision was then not made, the responsibility was theirs. For the present, Hamilton said, we shall weather all storms but those from real deficiencies in our public arrangements: the worst evil with which we can struggle is inefficacy in the governmental measures.[9]

The efficacy of governmental plans requires a corps of men not only for preparation but also for execution. Without proper organs for execution, good plans are made in vain; every new step to be taken is attended with embarrassment for lack of organization. Consider, for example, the execution of the business of procuring military supplies. This will grow, said Hamilton, with the growth of the country. It is a foolish attempt at economy to rely on the employment of many impermanent special agents in order to keep the officers of government few. For transacting public business whose object is likely to be permanent, regularly constituted officers of the government are more fit than are specially employed agents of a department. More effectual checks can be placed, by law, upon the regular officer. (This is particularly important in procuring military supplies, where the person entrusted ought to be prohibited, under penalties, from all dealing on his own account in the objects of supply.) Moreover, the duration and emoluments of mere agency being precarious, it would be more difficult, if possible at all, to find a well-qualified man disposed to make the necessary sacrifice of other pursuits in order to devote himself exclusively to the business. A mere agent who contracts to do public business, feeling little responsibility, executes carelessly. A good manager will be far less expensive than an agent under contract. To compensate an officer is an expense, but it is also an expense to employ and compensate an agent, and far more money than the officer's salary would be saved by the minute as well as extensive inquiries and investigations which a person can make when he is charged exclusively with an object that has his close, constant, undivided attention. Such attention would also greatly contribute to punctuality and dispatch. Efficacy would be promoted by assembling an organized apparatus of men entrusted with the transaction of public business.[10]

A legislature may regulate governmental establishments by establishing an organization with a general outline of duty, but a legislature should not insist on making detailed regulations. To vary as experience advises, detailed regulations will properly come from the executive departments, which are the great branches of administration, and from the chief executive, who presides over these great branches of administration.[11]

The administration of government is an affair of detail, but those who preside over the detailed preparation, execution, and modification of government plans must not be little men mastered by detail. The minister of a great department must subdivide the objects of his care, distribute them among competent assistants, and content himself with a general but vigilant superintendence. This course is particularly necessary when an unforeseen emergency has suddenly accumulated a number of new objects to be provided for and executed. Hamilton says that he knows from experience that no man, whatever his talents or diligence, can wade through a vast mass of details without neglecting the most material things and attaching to his operations a feebleness and sloth of execution. To be plunged into a vast mass of details is not to govern. A man who has probity, as well as talents for business within a sphere of action which admits of an immediate personal attention to everything that needs doing, may yet be incompetent to exercise an office which embraces extensive and complicated objects, in which system and arrangement and various combinations are necessary. The minister of a great department oversees other men who minister to him by attending to the details.[12]

The minister of a great department is not only a superintendent but an adviser; the greatest minister is a great adviser. The man who ministers to governmental business at the highest level presides over ministers, and the greatest man who presides over ministers is well advised to get advice from them. A President is not bound to conform to the advice of his ministers and is not even under any positive injunction to ask for or require it; but the Constitution presumes that he will consult them, and the spirit of our government and the public good recommend the practice. As the President nominates his ministers, and may displace them when he pleases, it must be his own fault if he is not surrounded by men who, for ability and integrity, deserve his confidence; and if his ministers are of this character, to consult them is always likely to be useful. Even if he is a man of talents superior to the collected talents of all his ministers (which can seldom happen, as the world has seen but few Fredericks), nonetheless he may often assist his judgment by a comparison and collision of ideas. Even the greatest genius, hurried away by the rapidity of his own conceptions, will occasionally overlook obstacles which ordinary and more phlegmatic men will discover, and which, when presented to his consideration, he himself will think decisive objections to his plans. Even the ablest men may profit by advice; but inferior men cannot dispense with it, and if they do not get it through legitimate channels, it will find its way to them through such as are clandestine and impure. When an ordinary man dreams himself to be a Frederick and through vanity refrains from counseling with his constitutional advisers, he is very apt to fall into the hands of intriguers, who put his self-love more at ease and slide without difficulty into his confidence and govern him. A presiding officer who thinks himself great enough to govern unassisted by advisers is likely to be governed by flattery.

The expression of these views on advice was occasioned by the practice of John Adams, successor to the President for whom Hamilton was first minister. Hamilton concluded these remarks by saying that the practice of John Adams was very different from that of the modest and sage Washington—who consulted much, pondered much, resolved slowly, resolved surely. Under Adams, Hamilton had earlier said, the country experienced feebleness and delay. Telling Rufus King the causes of this, Hamilton had remarked on how widely the business of government differs from the speculation of government, how widely the energy of the imagination dealing in general propositions differs from the energy of execution in detail. Hamilton expected the difficulty to be surmounted, however, and he anticipated, with King, that this country would ere long assume an attitude correspondent with its great destinies: majestic and effective—operative of great things. A noble career lies before it, he said. He then exclaimed: why does not Gouverneur Morris come home—his talents are needed; men like him do not superabound. Indeed, Hamilton wished that King were there at home rather than where he was, abroad; though King's position at that juncture was important, Hamilton thought, America needed to infuse more abilities into the management of its internal affairs.[13]

Able men are not enough, however. Such men need an effective government whose affairs they can manage. It was "excuseable," said Hamilton, for Americans to err at the beginning, when "good intentions, rather than great skill, were to have been expected from us"; "we began this revolution with very vague and confined notions of the practical business of government," for it was "a novelty" to "the greater part of us." Those who, under the former constitution, had opportunities of acquiring experience adhered in large proportion to the opposite side, and the remainder can only be supposed to have possessed ideas adapted to the narrow colonial sphere in which they had been accustomed to move—not ideas of that "enlarged" kind suited to the government of an independent nation. Exceptions there doubtless were, but their influence was too commonly borne down by the prevailing torrent of "ignorance and prejudice." There having been since then, however, time for reflection and experience, to persist in error becomes "disgraceful and even criminal."[14]

Good intents do not suffice for securing good effects, he said, and the tendency to produce good outcomes is essential to good government. To good intentions, America owed her independence; the outcome of the

struggle, insofar as it was not an immediate gift of fortune, was the product of a fortunate inspiration of enthusiasm. There is a certain enthusiasm
in liberty that makes human nature rise above itself in acts of bravery or
heroism. Transition to liberty inspires an enthusiasm that may possibly
substitute for the energy of a good administration as the spring of great
exertions, but the ebullitions of enthusiasm must ever be a precarious reliance. Reliance for good government on the good intentions of the people
had its source in an excessive distrust: the noble enthusiasm of liberty is
too apt to be infected with a spirit of narrow and illiberal distrust of governmental power, even though liberty cannot be secured without vigorous
government. Zeal for liberty is too often more ardent than enlightened. A
glorious struggle had been conducted in a disastrous manner; and "notwithstanding we have by the blessing of providence so far happily escaped
the complicated dangers of such a situation," Hamilton warned, it would be
unwise to hazard a repetition of the same dangers or to continue this extensive empire under a government unequal to its protection and prosperity.
But it was hardly to be expected that in a popular revolution the minds of
men should stop at that salutary mean between power and privilege which
combines the energy of government with the security of private rights. Too
little regard for the rights and liberties in defense of which the people fought
and suffered was not the American error; the American error was rather that
through excess of caution and impracticable zeal the public counsels were
devoid of consistency and stability. A new improved organization of power
was needed. This meant strengthening nation against state, and executive
against legislature.[15]

Americans suffered many evils because they confused popular government with governmental popularity. Government, however, is more truly
popular when the people like the long-lasting outcomes, which may be a
long time in coming, than when the immediately effective source of governmental outcomes is like the people or tends to what is immediately popular.
Such a principle was hard to make immediately clear to the people; and
many leaders of the people took the way more immediately pleasant to
themselves of immediately pleasing the people, that is, they became flattering demagogues. Instead of leading the people, they misled the people by
flattering the people's prejudices. In the American practice of taxation and
public finance, Hamilton found many examples of this pernicious popularity.

The little politicians who lack the capacity to govern but are consummate in the paltry science of courting and winning popular favor, he said,
stigmatize an enlightened zeal for the energy and efficacy of government as

the offspring of a temper fond of despotic power and hostile to the principles of liberty. But a dangerous ambition more often lurks behind the specious mask of zeal for the rights of the people, than under the forbidding aspect of zeal for the firmness and efficacy of government.

Hamilton, after helping to found the new government, sought to have it operate in a manner opposed to the feeble and contracted views of those who lacked the wisdom to plan and the spirit to adopt energetic measures. In every community there is a natural resistance to government, resulting from the human passions, but the people need to submit to present displeasures to avoid the more oppressive future burdens with which necessity will afflict those who, lacking foresight and fortitude, live under the delusion that they are free from necessity. Popular safety and prosperity require efficacious administration, but efficacious administration requires what is not immediately popular.

Popular prejudice against being governed, when it is formed into political opinion, operates under the name "republican jealousy"; its teaching is this: to grant power is to concentrate the capacity to harm the people and thus to contribute to erecting monarchy on the ruin of the republic. The politics of Jefferson exemplified for Hamilton the confusion of good government with popularity. "I am not a friend to very energetic government," wrote Jefferson to Madison; "It is always oppressive." Jefferson, not a friend to Hamilton, called the movement led by Hamilton "the *monocratic* party," and Jefferson used strong terms to characterize the difference that divided his own partisans from those that followed Hamilton:

> Were parties here divided merely by greediness for office, as in England, to take a part with either would be unworthy of a reasonable or moral man, but where the principle of difference is as substantial and strongly pronounced as between the republicans & the Monocrats of our country, I hold it as honorable to take a firm & decided part, and as immoral to pursue a middle line, as between the parties of Honest men & Rogues, into which every country is divided.

There is a certain aptness, to be sure, in the term "monocrat": *E pluribus unum* might be taken as Hamilton's motto in more ways than one. But the word "monocrat," used in contradistinction to "republican," was devised to be a weapon of revolutionary war: the popular prejudice against being governed was being enlisted by faction in a war of principles, thought Hamilton. The year after his armies lost the great battle of that war, an election address by Hamilton explained why the leaders he opposed could be called hostile to our national Constitution. To what end, he asked his fellow citizens, has your attention been carried to the revolution in France and to that fatal war of which it has been the source? To what end, he asked, are you told that it is a war of principles—a war between equal and unequal rights, between republicanism and monarchy, between liberty and tyranny? And then he said, of those whose ends he questioned, that "they have openly avowed their attachment to the excessive principles of the French revolution, and to leading features in the crude forms of government which have appeared only to disappear; utterly inconsistent with the sober maxims upon which our Federal Edifice was reared, and with essential parts in its structure." He concluded his address by saying of "these sects, which compose the pith and essence of the antifederal party," that "the contest between us is indeed a war of principles—a war between tyranny and liberty, but not between monarchy and republicanism"; "It is a contest between the tyranny of jacobinism, which confounds and levels everything, and the mild reign of rational liberty." This reign has as its basis a government that is "efficient and well balanced"; and "through the medium of stable laws" it "shelters and protects the life, the reputation, the civil and religious rights of every member of the community." It is against these sects that "all good men should form an indissoluble league"; "to resist and frustrate their machinations is alike essential to every prudent and faithful administration of our government, whoever may be the depositaries of the power."

According to Jefferson, the culmination of the struggle was a revolution. He said that though it was "not effected . . . by the sword . . . but by the rational and peaceable instrument of reform, the suffrage of the people," nonetheless "The Revolution of 1800 was as real a revolution in the principles of our government as that of 1776 was in its form."[16]

According to Madison, who was Hamilton's great collaborator in the effort to constitute a new government and his first great opponent in its operation, the prime source of this great party struggle was Hamilton's straining of *administration*:

> Mr. M., ". . . I deserted Colonel Hamilton, or rather Colonel H. deserted me; in a word, the divergence between us took place—from his wishing to *administration,* or rather to administer the Government (these were Mr. M's very words), into what he thought it ought to be; while, on my part, I endeavored to make it conform to the Constitution as understood by the Convention that produced and recommended it, and particularly by the State conventions that *adopted* it."[17]

Hamilton would not trust to fortune for splendid feats of virtue that would bless and keep the republic. He deemed it wiser to secure energetic administrative machinery that would operate reliably throughout an extended territory during a protracted time to produce one general interest from many most common interests. Good government—a system of liberty that is effective for protection and prosperity—must concentrate power and keep policy constant.

Those who are dominated by apprehension of being dominated, when they think of security from government, think mostly of how to secure the endangered people against government, and little of how to secure popular ends by means of government. Safety from government means keeping government from doing bad things. The powers needed to do much of anything are separated on the presumption that though the several depositories of power will have difficulty coming together, and staying together, in order to do bad things, they will nonetheless come together, and stay together, in order to do good. But the fear that leads to precautions against government's doing bad may lead to arrangements that keep government from doing much good. This is, literally, anarchy.

In a government amply arranged for safety against government, adequately arranging for energy of government is a problem. The problem is twofold: to concentrate power sufficiently for many wills to act as one at one time, and to stabilize policy sufficiently for many actions to be in concert during a long time for constant purposes. Governmental efficacy had two ingredients for Hamilton: unity and duration. Neither of these is characteristic of the numerous and short-lived representative body that is characteristic of free government and is also fundamental to good government. Nonetheless, both of the ingredients of efficacy could be infused into parts of a popular government properly partitioned. Unless the powers of government are apportioned to promote administrative efficacy, those who take part in the mutable affairs of the multitudes of men massed in political society will be uncooperative and improvident. America's new order of the ages would not last for ages if its founders could not find a way to make the means of safety also efficacious. The work of a founder is to lead men to agree to arrangements that will foster, among the leading men who will follow after them, the energetic wisdom which is leadership. There cannot be energetic wisdom without the two ingredients of efficacious administration: unity and duration.

VII
Unity

The first step in our acquiring internal consistency, said Hamilton, the first step in our acquiring a well-constituted and effective government, was to abandon that feeble and anarchical system which had brought us almost to the last stage of national nothingness. There is something diminutive and contemptible in the spectacle of a number of petty states having only the appearance of union, without any determined direction; jarring, jealous, and perverse; fluctuating and unhappy at home, and seen by other nations as weak and insignificant because of their dissensions. Governments are more or less energetic as their men are more or less united; the men are never simply united, and it is governmental arrangements that constitute them into a more or less perfect union.[1]

Unity is not easy to achieve perfectly. It is even hard to try to achieve an increase in unity. The critical moment for doing this was the summer of 1787: it was a "miracle" that the delegates to the Convention were there, exercising their tranquil and free deliberations on the subject, said Hamilton. He, if anyone, was the prime mover in providing that there would be such a convention, and he said it would be madness to trust to future miracles. Though there were imperfections in the plan that came forth from the Convention, efforts to amend the proposal should be postponed and brought forward one-by-one after ratification, for it is harder to achieve unity the more numerous are the points to be decided and the parties to the agreement. The difficult work of forming one from many is made easier by separating what is to be done all at one time and what is to be left to be done over a long time.[2]

The work of winning independence, though successful, had been precarious, because those who supported the common cause had to rely on the precarious concurrence of thirteen distinct deliberations. Hamilton expected that it would require arduous work to make independence a blessing by perpetuating the Union: the centrifugal force in the states was much stronger than the centripetal, the seeds of disunion much more numerous than those of union. After the War for Independence as before, the complete execution of every important measure that proceeded from the Union required thirteen distinct sovereignties to concur, with the foreseeable result that the measures of the Union were not executed.

Whenever a number of men compose a body, their being numerous makes them lose shame and become factious—and shirk their duty. But when a number of bodies compose a confederate body politic, their esprit de corps makes them seek power—and resist restraint upon their complete sovereignty; and so in this case the difficulties of any human cooperation in popular assemblies are compounded and multiplied by the multiplicity of components that must work together. The components, although themselves wholes of some kind, are also parts of a whole, which must itself be able to work as a whole. If only to defend the larger whole, plans and measures must be unified, but the component parts will not cooperate unless the powers to effect the common defense belong to the whole. The whole is a whole, moreover, not only with respect to its integrity over against other wholes like it outside of it, but also with respect to internal exchange—and a common market needs a government of the whole community.

The government of the whole must be truly a government. It must, that is, be able to obtain and employ men and money by legislating for its individual citizens. It must not try to govern governments. To bind by laws is coercive; to be bound by laws is not simply voluntary response to words. However, neither is it violent subjection by swords; it is a condition of liberty. The only alternatives to government by law are anarchy and despotism. The government of the Union must have what each state government has: it must not be a mere government over governments, but must have courts with jurisdiction over individuals, so that it may address itself immediately to the hopes and fears of individuals and be supported by the most influential passions. The state courts and the national courts must be parts of one whole—parts, however, of differing sorts, for one of the parts must speak for the whole: the last word on the rights of a part belongs to the jurisdiction of the Union.[3]

How to reconstitute the federal Union to keep it from dissolving into a plurality of confederacies—this was the urgent problem in Hamilton's America. He had to fight the fear that said that those who wished to form a more perfect union of the confederally united states would by their act dissolve these states into a perfectly consolidated unity. The most urgent work of unification in America was the "federalist" work that the words *E pluribus unum* first call to mind: from the point of view of urgency, *the* problem of unity was the problem of the Union—how to form a more perfect union. But a unity more intense than the consolidation of states in national union is the concentration of power *within* the more extensive government. The question most central was not the urgent federal question, the question of Union, but rather the republican question—the question of monarchy, and of aristocracy. To this let us now turn.

ii   The single-minded attention to security against concentrated power is most concentrated in the fear of monarchy, the arrangement that most facilitates authoritative action by authorizing action to proceed from one mind without requiring the concurrence of other minds. The single-minded attention to security from abuse of power, said Hamilton, does not attend with due care to the mischiefs that may be occasioned when the public business cannot go forward at critical seasons. When unanimity or something approaching it is required in public bodies, security is the intent, but the effect (besides an increased danger of foreign corruption) is always weakness, sometimes bordering on anarchy. When the concurrence of a large number is required by the constitution for doing any national act, Americans rest satisfied that all is safe, because nothing improper will be likely to be done—forgetting how much good may be prevented, and how much ill may be produced, by the power to hinder necessary action and to keep affairs in the same unfavorable posture in which they may happen to stand at particular times. Whenever two or more persons are engaged in any common enterprise, there is always a danger of difference of opinion, and there is peculiar danger of personal emulation and even animosity if it be a public trust or office clothing them with equal dignity and authority. Men often oppose a thing merely because they have had no agency in planning it or because it may have been planned by those whom they dislike or because they had once been consulted and happened to disapprove.

The principles of a free government require submitting to the inconveniences of dissension in the formation of the legislature. In the legislature, moreover, prompt decision is more often bad than good; there, deliberation and moderation are often promoted by the differences of opinion and the jarring of parties that may sometimes obstruct salutary plans. In the executive department, however, dissensions do no good that counterbalance the harm that dissensions do to what should be the executive department's characteristic features: vigor and expedition.[4]

iii   Hamilton very early argued that the Continental Congress should arrange for administration by a single man in each department of affairs, and he went on to complete the argument as a warm advocate on behalf of the executive power vested by the Constitution of the United States in a single man.

In 1780 he presented to a member of the Congress his thoughts on the defects of the system and the changes necessary to save America from ruin. Listed right after the fundamental defect, which is a want of power in Congress vis-à-vis the states (that is, the imperfection of the Union), the very next defect is want of method and of energy in the administration, which, though it partly results from the other defect, results in a great degree from prejudice and the want of a proper executive.

It is impossible, says Hamilton, for such a body as Congress, numerous and constantly fluctuating, to act with sufficient decision or with system. Congress, convinced at last that administration by a large assembly is a bad arrangement, adopted instead the practice of appointing boards. But this practice lately adopted by Congress is also bad, for boards partake of the inconveniences of larger assemblies. A greatly preferable plan would be to vest the great executive departments in the hands of individuals. Arguing in favor of making a single man the head in each department of the administration, Hamilton characterizes administrative boards. Their decisions are slower. Their decisions, one might say, are less decisive: they react instead of being active; that is, their energy is less. Their responsibility is more diffuse. Whatever else is bad about this characteristic last mentioned, it seems to be responsible for another bad characteristic: boards will not have the same abilities and knowledge as will an administration by single men. Their ability will be less, since men of the first pretensions will not so readily engage in boards, because they will have less opportunity of distinguishing themselves; and their knowledge will be less, since those who do become members of boards will take fewer pains to inform themselves and come to eminence, because they have fewer motives to do so. Since administration by single men in each department would give America a chance of more knowledge, more activity, more responsibility, and more zeal and attention, while of course these men would be at all times under the direction of Congress, this arrangement would "blend the advantages of a monarchy and republic in our constitution."

The heart of the difficulty seems to be the love of honor. A question has been asked: could single men be found to undertake these offices? Hamilton answers that they could, because everything would excite the ambition of candidates—if Congress, by their manner of appointing them and by the duties they mark out for them, show themselves to be in earnest about making them offices of real trust and importance. This appeal to the love of honor would, however, seem to frustrate the love of honor of those who would have to make the appeal: Hamilton fears that vanity has stood in the way of these arrangements, as though such arrangements would lessen the importance of Congress and leave the members of Congress nothing to do. But the frustration is imaginary: freed from vain imaginings, the members of Congress would have the same rights and powers as before, happily disencumbered of the detail. They would have to inspect the conduct of their ministers, deliberate upon the plans proposed by them, and themselves originate other plans for the public good—the only difference in such an arrangement being the rule that they ought to consult their ministers, getting from them all possible information and advice before entering into new measures or making changes in the old.

Further on in the letter, when Hamilton says what offices ought to be established and with what powers and duties, it becomes clear that his mention of the advantages of monarchy in connection with administration by single men is not a mere matter of terminology, for his express model is French administration under the ancien régime.[5]

When Hamilton, later on, urged adoption of the proposed Constitution, he declared in favor of a numerous legislature, as best adapted to deliberation and wisdom, and best calculated to conciliate the confidence of the people and to secure their privileges and interests—while declaring in favor of a single executive, because the proceedings of one man are most eminently characterized by decision, activity, secrecy, and dispatch. The persons to whose immediate management are committed those matters which constitute the administration of government properly understood, he said, ought to be considered as the assistants or deputies of the chief magistrate.[6]

iv   In one sense the executive is but a part of the government; in another sense the executive is the government. The First Congress under the new Constitution was warned by Madison that they ought not to look, for the meaning of terms used in the laws and Constitution of the United States, into the meaning accepted in other countries, whose situation and government are different from that of the United States: in monarchies, both absolute and limited, the residence of the monarch is the seat of government, but in such a government as ours the seat of government cannot be at a place other than where Congress sits, for the government comprehends Congress as well as the executive; and "so the term Administration, which in other countries is specially appropriated to the Executive branch of Government, is used here for both the Executive and Legislative branches."

Hamilton, however, in calling the executive "*the* Governor" (emphasis added) in the plan of government he presented at the Convention, was merely following previous state practice. And subsequent national practice, which measured governmental time by administrations defined by the terms of chief executives, seemed to confirm Hamilton's remark that "The administration of government, in its largest sense, comprehends all the operations of the body politic, whether legislative, executive or judiciary, but in its most usual and perhaps its most precise signification, it is limited to executive details, and falls peculiarly within the province of the executive department."[7]

Hamilton presented a list of the sorts of "executive details" that constitute what seems to be most properly understood by the administration of government: "the actual conduct of foreign negotiations, the preparatory plans of finance, the application and disbursement of the public monies, in conformity to the general appropriations of the legislature, the arrangement of the army and navy, the direction of the operations of war; these and other matters of a like nature."[8]

Central for Hamilton were the preparation of plans for getting money, and the spending of money following general appropriations. He spoke emphatically of the need, in preparing plans of finance, for the unity characteristic of executive power. It is impossible that the business of finance could be ably conducted by a body of men, however well-composed or well-intentioned. Although it is necessary to accommodate the diversity and crudity of the opinions and the passions and interests of the parties, which cause the public deliberations on matters of finance to be distracted between jarring and incoherent projects, nonetheless accommodation is not submission: there is need for a rallying point.[9] He was equally emphatic about the need to recognize that the business of administration cannot be as fully subordinated to rule as some would wish; the machinery cannot work without latitude in interpreting the rules for the expenditure of public money.[10] First and last on Hamilton's list are matters which cannot be simply prescribed by a general rule because what a government must do in respect to such matters must take into account the actions of men not subject to the authority of that government's laws: these matters are the actual conduct of foreign negotiations and the arrangement of armed forces and the direction of their operations in war.[11]

In the management of foreign negotiations the executive is the most fit agent, having the indispensable qualities of secrecy and dispatch, which come from unity. But a magistrate elected for a scant few years, not having that personal stake in the government which a hereditary monarch has, is in too much danger of being corrupted by foreign powers to be trusted alone to conclude treaties. And there is a peculiar propriety in vesting this power in an executive-legislative union. On the one hand, treaties are products that operate more like the products which are peculiarly legislative than like those which are peculiarly executive: a treaty once made operates as law. Hence it is unsafe to trust treaty-making to an agency without legislative participation. A treaty, however, is not a law in the strict sense. On the other hand, treaty-making calls for the operating qualities found in the executive, rather than in the legislature. Hence it is inefficacious to empower a legislative body to negotiate treaties. Making a treaty, however, is not an instance of the activities of executive power most strictly defined: it is not the execution of laws nor is it the employment of the common strength for law enforcement or for the common defense. Thus the heart of the argument against vesting the power to make treaties in the chief magistrate alone, without any requirement of legislative concurrence, is that while one can do it more efficaciously, this would be unsafe in a republic: in treaty-making the making is executive, while what is legislative is the concurring; and even the legislative share does not belong to the more representative branch, which is less fit.[12]

Finally, it is the direction of war which, of all governmental concerns, most peculiarly demands those qualities which distinguish the exercise of power by a single hand: it is of the nature of war to increase the executive at the expense of the legislative authority. Americans recognize this, for even those state constitutions which have in other respects coupled the chief magistrate with a council have nonetheless for the most part concentrated the military authority in him alone; and while, with republican caution, the Constitution of the United States does not place in a single hand the power of generating either the condition of war or the forces to fight war, it does designate as commander in chief the chief executive—placing in a single hand the power to employ, in a war already begun, forces provided by a body of men. Moreover, the energy of the unitary executive is an ingredient of good government not only in the conduct of the operations of war, but also with a view to being able to anticipate distant danger and prepare to meet the gathering storm. As Demosthenes said, a wise politician should be like a general, who marches at the head of his troops: the statesman should march at the head of affairs, not awaiting the event to know what measures to take, but taking measures which produce the event. While avoiding the exercise of authority only doubtfully constitutional, and being as accommodating toward foreign powers as honor and interest permit, the executive ought to be energetic as well as prudent; in times of crisis the executive ought to have a well-digested plan before Congress meet and ought to cooperate with them in getting it adopted. Energy is not, however, merely a necessary supplement to wisdom: energy at times *is* wisdom.[13]

The apportionment of power into several depositories is not an item-by-item distribution guided only by the wish to prevent abuse by equilibrating the capacity for abuse: there are sorts of work into which the various powers of government have a natural tendency to be sorted. The executive power has an inherent nature: the executive power is not a convention produced by the Constitutional Convention. What our Constitution did was to vest the executive power, with certain expressed exceptions and qualifications, in an official called the President; the executive powers it enumerates are not exhaustive of the President's powers. There is unanimous agreement that the vesting of the executive power in the President ought to be interpreted in conformity with other parts of the Constitution which express exceptions and qualifications. There is also unanimous agreement that it ought to be interpreted in conformity with the principles of free government. About the meaning of the latter, there is, however, antagonistic disagreement; its meaning is problematic. According to Hamilton, free government must not only be free; it must also be government: free government need not simply be popular; it may also be monarchical.[14]

V   The idea that a vigorous executive is inconsistent with the spirit of republican government is, to say the least, not without its advocates. Some of them are therefore not unfriendly to monarchy—but these are not those whom Hamilton seeks to persuade that the proposed Constitution ought to be adopted. Rather, he seeks to persuade those who are unfriendly to the proposal out of the belief that its executive is too energetic for its spirit to be sufficiently republican. Those unfriendly to the proposed Constitution because its executive is energetic are placed in a dilemma: they must choose between government that is republican but bad, and government that is good but nonrepublican.

Opposition to the energetic executive must be abandoned by enlightened well-wishers to republican government, for energy in the executive is a leading characteristic in the definition of good government. Energy in the executive is essential to the protection of the community against foreign attacks, and it is not less essential internally. Internally, it is essential to the steady administration of the laws; it is essential to the protection of property against those irregular combinations which sometimes interrupt the ordinary course of justice, and to the security of liberty against the enterprises and assaults of ambition, faction, and anarchy.

Whatever one's theory about the preferability of republican over monarchical government, practice shows the necessity of an energetic executive. Hamilton's problem is to persuade enthusiastic defenders of republicanism that a due dependence on the people and a due responsibility, the two circumstances which constitute safety in the republican sense, can consist with an executive attacked as monarchical because of its energy. At the root of the monarchical problem is the unity of the executive. The chief or central difficulty with which Hamilton must contend is the fear that a concentration of governmental power in one man, the chief executive, is not safe. In America, Hamilton finds ample concern for republican safety; the difficulty is in sufficiently providing the unity of power and the stability of policy necessary for energetic government. The Americans' habits and opinions in the situation impede the effort to protect their rights and promote their interests; they resist being governed because they fear to be oppressed.[15]

It is often best in a monarchy for the prince to relinquish a part of an excessive prerogative in order to establish a more moderate government, better adapted to the happiness or temper of his people. A government characterized by the absolutely unqualified monarchical principle is less truly energetic than is its antithesis, free government. But, though freedom has this tendency to energize government through the extensive feelings that identify public and private, it also has a tendency to enfeeble government through the fear and through the fear-manipulating envy which resist the concentration of power in men elevated above their fellows to exercise public authority. Freedom is not identical with energy: freedom energizes when the requirements of energy are not ignored. A country like Great Britain, in which the principle of freedom has been joined to the monarchical principle, may have both governmental energy and popular enthusiasm.[16]

vi   The opinions which led many Americans to desire an executive weaker than should be desired by an enlightened and reasonable people account for the arrangement of Hamilton's most extensive treatment of the executive, the discussion in *The Federalist*. The part of *The Federalist* which treats of the constitution of the executive department of the proposed government is the only part which begins with a long discussion of the slanders against the proposal. Number 67, the first paper

in the discussion, presents the proposed executive as having been so out-
rageously opposed that it is difficult to maintain the attitude appropriate to
civil argument.[17] The second paper on the executive, Number 68, pairs with
the first, which gave an instance of something that the outrageous opposition has misrepresented (an alleged power of appointment by the President
which was not in fact proposed),[18] by setting over against it an instance of
something that even the opposition has somewhat approved (the mode of
appointing the President which came to be called the "Electoral College").

What the most plausible opponents deign to admit is that the mode
of appointing the chief magistrate is pretty well guarded: their concern is
safety. Hamilton does not hesitate to venture somewhat further: the manner
of it is at least excellent, uniting in an eminent degree all the advantages to
be desired.

Putting aside consideration of what might not be perfect in it, Hamilton lists five advantages happily combined in the plan. The consideration
treated first and the two considerations treated last might be called "popular"; they initiate and conclude a discussion which contains two other considerations, of central concern to Hamilton, which might be called "non-
popular."

In the *first* place, the sense of the people should operate in the choice of
the person to whom so important a trust is to be confided by the people. It
is equally desirable, in the *second* place, to consider the superior efficacy of
operation when men are select and act in circumstances suitable for doing
their work. But it is also desirable to prevent what is dreadful. While it
is not dangerous that there be a magistrate with so important an agency
in the administration of the government as will belong to the President of
the United States, the process of electing him could be very dangerous; in
the election of such a magistrate, tumult and disorder are to be dreaded;
in the *third* place, therefore, it is desirable to afford as little opportunity as
possible to this evil. Effectual security against it is provided in part by an
arrangement that has already commended itself as most effectual for obtaining a man who may not be immediately popular but has qualities adapted
to the station: the people are to be not the immediate source but rather
the source of the source of the choice. Their making a preliminary choice
of several will be much less apt to generate any extraordinary or violent
movements than would their final choice of one: with the object of choice
more diffuse, because of the number of men immediately chosen, and the
final object more distant, because of the number of operations in the medi-
ated process of choice, the popular emotions will be less concentrated and
hence less likely to convulse the community with commotion as it moves

to concentrate power in one man. Further precautions are needed, however, just because there is an intermediate body of electors. The elite elected by the people to make the final election is itself susceptible to heats and ferments which might from them inflame the people. Hence the several persons chosen in the first of several operations are to meet not in one but in several bodies. Thus, the process is made less intense by its beginning with a choice of more than one man, it is protracted by its containing more than one step, and it is extended by its having the central step taken simultaneously in more than one place. It is desirable, however, not only to take precautions against the people's being inflamed by the elite they select, but also to set up obstacles against the people's being betrayed by those selected; in the *fourth* place, therefore, every practicable obstacle should be opposed to cabal, intrigue, and corruption—these most deadly adversaries of republican government. The danger is chiefly to be expected from the desire in foreign powers to gain an improper ascendant in our councils by raising a creature of their own to the chief magistracy. The guard against this danger is that there are to be no preexisting bodies of men to be tampered with: the choosing begins with an act of the people, and the immediate outcome of that beginning is the temporary appointment of persons for the single purpose of appointing a President. But the danger of corruption is not only that the electors of the President might serve foreign powers; the electors might also be subservient to the President already in office. All officials of the United States, including members of either branch of Congress, are therefore excluded from eligibility as electors, so that the people will not be betrayed because the electors of the next President lack independence from the President in office. This arrangement also secures another desideratum that is not less important, the *last* on Hamilton's list: that the people not be betrayed because the President in office, eager for reelection, himself lacks independence from the body of electors. This is another reason for giving the appointment of the President to persons temporarily appointed for that single purpose; the electors of the President are the elected officers furthest from having a considerable duration.

In Hamilton's list of five considerations, only the first desideratum might be called "popular" simply; the fourth and fifth desiderata with which Hamilton concludes his list might also be called "popular," but they are consequences of the second and third desiderata, which are "non-popular." The concluding considerations of popular safety arise from central considerations of what is requisite for governmental efficacy. While popular safety first requires that the sense of the people should operate at bottom, the people should not have an immediate operation on the outcome: operating intermediately between the sense of the people and the final choice should be those selected by the people because they are particularly capable of supplying the requisite information and discernment; this small number of men is to act under circumstances favorable to deliberation and to a judicious combination of considerations proper to govern choice.

After listing the advantages of the mode of appointing the President, Hamilton in Number 68 finds it no inconsiderable recommendation of the proposed Constitution that, because the process of election affords a moral certainty that the office of President will seldom fall to the lot of any man who is not eminently qualified, the office will therefore probably be filled by characters preeminent for ability and virtue. He finds this a considerable recommendation because he is one of those who are able to estimate the share which the executive in every government must necessarily have in its good or ill administration. "Though we cannot acquiesce," he says, "in the political heresy of the poet who says—'For forms of government let fools contest—That which is best administered is best'—yet we may safely pronounce, that the true test of a good government is its aptitude and tendency to produce a good administration." The poet was right to emphasize a good administration, but he was wrong to dismiss as an occupation of fools the contest for forms of government: forms of government differ in their aptitude and tendency to produce a good administration. It is not foolishness to take part in contentions to produce a form of government that has the aptitude and tendency to produce a good administration that is productive of good works. It is the work of statesmen to establish and foster forms of government in which there will flourish administrative energy, rather than talents for low intrigue and the little arts of popularity.[19]

Number 70 introduces Hamilton's presentation of the executive in itself.[20] After a brief statement that executive energy is essential to good government, however much it may be thought to be not republican, Hamilton devotes the rest of the 70th paper to unity, the first ingredient of executive energy.

This argument that an executive authority lacking unity would be exercised with a spirit habitually feeble and dilatory is an argument that applies with principal weight to one of the methods that destroys the unity of the executive: the arrangement for a plurality of magistrates of equal dignity and authority. This feeble arrangement is also unsafe, owing to the danger of differences that might split the community into the most violent and irreconcilable factions. Its advocates are not likely to be numerous.

More numerous are the advocates of the other method that destroys executive unity. This second method ostensibly vests executive power in

one man, but subjects him wholly or partly to the control and cooperation
of others who are the members of his council. Whereas Hamilton recurs
to ancient history for an example of the first method (the two consuls of
Rome), his examples of the second method are more recent and closer to
home, in the constitutions of several of the states. This is the more popular
method of destroying executive unity in America. To this arrangement that
makes a council's concurrence constitutionally necessary to the operations
of the ostensible executive, the argument that a plural executive is an executive lacking energy does not apply with equal weight, Hamilton concedes;
but, he says, it does apply with a weight that is considerable. Hamilton's
argument then goes on to turn against itself the argument for an executive
council. Not only is the executive in this method still quite feeble (even if
not so feeble as in that other plan found in the classical republic); an executive with a council also is unsafe. The method of an executive council, as
much as the other method for plurality in the executive, tends to conceal
faults and destroy responsibility, thus depriving the people of their secu-
rities against infidelity in elected officials: the removal and punishment of
wrongdoers, and—even more important in an elective government because
more commonly required—the censure of public opinion.

The implicit argument in favor of a council would seem to be something like this: since *even* a monarchy like England annexes to the executive
a constitutional council who may be responsible to the nation for the advice
they give, therefore a fortiori a republic like America should do so. Hamilton's reply is that such a council is needed in England *only because* it is a
monarchy: without a council, the British government would not be free,
for without a council the British executive would have no responsibility
whatever. The council in the monarchy increases responsibility—from no
responsibility whatever, to responsibility in some degree (though only in
some degree, for the English monarch is not bound to do as they say). But
the American executive with a council would be less responsible and would
therefore be more dangerous to republican liberty. The maxim of republican jealousy has been applied where it is inapplicable because consideration
has not been given to the proper combination of unity and multiplicity in
human affairs. To recognize that many cannot exercise executive authority
well, but to stop short of vesting that authority in one, is to reduce the security against infidelity to the people: a few may combine more easily than
many, but are harder to watch than one.

The state government of Hamilton's immediate audience, he points out,
has no council except for the single purpose of appointing to offices. The
republican fear of unity in the executive seems to make its last stand on this

ground of appointments: even if there is only one chief magistrate, there must be many other magistrates; to allow him to name them all alone would make him a lone magistrate, followed by his friends and servants.[21]

The discussion of the executive beginning with Number 67 is immediately preceded by the papers on the ultimate legislative check on what is most properly called administration: removal of the men who administer the government. What is discussed in the papers before these immediately preceding papers is discussed again in the concluding papers on the executive, the papers on executive powers: legislative participation in the executive powers of making treaties and appointing officials. As the reader approached the discussion of the executive, so the reader departs from it— noting how the executive is subject to the control of a branch of the legislative body.[22]

The executive is subject to control by legislators: the legislators themselves are not to be the holders of executive office; they themselves are not to constitute the administration. For a good administration the right men are needed to fill the offices. But the right sort of arrangement is better calculated to promote a choice of the right men than is some other sort of arrangement. What is the right sort of arrangement?

If the power of appointment is to be reposed in a body of men, that body must be not the people at large, but a select body of a moderate number. But, though the people collectively are too numerous and too dispersed to be regulated in their movements by a systematic spirit of cabal and intrigue, this spirit does regulate the movements of men in a select assembly of a moderate number. This systematic spirit of cabal and intrigue is the chief objection against reposing the power of appointment in a body of men. The resolutions of a collective body are frequently distracted and warped by diversity of views, feelings, and interests; and nothing is so apt to agitate men's passions as are personal considerations, whether relating to themselves or to others whom they are to choose or prefer. Hence, when an assembly of men exercises the power of appointing to office, the process will be a display of attachments and animosities which will result in a choice not for merit but for what gives to one party a victory or to many parties a bargain.

One man, by contrast, will have fewer personal attachments to gratify than will a body of men each of whom may be supposed to have as many as does that one man. Moreover, a single man with the sole and undivided responsibility will have a livelier sense of duty and a more exact regard for reputation. He will be led by the concentration of obligation and interest to investigate with care what qualities merit appointment and to prefer with

impartiality men who have those qualities. Hence, to analyze and to estimate the peculiar qualities adapted to particular offices, one man of discernment is better fitted than a body of men of equal or perhaps even of superior
discernment. (Not necessarily any one man, but one man of discernment;
in the case of the President, though, the mode of his own appointment is
such that there would always be great probability of having the place filled
by a man of abilities at least respectable.)

However, to reduce the danger of evils from one man's uncontrolled
agency in appointments, it would be well to restrain him by making it dangerous to his reputation, or even to his political existence, for him to play
favorites or to follow popularity: an efficacious check would be to require
the Senate's cooperation for appointment to office. Such a check would not
impair executive energy: the Senate restrains only by the power to concur
or not; the President retains the initiative.[23]

vii   Hamilton seeks to enlighten, but he does not seek to destroy the
concern for safety against concentrated power. He argues that a
government cannot be free if there is no responsibility in its executive department and that the security against an undue influence of the executive
ought not to be diminished. He argues against certain delegations of power
to the executive by the legislature.

To the suggestion that a discretionary power of pardoning for treason
might be occasionally conferred upon the President with a view to restoring
the tranquility of the commonwealth in seasons of insurrection or rebellion, Hamilton answers in the first place that it is questionable whether in a
limited constitution that power could be delegated by law. This remark is,
to be sure, part of an argument in favor of a delegation of this power to the
executive—but a delegation by the Constitution, rather than by an institution only holding its power from the people by constitutional delegation.
And less of a power to pardon is proposed for the President of the United
States than is possessed by the governor of the state of Hamilton's immediate audience: Hamilton repeatedly emphasizes the exception of cases of
impeachment from the President's power to pardon.

There is no question, Hamilton says, that government must contain a
power of pardoning: the necessary severity of governmental justice needs
to be mitigated by humane and politic mercy. The only question is which is
a more eligible dispenser of the mercy of government: one man or a body
of men.

Hamilton says why it appears better to vest the power in a single man.
The sense of responsibility is always stronger the less it is divided: so a

single man, reflecting that the fate of a fellow creature depended on his sole fiat, would be most ready, on the one hand, to attend to what pleads for a mitigation of the rigor of the law and, on the other hand, would be least apt to yield to the dread of being accused of weakness or connivance, which might otherwise shelter a man who was a fit object of the law's vengeance. A single man would be more circumspect; he would be more cautious on all sides. From numbers, however, men generally derive confidence—so they might, on the one hand, often encourage each other in an act of obduracy, and they might, on the other hand, be less apprehensive of censure for an injudicious or affected clemency. Hence the power of pardoning has been vested in the President.

Only in relation to the crime of treason, Hamilton believes, has the expediency of this been contested. The President's power to pardon for treason, it has been urged, ought to depend upon the assent of one or both branches of the legislative body. Hamilton says that he will not deny that there are strong reasons for requiring in this the concurrence of at least a part or even the whole of the legislative body. The legislative body seems more like the society it serves than does the chief magistrate, and he seems more likely than it to be the public enemy. But Hamilton not only does not deny, he positively asserts that the objections to such a plan are also strong.

There seems to be a fitness in referring the judgment of mercy to that numerous body the legislature; but it is not to be doubted that a single man, provided he has prudence and good sense, is better fitted than any numerous body whatever to do the work, balancing the pleas for and against in delicate conjunctures. And while the supposition of connivance by that single man the chief magistrate ought not to be entirely excluded, it deserves particular attention that treason will often be connected with seditions which embrace a large proportion of the community and that in every such case we might expect the representation of the people to be tainted with the same spirit which had given birth to the offense. And thus, on the one hand, when parties were about equal, then the sympathy of friends and favorers, availing itself of the good nature and weakness of others, might frequently bestow impunity on a condemned man where the terror of an example was necessary; but, on the other hand, when the major party was inflamed with resentment against the sedition, then they might often be obstinate and inexorable when forbearance and clemency were politic. What is most to be feared is not a single thing: while it is the connivance of the single man when the traitors are few, it is the party spirit of the numerous body when the traitors are many.

But the principal argument for placing the power of pardoning treason in the single chief magistrate, rather than in the numerous legislative body, has to do not with safety against betrayal of duty by those in whom the power is placed, but rather with the inefficacy that would result from dilatory response to fleeting opportunity: a well-timed offer of pardon to insurgents or rebels may often restore tranquility at critical moments. To the observation that a discretionary power with a view to such contingencies might be conferred upon the President occasionally, Hamilton's first answer, as we have seen, has to do with safety, with what is essential to a limited constitution; but his last word on the subject has to do with the inefficacy resulting from premature disclosure of secret intent. The power of pardoning treason is another instance where an enlightened concern for safety, which seeks to promote responsibility, would combine with a concern for efficacy, which requires secrecy and dispatch, in order to repose authority in a single man.[24]

VIII

Unity and Duration

Effective government requires not only that one will be composed from many wills in time to do what must be done for the public safety and prosperity; it requires also that the one will not decompose into many wills over time. Brief efficacy is little efficacy: the efficacy derived from unity must be protracted. *Unity* at an instant in time must be combined with *duration* through a long interval of time. For energetic government, power must be concentrated for action that is soon enough; for wise government, policy must be kept constant for action that lasts long enough. Men are feeble (though many) if they cannot consist; if they cannot persist, they fall into folly. Republican governments are naturally liable to change, to vibrations of power. This tends to their destruction. Hence, in Hamilton's project for republican effectiveness the second element is stability.[1]

ii   Deficiencies of constancy were early mixed with defects of consistency in the misfortunes and embarrassments that attended the Americans' conduct of their War for Independence. In 1780, as we have seen, Hamilton (then serving in the army) presented to a member of Congress his thoughts on the principal defects of the system and the changes necessary to save the Americans from ruin. After listing two defects of unity in America's civil constitution, Hamilton then completes his list by presenting two defects in America's military arrangements. (He says that he omits listing inferior defects in the organization of particular departments, as well as errors of administration, because it would be a tedious and troublesome task, and it would be easy to remedy *them* if the *principal* defects were remedied.)

The fluctuating constitution of the American army is the third defect listed by Hamilton, after the two defects of unity. To this fluctuation, he says, is to be ascribed all of our military misfortunes and three-fourths of our civil embarrassments. It is therefore an immediate necessity to recruit for the duration of the war, or at least for the relatively long term of three years. In the long run the fundamental law ought to have a provision for such long-term recruitment; something can be done for now, however, because the people wish a change from the expense of the heavy bounties which are frequently demanded as pay for a brief few months' term of service. The remedy for the fluctuating constitution of the army would, as we shall see, greatly contribute to providing a remedy for another defect.

The fourth defect on Hamilton's list concerns the provision made for the army. This provision, Hamilton says, is imperfect and unequal. Unless Congress better looks to the future, and does so in the immediate future, the army will be a thing of the past. Without a speedy change the army must dissolve. Indeed, the Union itself, held together by the slenderest ties, is ripening for a dissolution; so that even apart from winning the War for Independence, America—whatever may be the visionary speculations of some men at this time—will find it indispensable to keep on foot a considerable body of troops after the war. If the American army does not endure, neither will the American union. It is an axiom for Hamilton that an army is essential to the American union; with a real American army, Congress will have a solid basis of authority and consequence. The army now, he says, is not an army but a mob—without clothing, without pay, without provision, without morals, without discipline.

This statement of the last defect lists five items from lack of which the army is a mere armed mob. Later in the letter, when discussing remedies for these defects, he says that Congress should endeavor, both upon their credit in Europe and by every possible exertion in this country, to provide the officers with clothing. Congress should, moreover, not leave to the states but should itself immediately take up making good the depreciation of the currency and all other compensations to the army. And it would be a great stroke of policy to place the officers upon half pay during life; this permanent provision, which would be preferred to any temporary compensation, would give Congress a stronger tie upon them than anything else that can be done. By securing the attachment of the army to Congress, he says, we then should have an army not only in name but also in reality; we should then have discipline.

Thus a remedy for the first two lacks on the list, clothing and pay, will also remedy the last one, discipline: the lacks with which the list opens and concludes belong together from a provident point of view. Insubordination to military authority follows from the hesitance of civil authority, according to Hamilton's statement of defects: Congress have long been jealous of us, he says, and we have now lost all confidence in them and give the worst construction to everything they do. The central lacks on the list, provision and morals, go together: we begin to hate the country for its neglect of us, he says, and the country begins to hate us for our oppressions of them.

There is improvidence toward the army, and it will continue, because the channels of provision are multitudinous: the present mode of supplying the army—by state purchases—is not among the least considerable defects of our system, he says; it is too precarious a dependence. Each state will make its own ease a primary object, and the supply of the army a secondary one. The variety of channels through which the business is transacted will multiply the number of persons employed and the opportunities of embezzling public money. From the popular spirit on which most of the governments turn, the state agents will be men of less character and ability, nor will there be so rigid a responsibility among them as there might easily be among those in the employ of the continent, and of course there will not be so much diligence, care, or economy. Very little of the money raised will go into the Continental treasury (it will be pretended that all of it has been exhausted in providing the quotas of supplies), and funds will be lacking for other government demands.

Later, when discussing remedies for the defects stated earlier, Hamilton says that the provision of supplies is the pivot of everything else (though a well-constituted army would conduce to this provision, he says, by giving consistency and weight to government). He proposes that the whole system of state supplies should be abolished by Congress in four ways, all of which must be united. Hamilton lists the items of this fourfold way: a foreign loan, heavy pecuniary taxes, a tax in kind, and a bank formed on public and private credit. Taxation is central in this listing; listed first and last are items which suggest another aspect of the question of stability: public credit.[2]

iii   This letter to a leader was followed up by Hamilton with efforts at persuasion in the public prints. The Articles of Confederation did not remedy the defects of the feeble Union; Congress lacked the central power to tax. On the seventh anniversary of American independence, Hamilton wrote that the government of the Union ought not to be too much dependent on the states: occasional supplies are insufficient for a government to maintain itself. A permanent government needs permanent funds.

Indeed, he pointed out, a permanent access to money is necessary to have access to the temporary use of money: the power to tax is the basis of the ability to borrow.[3]

When the power to tax was finally vested in the government of the United States, it became Hamilton's great official project—a project which was foreshadowed in his early writings—to render the credit of the United States solid and enduring.

A permanent source of independent revenue is necessary for obtaining credit. Halfway through *The Continentalist*, the first great series of papers in which he sought to show what governmental changes were required by the American Union, Hamilton remarked that the preceding numbers had been chiefly intended to confirm an opinion, already pretty much received, of the necessity to augment the powers of the confederation—but there yet remained, he said, the principal difficulty: to fix the public judgment definitively on the points that should compose that augmentation.

He gave a list of six articles—nothing short of them could be sufficient. The first was the power to regulate trade, and the last was the power to appoint all officers of every rank in the armed forces; all the others had to do with revenue for the federal government, and of these, all but one concerned revenue of perpetual duration.

The first three articles, he said, are of immediate necessity; the last three would be of great present but of much greater future utility; the whole combined would give solidity and permanence to the Union. The Union cannot be solid and permanent without a power to govern it, but power without revenue in political society is a mere name. It is the great defect of the confederation, he said, that it gives the United States no property—or in other words no revenue or means to acquire it that inheres in the Union and does not depend on the temporary pleasure of the different members. Congress must cease to be dependent on the occasional grants of the several states for the means of defraying the expenses of the federal government; otherwise it cannot have credit, which supposes specific and permanent funds for paying interest and redeeming principle. The property in such funds must be in the contractor himself, and the appropriation must be dependent on his own will. If, instead of this, the possession or disposal of them is to float on the voluntary and occasional concurrence of a number of different wills not under his absolute control, then both the one and the other will be too precarious to be trusted. The lack of its own revenue operates powerfully against the Union's obtaining credit not only directly but also indirectly: if the Union had its own revenue, there would be less distrust of our continuing united; both foreigners and thinking men among ourselves would have much more confidence in the duration of the Union.[4]

The establishment of a new foundation to support the Union was only the beginning of the provision for establishing the credit of the United States. Even if they do have their own sources of revenue, governments experience difficulty in obtaining credit. Hence, reported Hamilton to Congress from the Treasury, some men speak of a National Bank—many of these having a wish, suggested by considerations of public advantage, that the bank could be established upon principles which would cause its profits to redound to the immediate benefit of the state. But to establish it upon such principles would deprive the institution of an essential ingredient in its structure. To attach full confidence to an institution of this nature, it must be under a private direction—under the guidance of individual interest, not of public policy.

Public direction would be supposed to be, and in certain emergencies under a feeble or too sanguine administration it really would be, too much influenced by public necessity. The suspicion of this would most probably be a canker that would continually corrode the vitals of the bank's credit and would be most likely to prove fatal in those situations in which the public good would require these vitals to be most sound and vigorous. Were the bank's credit to be at the government's disposal, it would be little less than a miracle if over a long time there were not a calamitous abuse of it. The bank must be established on a basis which will allow it to be maintained, but a government authorized to take immediate benefit from it will over a long time be governed by momentary exigencies. No nation is blessed by a constant succession of upright and wise administrators. Enduring public advantage from a bank must not be based upon a wish for immediate benefit to the state. To furnish enduring public advantage, the bank must have directors invariably directed to the prosperity of the institution by a keen and steady sense of their own interests: this is the only security that can always be relied upon for a careful and prudent administration.

Even though its management be in the hands of private individuals, a bank will be, within proper limits, as much of an aid to a good government as might be wished. Even apart from general considerations, there are the more particular benefits that government will have in its power to confer—some of them conferred from time to time, some of them immediate. Because the institution, if rightly constituted, must depend for its renovation from time to time on the pleasure of the government, it will not be likely to feel a disposition to render itself, by its conduct, unworthy of public patronage; moreover, the government in the administration of its finances is able to reciprocate benefits to the bank as important as those which the bank affords to the government, and which, besides, are never unattended with an immediate and adequate compensation. But independent of these more particular considerations, the natural weight and influence of a good government will always go far toward procuring a compliance with its desires; and as the directors will usually be composed of the most discreet, respectable, and well-informed citizens, it can hardly ever be difficult to make them sensible of the force of the inducements which ought to stimulate their exertions.

The state may profit from owning part of the bank's stock. It must not, however, own the whole or a principal part; for if the mass of the property should belong to the public while the direction of it be in private hands, the interests of the state would be committed to persons not interested, or not enough interested, in their proper management. The state, moreover, while excluding all pretensions to control, must reserve a right of ascertaining, as often as may be necessary, the condition of the bank: it becomes a national concern of the first magnitude if the bank's paper is permitted to insinuate itself into all the revenues and receipts of a country or is tolerated as the substitute for gold and silver in all the transactions of business; and the ordinary rules of prudence require that the government should have the means to ascertain, whenever it thinks fit, that so delicate a trust is being executed with fidelity and with care. This right is desirable not only for the government but equally for all those concerned in the institution—as an additional title to public and private confidence, and as something which can be formidable only to practices that imply mismanagement. There is need, moreover, for precautions to guard against a foreign influence insinuating itself into the direction of the bank: a due caution would scarcely permit any but citizens to be eligible as directors of a national bank or enable nonresident foreigners to influence the appointment of directors by the votes of their proxies. Such a bank is to be considered not a mere matter of private property, but a political machine of the greatest importance to the state.

The bank's constitution needs a principle of rotation in the directing officers. In the constitution of a country, there are reasons which militate against this principle, but scarcely one of these reasons applies to the constitution of a bank; while there are strong reasons in favor of the principle in relation to a bank, which do not apply to a country.

The only thing common to both which pleads against rotation in the directing officers of a bank is the knowledge to be derived from experience.

But the objects of the government of a nation and those of the government of a bank differ so widely as to weaken greatly the force of that consideration in reference to a bank. In almost every important case of legislation, right decision requires a general and accurate acquaintance with the affairs of the state, and habits of thinking seldom acquired but from a familiarity with public concerns; whereas the administration of a bank is generally a constant succession of the same details regulated by a few simple fixed maxims, the application of which is not difficult for any man of judgment, especially if he has been instructed in the principles of trade. But the advantages of experience are not to be utterly slighted: to leave room for the regular transmission of official information, the head of the direction ought to be excepted from the principle of rotation. With this exception, and with the aid of the information of the subordinate officers, there can be no danger of any ill effects from lack of experience or knowledge, especially as the periodical exclusion ought not to reach the whole of the directors at one time. Thus, a closer consideration *weakens* the force of the argument *against* the principle of rotation.

The argument *in favor of* the principle of rotation is that it will render the public confidence more firm, stable, and unqualified—by lessening the danger that the directors would form combinations to make the institution subservient to party views or to accommodate any particular set of preferred men. The directors of the bank are elected, not by the great body of the community, in which a diversity of views will naturally prevail at different conjunctures, but by a small and select class of men, among whom it is far easier to cultivate a steady adherence to the same persons and objects; and those directors have it in their power immediately to conciliate, by obliging, the most influential of this class. Without the principle of rotation, therefore, changes in that body can rarely happen, but as a concession which they may themselves think it expedient to make to public opinions. But the continual administration of an institution of this kind by the same persons will never fail—with or without cause from their conduct—to excite distrust and discontent: the necessary secrecy of their transactions gives unlimited scope for imagination to infer that something is or may be wrong. This inevitable mystery is thus a solid reason for inserting in the constitution of a bank the necessity of a change of men. Neither the mass of the interested parties nor the general public can be permitted to be witnesses of the interior management of the directors, so both should have that check upon the directors' conduct, and that security against the prevalence of a partial or pernicious system, which will be produced by the certainty of periodical changes. There is such delicacy in the credit of a bank that everything which can fortify confidence and repel suspicion, without injuring its operations, ought carefully to be sought in forming it.[5]

But as necessary as credit may be, credit is also dangerous. A tendency to the progressive accumulation of debt is perhaps the natural disease of all governments. One exigency rapidly succeeds another in the life of a nation, producing new causes of expenditure, as well from its own as from the ambition, rapacity, injustice, intemperance, and folly of other nations. And in those who administer a government's affairs there is a propensity to shift off the burden from the present to a future day.

This propensity is general, says Hamilton, for it is founded in the constitution of man, but it may be expected to be stronger the more popular is the form of the state. Human nature has within it contradictions: public feeling and opinion almost always favor the extinction of existing debt and the avoidance of contracting more, but the only means for doing so, the payment of taxes, is always more or less unpopular. A country's lot would indeed be enviable if there were not always men ready to turn these contradictions of human nature to the account of their own popularity or to some other sinister account. Such men clamor for occasions of expense, when these happen to be in unison with the present humor of the community, whether well or ill directed, and they declaim against a public debt and for the reduction of it as an abstract thesis; yet they are vehement against every plan of taxation proposed to discharge old debts or to avoid new ones by defraying the expenses of exigencies as they emerge. These unhandsome arts that play upon popular propensities throw artificial embarrassments in the way of the administrators of government, but they do this while cooperating with the propensities of the administrators of government, for the administrators of government themselves are too apt to feel a desire to conciliate public favor by declining to lay even necessary burdens or too apt to feel a fear of losing public favor by imposing them with firmness. Thus, existing debt is left without adequate provision for its reimbursement, and new taxes are not laid with energy when new occasions of expense occur.

In consequence the public debt swells till its magnitude becomes enormous, and the burdens of the people gradually increase till the weight becomes intolerable. The natural offspring of such a state of things are great disorders in the whole political economy, convulsions, and revolutions of government. Indeed, it is not easy to conceive anything more likely than this to lead to great and convulsive revolutions of empire. The public agents of a nation have no more sacred obligation than to guard with provident foresight and inflexible perseverance against so mischievous a result.

The public agents of the United States at the present juncture, Hamilton says, should improve very efficaciously the very favorable situation in which they stand, first, for extinguishing with reasonable speed the actual debt of the country, and second, for laying the foundations of a system which may shield posterity from the consequences of the usual improvidence and selfishness of its ancestors—a system which, if possible, may give to public credit immortality.

For the first object, fortunately, he says, the circumstances in our foreign affairs, which during the last session impelled to an extension of the national revenues, have left little more to do than to apply the existing means with decision and efficacy; but the second object will depend on the establishment of wise principles in that application—principles fitted to become a permanent precedent in the fiscal system of the country. Hamilton points out that the Secretary's first report on the subject of the public debt (9 January 1790) suggested incorporating in the system of public credit of the United States, as a fundamental maxim, the principle that the creation of debt should always be accompanied with the means of its extinction— this being the true secret for rendering public credit immortal. The Secretary, he says, has lost no opportunity to put this principle into practice, and the legislature has from time to time taken important steps toward it; but much remains to be done to give it full effect—and the Secretary, about to leave the office that he holds, feels it a peculiar duty to make a final effort to promote that invaluable end.[6]

Thus, a government unprovided with sources of revenue cannot endure, for it cannot obtain credit; and a government improvidently given to postponing payment of its expenses cannot endure, for its credit will cease, if it itself does not collapse before its credit does. But there is yet another danger to consider: a government may also shortsightedly ruin the public credit that supports it by lightly disregarding the rights of its creditors, even though honesty is the best long-term policy.

In his farewell report on the public credit, Hamilton advises the United States to observe with delicate caution the maxims of credit, as well toward foreigners as toward their own citizens, in connection with the general principles of an upright, stable, and systematic administration. If they do so, then the strong attractions which they present to foreign capital will be likely to ensure them the command of as much capital as they may want in addition to their own for every species of internal amelioration. From this, in the course of time, they will derive advantages incomparably greater than any, however tempting, that could partially result from a disregard of those maxims, or from the exercise of a questionable right which might even appear to derogate from them. Credit, he warns, is an entire thing: every part of it has the nicest sympathy with every other part; wound one limb, and the whole tree shrinks and decays; the security of each creditor is inseparable from the security of all creditors. The boundary between foreigner and citizen would not be deemed a sufficient barrier against extending to the citizen the precedent of an invasion of the rights of the foreigner: the most judicious and cautious would be most apt to reason thus and would only look for stronger shades of apparent necessity or expediency to govern the extension, but in affairs of credit the opinion of the judicious and cautious may be expected to prevail; hence the government, by sequestering the property of foreign citizens in the public funds at the commencement of a war, would at least impair if not destroy that credit which is the best resource in war.

Hamilton's fears that his policy was not yet a permanent precedent soon received confirmation. A year after leaving office, he wrote to the President concerning a bill, recently passed by Congress, authorizing a sale of bank stock to pay off a sum due to the bank. Because Congress had earlier solemnly appropriated the dividends of the bank stock to the sinking fund for redeeming the public debt, this was a formal violation of the public faith. It will ruin public credit, he warns: all that the President's administration has effected for establishing the credit of the country will be prostrate at a single blow. It grieves my heart to see so much shocking levity in our representative body, he says, suggesting that the President refuse his assent to the bill.[7]

Early in his tenure of office, Hamilton had envisioned that sort of remedy for levity in the handling of so grave a matter as public credit. One argument which should weigh on our behalf in obtaining foreign loans, he said, is the reliance which may be had on the stability of our pecuniary arrangements *once made*, from the nature of our government in respect to the mutual checks inherent in its organization. As he told the public creditors, the nature of our government is such that, though obstacles and delays will frequently stand in the way of the adoption of good measures, yet when once adopted, they are likely to be stable and permanent: it will be far more difficult to undo than to do. It cannot be supposed, he says, that if one of the two branches of Congress should hereafter be disposed to do so disgraceful and ruinous a thing as to repeal a law on which the credit of the government was at stake, that the other branch would be willing to concur in a measure so pernicious; or if both branches of Congress should be so unwise and dishonest, that the President of the United States would give his assent to it, or, if he refused assent, that two-thirds of both houses of Congress would be inclined to persist in spite of his disapprobation.[8]

His farewell report on public credit spoke to the point more fully. In this report Hamilton argues that when property in public debt rests on specified and competent funds firmly pledged for the satisfaction of the creditor, it is more valuable, intrinsically and to a considerable extent, than when it depends on annual provision. His argument is directed against those who argued that if there is a steady preservation of faith by the government, it is a matter of indifference to the creditor whether his demand stands upon the basis of an annual provision or upon that of mortgaged funds.

Hamilton says that those against whom he argues substitute theory for fact. There is, in the nature of things, an intrinsic difference between the value of a debt bottomed on mortgaged funds and that of a debt resting on what is called personal security. A debt not bottomed on mortgaged funds is a debt resting on personal security—at least this is what it is called in the case of an individual, and so it may be called also in the case of a government. The degree of this difference, and some of the circumstances on which it depends, may differ in the case of a government, but even so, its existence is undeniably real.

Government, being administered by men, is naturally subject, like individuals, to particular impulses, passions, prejudices, vices; it is subject, says Hamilton, to inconstancy of views and mutability of conduct. Necessarily, therefore, a kind of property of which the essence is contract must be more or less valuable, because more or less secure, in proportion as it is little or much exposed to the influence of that inconstancy or mutability. But if a provision is to be made by a new resolution every year, that resolution, being always liable to be affected by momentary circumstances, is always casual—whereas if it is made once for all, it continues unless revoked by some positive act and has for that reason a "moral certainty" of stability.

But, it might be asked, if there should exist a disposition unfaithful to the public engagements or unfriendly to the public credit, why would it not operate as well to produce a violation of a provision already made as to prevent the making of a new one? Hamilton explains how the two things widely differ: to undo, which is to act, and (in such a case) to act with violence, requires more enterprise and vigor, and presupposes greater energy or a stronger impulse, than not to do, or to forbear to act—and this is particularly true where a number of wills is to concur. Many men who will not rouse to the effort or encounter the responsibility of doing mischief by positive acts will readily enough slide into it by a negative conduct— that is to say, by omitting to act. Merely from easiness of temper or lack of active fortitude, many men will suffer evil to take place which they do not desire and which they themselves would not commit. In collective bodies, though votes are necessary to action, mere absences may produce inaction; and it often happens, moreover, that a majority of votes could not be had for a resolution to undo or reverse a thing once done, which there would not be a majority of voices to do in the first place.

This reasoning acquires a tenfold force when applied to a complex government like ours—a government distributed into departments, acting through different organs which must concur to give it motion (as—in our Constitution—the House of Representatives, the Senate, and the President). In cases that are delicate and difficult, whether to issue in good or ill, a suspension of action is far more natural to such a government than action is. It can hardly happen that all the branches or parts of it can be infected at one time with a common passion or disposition manifestly inimical to justice and the public good—such as to prostrate the public credit by revoking a pledge given to the creditors. It is far more probable that such a disposition should possess one part at one time, at another time another part. Possessing either part, it might be sufficient to obstruct a provision which was to be made—but without possessing all the parts, it could not subvert one which had been already made. This last can hardly be supposed, says Hamilton, except in one of those extraordinary crises of nations which confound all ordinary calculations.[9]

Afterward defending the funding system, upon his retirement from office, Hamilton explained how wisdom might make use of a complex government like ours to promote constancy in matters so grave as the credit of the nation. He wrote that while he was in office he had aimed at establishing public credit efficaciously while guarding against its abuses; as a first step to this great result, he said, he had proposed the funding of the public debt; and in telling why the funding was essential in the plan of providing for the public debt, the second reason that he gave was that it was desirable to guard the government and the creditors against the danger of inconstancy in the public councils.

The debt being once funded, to shake the provision would require a condition of which there was a moral impossibility or at least the highest degree of improbability: the concurrence of both branches of the legislature and of the President, or of two-thirds of both branches overruling the opposition of the President. The alternative to providing for the public debt by funding was to make a provision annually; this, however, would require the like concurrence in its favor and so of course would be continually liable to be defeated by improper views in either of the branches or departments. As is clear from the course of our public councils and from the dispositions which have been manifested in them, he says, in this case there was real danger: there was good ground to apprehend that the accidental result of a single election and the accidental prevalence of ill humors in parts of the community might violate the justice and prostrate the credit of the nation. Justice and expediency both require a certain steadiness which should not be left to accident when precautions are available against the chances and changes of time; it is not wise to ignore infirmities when foresight may contrive to make respectability, if not virtue, almost a necessity. It is the part of wisdom in a government as well as in an individual to guard against its own infirmities, and, having taken beforehand a comprehensive view of its duty and its interest, to tie itself down by every constitutional precaution to pursue them in a steady way.[10]

Earlier, urging adoption of the proposed Constitution, Hamilton had discussed how the steady pursuit of the nation's duty and interest would be served by the complicated arrangement of powers separated and shared. In an early number of *The Federalist*, he asked whether it has not invariably been found that momentary passions and immediate interests have a more active and imperious control over human conduct than general or remote considerations of policy, utility, or justice; and in a later paper he discussed one of the remedies for this human failing: the President's power of a qualified negative upon acts or resolutions of the Congress.

Although the primary inducement or chief design of conferring this power upon the executive is to enable him to defend himself against immediate attacks upon his constitutional rights, says Hamilton, the power not only serves as a shield to the executive, but it has a further use, a secondary use: it furnishes an additional security against evident and palpable sacrifice of the public good by the enactment of improper laws. This negative establishes a salutary check upon the legislative body, calculated to guard the community against the effects of faction, of precipitancy, or of any impulse unfriendly to the public good which may happen to influence a majority of that body. Thus, such a check is needed to guard against the effects not only of faction but also of precipitancy: it reduces the chances that bad laws will be passed through haste and inadvertence as well as through design.

A negative is sometimes said to be improper on the ground that giving the executive magistrate any species of control over the legislative body presumes what should not be presumed—that a single man would possess more virtue or wisdom than a number of men. But the propriety turns not upon the supposition of superior wisdom or virtue in the executive, says Hamilton, but upon the supposition that the legislative will not be infallible. The supposition about the legislative is not only that the love of power may sometimes betray it into a disposition to encroach upon the rights of the other members of the government (which has to do with the primary inducement to conferring the power in question upon the executive) and that a spirit of faction may sometimes pervert its deliberations; the supposition is also that the impressions of the moment may sometimes hurry it into measures which itself on maturer reflection would condemn.

That culpable views of any kind should infect all the parts of the government at the same moment, and in relation to the same object, is far less probable, says Hamilton, than that they should govern and mislead every one of them by turns. Hence, the oftener a measure is brought under examination, and the greater the diversity in the situations of those who are to examine it, the less must be the danger not only of those missteps which proceed from the contagion of some common passion or interest, but also of those errors which flow from want of due deliberation. Constancy and stability will be promoted by an arrangement in which laws are made not by a single governmental agency but by the concurrence of departments of government, several and diverse, so that proposals are considered many times in different situations.

Inconstancy and mutability in the laws, says Hamilton, form the greatest blemish in the character and spirit of the American governments. Hence, those who can properly estimate the mischiefs of that inconstancy and mutability will give little weight to the objection that the power of preventing bad laws may be used to prevent good ones. The answer to the objection is that the injury which may possibly be done by defeating a few good laws will be amply compensated by the advantage of preventing a number of bad ones. Every institution calculated to restrain the excess of lawmaking and to keep things in the same state in which they may happen to be at any given period is much more likely to do good than harm—because it is favorable to greater stability in the system of legislation.[11]

iv Governmental complexity promotes steadiness of measures and helps make constitutions lasting. Partly it does this merely by having *several* parts that must concur to undo old measures as well as to pass new ones. However, stability requires not only that the governmental whole contain several independent parts, but that the several parts be *diverse* as well.

It has been sufficiently emphasized that safety against government, which requires that government be representative, requires also that the power of representative government be partitioned among several depositories: bad works are impeded when separated depositories of power share the exercise of power. But it has not been sufficiently explained how efficacy of government requires that the organs of government be diversified.

We have examined this diversification with respect to the theme of unity, the organization of power so that its active operation will lead the multitudinous wills of an extensive country to consist with each other in time to meet present urgencies. Now we need to examine this diversification with respect to the theme of duration, the organization of power so that its active operation will lead the shortsighted wills of a mutable populace to persist through time in making provision for a long future.

The chief departments of power, which differ in the number of officials who compose them, differ as well in the term for which officials stay in office in them. To diversify the duration of office-holding in a complex representative government is to prolong the terms of those who are not members of the body most strictly called representative. This helps to fortify general and remote considerations against momentary passions and immediate interests.

v The Presidency is an instance. The President has a longer duration in office than does a representative. It is believed by many, however, that a short term of office for the executive gives greater security against the evil designs of ambition and of avarice. But the time during which a man holds the office of President may be prolonged without limit by multiplying the number of his terms of limited length, and the reasons against prohibiting such re-eligibility suggest reasons for each term itself to be long.[12]

One advantage supposed to result from prohibiting re-eligibility is greater security to the people. But popular security would not be increased by the exclusion. The people, attached to a favorite and disgusted by what they might be induced to consider an odious and unjustifiable restraint, might sacrifice their permanent interest in constitutional liberty to their temporary inclination to perpetuate their favorite in office. The executive himself would be tempted by the exclusion to sordid views, to peculation, and in some instances to usurpation.

Consider a man in office with the prospect of inevitable exclusion at the end of his term. If that man were avaricious, he would feel a propensity to use his opportunity while it lasted; by employing corrupt expedients he would make the harvest as abundant as it was transitory. But with a different prospect he might be content to enjoy the regular perquisites of his station and might be unwilling to risk the consequences of abusing his station; his avarice might thus guard against his avarice. If the man were vain or ambitious as well as avaricious, his avarice would be likely to overcome his caution and his vanity or ambition. But with the expectation that good conduct would prolong his honors, he might hesitate to lose honors for the sake of gain; one appetite might thus guard against the other. If the man were simply ambitious, he would be tempted to embrace at every personal hazard a favorable conjunction for attempting to prolong his power—much more violently tempted than if he could probably achieve the same end by doing his duty. And consider the situation, not of one man who is still in office with the prospect of his inevitable descent from eminence, but of a number of men who, having had credit enough to ascend to the supreme magistracy, had descended from office but yearn for a forbidden re-ascent: the mandatory rotation in office would disturb the peace of the community and would even threaten the stability of the government.[13]

Another advantage supposed to result from prohibiting re-eligibility is greater independence in the magistrate. But the prohibition would be no more likely to render the magistrate more independent than to render the people more secure. That outcome would be very doubtful. It is to be doubted that there would be greater independence in the magistrate if the exclusion were only temporary. It is even to be doubted if the exclusion were perpetual: for the magistrate will have friends, after all, for whom he might sacrifice his independence; and he would be less willing to make enemies, on the other hand, when he must see himself, in the time fast approaching, their equal, or perhaps their inferior, while exposed to their resentments.

It is not to be doubted, however, that greater independence in the magistrate is an advantage. This is so if only for the sake of safety, since the abuse of governmental power cannot be checked internally unless the several depositories of power that are balanced against each other are independent of each other. But Hamilton's concern for executive independence, while taking into account the situation of the executive when the legislature is outraging its constituents, chiefly considers another situation.[14]

Prior to discussing re-eligibility, Hamilton discusses the decision fixing a limited term. In arguing that the executive should have considerable time before the end of his limited term, Hamilton says that in order to regard the executive's best recommendation as his servile pliancy to a prevailing current in the legislature, or even in the community at large, one must entertain very crude notions both of the ends for which government was instituted and of the true means by which the public happiness may be promoted.

Hamilton, who rejects notions that are "very crude" as well as ideas in which there is an "excess of refinement," then goes on to interpret, not to question, the republican principle. The republican principle seems to reveal the end for which government was instituted or the fundamental equality of men: the interests of the people are to be served by those to whom they choose to entrust the management of their affairs. But intention is not effect. The republican principle must be properly interpreted to reveal the means for making operative the means to effect that end.

Those who would move the public business forward must do it by looking far ahead. Leadership is necessary to place impediments in the way of sudden passions, of temporary delusions, and of persistent prejudices, so that right reasoning may prevail in the choice of means. The people have the dangerous prejudice, which is flattered by would-be tyrants, that the institutionalization of leadership is dangerous and even tyrannical. Republican leadership is government that is itself governed by the deliberate sense of the community. To be governed by the *deliberate* sense of the community is *not* however, to be governed by transient popular impulses— impulses excited by the flattering arts and deceptive artifices of cowardly or mean-spirited men who prefer to rule by manipulating popular inclinations, rather than by insisting upon arrangements that give the people time and opportunity for more sedate reflection. To avoid courses which may be temporarily attractive but are eventually fatal, the people must be led. The reward of leadership is the pleasure of receiving, at last, lasting monuments of popular gratitude for serving, with courage and with magnanimity, the lasting interests of the people. The price of leadership is the pain of suffering, in the meantime, the immediate perils of popular displeasure for withstanding the people's temporary inclinations toward means that do not promote their interests.[15]

The longer the duration in office of the executive magistrate, the more probable is his personal firmness in the employment of his constitutional powers. A man will be more attached to what he enjoys by a durable or certain title than by one that is momentary or uncertain. He is apt to take less interest in an advantage he holds precariously. For what he holds by a tenure more firm, a man will more firmly take risks and endure pains. A short-lived advantage affords him little inducement to expose himself, on account of it, to any considerable hazard or even inconvenience. Hence, an executive with a short duration in office will be feeble and irresolute.

A man acting as chief magistrate, under the consciousness that in a very short time he must lay down his office, will be apt to feel too little interested in it to hazard any material censure or perplexity from exerting his powers independently, or from encountering the ill-humors which may happen to prevail, however transiently, in a considerable part of the society itself, or even only in a predominant faction in the legislative body. And if the case should be, not that he must lay it down at the end of his brief term, but only that he must lay it down if he is not continued by a new choice, then the tendency would be still more powerful for his wishes, conspiring with his fears, to corrupt his integrity or debase his fortitude.

Though it cannot be affirmed that any limited duration would completely answer the end proposed, still, a duration of four years, while not long enough to endanger the public liberty, would be long enough to make a very valuable contribution to the firmness of the executive. During the interval between the commencement and the termination of such a period, the prospect of annihilation would be remote enough to have no improper effect upon the conduct of a man imbued with a tolerable portion of fortitude, for it would be remote enough to have the effect of making the community sensible of how proper are the measures he might incline to pursue. And though, as the moment approached when the public were by a new election to signify their sense of his conduct, his firmness would probably decline, yet it would still derive support from the opportunities he had had, from his previous continuance in office, of getting the esteem and the good will of his constituents by giving proofs of his wisdom and of his integrity.[16]

The people must be led; hence some of the people must be led to undertake the task of being leaders. Men need inducements to become leaders. Their courage and their magnanimity must be activated. Virtue may be its own reward, but exertion of virtue on behalf of multitudes requires the prospect of another reward. Even the noblest minds will hesitate to exert themselves in ruling if their ruling passion, the love of fame, cannot hope to be rewarded. Virtue practically takes the form of excellence; only the desire to excel will sufficiently prompt the exertions of self on behalf of countless others; political excellence is that laudable ambition which takes gratification from popular gratitude for promoting vast projects of public benefit. Few officials will last in the struggle to do their duty if they cannot hope to last in office; few officials will engage themselves in long-lasting effort to plan and undertake vast enterprises unless they can hope to have their merit acknowledged by lasting monuments, and this requires lasting in office long enough to have something to show for the effort. Arrangements must be such that officials will be induced by their own passions and interests not only to resist firmly the transient errors of others, but also to persist arduously in their own provident long-term projects.[17]

The longer his duration in office, the more probable it is that an executive with a merely tolerable portion of fortitude will resist the transient errors of others; but so long as the duration in office is limited, re-eligibility is necessary to counter what deters the generality of men in such a situation from planning and undertaking ambitious projects requiring for their completion persistence through a long time. The passionate regard for reputation which distinguishes noble minds acts as an inducement to such public enterprise only in situations where the initiators can hope for the reward of the fame which follows upon the work's completion. Arrangements must be made not with a view to what very few men might do, but with a view to what is to be expected from the generality of men. To make men's interest coincide with their duty is to rely on the best security for their fidelity. Arrangements must provide incentives to be provident; perhaps a very few of the very best minds might rise even above the ruling passion of the noblest minds, but it is more rewarding for the public to base political hopes on one of the strongest incentives of human conduct, the desire of reward. A long enough term of office diminishes the incentives to collaborate with public enemies or to become oneself a public enemy; exclusion from office after a limited term would diminish the inducements to become a public benefactor. Lacking incentives to provide for ends a long time off, the governors will improvise means that merely look good in the meantime. They will choose specious means to the general good.[18]

Duration in office as requisite to the energy of the executive authority, writes Hamilton at the beginning of the first of two *Federalist* papers on the subject, relates to two objects: the personal firmness of the executive magistrate in the employment of his constitutional powers (discussed in Number 71 in connection with the need for a term of considerable extent), and the stability of the system of administration which may have been adopted under his auspices (discussed in Number 72 in connection with the need for re-eligibility). The two objects of executive duration are firmness and stability: with a view to duration the executive is to be characterized by resistance and persistence. Arrangements for the executive must consider the relation between time and incentives—incentives that encourage (or enfeeble) resistance against transient impulses toward harmful measures and incentives that inspirit (or deter) persistence in great projects for long-term benefit. In both cases the longer a time that the executive can count on his holding the office, the longer a time that will count in his handling of the office. The intention of increasing safety by decreasing the duration of the executive, like the intention of increasing safety by increasing the number of the executive, would have the ill effect of decreasing safety. Executive responsibility to the people is essential to republican safety, but a short-sighted attention to the requisite responsibility for short-term effects loses sight of the requisite responsibility for effects that are long-term.[19]

Because the administration of government is most properly located within the executive department, the duration of the executive magistrate in office is intimately connected with the stability of the system of administration: permanence in a wise system of administration requires that the duration of the executive magistrate in office be considerable. It is not generally to be expected that men will vary and measures remain uniform. A man new to an office wishes to prove his capacity; and he wishes, in addition, to assure those upon whom he depends for his position that he is a man after their own heart. To undo what a predecessor has done is very often considered by a successor the best proof he can give of his own capacity; and, if the successor was substituted for his predecessor by public choice, he supposes that this predecessor was dismissed because his measures were disliked, and hence that the successor will be the more liked by his constituents the less he resembles his predecessor. Moreover, a new chief executive's propensity to change measures from these considerations will join with a propensity to place those who depend upon him personally for position; and these propensities together will give him a propensity to change men in subordinate positions, thus multiplying the mutability of measures. Excluding men from re-eligibility for the presidency would therefore have the ill effect of operating as a constitutional interdiction of stability in the administration. By necessitating a change of men in the first office of the nation, it would necessitate a mutability of measures. There will be little enough stability when popular constancy is permitted; to interdict it constitutionally would be fatal. In particular situations of crisis, replacing an experienced man by an inexperienced man of even equal merit would dangerously unsettle the train of the administration; but even in ordinary times, there is need for permanence in a wise system of administration—and the parent of wisdom is experience, which comes with time.[20]

vi   It is in suggesting the intimate connection between the duration of the executive magistrate in office and the stability of the system of administration that Hamilton says that the persons having immediate management of those matters which constitute "the administration of government . . . in its most precise signification" ought to be considered the assistants or deputies of the chief magistrate. On this account, he says, they ought to derive their offices from his appointment or at least from his nomination, and ought, Hamilton also says, to be subject to his superintendence. Hamilton does not say what might be expected—that they ought to be subject to removal by him.

A few papers later, in discussing the mode of appointing the officers of the United States, Hamilton says that to require the cooperation of the

Senate, besides being an excellent check upon a spirit of favoritism or of popularity in the President, will in addition be an efficacious source of stability in the administration. He then begins the next paper by recalling having mentioned this contribution to administrative stability which can be expected from the Senate's cooperation in the business of appointments, and he goes on to add that the consent of the Senate will be necessary not only to appoint but to displace as well. If the chief magistrate were the sole disposer of offices, then a change of the chief magistrate would occasion a more violent and more general revolution in the officers of the government, but administration will be made steadier by the provision that connects the official existence of public men to the approbation and disapprobation of that part of the government most permanent in its composition and hence in all probability least subject to inconstancy. The consequence is that, where a man in any station had given satisfactory evidence of his fitness for it, a new President would be restrained from attempting a change in favor of a man more agreeable to himself by the apprehension that the Senate's discountenance might frustrate his attempt and discredit himself.[21]

vii   Because of certain statements made by Hamilton in the first "Pacificus" paper, it has been contended that Hamilton changed his mind on where the power of removal resides. In that paper Hamilton says that the appointing power is in itself an executive power, but that by the Constitution it is a power specifically excepted from the executive power vested in the President alone and is vested instead in the President with the consent of two-thirds of the Senate. He does not say, however, that the removal power is an incident to the appointing power. What he does say is that the power of removal from office is an important instance of recognition by Congress of the true construction of the clause vesting executive power in the President—the construction according to which the President has all executive power that the Constitution does not specially except or qualify. Two of these exceptions or qualifications, Hamilton reminds his readers, he had noticed earlier in the paper—the Senate's participation in the appointment of officers and its participation in the making of treaties; he now mentions as a third the legislature's right to declare war and grant letters of marque and reprisal. Otherwise, he says, the executive power of the Union is completely lodged in the President—as Congress recognized when, in formal act upon full consideration, it allowed that the President alone might remove officers even though the power to appoint is vested in the President with the Senate's consent.[22]

Perhaps rather than changing his mind about the power of removal,

Hamilton thought that the question of the power of removal was a matter relatively minor compared to the recognition by Congress of an important general doctrine for construing the Constitution with respect to executive power, so that he was willing to accept a more questionable interpretation of a less important point to confirm a principle of the utmost importance. Perhaps Hamilton had earlier adopted an interpretation to which he was not firmly committed but which was the interpretation most likely to seem plausible to those whose consent was needed to ratify the proposed Constitution and whose dominating concern was republican safety—an interpretation which was, moreover, capable of being put to use in promoting the unpopular cause of administrative stability.[23]

In any case, discussing the removal power in *The Federalist*, Hamilton does speak of the Senate as that body which, from the greater permanency of its own composition, will in all probability be less subject to inconstancy than any other member of the government, and he says elsewhere that stability is a principle even more essential to the Senate than to the President.[24]

Before turning to this, we should consider here a matter related to the doctrine of "Pacificus." According to the first of the "Pacificus" papers, the power of appointing officials is one among several powers which the Constitution makes a specific exception from the executive power vested in the President alone. Another exception is the power to declare war and grant letters of marque and reprisal; this power, however, is not even vested in the President with nonpresidential participation: it is vested in the Congress alone. The Constitution does make another exception from the executive power vested in the President alone. The power of making treaties, like the power of appointing officials, is vested in the President with the advice and consent of the Senate. A few years after setting out the Pacificus doctrine, Hamilton discussed the relations between the parts of government with respect to the power of making treaties. The occasion was a dispute about the Jay Treaty in the House of Representatives.

This occasion not only evoked an exposition of Hamilton's views on the parts of government and their work; it was also one of two great crises in the attempt to give those views effect in the administration of the newly founded Constitution. In Part Three, chapter XII, we shall examine the other crisis at length. Now let us consider this one at some length.

The Jay Treaty received the consent of the Senate in June 1795. In August the United States ratified it. In October the British also ratified it, and the ratifications were exchanged. At the end of February 1796 the President proclaimed it, and the next day he sent a message communicating the treaty to both houses of Congress. But although the treaty had already been ratified and proclaimed, its fifth through seventh articles (which provided for several commissions to resolve certain disputes) could not be put into effect unless Congress voted appropriations.

On 2 March 1796, the day after Washington's message to Congress, Edward Livingston, an opposition member from New York City, made a motion in the House of Representatives, resolving that the President of the United States be requested to lay before the House a copy of the instructions given to the minister of the United States who had negotiated the treaty, together with the correspondence and other documents relating to the treaty. Livingston said that some important constitutional questions would be discussed when the treaty was considered and that therefore it was very desirable to have before the House every document that might tend to throw light upon the subject. On 7 March, Livingston amended his motion, in deference to gentlemen to whose opinions he said he paid the highest respect; the following words were to be added: "excepting such of said papers as any existing negotiation may render improper to be disclosed."

Madison, who opposed the treaty, but who said he wished to throw the resolution into such a form as not even to appear to encroach upon the constitutional rights of the executive, suggested a different amendment: "except so much of said papers as, in the President's judgment, it may not be consistent with the interest of the United States, at this time, to disclose." But Madison's proposal was defeated, and the House turned to consider the resolution made and amended by Livingston.

Washington, reading of Livingston's resolution in the newspaper the morning after it had been introduced, sought advice from Hamilton, who already had left office. On 7 March, Hamilton sent to the President "a hasty and crude outline" of what had struck him as an eligible course. The motion, if it succeeds, he said, ought not to be complied with: in a matter of such a nature, the production of the papers cannot fail to start a new and unpleasant game; but besides that, it will be fatal to the negotiating power of the government if it is to be a matter of course for a call of *either* House of Congress to bring forth all the communication however confidential. Thinking that while a too easy compliance would be mischievous, nonetheless a too peremptory and unqualified refusal might be liable to just criticism, Hamilton sent along "something like" the answer that it would be advisable to make.

It cannot be admitted without danger of much inconvenience, he said, that the House of Representatives has a right to demand and have as a matter of course, without specifying any object, all communications respecting a negotiation with a foreign power. It is essential to the due conduct of foreign negotiations, and to preserving the limits between the legislative and executive departments, that the executive have discretion over how far and where to comply in such cases. The present call is altogether indefinite and without any declared purpose, and the executive has no cases on which to judge of the propriety of compliance with it, so the executive cannot, without forming a very dangerous precedent, comply.

The answer went on: an impeachment seems to be the only purpose within the competence of the House of Representatives to which a view of the requested papers can relate; but the grounds for an impeachment in every case of a foreign treaty must primarily be deduced from the nature of the instrument itself and not from anything extrinsic. If at any time the House of Representatives shall have pronounced that a treaty presents such grounds and a further inquiry shall be necessary to ascertain the culpable person, there being then a declared and ascertained object, the President would attend with due respect to any application for necessary information.

On the day that Hamilton wrote Washington, Madison spoke in the House of Representatives on Livingston's motion. Madison said that the proposition before the House raised the question whether the general power of making treaties supersedes the powers of the House of Representatives particularly specified in the Constitution, so as to take to the executive all deliberative will and leave to the House an instrumental agency merely executive and ministerial. Madison also said he was not satisfied whether it was expedient at this time to go into a consideration of this very important question.

Three days later, on 10 March, Hamilton wrote to William Loughton Smith, a representative from South Carolina who had been a leading advocate in the House of the policies which Hamilton had introduced as Secretary of the Treasury. Hamilton says that the power of the House of Representatives in the case of a treaty is brought by Madison to the question whether the agency of the House of Representatives on this subject is deliberative or executive; and on the sophism that this legislature and each branch of it is essentially deliberative, and consequently must have discretion, Madison will maintain the freedom of the House to concur or not.

But, says Hamilton, this sophism is easily refuted. The legislature, and each branch of it, *is* deliberative—*but* with various restrictions, not with unlimited discretion. All the injunctions and restrictions in the Constitution abridge its deliberative faculty and leave it, as to these, merely executive. Thus, the Constitution enjoins that there shall be a fixed allowance for the judges which shall not be diminished, and the legislature therefore cannot deliberate whether they will make a permanent provision—nor whether, once the allowance is fixed, they will appropriate and pay the money. The only matter of deliberation that remains to them is the mode of raising and appropriating the money. So likewise, the Constitution says that treaties shall be made by the President and Senate, and shall be supreme laws. But it would be a contradiction to call a thing a law which is not binding; and therefore by constitutional injunction, as in the case respecting the judges so also as to the stipulations of treaties, the House of Representatives is not deliberative but is merely executive—except as to the means of executing. Any other doctrine, says Hamilton, would vest the legislature and each of its houses with unlimited discretion—and would thus destroy the very idea of a constitution which limits its discretion. "The Constitution would at once vanish." A constitutional apportionment of power which gives to the executive the work it is most fit to do is not compatible with a doctrine which asserts that the work of the legislature, and only of the legislature, is deliberative, while the work of the executive, and only of the executive, is to execute.

And, besides, Hamilton argues, the power to repeal a law is not vested in the House alone, but the legal power to refuse the execution of a law is a power to repeal it. Hence by Madison's doctrine the House of Representatives would, as to treaties, concentrate in itself the whole legislative power—for it would undertake, without the Senate, to repeal a law that was complete by the action of the President and Senate.

And again, Hamilton argues, the legal discretion of even the whole legislature does not absolve it from the moral obligations of the government. A treaty, being a contract between nation and nation, abridges the discretion of even the whole legislature by the moral obligation of keeping faith, and so a fortiori it abridges the discretion of only one branch of the legislature. In theory a treaty can be annulled only by mutual consent of the contracting parties—or by such a revolution of the government as changes the condition of the parties so as to render the treaty inapplicable—or by bad faith in one of the parties.

Almost a week later, on 16 March, Hamilton replied to a letter from Rufus King. Hamilton first reports his opinion about Livingston's resolution when it first appeared; he then thought that the President should answer in substance as follows: It cannot be admitted as a right of course in the House of Representatives to call for and have papers in the executive department relating to foreign negotiations, which frequently embrace confidential matters. Under all the circumstances and upon so indefinite a call, without any declared specific object, it is not proper, nor consistent with what the President owes to a due separation of the respective powers, to comply with the call. If, in the course of the proceedings of the House, a question within their competence shall arise for which any of the papers in question might be necessary, an application made on that ground will be considered with proper respect.

Hamilton goes on to say that after what has taken place in the discussion, however, if it can be done with proper form, a stand should be made by the President against the usurpation. As grounds for such a stand, he gives thirteen propositions. "On these grounds with the President's name a bulwark not to be shaken is erected." These propositions amount to "irresistible" demonstration.

The Constitution, begins the demonstration, empowers the President with the Senate to make treaties. A treaty is a perfected contract between two nations, obligatory on both. But that cannot be a perfected contract or treaty to the validity of which the concurrence of any other power in the state is constitutionally necessary.

And yet again: The object of the legislative power is to prescribe a rule of action for our own nation (including foreigners who come among us), whereas the object of the treaty power is to settle by agreement a rule of action between two nations binding on both. These objects are essentially different and cannot constitutionally interfere. Hence, the treaty power binding the will of the nation must, within its constitutional limits, be paramount to the legislative power which is that will. Or at least a treaty, being the law last made, must repeal an antecedent contradictory law; and if the legislative power is competent to repeal by a subsequent law this law last made by treaty, then this must be done by the whole legislative power, by a solemn act in the forms of the Constitution—not by one branch of the legislative power by disobeying the law.

The foregoing construction thus reconciles the two powers, assigning them distinguishable spheres of action. The other construction destroys the treaty-making power: it negates two propositions in the Constitution—that a treaty can be made by the President with the Senate and that a treaty is a law.

On 24 March, after more than two weeks of debate, the House of Representatives adopted Livingston's resolution, by a vote of sixty-two to thirty-seven. The press of business kept Hamilton from sending a reply to Washington as quickly as he wanted to, but he finally was able to send off a draft on 29 March. In his accompanying letter he says he wishes that it would have been possible to send the draft in a more perfect state. He hopes, however, it can be made out and may be useful; to say all that was proper in a more condensed form required more time.

Affairs, however, had not been standing still while Hamilton composed his draft. On 25 March, the day after Livingston's resolution had been adopted by the House of Representatives, a committee composed of Livingston and Albert Gallatin (the man who was later to hold, under Thomas Jefferson, the cabinet office Hamilton had held earlier under Washington) delivered the resolution to the President, who told them that he would take it into consideration. A message refusing the request of the House, both on constitutional grounds and for reasons of expediency, was then drafted for Washington by Secretary of State Timothy Pickering. After slight revision by Attorney General Charles Lee, the only cabinet member who thought that the President should comply with the request of the House, Pickering's draft was delivered to Washington the day that Hamilton sent his draft. The next day Washington received Hamilton's draft but sent to the House the message which Pickering had drafted; the next day after that, he wrote to Hamilton to express his thanks and to give Hamilton an account of the business, which concluded with these words:

> Finding that the draft I had prepared, embraced most, if not all the principles which were detailed in the Paper I received yesterday; though not the reason[in]gs—That it would take considerable [t]ime to copy the latter—and above all, hav[ing] understood that if the Papers were refused a fresh demand, with strictures might be expected; I sent in the answer whch. was ready; reserving the other as a source for reasoning if my information proves true.

A response to the President's message was proposed in the House by Thomas Blount of North Carolina, who introduced two resolutions:

[1] the House of Representatives do not claim any agency in making Treaties, but, . . . when a Treaty stipulates regulations on any of the subjects submitted by the Constitution to the power of Congress, it must depend, for its execution, as to such stipulations, on a law or laws to be passed by Congress. And it is the Constitutional right and duty of the House of Representatives, in all such cases, to deliberate on the expediency or inexpediency of carrying such Treaty into effect, and to determine and act thereon, as, in their judgment, may be most conducive to the public good . . . ;
[2] it is not necessary to the propriety of any application from this House to the Executive, for information desired by them, and which

may relate to any Constitutional functions of the House, that the purpose for which such information may be wanted, or to which the same may be applied, should be stated in the application.

Blount's resolutions were approved by the House the next day, 7 April, by a vote of fifty-seven to thirty-six.

After a week of considering other matters, the House finally took up the question of appropriations for implementing the fifth through seventh articles of the Jay Treaty. Then, after two weeks of debate, the Committee of the Whole House on 29 April divided forty-nine to forty-nine on a resolution affirming the expediency of making the appropriations necessary for giving effect to the treaty. This tie was broken by the chairman, who said that though he was not satisfied with the resolution as it stood, he would vote for it so that it might go to the House and be modified there. On 30 April the House defeated a preamble to the motion—a preamble stating, among other things, that the treaty was highly objectionable. The House then passed the resolution of the Committee of the Whole by a vote of fifty-one to forty-eight. On 2 May a bill was reported, which was passed by the House on 3 May. The next day, this House bill was adopted by the Senate, and two days after that it became law.

Before we turn to consider the draft prepared by Hamilton for the President, let us for a little while longer consider the context of the text. A few days before Blount introduced his resolutions in the House and, again, a few days after the House took up the question of appropriations, Madison, the opposition leader in the House, indicated to Jefferson as well as to Monroe his belief that Hamilton was the author of the President's message. Madison was mistaken, but there was reason for the suspicion. Hamilton had played a very large part in the public controversy over the Jay Treaty, and two months before the resolution that called for papers was introduced in the House, the thirty-seventh of Hamilton's extensive "Camillus" papers defending the Jay Treaty had answered certain constitutional objections to the treaty's provisions.

On 10 March, the day that Hamilton wrote to Smith, Madison gave a speech in the House considering that construction of the Constitution which left the President and Senate the power of making treaties, but which required at the same time the legislative sanction and cooperation in those cases where the Constitution had given express and specific powers to the legislature. In all such cases, Madison argued, it was to be presumed that the legislature would exercise its authority with discretion, allowing due weight to the reasons which led to the treaty and to the circumstances of the existence of the treaty; but still the House must, in its legislative capacity, exercise its reason—it must deliberate, for deliberation is implied in legislation. If it must carry into effect all treaties, then it would no longer exercise a legislative power; it would be the mere instrument of the will of another department and would have no will of its own. Where the Constitution contains a specific and peremptory injunction on Congress to do a particular act, then of course Congress must do the act—because the legislative discretion of Congress has here been expressly taken away by the Constitution, which is paramount over all the departments. But the case is essentially different where the act of one department of government interferes with a power that is expressly vested in another and is nowhere expressly taken away: here the latter power must be exercised according to its nature, and if it be a legislative power, then it must be exercised with that deliberation and discretion which is essential to the nature of legislative power.

On this same day, Smith, the recipient of Hamilton's letter, spoke in the House in reply to Madison. And while the House debated, Hamilton and his friends "went to work out of doors in the most intensive campaign of pressure politics the nation had yet known." [25]

It should be noted that in the letter to Smith of 10 March 1796, when Hamilton argues, by *implication* from constitutional provisions, that the House has a limited discretion in appropriating money for carrying treaties into effect, he gives, as his example of an *express* constitutional provision limiting the discretion of the House in appropriating money, the injunction that the judges shall have a fixed allowance which shall not be diminished. He says that any constitutional doctrine other than the one for which he argues would destroy the Constitution.

Not very many years later, Hamilton saw constitutional destruction threatening again, in a controversy about legislative discretion with respect to this matter of the judiciary and its compensation. As has been already indicated, a later chapter will consider that controversy about the judiciary, which was the great defensive operation in Hamilton's reaction against the movement called "The Revolution of 1800" by Jefferson, the man presiding over it. The man presiding over the judiciary when that revolution later moved against it, John Marshall, in his most famous opinion as a judge, asserted a judicial claim of independent power to judge the validity of legislative acts, in a case involving a legislative claim of power to abolish judicial offices.

About the earlier skirmish that we are now considering (Washington's refusal of the House demand to see papers before appropriating money to implement the Jay Treaty), Marshall said that it "appeared to break the last cord of that attachment which had theretofore bound some of the active leaders of the opposition to the person of the President. Amidst all the agitations and irritations of party, a sincere respect and real affection for the Chief Magistrate, the remnant of former friendship, had still lingered in the bosoms of some who had engaged with ardor in the political contests of the day. But, if the last spark of affection was not now extinguished, it was at least concealed under the more active passions of the moment."

Washington himself wrote that this was "one of those great occasions than which none more important had occurred or probably may occur again," for "the *real* question" was not the unpopular treaty but whether the popular branch of government could increase its own power.

Jefferson wrote Monroe that he was willing to risk bringing on "an embarrassing and critical state in our government," for "on the precedent now to be set will depend the future construction of our Constitution"; "It is fortunate," he wrote, "that the first decision is to be in a case so palpably atrocious as to have been predetermined by all America."

Jefferson wrote to Madison, when Hamilton's overwhelming series of *Camillus* papers threatened to change the appearance of the case and thus to master fortune: "Hamilton is really a colossus to the anti-republican party. Without numbers he is an host within himself. They have got themselves into a defile, where they might be finished; but too much security on the republican part will give time to his talents and indefatigableness to extricate them. We have had only middling performances to oppose them. In truth, when he comes forward, there is nobody but yourself who can meet him."

Jefferson said of Washington, when the House, assailed by protests from its constituents, at last gave in: "one man outweighs them all in influence over the people, who have supported his judgment against their own and that of their representatives. Republicanism must lie on its oars, resign the vessel to its pilot, and themselves to the course he thinks best for them."

However, those who called themselves "the republican part" had no intention of surrendering the ship of state to those whom Jefferson thought would let it drift toward slavery. According to the clerk of the House, whom one historian calls the "ex-officio national chairman of the Republican party," they had hoped by defeating the treaty to pave the way for "a Republican president to succeed Mr. Washington." Madison wrote Monroe, in May 1796, in cipher: "It is now generally understood that the President will retire, and Jefferson is the object on one side, Adams apparently on the other."

But let us now consider the draft which Hamilton prepared for the President. In it the executive begins by acknowledging his receipt of the resolution and his respect for the House—and for the other branch of Congress as well, which he alludes to but does not name as such. He then refers to the duty of both the executive and the body of representatives to preserve that which, by constituting both of them, thereby limits the disposition of the executive to defer to the body of the representatives. Then, acknowledging the fact which the House wished undone, he indicates in a phrase, subordinate but final, that there were decisive reasons for it. He then gives an account of the reasons.

He speaks first of general reasons against transmitting the papers with the treaty. The reasons are general because they explain the grounds of a general practice of governments. Among prudent governments there prevails this rule of conduct: do not promulgate without weighty and special reasons, or due reserves, the particulars of the intermediate transactions of a foreign negotiation. The general reasons show how powerful are the motives for great delicacy and reserve on this point. The general reasons exhibit why it is that to exhibit the particulars of a foreign negotiation requires reasons which are special.

What one party to a negotiation says to another party in private might injure the first party if made public by the other. The injury might be a tendency to embarrassment and mischief internally, or, externally, it might be a provocation to the resentment or jealousy or inexpedient pretensions of a third power. Either way, a nation that freely communicates to all other nations what was said to it in past negotiations to which it was a party will find that no other nation will communicate freely with it in future negotiations. Thus will harm be done to the accommodation and adjustment which are the ends of communication between governments. Yet further harm will be suffered by a nation with this habit of indiscreet publicity. The agents of another nation in negotiations with it, fearing exposure to the criticism of their political adversaries at home, will be less accommodating to the agents of the indiscreet, who will not have the same motive to be tough toward the agents of the reserved—and thus the agents of the indiscreet will obtain worse bargains. A nation's habit of freely communicating its negotiations will provide strong inducements for its own agents to be reserved in communicating with it. This habit will also give the nation reason to regret communicating freely with its agents, since what it tells them, if made public after amicable settlement, will often undo good will, will give occasion for suspicion and pretext for discontent, or will prejudice future negotiations with the same or different powers.

After he presents these general reasons against transmitting the papers with the treaty, but before he considers whether any special reasons rec-

ommend in this particular case a departure from the rule, he concedes that
many of the general reasons have no immediate application to the case of
the present treaty, but he says it would be extraordinary if some of them
did not operate—and it would be inadvisable to discriminate here between
such as may apply and such as may not.

When he turns to considering whether there are any special reasons
which recommend in this particular case a departure from the rule governing the general practice of governments, the question of special reasons is
especially a question having to do with the particular species of government
which the Constitution has established.

The first part of the constitutional argument shows that the express
terms which regulate deposit of the treaty-making power have the force of
negating any alleged discretionary right in the House of Representatives to
give or refuse assent to a treaty or, what is equivalent, to execute it or not.
Hence, if there is a discretionary right in the House to execute a treaty or
not, it must be because there is something in the Constitution which by
necessary implication changes the force of the express terms that regulate
the deposit of the treaty-making power.

The second part of the constitutional argument raises the question
whether there is any such thing. The answer is *no*. Such a thing, if it exists,
must be found in those clauses which regulate the deposit of the legislative
power. Here, therefore, the question splits, and two questions arise. First,
can the power of treaty reach and embrace objects upon which the legislative power is authorized to act, such as the regulation of commerce and the
definition of piracy? The answer is *yes*. Second, if it can reach and embrace
those objects, is there any principle which (as to them) gives Congress, or
more properly the House of Representatives, a discretionary right of assent
or dissent? The answer is *no*. Elaborate argument is presented in support of
these answers.

At the end of the course of reasoning, Washington, present President
of the United States and former President of the Convention which planned
the Constitution of the United States, is to state that "While I can discover
no sufficient foundation in the constitution for the claim of a discretionary right in the House of Representatives to participate in giving validity to
Treaties; I am confirmed in the contrary inference by the knowledge I have
that the expediency of this participation was considered by the Convention
which planned the Constitution and was by them overruled."

Washington is then to go on to justify the Constitution in this respect
as follows. The greatness of the power of treaty under this construction is

no objection to its truth. It is doubtless a great power, and necessarily is it so—else it could not answer those purposes of national security and interest in the external relations of a country for which it is designed. Nor does the manner in which it is granted in our constitution furnish any argument against the magnitude which is ascribed to it—but rather the contrary. A treaty cannot be made without the actual cooperation and mutual consent of the executive and two-thirds of the Senate. This necessity of positive cooperation of the executive charges him with a high responsibility, which cannot but be one great security for the proper exercise of the power, and the proportion of the Senate requisite to their valid consent to a treaty approaches so near to unanimity that it would always be very extraordinary were it given to a treaty really pernicious or hurtful to the State. These great guards are manifest indications that a great power is meant to be deposited. The manner of its deposit, therefore, is an argument *for* its magnitude rather than an argument against it—and is an argument *against* the intention to admit, with a view to security, the discretionary cooperation of the House of Representatives, rather than being an argument in favor of such a right in them. According to our Constitution, two-thirds of the two houses of Congress may exercise their whole legislative power, not only without but even against the consent of the executive. It is not evident on general principles that this arrangement gives much greater security against a bad law than the other arrangement gives against a bad treaty. The frequent absolute necessity of secrecy not only in the conduct of a foreign negotiation, but at certain conjunctures even as to the very articles of a treaty, is a natural reason why only a part, and that the least numerous part, of the legislative body was united with the executive in the making of treaties—in exclusion of the other and the most numerous.[26]

The Senate is less numerous than the House of Representatives. With a view to secrecy this matters most. With a view to dispatch it matters too. With a view to both, the Senate rather than the House of Representatives cooperates with the President in making treaties. But government must work not only silently and swiftly, but steadily as well. Hamilton argued, as we have seen, that there would be more constancy under the proposed Constitution because the Presidency would be a seat of resistance and persistence. But the feature most characteristic of the Presidency was unity, not duration. And another part of government received the name that indicates lasting a long time—the Senate. With respect to number, the few Senators are more than one but less than many; with respect to number the Senate and the House of Representatives differ from each other only in degree, while both differ in kind from the President: bodies of men are more or less numerous, but unity is not numerous at all. The Senate is distinguished by duration: the Senate is a continuing body, for at no time can its membership entirely, or even mostly, change; and its members remain in office longer than do any other officials elected in the republic. As the President is the incarnation of unity, so the embodiment of duration is the Senate.

IX
Duration

In considering what Hamilton says about the institution of a Senate, we must not forget his belief in popular representation as the foundation of good government. It is because a representative body has its own essential features which are essential to good government that such a body cannot provide other features which are also essential to good government. Among the reasons why a representative body by itself does not suffice for durable liberty is this: the embodiment of representation which is essential to liberty cannot be a body of enduring character.

Even in the case of the House of Representatives, however, Hamilton did not think that the more rapid the turnover the better. In the Constitutional Convention he opposed the motion to reduce from three to two years the term proposed for representatives. The elections, which must not be infrequent, must also not be too frequent. When elections are too frequent, not only do the people become so listless that factious cabals more easily succeed, but the representatives become too dependent on the popular sentiments. Too great dependence of the representatives on the popular sentiments is, like too little dependence, bad. The representative must think his way to an opinion of his own—he is to engage in deliberation while conveying popular sentiments.

The body of the people's representatives is contrasted with the Senate in Hamilton's *Federalist* discussion of the constitutional provision which places in the national legislature the authority to regulate elections to the national legislature. The authority is so placed in order to get uniformity in the time of elections, such uniformity being doubly desirable.

On the *one* hand, it provides a cure for the diseases of faction and a security against the perpetuation of the same spirit in the House of Representatives. If there were as much diversity in the times of election for the House of Representatives of the United States as there is in the times of election established in the several states for local purposes, then there could never be at one time a total dissolution or renovation of the representative body. Hence, any kind of improper spirit which should happen to prevail in it would be apt to infuse itself into the new members as they come forward in succession, there being a contagion in example which few men have sufficient force of mind to resist. For this reason three times the duration in office, with the condition of a total dissolution of the body at the same time, might be less formidable to liberty than one-third of that duration, subject to gradual and successive alterations.

On the *other* hand, this uniformity in the time of elections would be needed just as much for executing the idea of a regular rotation in the Senate. By this rotation, the Senate, unlike the House constituted of representatives in the strictest sense, is to be incapable of total dissolution or renovation at one time. It is rather to remain nearly the same, constantly assimilating to itself gradual accretions. The idea of rotating the members of the Senate is to make its alterations gradual and successive.[1]

ii The senatorial part of the legislature is most prominently distinguished from the representative part of the legislature by the powers allotted to it in a distinct capacity. The distinctively senatorial powers are these: to participate with the executive in the appointment to offices and in the making of treaties and to have a judicial character as a court for the trial of impeachments.[2]

Because in the business of appointments the principal agent will be the executive, the provisions relating to appointments will be discussed most properly in the examination of the executive department, says Hamilton at the beginning of *Federalist* Number 65 before going on to discuss the Senate's judicial character as a court for the trial of impeachments. Since we have already considered the advantages to be expected from the Senate's cooperation in the business of appointments, we now need only see how Hamilton concluded that discussion. He says that he could not properly conclude his observations on the subject of appointments without taking notice of a scheme for uniting the House of Representatives in the power of making them. He says, however, he'll do little more than mention it, for the example of most of the states in their local constitutions encourages us to reprobate the idea, which is one not likely to gain the countenance of any considerable part of the community. He gives two reasons why such a body can never be deemed proper for the exercise of that power. One reason is that such a body is so numerous: this would occasion infinite delays and embarrassments—indeed, its unfitness will be manifest to all who are reminded that in half a century it may consist of three or four hundred persons. The other reason is that such a body is so fluctuating: this uniting of the House of Representatives with the Senate and the executive in the power of appointment would defeat all the advantages of the stability of both the executive and the Senate.[3]

The Senate not only participates with the executive in *appointments* to office—it acts also in a judicial character, as a court of impeachments, impartially to decide upon permanent *removals* from office. Impeachment is an institution designed as a method of national inquest into the conduct of public men, and the most proper inquisitors for the nation are the nation's representatives. Where to place the power of originating the inquiry is not a matter in dispute: it is everyone's opinion that one branch of the legislative body ought to have the power of preferring the impeachment. But what is in question is where to place the power of completing the inquiry.

It was the Convention's opinion that the Senate would be the most fit depository of the power of deciding upon the impeachment. Questioning the Convention's opinion, Hamilton relies heavily on rhetorical questions in his effort to show why those who can best discern the intrinsic difficulty of the thing will be least hasty in condemning that opinion and will be most inclined to allow due weight to the arguments which may be supposed to have produced it. Hamilton devotes two paragraphs to these arguments, after which he devotes the rest of *Federalist* Number 65 to showing that none of the alternatives to the Senate would be as good a depository.

The first of the paragraphs begins with four rhetorical questions, each longer than the one before, culminating in a complicated sentence. Having asserted that there has been no dispute about the deposit of the power to originate the inquiry in one branch of the legislative body, it asks this question: do not the reasons which indicate the propriety of this arrangement plead strongly for admitting the other branch of that body to a share in the inquiry? Then follow four sentences of assertion about the source of the institution of impeachment. Admission of the other branch of the legislative body to a share in the inquiry was suggested by the model from which the idea of this institution was borrowed. The model is British: in Great Britain it is the province of the House of Commons to prefer the impeachment and of the House of Lords to decide upon it. But the practice is not an alien one: several of the states have followed the example. Not only is the practice common to these diverse constitutions, but they have a common opinion about it: the Americans as well as the British before them seem to have regarded the practice of impeachments as a bridle in the hands of the legislative body upon the executive servants of the government. The assertions are followed by a question, which concludes the paragraph by asking whether this is not the true light in which the practice ought to be regarded. The common opinion, it seems, is correct. The diversity of constitutions is irrelevant to the matter, or perhaps it is relevant—not, however, as weakening the argument but rather as adding an a fortiori.

In the second of the paragraphs are two more questions indicating the Senate for the work of trying impeachments. The Senate, like the House of Lords, is not merely part of the legislature; it is also alone sufficiently dignified or sufficiently independent: no other body is likely to feel self-confidence enough to preserve, unawed and uninfluenced, the necessary impartiality between an accused individual and his accusers, who are the representatives of the people. A court of impeachments has the power to doom to honor or to infamy the most distinguished characters of the community, those in whom the community itself has placed the most confidence. Earlier in the paper, speaking of this trust which so deeply concerns the political reputation and existence of every man engaged in the administration of public affairs, Hamilton says that the delicacy and magnitude of the trust speak for themselves; what does not speak for itself, but will as readily be perceived only when Hamilton's speech about it is considered, is the difficulty of placing the trust rightly in a government based entirely on periodical elections.

In such a circumstance a well-constituted court for the trial of impeachments is as hard to get as it is desirable. The subjects of the jurisdiction of a court for the trial of impeachments are in their nature political. Being offenses which proceed from the misconduct of public men, that is, from the abuse or violation of some public trust, they may with peculiar propriety be denominated "political": they relate chiefly to injuries done immediately to the society itself. For this reason the prosecution of offenses that are subject to impeachment will seldom fail to agitate the passions of the whole community and to divide it into parties more or less friendly or inimical to the accused. This passionate partisanship will often be only an intensification of the previous factious state of affairs—the prosecution in many cases connecting itself with the preexisting factions, all of whose animosities, partialities, influence, and interest are thus enlisted on one or the other side. In such cases there is always the greatest danger that the partisanship intensified by the inquiry prior to impeachment will prevail in the judgment subsequent to impeachment, the decision being regulated more by the comparative strength of the parties than by real demonstrations of innocence or guilt. If a government is based entirely on periodical elections, the most conspicuous characters in the impeachment proceeding will too often be the leaders or the tools of the most cunning or the most numerous faction and hence will lack the requisite neutrality toward those whose conduct may be under scrutiny.

Perhaps it might be thought that the court for the trial of impeachments should be composed of persons wholly distinct from the other departments of the government. The state, however, then could suffer harm from the prolonged inaction of men whose firm and faithful execution of their duty might have exposed them to the persecution of an intemperate or designing majority in the House of Representatives. Harsh though it may be to suppose this, and unlikely though it may be to happen often, yet at certain seasons faction will prevail in all numerous bodies of men. A court of impeachment composed of persons wholly distinct from the other departments of the government would be too vulnerable to factious attack by the multitudinous body which is immediately representative of the people.

Then perhaps it might be thought that this court should be a body not at all distinct from the highest court within the department which is entirely composed of courts. The Supreme Court, however, by itself would not be a proper court for impeachments—even apart from the loss to the accused of the double security that is furnished by having separate trials for his office and for his life, liberty, and estate. Apart from this loss, there is another reason: the nature of the proceeding makes it necessary that a court for the trial of impeachments be numerous. It must be numerous because neither in the delineation of the offense by the prosecutors nor in the construction of it by the judges can an impeachment proceeding be tied down by such strict rules as in common cases limit the discretion of courts in favor of personal security. Even though the execution of this task of trying an impeachment cannot be strictly governed by preexisting rules, and thus is execution that cannot follow legislation, nonetheless it can be followed by a punishment so severe that it might with propriety be denominated "political execution." And yet there will be no jury to stand between the judges who are to pronounce the sentence of the law and the party who is to receive or suffer it. Thus, a court of impeachments must necessarily have an awesome discretion that cannot be placed in a small Supreme Court without personal danger to the accused. But a Supreme Court large enough to reconcile the requisite discretion of the court with the personal security of the accused would be unreasonably expensive.

There is a further consideration why making the Supreme Court the court of impeachments would have required the size of the Supreme Court to be multiplied beyond what would consist with a reasonable attention to economy. Not only must a court of impeachments have an awesome discretion; it must also be unawed by the people's representatives. To execute a task as difficult as the trial of impeachments, the members of the court must be endowed with so eminent a portion of fortitude as to be capable of finding an individual innocent despite an accusation brought by the immediate representatives of the people. A deficiency in this fortitude would be fatal to the accused.

Fortitude, however, while necessary is not sufficient. The members of the court of impeachments would also have to possess the degree of credit and authority which might sometimes be indispensable for reconciling the people to a decision that happened to clash with an accusation brought by their immediate representatives. If the members of the court of impeachments had a sufficiency in fortitude, their deficiency in credit and authority would endanger the public tranquility.

If the Supreme Court were to be the court of impeachments, it is much to be doubted whether they would always have sufficient fortitude, and it is still more to be doubted whether they would have sufficient credit and authority. This twofold hazard—to personal security and to public tranquility—could only be avoided, if at all, by rendering that tribunal so numerous as to be unreasonably expensive. This very hypothetical "if at all" seems to indicate that even if the membership of the Supreme Court were made so numerous as to be made unreasonably expensive, this would not avoid the double lack of fortitude and credit necessary to an impartial court of impeachment.

The Senate, however, combines the fortitude of independence with the credit and authority of its peculiar dignity. If the Supreme Court were to be united with the Senate to form the court of impeachments, this would diminish the credit of the Supreme Court by augmenting its authority so much as to afford additional pretext for clamor against the judiciary, and the benefits of such a union are to some extent obtained from the provision that makes the Chief Justice of the Supreme Court the president of the court of impeachment that would try an impeached President of the United States.[4]

iii   The Senate's participation with the executive in making treaties is the subject of *Federalist* Number 64, of which Jay is the undisputed author. Hamilton's *Federalist* Number 75, which is among the papers on the executive, replies to objections raised against the arrangements for the treaty power; in this paper Hamilton remarks on his own allusion to remarks made by Jay in Number 64: "The remarks made in a former number,

which has been alluded to in another part of this paper, will apply with conclusive force against the admission of the house of representatives to a share
in the formation of treaties."

He gives a twofold reason why we may expect the representative body
to lack those qualities which are essential to the proper execution of such
a trust. It is the same twofold reason for excluding the representative body
that he gave when he discussed the Senate's participation with the executive in making appointments to office: the composition of the body will be
fluctuating and (taking into account its future increase) multitudinous.

Elsewhere he treats as an advantage the mere multiplicity of parts
of government that must concur to do something, but here in discussing
treaties he says that the very complication of the business, by introducing
a necessity for so many different bodies to concur, would of itself afford a
solid objection to participation by the House of Representatives along with
the Senate. To have included in treaty-making any other body in addition
to the Senate would have been objectionable merely as a complication; to
have included a body like the House would have been objectionable of itself,
however. The work of treaty-making requires decision, secrecy, and dispatch—qualities incompatible not only with requiring the concurrence of
a number of bodies, but incompatible as well with the spirit of a body so
numerous as the representative body.

These qualities of decision, secrecy, and dispatch are possessed to a
higher degree by the Senate than by the House, but they are possessed to
an even higher degree by the single man who is President. The Senate is
to participate with the executive, not in order to supply these qualities, for
the executive alone would have them, but because the Senate, while having
these qualities to a higher degree than does the body of representatives, has
other qualities to an eminent degree. The qualities proper to the Senate that
are essential to the proper execution of the work of treaty-making are these:
an accurate and comprehensive knowledge of foreign politics, a steady and
systematic adherence to the same views, and a nice and uniform sensibility
to national character—qualities which are incompatible with the spirit of a
body so *variable* as the body of representatives.

A senator, being elected for a term which is longer than a representative's, will have his mind on long-term matters—that is, he will have an
incentive steadily to acquire knowledge of foreign affairs, will be steady in
his views, and will be concerned to be viewed by foreigners as steady. And
the Senate, being elected only a little at a time, will take more time to change
its mind than will the House of Representatives. The term for which a senator is elected and the rotation in election among the senators also make

the Senate steadier than the President. Moreover, there being a number of senators makes the Senate steadier than the single man who is President, while the senators' being few in number makes the Senate steadier than the multitudinous House of Representatives.[5]

Jay's Number 64, which is among the papers on the Senate, gives the reasons why the President is to have power by and with the advice and consent of the Senate to make treaties, provided two-thirds of the senators present concur. Reasons for this are also given by Hamilton's Number 75, which is among the papers on the executive. In giving these reasons in Number 75, Hamilton says he will content himself with offering only some supplementary remarks, principally with a view to the objections—as the observations made in a preceding number, upon this part of the plan, must have sufficed to place it to a discerning eye in a very favorable light. What Jay has said shows at the least what Hamilton says will to a discerning eye cast a very favorable light upon this part of the plan.[6]

The power of making treaties is so important, says Jay—especially as it relates to war, peace, and commerce—that it should only be delegated in such a mode and with such precautions as to secure its being exercised by the men best qualified for the purpose and in the manner most conducive to the public good. Under the proposed Constitution, our negotiations for treaties would have every advantage which can be derived, on the one hand, from talents, information, integrity, and deliberative investigations and, on the other, from secrecy and dispatch.

Two sorts of requirements must be satisfied by the manner in which the power is exercised. It is because of the agency of the President that the requirement having to do with secrecy and dispatch is satisfied: with respect to this requirement, as we have seen, the senators, though few in number, compose a body which is different only in degree from the body composed of the many representatives, but which is different in kind from the single President. Thus, one sort of requirement that must be satisfied by the manner in which the power is exercised has to do with number. The other sort of requirement that must be satisfied by the manner in which the power is exercised has to do with duration—as does, in a way, the requirement that the men by whom the power is exercised be those best qualified for the purpose.

Let us first consider the requirement of the men best qualified. The power is to be exercised by the President with the Senate—the President to be chosen by select bodies of electors deputed by the people for that express purpose, and the senators to be chosen by the state legislatures. Jay explains why this mode in such cases is vastly better than elections by the people in their collective capacity.

In elections by the people in their collective capacity, men are often placed in office by the activity of party zeal that takes advantage of the supineness, the ignorance, and the hopes and fears of the unwary and uninterested. By contrast, those who choose the men who will exercise the treaty power are themselves of the sort who will consider and choose only the sort who are already time-tested. Because the select assemblies for choosing the President, as well as the state legislatures who appoint the senators, will in general be composed of the most enlightened and respectable citizens, their attention and their votes will therefore be directed to those men only who have become the most distinguished by their abilities and virtue and in whom the people perceive just grounds for confidence. Thus, only those will receive the distinction of office who in the course of time already have become the most distinguished. Indeed, the Constitution manifests very particular attention to this object: by excluding men under thirty-five from the office of President and under thirty from that of senator, the Constitution confines eligibility to men of whom the people have had time to form a judgment and with respect to whom they will not be liable to be deceived by those brilliant appearances of genius and patriotism which like transient meteors sometimes mislead as well as dazzle. Thus, the Constitution positively guarantees that the choosers of the men who exercise the treaty power will themselves be men of whom the people, who choose the choosers, have had time to form a judgment rather than a transient impression. It has been observed that wise kings will always be served by able ministers, but in this respect the electors can better serve the electorate than kings can serve their kingdoms. Being an assembly coming from the people, the electors will have means of getting more extensive and more accurate information about men and characters than kings do; and being themselves select men, the electors themselves will select men at least as discreetly and discerningly as kings do.

From these considerations there naturally results this inference: the President and the senators so chosen will always be of the number of those who best understand our national interests in relation both to the several states and to foreign nations, who are best able to promote those interests, and who also by their reputation for integrity inspire and merit confidence. With such men the power of making treaties may be lodged safely. But this does not seem to be the chief thing. Earlier he had said that the power should be delegated only in such a mode and with such precautions that it will be exercised by the men best qualified and in the manner most beneficial. Earlier he had also said that the mode of choosing the men by select electors was more advantageous than election by the people collectively. The mode of choosing the men is a refinement of that precaution of republican government which is popular election, but the sort of mode that is less a matter of precaution and more a matter of performance is the manner in which the power is exercised. Having considered previously that aspect of manner which is related to number, let us consider now that aspect of manner which is related to duration.[7]

Those great objects involved in the power now under consideration need to be contemplated steadily in all their relations and circumstances; and, moreover, to concert and execute the measures needed for approaching and achieving them, not only are talents necessary, but also exact information, and often much time. A popular assembly, however, composed of members constantly coming and going in quick succession, must be inadequate to attain such objects. Those who wish to commit the power under consideration to such a body seem not to recollect this. It is universally known and acknowledged that system is an absolute necessity in conducting any business, but it has not yet become sufficiently impressed on the public mind that system is of high importance in national affairs. In particular, the affairs of trade and navigation should be regulated by a system cautiously formed and steadily pursued, and both our treaties and our laws should correspond with and be made to promote it. It is of much consequence that this conformity and this correspondence be carefully maintained. This will be admitted by all but a few, and those who admit it will also admit that such system is well provided for by making the concurrence of the Senate necessary both to treaties and to laws.

Provided with this opportunity to recollect a truth of great consequence which is known and is acknowledged universally, the reader will draw the consequence. The truth about the need for persistence, which did not persist in his mind long enough to be of consequence, needs to be recalled so that he will see far enough into the future to accept what provident men have prescribed to meet the present need for making arrangements favorable to foresight and persistence. Whereas the negotiation of treaties of any nature almost always requires the secrecy and dispatch to which unity conduces, affairs of trade and navigation, which are regulated by legislation as well as by treaty-making, especially require the systematic steadiness to which duration conduces.

The Convention was wise to provide as they did. They went beyond committing the power of making treaties to able and honest men: they provided not only that the power be committed to such men, but also that those men should continue in place a sufficient time. The time for which those men will continue in place suffices for them to become perfectly acquainted with our national concerns and to form and introduce a system for the management of them. Such duration is prescribed as will give them an opportunity greatly to extend their political information and to render their accumulating experience more and more beneficial to their country.

The Convention's provident prudence was shown as much in another arrangement for duration which is conducive to the power's being exercised in the manner most conducive to the public good: they provided for the frequent election of senators in such a way as to leave a considerable remainder of the old ones in place, thus obviating the inconvenience of periodically transferring these great affairs entirely to new men, with the result that uniformity and order, as well as a constant succession of official information, will be preserved.[8]

To Hamilton what Jay had said about the Senate's constitutional character should lead the discerning to be very favorable to the plan which would establish it. Hamilton expected the Senate under that plan to have a considerable part in foreign policy. A great part of the business which, prior to the adoption of the Constitution, kept the Congress sitting through the year was, under the new Constitution, to be transacted by the President— even the management of foreign negotiations was naturally to devolve upon him—yet nonetheless, Hamilton said, foreign negotiations were to be managed not only subject to the Senate's final concurrence but also according to general principles concerted with them. The legislative sanction, that is to say, was not to be a simply take-it-or-leave-it matter at the final stage of a treaty: one of the objections raised by Hamilton against admitting the House of Representatives to a share in the formation of treaties along with the Senate was the great inconvenience and expense of more frequently calling together the House of Representatives, and often of keeping them together a longer time when convened, in order to obtain their sanction in the progressive stages of a treaty.[9]

iv   Numbers 62 and 63, the first two of the five *Federalist* papers on the Senate, form a single discussion, divided between the parts of a single subdiscussion. Whereas in Numbers 64 to 66 "Publius" discusses the provisions for the Senate's distinctive powers, in Numbers 62 and 63 he discusses the provisions for the Senate's composition, especially those concerning the number of senators and their duration in office, with an emphasis on duration.

The discussion of the number and especially the duration of the senators, which is followed by the three papers discussing the distinctive powers of the Senate, is preceded by a brief discussion of what is said to need no dilation in considering the composition of the Senate: the qualifications of the senators and the role of the states.

The qualifications of the senators are considered in contrast to those of the representatives, and the point of comparison is time. They must for a longer time have been alive and also for a longer time have been citizens—the one qualification is to make their information more extensive and their character more stable, and the other is to make them freer of foreign influence.

The role of the states with respect to the Senate is twofold. In the *first* place their legislatures appoint the senators. This suits public opinion; it also has the advantages of being selective, and of drawing in the states by securing their authority while linking them together. And in the *second* place their representation is equal. While this is a compromise, making concessions to the small states' principle of a league in contradistinction to the principle of a people thoroughly incorporated into one nation, it appears to have some reason in the mixing of principles that constitutes a compound republic, and it is, if evil, the least evil that is acceptable; moreover, it has its advantages, for it gives the big states (which also claim sovereignty) the guard they wish against consolidation into a simple republic, and it impedes legislation. Improper legislation will probably fail to get a majority of states as well as of people, and good legislation will in practice not fail for this reason, for the big states can use the power of supplies in the House to push the Senate; in any case the American disease is too much legislation too easily passed.

After this brief prelude at the beginning of Number 62, "Publius" moves on to his chief theme with respect to the Senate. He stays with this for the remainder of Number 62 and for most of Number 63, concluding Number 63 with a brief statement approximately as long as the prelude, in reply to the objection that a body whose members do not come to office by immediate appointment of the people, nor finish their term in a short time, will gradually come to dangerous preeminence and finally become a tyrannical aristocracy.

The reply has a general part: what is feared, the abuse of power, is not the only danger to liberty. Liberty may also be endangered by the abuse of liberty itself; this in fact has happened many times, and this, rather than the abuse of power that is feared, seems to be what is most to be feared here in the United States. This country in particular is subject to the general danger. The reply also has a particular part. What is feared will not happen here. Reason suggests that the Senate could not succeed in corrupting itself as well as corrupting the state legislatures, and the House, and the people; and experience provides instructive examples at home in our own time (the Maryland Senate), elsewhere in our former home (the British House of Lords), and long ago and far away (in classical antiquity—Sparta, Rome, and Carthage). And if what is feared did happen here, a restoration would arise from the popular House of Representatives.[10]

The chief theme of "Publius" with respect to the Senate, on which (except for a brief prelude) he dilates through Number 62 and continues on through Number 63 (except for a brief conclusion), is this: how the senators, being few in number and especially long-lasting in duration, will serve the purposes of a senate.[11]

Our experience enforces what our reason suggests, says "Publius," that every republic which lacks a senate suffers certain inconveniences, and historical examples show that every republic which lived long had a senate. For long duration a government having as its special characteristic popular liberty has special need of a body whose members are characterized by long duration in office; the ancient examples of the only long-lived republics (Sparta, Rome, and Carthage) teach the need to blend stability with liberty. But, someone might object, examples from the ancients are not relevant to us; the reply to this should be that though their differences from us make them unfit for imitation and repugnant to the spirit of America, nonetheless their similarity to us makes examples from them relevant to us. A senate among us supplies the defects of a numerous assembly that is frequently elected by the people. Some of these defects are defects of the people themselves; that is to say, we need a senate for the very reasons we need representatives instead of government by the people in their collective capacity. And others of these defects are defects peculiar to a representative body; that is to say, we need a senate if only because we have representatives instead of having government by the people in their collective capacity. The experience of the ancients can show us the defects, which are remedied by a senate, of government by the people in their collective capacity; and the experience of the ancients can also show us something about government by representatives, for the difference between the ancient republics and the American republics is not that there was no representation at all in the ancient, but that there is only representation in the American, which have no participation at all by the people in their collective capacity.[12]

What inconveniences are suffered by a republic that lacks a senate? The discussion of these inconveniences is the heart of the discussion by

"Publius" of the Senate. A senate guards the people by supplying a remedy
against seven defects, six being deficiencies of their representatives and one
being a deficiency of their own. Of the six deficiencies of the popular representatives, the first and last may be considered a pair; so also may the
second and the next-to-last; and the two central deficiencies come together.

The *first* defect of representatives of the people is that they may be unfaithful to the people. To add another body adds a guard on their fidelity,
and the guard is the more reliable, the more dissimilar is the additional
body—so long as the arrangement preserves due harmony and republican
principles. The *last* defect of the popular representatives is that as a changeable body they have little responsibility to the people for long-term consequences. Thus, the list of six begins and ends with defects that are peculiar
to a body that is representative, a body constituted not by the presence
of the assembled people but by a frequently renewed tie to the multitude
represented. The people can easily recognize that men are not well served
whose servant slips loose from his tie to them or is so closely tied to them
that he cannot be made to answer for neglecting to look further than they.[13]

After speaking of the infidelity of a body that is representative, "Publius" moves *next* to the deficiency of a body that is numerous: its propensity
to passion and faction. To add another such body would merely duplicate
the propensity, but there would be less propensity to passion and faction
in a body which differed in having a membership that is less numerous—
although the less numerous body's lesser propensity to passion and faction
would be a remedy for the more numerous body's greater propensity to passion and faction only if the less numerous body were made a firmer body
by the additional difference of having a membership with greater duration.
Corresponding to this arrangement for counteracting vicious political behavior which unwisely rises up against the rule of reason, and which stoops
to grasp dishonorably for partial and for transient advantage, is the *next-
to-last* defect: the lack of a due sense of national character. The possession
of such a sense is a desideratum (this is the only item listed positively as
a desideratum) because it is useful to appear wise and honorable to other
nations and also because it is proper to test one's own policy by looking to
its appearance in the opinion of impartial others. For such a sense to characterize a body of men, they must feel individually the praise or blame of
public measures, a feeling which comes with their being few in number;
they must also feel individually the pride in public prosperity which comes
with having a tenure in office of sufficiently long duration.[14]

After having considered, with a view to the Senate as a corrective,
first the representative body's ties to the people and then the representative

body's moral character, "Publius" arrives at the representative body's central pair of deficiencies, its deficiencies of competence. Incompetence is the core of the deficiencies of popular representation. Both ingredients in the incompetence for which a senate may supply a remedy have to do with duration. The *third* deficiency of the popular representatives is a lack of acquaintance with the objects and principles of legislation: knowledge of means is as needful as fidelity to ends. In order to supply public servants with both the motive and the opportunity to learn, their tenure of office must have a long duration. They will not know how to achieve the popular ends if the long time needed to learn the know-how is not supplied by a long time in office. Without the prospect of a long tenure, they do not try to learn and are not able to learn what they need to know. Their lack of know-how shows itself in the changes in the laws that are necessitated by their errors. But even if the men in office do have the know-how, the consequence of their short duration in office is mutability of measures. Thus, consideration of the third deficiency leads us to the *fourth*: the mutability of measures that results from the rapid succession of new members. This fourth deficiency, part of the central pair of deficiencies of the people's representatives, receives the longest discussion of all the deficiencies of the people's representatives; it is the central deficiency of the entire list of deficiencies (comprising deficiencies of the people's representatives together with those of the people themselves) for which the Senate supplies some remedy, and discussion of it is the conclusion to the first of the two papers in which "Publius" explains why popular government needs a senate.[15]

The mutability of measures is produced by mutability in the body of men who adopt the measures. The mutability of measures, an effect produced by insufficient duration, itself has many effects. Externally, it causes the nation to forfeit other nations' respect and confidence, thus harming the nation's honor and its interests. Internally, its many effects are worse. Although mutability of measures is the deficiency of the people's representatives which is discussed at greatest length, the discussion might be very much longer: it would fill volumes to list more than only a few of its mischievous effects, even giving only a hint about those listed, and the effects of the mischievous effects are innumerable.

Four of these mischievous effects of mutability of measures are indicated. First, since the rule of laws made by men chosen by the people turns into lawlessness when the people cannot know what the law requires, liberty ceases to be of much avail to the people; mutability of measures takes from the people the blessings of liberty. In the next place it gives advantages to the few over the many; moneyed and sagacious enterprise, watching the many changes in the laws and able to trace their consequences, will profit at the expense of the industrious and uninformed mass. And in the next place it discourages that useful private enterprise which requires steady national policy; productive busyness depends on governmental steadiness. Finally, popular liking for and looking up to government requires that government be businesslike: mutability of measures diminishes the people's attachment to and their reverence for their political system, since a government will not be long respected if it is not respectable, and it will not be respectable if it does not have order and stability—that is, if it does not long persist in systematic steadiness.

Of those indicated mischievous effects of mutability of measures, the first item is the loss of what the people have an attachment to because it protects them against the fear that government will depart from its proper purpose, and the last item is the loss of what government must have in order to function properly enough to have the attachment and the reverence of the people; these two items surround two items that have to do with the dependence of private enterprise on public policy—the improper profit that depends on governmental mutability and the proper profit that depends on governmental steadiness.[16]

The *last* deficiency of *all* those on the list of deficiencies for which a senate may supply a remedy is a deficiency of the people themselves: the people are subject to passion, to temporary error and delusion—thus the need for a body of considerable duration which will stand firm against the popular errors and delusions that temporarily seize the popular representatives because they seize the people themselves. Against the objection that what counters the people's susceptibility to temporary error and delusion is the extent of the republic, the reply is that there is need for auxiliary precautions, because extent is not a sufficient reliance; and extent itself, though it impedes the distributing of errors and delusions, also impedes their removal once distributed, thus prolonging their duration.[17]

v   Numbers 62 and 63 of *The Federalist* were claimed by Madison as well as by Hamilton. According to Jacob E. Cooke, the editor of the definitive edition of *The Federalist*, internal evidence "indicates" that Madison "probably," though not "surely," wrote Numbers 62 and 63; and the "more reliable" evidence of the claims made by the disputants themselves (that is, the facts showing that Madison's claim was made less casually than was Hamilton's) "clearly suggest," says Cooke, the superiority of Madison's claim to the authorship of these disputed papers, though the facts "do not conclusively controvert" Hamilton's claim. Not only may Hamilton have erred in claiming to have written them, but his claim may even have been made, indeed "probably was made," says Cooke, without referring to the essays.

But even if Hamilton did err in his claim, he nonetheless did make it, and thus he lent his authority to what "Publius" said in Numbers 62 and 63. Moreover, what "Publius" in those papers told the people of the state of New York, on the points of interest here, consists with what Hamilton in convention shortly afterward told the delegates chosen by the people of the state of New York to debate and decide the ratification of the proposed Constitution.[18]

When the New York Ratifying Convention on 24 June 1788 discussed the provisions for the Senate in the third section of Article I of the proposed Constitution, Gilbert Livingston proposed an amendment: no person should be eligible as senator for more than six years in any term of twelve years, and the legislatures of the several states should have power to recall their senators (either one or both of them) and to elect others to serve for the remainder of the time for which those recalled had been appointed. After several other speakers, Hamilton spoke against the amendment.[19]

He began by speaking of the noncontroversial end. We all are eager to establish a republican government on a safe and solid basis, he said. This is the object of the wishes of every honest man in the United States, and it is of all objects the nearest and dearest to my own heart, he said. But much mental effort is required for choosing the best and most effectual means of accomplishing this end, the most important study which can interest mankind. We must mix the ingredients that make for safety with those that make for solidity; we must not think that we have established good government when we have provided only for republican safety. The choice of means to the noncontroversial end is most controversial.

Nothing was more natural than that, in the commencement of a revolution which received its birth from the usurpations of tyranny, the public mind should be influenced by an extreme spirit of jealousy. To resist these tyrannical encroachments and to nourish this jealous spirit was the great object of all our public and private institutions—and it was certainly a valuable object, he said. But the zeal for liberty became excessive. In forming our confederation, this passion alone seemed to actuate us, and we appear to have had no other view than to secure ourselves from despotism. Safety from despotism is indeed one important object of good government. But there is another object, equally important, which enthusiasm kept us from attending to. Our exclusive attention to tying the representative to the people has kept us from seeing the need also to embody in our government another principle: a principle of strength and stability in the organization of government and vigor in its operations.

In every republic, he said, there should be some permanent body to correct the prejudices, check the intemperate passions, and regulate the fluctuations of the popular assembly. A body instituted for these purposes must be so formed as to exclude as much as possible from its own character those infirmities and that mutability which it is designed to remedy. It is therefore necessary that it should be small, and that it should hold its authority during a considerable period. (It should also have so much independence in the exercise of its powers as will divest it as much as possible of local prejudices.) It should be so formed as to be the center of political knowledge, to pursue always a steady line of conduct, and to reduce to system every irregular propensity. This purpose cannot be accomplished without establishing some select body formed peculiarly upon its own principle of strength and stability. We shall never have an effective government unless our government has within it some stable body which will pursue a system, will guard against innovations that lead to instability, and will have the opportunity to know what must be known for directing public affairs.

The people do not possess the discernment and stability necessary for systematic government, and a community will always be especially incompetent in that branch of administration which involves our political relation with foreign states. Lacking necessary information respecting public measures, the people are frequently led into the grossest errors of misinformation and of passion besides. To deny this would be flattery which their own good sense must despise. Yet these truths are not often held up in public assemblies—although they cannot be unknown to any who hear me, said Hamilton. The reason for this seems to be that the people are not only lacking in information but are also misled by artful men or by men of influence whose views are partial. The body of the people in every country intend the good end; it almost goes without saying that the populace desires public prosperity. The people's leaders in America, however, need to be told that the people's deficiencies do not include an incapacity to be told that they have deficiencies. The people are capable of recognizing that it is misleading flattery to tell them that they need not provide against their own deficiencies. A part of the misleaders are misled by partial views that can be enlarged; a part of them, artful and ambitious, may be overcome by leadership that holds up in public assemblies the truths not often publicized in enthusiastically republican America. Because two objects need to be conciliated, there ought to be two distinct bodies in our government. One of the two bodies is to be immediately constituted by, and peculiarly to represent, the people. Being dependent on the people, and possessing all the popular features, it will have a quick sensibility of the ideas of the people. This body, being made up of representatives elected for a short term who shall be closely united to the people, is the representative body. In addition to the representative body, there is to be another body: a permanent body with the firmness to stand against popular fluctuations and to pursue the public interest, the true interest of the people, as the arts of demagogues and designing men play upon and generate popular dissatisfactions.[20]

Such an embodiment of the twofold principle of safety and solidity was not unprecedented in republican America. Why, Hamilton asked, have we in New York a Senate with a four-year duration of membership, one-third going out every year: because the men of the convention that formed the state constitution of New York had been taught by the history of ancient and modern republics that many of the evils which these republics suffered arose from the lack of a certain balance and mutual control indispensable to a wise administration. They were convinced that popular assemblies are frequently misguided by ignorance, by sudden impulses, and by the intrigues of ambitious men—and that some firm barrier against these operations was necessary. They therefore instituted your Senate, Hamilton said, and the benefits we have experienced have fully justified their conceptions. As they did then, now we too should look at truth firmly and without prejudice. The tendency of the amendment now proposed, he said, would be to take away the stability of government by depriving the Senate of its permanence. It would subject this body to the weakness and prejudices incident to popular assemblies, the very things which it was instituted to correct. By thus assimilating the complexion of the two branches, the amendment would destroy the balance between them, rendering the senator a slave to all the capricious humors among the people.

Hamilton anticipated that here it would probably be suggested that not the people but the state legislatures were to have the power of recall. He replied that in respect to federal affairs the state legislatures must be very much the image of the multitude, with the same prejudices and factions prevailing, but he insisted that in whatever body there was vested the power of recall, the senators would feel themselves so dependent that they could never have that firmness and stability needed to discharge their duty to the Union. At this place in the speech, the emphasis shifted from stability amid popular mutability to firmness against such local partiality as the states embodied, and Hamilton discussed at length the unhappy effects of making the senators more dependent on the state governments.[21]

Hamilton then replied to the argument that although the several states had had the power to recall their delegates to Congress, the states nonetheless had not exercised the power. That, he said, has been the experience of only a few years, under peculiar circumstances: a seat in Congress has been less an object of ambition, and consequently the arts of intrigue have been less practiced—indeed, it has been difficult to find men willing to suffer the mortifications to which they are exposed by so feeble a government and so dependent a station. Under the proposed Constitution, by contrast, the government of the United States is to be not a feeble congress of ambassadors but a government, and the Senate is to transact its vast affairs. A moment's consideration of the purposes for which the Senate is instituted, and the nature of the business which they are to transact, will show the necessity of giving them permanence or duration. In this consideration there are three items: knowledge, responsibility, and sense of national character.

New and unqualified members should not be continually thrown into the body of those who, together with the President, are to manage all our concerns with foreign nations. To make treaties, manage commerce, and direct the foreign interests, they must understand all the interests of foreign nations and their political systems. This knowledge is not soon acquired, and only a very small part is gained privately. It is acquired by experience. A knowledge of the powers of Europe—their commerce, politics, and interests—a knowledge of your own country's commercial interests, products, and finances: all this requires time.

With a view to responsibility also, the Senate needs duration or permanence. They must have a hold on office that lasts some while if they are to be held responsible for the effect of their measures. When public bodies are engaged in the exercise of general powers, you can judge the propriety of their conduct only from the result of their systems. They may be forming plans which require time and diligence to bring to maturity. They must therefore have a considerable and fixed duration in order that they may calculate accordingly. In bodies subject to frequent changes, great political plans must be conducted by members in succession; a single assembly can have but a partial agency in them and consequently cannot properly be answerable for the final event. A Senate in perpetual flux could never have that responsibility which is so important in republican governments.

There is a final view in which duration will appear necessary in the Senate: a government whose policy is changeable must soon lose its sense of national character. Senators will not be solicitous for the reputation of public measures in which they have had a merely temporary concern, and they will feel more lightly the burden of public disapprobation the greater is the number of those who share the censure. Such senators will forfeit the respect of foreigners. Our political rivals, seeing our mutable counsels as evidence of deficient wisdom, will be little apprehensive of our arriving at any exalted station in the scale of power. The Senate must have the national character lacking in a body that transacts temporary measures from day to day, and the senators must have a sensibility of national character. Senatorial permanence will foster not only knowledge and responsibility, but also that firmness which constitutes national character.[22]

Thus, Hamilton concluded, the amendment if adopted would make the senators so dependent as to disqualify or render them useless as senators. The country would suffer grave disadvantages, internal and external. History shows that wherever there has operated the fatal principle of subjecting the head to the control of the members, it has proved a fruitful source of commotions and disorders; and if the amendment were admitted, prejudices would govern and passions rage in the counsels of the union, for state interests and factions would be thrown into the national government. Beyond the federal question, however, is the republican question: the amendment would create a mutability of measures. Let us, pleaded Hamilton, rescue republican government from the mutability and inconstancy charged against it. Instability has been a prominent defect in most republics, so baneful a feature of our own infant republics that a lawyer in our states has to learn a new system at the end of every session. This is the first fair opportunity of deliberately correcting governmental error. We must apply an immediate remedy to eradicate the poisonous principle of instability from our government. If we do not do so, we shall feel, and posterity will be convulsed by, a painful malady. Without blending liberty and stability, he said, we cannot establish a good republican government.[23]

The next day, 25 June 1788, after Melancton Smith spoke against the proposed Constitution's provision for a Senate, and on behalf of Livingston's amendment, the New York Ratifying Convention again heard Hamilton speak.[24]

Hamilton began again by pointing out the source of the difficulty: truth in the matter under debate resided not in a single principle but in a judicious combination of principles. In debates of this kind it is extremely easy, on either side, to say many plausible things. Indeed, there is even some truth in the reasonings on both sides. In this situation, judgment and good sense should determine their force and application. There is a double object in forming systems of government—safety for the people and energy in the administration. When these two objects are united, the system will tend to the public welfare, but if energy be neglected, the people's security will be as certainly sacrificed as by disregarding safety. Good constitutions are formed upon a comparison of the liberty of the individual with the strength of government; if the tone of either be too high, the other will be too much weakened. But one element in administrative energy or governmental strength is stability: without stability as well as security for the rights of the people, government is not government. The principle of stability in government and the principle of safety for the people are best combined by instituting one branch peculiarly endowed with sensibility and another with knowledge and firmness. Through the opposition and mutual control of these bodies, the government will perfectly·combine, in its regular operations, individual liberty with governmental strength. The principle of caution, of a laudable anxiety for the safety of the people, is the principle justly applied in reasoning about the representative house. We have it constantly held up to us, however, that as it is our chief duty to guard against tyranny, it is our policy to form all the branches of government for this purpose. But, Hamilton replied, experience shows that when the people act by their representatives, they are commonly irresistible; when the people have an organized will which pursues measures, they will always prevail. And to impose upon a senatorial body the principle of caution, which properly applies to the operation of a representative body, would destroy the essential qualities of a senate, whose proper principle is stability.[25]

It does not deprive this argument of force, he said, to point out that not the people but the legislatures of the states are to appoint the senators. The state legislatures are the immediate representatives of the people and are so constituted as to feel all the people's prejudices and passions and to be governed in a great degree by the people's misapprehensions. The history of the state legislatures is a history of factions arising from the most trifling causes and of intrigues practiced for the most illiberal purposes. One example is furnished by the state of Rhode Island, struggling under difficulties and distresses for having been led blindly by the spirit of the multitude, her legislature the picture of a mob, having carried with violence a depreciating paper medium. But there are in many of the other states only annual bodies which represent the violence and passions of the people, who at times are deceived for lack of information. Although in the state of New York, Hamilton said, we have a Senate with the proper qualities of a permanent body, as do Virginia, Maryland, and a few other states, the rest are either governed by a single democratic assembly or have a senate constituted entirely upon democratic principles. These have been more or less embroiled in factions and have generally been the image and echo of the multitude. It is difficult to reason on this point without touching on certain delicate chords, said

Hamilton: I could refer you to periods and conjunctures when the people have been governed by improper passions and led by factious and designing men, and I could show that the same passions have infected their representatives. Let us beware that we do not make the state legislatures a vehicle in which the evil humors may be conveyed into the national system. To prevent this the Senate must be so formed as in some measure to check the state governments and to preclude the communication of the false impressions which they receive from the people. The legislatures of the states can have only a partial and confined view of national affairs; they can form no proper estimate of great objects which are not in the sphere of their interests.[26]

The states, and the local views and interests they embody, would have sufficient influence over the senators without the check which Livingston's amendment would add. In the midst of that part of his speech which argued that this was so, Hamilton returned to the general point about the need to reconcile the two principles of dependence (required for safety) and permanence (required for energy).

Six years, he said, is a period short enough for a proper degree of dependence. More dependence would destroy stability, as may be seen by considering under what impressions they will act. One-third of them are to go out at the end of two years, two-thirds at four years, and the whole at six years. When one year is elapsed, there are some who are to hold their places for one year, others for three, and others for five years. Thus, there will be a frequent enough change of members, and those whose office is near the point of expiration will have a lively sense of their dependence. The biennial change of members is an excellent invention for increasing the difficulty of combination. Any scheme of usurpation will lose, every two years, a number of its oldest advocates, and their place will be supplied by an equal number of new, unaccommodating and virtuous men. This goes as far as is consistent with any degree of energy in the general government and gives a due degree of dependence; besides, the House of Representatives will also have a due degree of dependence. When two principles are equally important, we ought if possible to reconcile them and sacrifice neither; we must reconcile safety and permanence in government.[27]

Having considered the principle of recall, Hamilton concluded by considering the other principle in Livingston's proposal: the requirement of rotation. Those who contend for rotation, he said, carry their zeal beyond all reasonable bounds. To make the senators so dependent will destroy the very use of the Senate. A rotation might, under particular circumstances, be fatal to the prosperity of the country, and even when not dangerous will be very inconvenient; it will banish men perhaps most useful and send in new men who may be imposed on for lack of information or experience. In this connection Hamilton makes three points.

In the first place the amendment would defeat the design of its advocates: rotation lessens the motives to good behavior. Men will pursue their interests. It is a task like trying to change human nature to oppose the strong currents of the selfish passions. A wise legislator will divert the channel gently, directing it if possible to the public good. The interest of the officer in many cases may interfere with the interest of the community. The amendment opposes the current of the human heart too violently. When a man knows he must quit his station, let his merit be what it may, he will turn his attention chiefly to his own emolument. If he is ambitious, he will be influenced to go along with ambitious designs; he will feel temptations, furnished by few other situations, to perpetuate his power by unconstitutional usurpations.

Notice must be taken, in the next place, of the argument that it is not possible there should be only two men qualified for senators. The question, however, is not whether there may be no more than two men, but whether in certain emergencies you could find two equal to those whom the amendment would discard. Important negotiations, or other business to which they shall be most competent, may employ them at the moment of their removal—these things happen often. To obtain men capable of conducting the affairs of a nation in dangerous times is much more serious a difficulty than is imagined. More frequently than is supposed, nations are harmed by the changing of men. The amendment would make it possible for the most useful individuals all to be removed at the same time. The state legislatures should not be prohibited from returning to the Senate those men they think best able to serve the country.

Finally, there is the argument as to corruption: it is argued that the executive will have at his disposal a great number of offices, while one-third of the Senate must go out, so the executive will promise offices to those who answer his purposes before they go out. But, admitting in the President a disposition to corrupt, what are his instruments of bribery—are there many offices for which a man would relinquish the senatorial dignity? There may be some in the judicial and some in the other principal departments; however, few men will be fit to accept a judgeship, and foreign ambassadors will seldom be changed. Very few offices are as respectable as the office of a senator. Men who have been in the Senate once and have a reasonable hope of reelection will not easily be bought by offices. Gross corruption or gross seduction is much less extensive than is supposed.

Making all these arguments against rotation, Hamilton said that no government can operate well if founded on a principle so feeble.[28]

Hamilton contended for another principle. We should not, he argued, impose the same principle upon branches of government designed for different operations. The two houses were built for different kinds of work. The differences laid down in building them were meant to be embodiments of differences in nature. The House of Representatives was designed primarily to keep the people safe; the Senate, to keep the government steady.

X

Republican Constitution

Unity and duration were two aspects of a single problem: how to give constitutional efficacy to republican liberty in America. Hamilton, the man who most sharply posed the problem, tried to show the way to a solution—by teaching what it takes to *administer* a republic. Republican statesmanship required that American principles be restated.

Hamilton told the Constitutional Convention a week or so before it finished that he'd been kept from entering the discussions earlier by his dislike of the scheme of government in general, but that since he meant to support the plan now to be recommended, he wished to make a few remarks. He spoke in particular about the mode of electing the President. He said that in the printed report of the Committee of Detail a month before, the President was a monster, elected for seven years but afterward ineligible: the constitutional plan reported would give the President great powers in appointments to office, while subjecting him to a disqualification which would continually tempt him to abuse his powers and subvert the government in order to remain in power. The printed report, moreover, placed the election of the President in the legislature, so that even if he were to be reeligible, he would still be tempted to make use of corrupt influence in order to be continued in office. Hamilton said that on the whole he preferred the mode of election more recently reported by the Committee of Eleven. In this the President was to be chosen for four years by electors in such a manner as the legislature in each state should direct. In this mode, however, as it now stood, the choice would devolve on the Senate if no candidate received a majority of the electors' votes. Unless this new mode were altered, Hamilton warned, the President would use his power of appointment to influence the Senate to perpetuate him, thus aggrandizing both President and Senate. Under this mode the Senate would as a matter of course appoint the President because the electoral votes for President would not be concentrated. The best remedy would be to let the President be that candidate who received the highest number of ballots, even if not a majority. It is a weak objection to say that too small a number might then elect—for under the new mode without this remedy, the candidate who had received the smallest number of votes might be chosen President by the Senate.[1]

Two days later Hamilton returned to this theme of danger from the President and the Senate. Madison reports that Hamilton "expressed himself with great earnestness and anxiety in favor of the motion" that, before sending to the Committee on Style the articles which had been agreed upon, they reconsider the clause relating to the number of the House of Representatives—for the purpose of increasing its size. Hamilton avowed himself a friend to vigorous government, but he declared that at the same time he held it essential for its popular branch to stand upon a broad foundation. His serious opinion was that so narrow a scale in the clause made the House of Representatives really dangerous; it would warrant a jealousy in the people for their liberties. And he remarked on a special reason for apprehension: the connection between the President and Senate would tend to perpetuate the President, by corrupt influence, making it all the more necessary to establish in the other branch of the legislature a representation that would be numerous. The motion was defeated; but on the last day of the Convention, between the motion for signing the proposed Constitution and the signing itself, there was a last-minute proposal to increase the ratio of representatives to people; and after Washington, the president of the Convention, intervened in favor of the proposal, with his only speech during the deliberations, it passed unanimously.

So Hamilton could argue later, at the New York Ratifying Convention, that the number was sufficient—a month after defending the arrangement in a paper of *The Federalist* which insisted that, expensive though it be, it would be impossible with any degree of safety to narrow the foundation upon which the system was to stand: the representative body must be numerous.[2]

When the engrossed Constitution was read on the final day of the Federal Convention, Hamilton "expressed his anxiety that every member should sign": a few characters of consequence, he warned, by opposing or even only refusing to sign might do tremendous mischief. His last recorded speech to the Convention was this rhetorical question: though no man's ideas were more remote from the plan than his were known to be, is it possible to deliberate between anarchy and convulsion on one side and, on the other, the chance of good to be expected from the plan? If Hamilton could sign, he suggested, everyone must. (And every *state* must too: the names of the states listed before the signatures are in Hamilton's writing.)[3]

Hamilton's enemies did not afterward point to the remarks that he made near the end of the Convention about the need to provide against the danger of corrupt influence employed by the executive; they pointed rather to remarks made earlier in the Convention. Reports about his speech of 18 June were aduced as prime evidence of his allegedly subversive designs,[4] and reports about his speech a few days thereafter made him out to be a friend of corruption.

This latter speech was made on 22 June, when the Convention was considering the organization of the first branch of the legislature, which became the House of Representatives. In adopting the Virginia Plan, the Convention had resolved that members of the first branch would be ineligible for other offices not only during their term in the legislature but also for one year after. Gorham of Massachusetts moved to strike this out. Although it might seem from Madison's notes that he moved to strike out the whole of it, the notes of Yates make clear that he moved to strike out only the provision regarding the one year after the term.[5]

Hamilton was the last speaker before the vote. His remarks to the Convention on 22 June seem very different when the context is considered and when the notes of Yates are read beside those of Madison. Hamilton was not quoting Hume to advocate that a system of reliance on patriotism be replaced by a system of influence in which the executive would corrupt the members of the legislature, gaining the support of their votes by bribing them with offices; Hamilton, rather, was arguing that the question is complex.

Men as they are in general, he said, are less than honest or firmly patriotic; they are vicious or moved by passions of ambition and interest. Hence it is dangerous to allow them to sit as members in the representative assembly while also holding offices in the government. We have been taught to reprobate the influence of the British government, but we have not duly reflected how far that dangerous influence may be necessary to support a good government, nor how often a corrupt government is shaken by the body of firm patriots that always exist. According to the very brief notes of Madison, Hamilton cites Hume to suggest that constitutional equilibrium requires the influence of the crown which is called corruption; according to the much more extensive notes of Yates, Hamilton cites Hume to confirm that there is always a body of firm patriots who often shake a corrupt administration.

Yates reports, as Madison does not, that Hamilton advocated an exclusion. There is a danger where men are capable of holding two offices, he said (since, mankind being in general vicious, their passions may be operated upon); therefore when a member takes his seat, he should vacate every other office. But to put into effect any exclusion more than this is difficult; indeed, it is more than difficult—it is unwise. There is another inconvenience besides the inconvenience of corruption.

It is on this other inconvenience that Hamilton places his emphasis in the speech of 22 June as reported by Yates. In the place where, and at the time when, the speech was given, corruption was less of a danger than was insufficient motivation for public service. A few choice spirits may act from motives more worthy than ambition and interest, but it is the latter motives that induce to action men in general as they are. This being so, some exclusionary regulation is needed to prevent the evils of corruption. But an excessively refined exclusionary regulation will destroy, in men who do not hold government office but might, the motive to become members of the legislature.[6]

ii   Soon after the Convention disbanded to lay its proposal before the people, Hamilton spoke further on the topic when arguing that favoritism in appointments by the President would be checked by the necessity for the Senate to consent. Against this provision it had been objected that the President would exert influence over the Senate by using his power of nomination to make them complaisant to his views. But there are, said Hamilton, constitutional safeguards against this danger of executive influence upon the legislative body: no office-holder shall, during his continuance in office, be a legislator; and no legislator shall, during the time for which he was elected, be appointed to any civil office created during, or having had its emoluments increased during, such time.

To suppose that this does not suffice—to suppose that the executive could go beyond occasionally influencing some individuals in the Senate and could succeed in generally purchasing the integrity of the whole body—is to deny the presupposition of the institution of delegated power: men, while not all good, are not all bad either; mankind is partly good. This is a true view of human nature; it neither flatters the virtues nor exaggerates the vices of mankind. This theory that there is some goodness in mankind is justified by experience, even in the most corrupt periods of the most corrupt governments. Though Hamilton is silent about examples from the most corrupt times and places, he does discuss an example of venality long a topic of accusation not only in its own country but also in America: in the case of the British House of Commons, he says, the charge of venality is to a considerable extent well founded. And yet, venal though the House of Commons undoubtedly is, it equally undoubtedly contains enough independent and public-spirited men to check the monarch's inclinations.

In any case, what has been suggested as the alternative to participation by the Senate (appointment by a council) would be a bad arrangement. It would in fact diminish the security against an undue influence of the executive.[7]

Later, a year and a half after the Constitutional Convention, Hamilton as chairman of a committee of correspondence was suggesting that George Clinton's undue and even dangerous influence was among the reasons he ought not to be reelected governor of the State of New York after a dozen years in office. The council of appointment, which provided the governor with great opportunity to affect for good or ill the conduct of the public business, was a powerful engine by which the governor might remove himself from control by the opinions of the people and might perpetuate himself in office despite the efforts of the virtuous to remove him. It is true, Hamilton grants, that the governor is, by the state constitution, only one member of the council of appointment and has no vote except in case of a tie, while the four other members are senators, each from a different district of the state, elected by the Assembly. But the governor has constantly claimed the right of previous nomination and has extensively practiced upon that pretension. From the usual course of things, it may be presumed that this pretension would give the governor a prevailing influence in appointments; and, independent of this pretension, merely to be a standing member of so small a council with a casting vote might give a man of even tolerable address a preponderating weight in its arrangements, and consequently an extensive influence from the distribution of offices. The conclusion of this reasoning corresponds with public opinion, for office-seekers generally believe that they are sure of success if they are sure of the governor's cooperation.

The council is therefore a powerful engine in the hands of the governor. The question is whether an improper or excessive influence has in fact been derived from the use of that engine. If members of the legislature have been seen to change one party or system disagreeable to the governor for another party or system agreeable to him, and if that change of conduct has been seen to be speedily followed by the reception of lucrative appointments, the conclusion would be irresistible. Indeed, if appearances render the conclusion only probable, the rules of republican caution admonish us to seek a change. To suppose, contrary to all experience of human nature, that our representatives cannot be improperly influenced would destroy that watchfulness in the people over the conduct of their representatives which is an indispensable security of republican government. The committee of correspondence is acting out of republican caution, not out of the belief that many of its countrymen have been corrupted; for by exerting a sinister influence over only a few who, by their advice and example, operate upon others, the governor may unite in his views a majority which he might otherwise not have had.

Nor does the committee of correspondence say that one man ought never to continue long in office as chief magistrate. The committee acts from republican caution, which is not identical with that fearfulness which would make it constitutionally impossible for the people to concentrate executive power in one man and continue him in office. Prudence is not timidity.[8]

It was not simply to get things done that Hamilton was a proponent of constitutional arrangements for energizing and stabilizing the exercise of governmental power. Things may get done, soon and so as to last a long time, even when a constitution makes for fragmented and mutable government. If the constitutionally provided machinery of government lacks efficacy, an extragovernmental political machine unknown to the constitution may be improvised to do the job: effective decisions can be made and enforced by a boss sitting in the back room, then sent up front for dignified promulgation by those who formally preside; or the man who presides up front with a popular air of republican humility may himself do the effective work, operating his own machine in the back room. But the constitutional arrangements that necessitate such extraconstitutional arrangements in order that the public business may in some way go forward are dangerous and demeaning.[9]

iii   Hamilton's enemies in the first decade under the new Constitution charged him with being a menace to the liberty of the republic. He was called a "monocrat." He was accused of leading a movement to establish a consolidated government in place of a compound system. He sought, they said, to abolish the states by removing the federal and leaving only the national features of the American Union. The union of American states would thus become a unitary American state. In Hamilton's view, however, America was threatened not so much by an eventually unitary state as by an immanent dissolution of the union of states. He was willing to try, he said, a compound system with a truly national government that would be strong; the difficulty was, however, that those who were preoccupied with taking precautions against consolidation favored arrangements that verged on pure confederation, which could not be adequate to preserve the Union. In any case, a charge more central than the charge that Hamilton sought to centralize the government of the Union in a unitary government, extending an all-powerful hand over the country's periphery, was the charge that he sought to concentrate the power of the national government in one man's hands—that he sought with aristocratic support to erect a monarchy on the ruins of republican government.

Hoping to unite energetic administration with republican safety, Hamilton accepted office under the new Constitution of the United States. Within a few years, reluctantly concluding that Madison, cooperating with Jefferson, was at the head of a faction decidedly hostile to him and to his administration and was actuated by views subversive of the principles of good government and dangerous to the union, peace, and happiness of the country, Hamilton wrote a letter on the state of political parties and views at the time to Edward Carrington, the supervisor of revenue for the District of Virginia. This man, Hamilton believed, had the same political creed as he on two essential points: "the necessity of *Union* to the respectability and happiness of this Country," and "the necessity of an *efficient* general government to maintain that Union." This friend had presumably not been persuaded by Hamilton's enemies, who had persuaded themselves of what they had told others—"namely, that there is some dreadful combination against State Government and republicanism; which according to them, are convertible terms."

After giving a long account intended to alert his friend to the conduct of the men hostile to Hamilton's administration, Hamilton concluded in defense of himself and his associates. Serious apprehensions were disseminated in Virginia as to the existence of a monarchical party which was meditating the destruction of state and republican government, but Hamilton, on his private faith and honor as a man, unequivocally denied that any such party existed. The absurd idea must be combated, he said.

First he characterized the group of men about whose alleged anti-republicanism there were apprehensions. A very small number of men indeed may entertain theories less republican than Jefferson and Madison—but none among them would not regard as both criminal and visionary any attempt to subvert the republican system of the country. Most of them rather fear that it may not justify itself by its fruits, than feel a predilection for a different form; and their fears are not diminished by the factions and fanatical politics which they find threaten to disturb the tranquility and order of the government. And, as to the destruction of state governments, he said, the great and real anxiety is to be able to preserve the national government from the too potent and counteracting influence of those governments.

Second he said he would give with the utmost sincerity his own "political creed": "I am *affectionately* attached to the republican theory. I desire *above all things* to see the *equality* of political rights exclusive of all *hereditary* distinctions firmly established by a practical demonstration of its being consistent with the order and happiness of society."

And, as to state governments, he said, the prevailing bias of his judgment was that if they could be circumscribed within bounds consistent with the preservation of the national government, they would prove useful and salutary. This was a big *if*. He would have preferred things to be otherwise: if the states were all the size of Connecticut, Maryland, or New Jersey, he would decidedly regard the local governments as both safe and useful, he said. As the thing was then, however, he acknowledged the most serious apprehensions that the government of the United States would not be able to maintain itself against their influence, which was already penetrating into it.

The most preferred situation not prevailing, he feared that things were sliding toward catastrophe: hence a disposition on his part toward a liberal construction of the powers of the national government, a disposition to erect every fence, consistent with constitutional propriety, to guard it from depredations. His disposition to go to the limit in liberally construing the powers of the national government, and in firmly fortifying it against assault, was apprehensively misconstrued by those defending the familiar fortifications nearer home. His disposition to go all the way up to the constitutional limit, they mistook for a plot to go even beyond the constitutional bounds laid down. But he disavowed and denied any combination to prostrate the state governments. The existing constitution set bounds which he hoped might sufficiently confine the state governments—if the national government were energetically administered.

Apprehension did make him favor an improvement in the existing constitution. Lest the judiciary should not work efficiently or harmoniously, he had desired the adoption, as an amendment to the constitution, of some rational scheme of connection between the national and the state judiciaries. But otherwise he was for maintaining things as they were, though he doubted much the possibility of it, from a tendency in the nature of things toward the preponderance of the state governments.

After discussing his preferences, fears, and doubts as to the state governments, Hamilton went on to reaffirm in this letter the really heartfelt sincerity with which he was "*affectionately* attached to the Republican theory," adding that he had "strong hopes of the success of that theory," but in candor ought also to add that he was "far from being without doubts." A fond attachment to the republican theory would be folly unless it were *not* folly to have strong hopes of the success of that theory, but to have such hopes without having some doubts about the republican theory would also be folly: "I consider its success as yet a problem," he said. As yet, successful republican government is not an accomplished fact but a project to be accomplished, for "It is yet to be determined by experience whether it be consistent with that *stability* and *order* in Government which are essential to public strength & private security and happiness."

His hopes that his preferences might prevail were assailed by his doubts, doubts arising from his fears:

> On the whole, the only enemy which Republicanism has to fear in this Country is in the Spirit of faction and anarchy. If this will not permit the ends of Government to be attained under it—if it engenders disorders in the community, all regular & orderly minds will wish for a change—and the demagogues who have produced the disorder will make it for their own aggrandizement. This is the old Story.
>
> If I were disposed to promote Monarchy & overthrow State governments, I would mount the hobby-horse of popularity—I would cry out usurpation—danger to liberty &c—I would endeavor to prostrate the National Government—to raise a ferment—and then "ride in the whirlwind and direct the Storm."

"That there are men acting with Jefferson and Madison who have this in view," he said he "verily" believed. He said he "also verily" believed "That Madison does *not* mean it." And he said he "rather" believed "the same of Jefferson"—"but I read him upon the whole thus—'A man of profound ambition & violent passions.'"[10]

iv   A couple of months later Washington transmitted to Hamilton certain objections that had been made against the administration of the government, and he requested Hamilton's thoughts in writing so that the President might have before him explanations as well as complaints. Hamilton sent back answers to the objections. The objections had to do with Hamilton's financial policies.

The twelfth objection charged that the funding system furnished effectual means of corrupting enough of the legislature to turn the balance when it voted, and the thirteenth objection charged that this corrupt squadron were disposed to get rid of the limitations on the general legislature which the Constitution had imposed and which had been relied upon by states in ratifying the Constitution. After denying these charges, Hamilton turned to the fourteenth objection, which makes this charge: the ultimate object of all this is to prepare the way for a change from the present republican form of government to that of a monarchy, of which the British Constitution is to be the model.

Hamilton answers that, except for a flat denial, one can only say that the project, from its absurdity, refutes itself. None but a madman could meditate, and no wise man will believe, so visionary a thing as the idea of introducing a monarchy or aristocracy into this country by employing toward it the influence and force of a government continually changing hands. That this could be done at all is utterly incredible. But let us suppose that it could be done.

In the first place it would require a long time, certainly beyond the life of any individual to effect it: who then, he asks, would enter into such a plot—for what purpose of interest or ambition? Hamilton assumes that the plotter in such a project could have none but a low motive of interest or ambition, and so, since circumstances postpone the successful outcome of the plot till long after the death of the plotter, there could be no such plot. It would be irrational to enter into such a plot in the hope of satisfying interest or ambition, for its success could not come while the plotter was still alive to enjoy it.

In the second place it is still more chimerical to hope that the people may be cajoled into giving their sanctions to such institutions, for the people of this country are so enlightened and diversified that they surely could be brought to sanction such institutions only from convulsions and disorders, in consequence of the arts of popular demagogues: "unquestionably . . . the only path to a subversion of the republican system of the Country is by flattering the prejudices of the people, and exciting their jealousies and apprehensions, to throw affairs into confusion, and to bring on civil commotion. Tired at length of anarchy, or want of government, they may take shelter in the arms of monarchy for repose and security."

Hamilton first *re*-stated the charge; the objection itself had spoken of changing a republican form of government into a monarchy modeled on the British Constitution, but only after the answer has spoken of introducing a monarchy *or* aristocracy, is it clear again that the only alternative to a republic is a monarchy. The people will not sanction an aristocracy. They might, however, eventually, as a lesser evil, sanction monarchy.

The republican problem could be solved only by the development of a republican form of government which did not lack the aptitude and tendency to produce a good administration. If such a form were not developed, Hamilton warned, if popular prejudices against being governed were flattered to the point of inciting those popular propensities which bring on the self-destruction of popular government, then monarchy would after all prevail.

"Those, then, who resist a confirmation of public order, are the true Artificers of monarchy," says Hamilton. Although the manufacture of monarchy is not the intention of the generality of them, yet it would not be difficult to lay the finger upon some of their party who may justly be suspected:

> When a man unprincipled in private life desperate in his fortune, bold in his temper, possessed of considerable talents, having the advantage of military habits—despotic in his ordinary demeanor—known to have scoffed in private at the principles of liberty—when such a man is seen to mount the hobby horse of popularity—to join in the cry of danger to liberty—to take every opportunity of embarrassing the General Government & bringing it under suspicion—to flatter and fall in with all the nonsense of the zealots of the day—It may justly be suspected that his object is to throw things into confusion, that he may "ride the storm and direct the whirlwind."

To flatter the people into anarchy that they may be cajoled into despotism is an old story: "It has aptly been observed, that *Cato* was the Tory—*Caesar* the whig of his day. The former frequently resisted—the latter always flattered, the follies of the people. Yet the former perished with the Republic, the latter destroyed it. No popular government was ever without its Catalines and its Caesars. These are its true enemies."

What, then, of those who have been accused of constructing and operating an engine for the introduction of monarchy? As far as he is informed, Hamilton says, those who have been calumniated are anxious to keep the government in the state in which it is, which they fear will be no easy task, from a natural tendency in the state of things to exalt the local on the ruins of the national government. It is true that among those men there is some desire for change, but this is nothing to worry about. Some of them appear to wish, in a constitutional way, a change in the judiciary department of the government, from apprehension that an orderly and effective administration of justice cannot be obtained without a more intimate connection between the state and national tribunals. But even this is not an object of any set of men as a party; among those who have generally acted together, there is a difference of opinion about it on various grounds. And as to any other change of consequence, Hamilton says that he believes that nobody dreams of it.

He concludes his answer to the objection by remarking that it is curious to observe the anticipations of the different parties. He then characterizes the two sides, and impartially observes that both sides may be equally wrong and that their mutual jealousies may be what naturally causes the appearances which mutually disturb them and sharpen them against each other. His characterization is not, however, characterization by a neutral. "One" side "appears to" believe that there is a serious plot of subversion: the "other" side "firmly" believes that there is a serious plot of subversion. The plot in the existence of which the one side appears to believe (a plot to overturn the state governments and substitute a monarchy for a republican system) could be meditated by "none but a madman" and would be believed by "no wise man"; and its object could only be effected, albeit unintentionally, by those who, acting as if they were struggling against it, act like those would act who had entered into the plot in the existence of which the other side firmly believes (a plot to overturn the general government and elevate the separate power of the states upon its ruins). Unless there had been the "one side" first, there would not have been the "other side."

The answer to the fourteenth objection suggests that those who oppose the administration are acting as a party to promote subversion. The answer to the next objection, the fifteenth seeks to establish this. The fifteenth objection asserted, in effect, that those who oppose the administration are reacting against an already active partisan movement of subversion. The previous objection, the fourteenth charged that the funding system prepared the way for a change from the republican form of government to a monarchy modeled on the British Constitution, and then the fifteenth objection spoke of the beginning of the preparations for this change: that this was contemplated in the Convention, the fifteenth objection charged, is no secret, because its partisans have made no secret of it; to effect it then was impracticable—but they are still eager after their object and are predisposing everything for its ultimate attainment.

Hamilton answers that he knows of no man who contemplated introducing into this country a monarchy. All the members of the convention agreed that a constitution for America could be like Britain's only in having, in addition to a frequently elected representative assembly that was numerous, a second smaller legislative chamber of some duration, and an independent executive magistracy. True, some opinions favorable to a constitution more like Britain's were heard. These opinions, however, were to this effect: surely Britain's constitution is a good one, and perhaps none different from it can be as good, but it nonetheless would not be good in these circumstances here and now. Such opinions were merely theoretical and favorable in the abstract. And they were manifested by very few of the members. (It might be said that it matters very much who those few were: one of them, in fact the one most explicit on this point, was a member from New York who afterward became the chief minister of the first chief executive under the new constitution; the funding system was his program.)

Hamilton goes on to report that "the Member who was most explicit on this point (a Member from New York) declared in strong terms" that in the circumstances republican theory ought to govern governmental practice; it ought not to be abandoned unless its failure is certain. "In the abstract," or neglecting the circumstances here and now, the nonrepublican theory may seem to be better. "Permanent or hereditary distinctions" of political rights are an essential part of the British constitution, a constitution that is good as well as being the best that has yet been. Experience thus shows that the *non*republican theory *can* be successful in practice. Experience, moreover, gives cause to *doubt* whether the *republican* theory as well can be successful in practice. But "every good man" ought to have "good wishes" for the republican theory's essential "idea of a perfect equality of political rights among the citizens"; the republican theory has a more desirable constitutive principle than does the nonrepublican theory. The republican theory would seem to be less practicable. The republican theory merits "the best efforts to give success to it in practice." It has "hitherto from an incompetent structure of the Government . . . not had a fair trial, and . . . the endeavor ought to be to secure it a better chance of success by a government more capable of energy and order." Indeed, "the republican theory ought to be adhered to in this Country as long as there was any chance of its success"—so "declared in strong terms" the member from New York.

And the Secretary of the Treasury, after all, merely proposed the financial measures that are alleged to be the vehicle for restoring monarchy modeled on the British constitution; it is the legislature that disposes— and what of them? Hamilton goes on to say that he recollects not a man at present in either branch of the legislature who held language in the Convention that was favorable to monarchy, and he concludes that the basis of the suggestion fails.[11]

V   Between the time Washington transmitted the objections to Hamilton and the time Hamilton sent back his answers, Hamilton published, under the pseudonym "An American," two articles in which he attacked Jefferson for being the covert patron of a paper the object of which was to attack the administration in which Jefferson himself held office as head of a principal department. Jefferson had hired Philip Freneau at the State Department, ostensibly as a translator but actually to publish the *National Gazette*. Hamilton's "American" accused Jefferson of using improper means to promote his ambition to be the head of a party whose politics have constantly aimed at elevating state power upon the ruins of national authority. He accused Jefferson of being the prompter, open or secret, of unwarrantable aspersions on men who—as long as actions, not merely professions, shall be the true test of patriotism and integrity—need never decline a comparison with Jefferson of their titles to the public esteem. A few weeks after Hamilton's reply to Washington, there appeared two replies to Hamilton's "American," to both of which he in turn replied.[12]

In the *National Gazette* appeared the *first* reply to Hamilton: an unsigned defense of Jefferson against "An American" concluded with a counterattack. Hamilton responded to this under the pseudonym "Amicus," taking particular notice of the charge that a certain public character, according to uncontradicted fame, opposed the Constitution in the Grand Convention because it was too republican and advocated the British monarchy as the perfect standard to be approached as nearly as the people could be made to bear.

Hamilton's "Amicus" affirmed this to be a gross misrepresentation and said that appeal to a single fact was sufficient to prove it so: "the gentleman alluded to, was the only member from the state to which he belonged who signed the Constitution, and, it is notorious, against the prevailing weight of the official influence of the state, and against what would probably be the opinion of a large majority of his fellow-citizens, till better information should correct their first impressions." How then, Hamilton's "Amicus" asked, can he be believed to have opposed a thing to which he actually agreed—and in so unsupported a situation and under circumstances of such peculiar responsibility?

He added two more facts. One was that the member in question never made a single proposition to the Convention that was not conformable to the republican theory. The other fact was that the highest-toned of any of the propositions made by him actually received the votes of the representatives of several states, including some of the principal ones—and including individuals who, in the estimation of those who deem themselves the only republicans, are preeminent for republican character.

More than this, said Hamilton's "Amicus," he was not at liberty to say. He was, however, at liberty to say why he was not at liberty to say more. It is a matter generally understood that the deliberations of the Convention, which were carried on in private, were to remain undisturbed. The fact *that* this was so may be generally understood, but the reason *why* it was so may not be so generally understood. The public may not appreciate why the deliberations were not held in public and why they were not to be given subsequent publication; perhaps not every man, but at least "every prudent man" must be convinced of the propriety both of the one and of the other. Hamilton's "Amicus" explains the propriety of both, with emphasis on the latter. Had the deliberations been open while going on, the clamors of faction would have prevented any satisfactory result, and had they been afterward disclosed, much food would have been afforded to inflammatory declamation. Propositions made without due reflection, and perhaps abandoned by the proposers themselves on more mature reflection, would have been handles for a profusion of ill-natured accusation. Every infallible declaimer, taking his own ideas as the perfect standard, would have railed at every member of the Convention who had gone a single line beyond his standard.[13]

The *other* reply to Hamilton's "American" was a series of articles, under the signature "Aristides," which proposed to answer the question why Jefferson for the first time was being distinguished as the Cataline of the day, as the ambitious incendiary who would light a torch to the ruin of his country—is it, "Aristides" asked, because of the manly freedom with which he declares his abhorrence of some of the leading principles of Hamilton's fiscal administration, or is it because his known attachment to republicanism makes him feared as the decided opponent of aristocracy, monarchy, hereditary succession, a titled order of nobility, and all the other mock-pageantry of kingly government? "Aristides" hinted that he would disclose facts and principles in relation to public men, important for the public to know, but now concealed in the arcana of a certain convention or obscured by political mystery and deception.

Hamilton replied to this "Aristides" in a series of articles under the pseudonym "Catullus," the third number of which gives examples of Jefferson's unwarrantable aspersions on men whose actions show their patriotism and integrity. One circumstance which shows Jefferson to be the prompter or instigator of detraction is his patronage of the *National Gazette*—for that paper has as a main object to destroy the public confidence in a particular public character who is, it seems, to be hunted down for having been the steady and decided friend of broad national principles of government. The attacks on the officer alluded to (i.e., Hamilton) proceed from a man hitherto regarded as the quiet, modest, retiring philosopher, as the plain simple unambitious republican—but a man now unveiled as the intriguing incendiary, the aspiring turbulent competitor: Jefferson. This voluptuary concealed in the plain garb of Quaker simplicity, this Epicurean disguised under the vizor of stoicism, is a Caesar. Coyly refusing the proferred diadem, he only rejects the trappings but tenaciously grasps the substance of imperial domination.

"Aristides" had defended Jefferson by attacking Hamilton for an alleged attachment to the mock-pageantry of kingly government. This allegation, says Hamilton's "Catullus," is no more than what has long been matter for malevolent insinuation—but "I mistake . . . the man, to whom it is applied" if the following is not true of him. In the *first* place, "I mistake him"—if he fears the strictest scrutiny into his political principles and conduct, and if he does not wish that there were windows in the breast through which America assembled might witness the inmost springs of his public actions. In the *second* place, however much he may have been led to speculative doubts concerning the probable success of the republican theory, by a turn of mind less addicted to dogmatizing than to reasoning, less fond of hypotheses than of experience, nonetheless, "I mistake him"—if he has not uniformly and ardently, since the experiment of it began in the United States, wished it success; and if he is not sincerely desirous that the sublime idea of a perfect equality of rights among citizens, exclusive of hereditary distinctions, may be practically justified and realized; and if, among the sources of his regret at the overdriven maxims and doctrines that too long withstood the establishment of firm government in the United States, and now embarrass the execution of the government which has been established, a principal one has not been their tendency to counteract a fair trial of the theory to which he is represented to be adverse. In the *third* place, "I mistake him"— if his measures, proceeding upon the ground of a liberal and efficient exercise of the powers of the national government, have had any other object than to give it stability and duration, the only solid and rational expedient for preserving republican government in the United States. Concluding his counterattack, Hamilton's "Catullus" recalls a judicious writer's remark (cited earlier) about Cato and Caesar.[14]

vi For the role of Caesar, in the end, Jefferson was not most likely. As we saw earlier, the man upon whom "it would not be difficult to lay the finger" was a man "having the advantage of military habits" and "despotic in his ordinary demeanor," the kind of man who would fight a duel: "if we have an embryo-Caesar in the United States 'tis Burr." Burr "is for or against nothing, but as it suits his interest or ambition . . . and I feel it a religious duty to oppose his career," said the kind of man who would be capable of getting into a duel with such a man and throwing away his own fire. In Hamilton's death by the hand of Burr, there was at work a strange effective mixture of honor and humility. Burr effected Hamilton's intent. Burr failed—unlike Caesar, who in a way succeeded: Caesar became more than an embryo-Caesar. Hamilton also in a way succeeded—unlike Cato, who failed: Cato died by Cato's hand, and the republic fell to Caesar.[15]

But there was a kind of greatness in Caesar; even Burr was not so much a Caesar—he was more a Cataline. It sometimes seemed that there were many Catalines around. As "Tully," Hamilton wrote to his fellow citizens, in defense of suppressing the insurrection against the excise tax on whiskey, that "Those who . . . dissuade you from exertions adequate to the occasion . . . treat you either as fools or cowards, too weak to perceive your interest or your duty, or too dastardly to pursue them"—concluding the paper by urging them to become a multitude of Tully's: "To the plausible but hollow harangues of such conspirators, ye cannot fail to reply, How long, ye Catalines, will you abuse our patience?" But it was Burr who most represented the menace of Cataline, or, it might be said, of Bonaparte: "There seems to be too much probability that Jefferson or Burr will be President. The latter is intriguing with all his might in New Jersey, Rhode Island & Vermont. He counts positively on the universal support of the Antis: & that by some adventitious aid from some other quarters, he will overtop his friend Jefferson. . . . [T]he conclusion may be realized. And if it is Burr will certainly attempt to reform the government *à la Buonaparte.* He is as unprincipled and dangerous a man as any country can boast; as true a *Cataline* as ever met in midnight conclave."[16]

Earlier, opposition to Jefferson's becoming President had priority over the promotion of anyone in particular to the office. And later as well, Jefferson had still to be opposed, even by extraordinary measures. But Jefferson's associations were a greater menace than he was in himself; his party contained those who would foster "revolution, after the manner of a Buonaparte" as well as those who would "overthrow . . . the government, by stripping it of its due energies."[17]

The greatest menace among the enemies of the Federalists was a man who "thinks everything possible to adventure and perseverance." This man, Burr, was daring and resolute enough to become a usurper: in *this* respect he had the stuff of a Bonaparte. But Burr was altogether more of a Cataline than a Bonaparte: indeed, "Every step in his career proves that he has formed himself upon the model of *Cataline.*" The real Bonaparte was probably then using and would undoubtedly in the future use Burr. Bonaparte was at least a man of real ability, but "really the force of Mr. Burr's understanding is much overrated. He is far more *cunning* than *wise,* far more *dextrous* than *able.* . . . [H]e is far inferior in real ability to Jefferson." [18]

Forced to choose between Jefferson and Burr, after a tie vote in the Electoral College threw the presidential election into the House of Representatives, the Federalists were inclining toward Burr, when Hamilton wrote to Representative James A. Bayard: "I was glad to find . . . that you had not yet determined to go with the current of the Foederal Party in support of Mr. *Burr*; . . . if the Party shall by supporting Mr. Burr as President adopt him for their official Chief—I shall be obliged to consider myself as an *isolated* man. It will be impossible for me to reconcile with my notions of *honor* or policy, the continuing to be of a Party which according to my apprehension will have degraded itself and the country."

He would not unsay what he had said against Jefferson: "Perhaps myself the first, at some expense of popularity, to unfold the true character of Jefferson, it is too late for me to become his apologist. Nor can I have a disposition to do it. I admit that his politics are tinctured with fanaticism, that he is too much in earnest in his democracy, that he is not very scrupulous about the means of success, nor very mindful of truth, and that he is a contemptible hypocrite."

On the other hand, he said, Jefferson was not an unmitigated menace: "it is not true as alleged that he is an enemy to the power of the Executive, or that he is for confounding all the powers in the House of Rs. . . . I have more than once made the reflection that viewing himself as the reversioner, he was solicitous to come into possession of a good Estate." "Nor is it true that Jefferson is zealot enough to do anything in pursuance of his principles which will contravene his popularity, or his interest. He is likely as any man I know to temporize—to calculate what will be likely to promote his own reputation and advantage; and the probable result of such a temper is the preservation of systems, though originally opposed, which being once established, could not be overturned without danger to the person who did it . . . a true estimate of Mr. J's character warrants the expectation of a temporizing rather than a violent system." "Add to this, that there is no fair reason to suppose him capable of being corrupted, which is a security that he will not go beyond certain limits."

"As to Burr," said Hamilton, "he is a man of *extreme & irregular* ambition." It was bad enough that "he is *selfish* to a degree which excludes all social affections & . . . is decidedly *profligate*"—for "Unprincipled selfishness is more apt to seek rapid gain in disorderly practices than slow advantages from orderly systems." But there was worse: Burr was the greatest of menaces, for "Mr. Burr has never appeared solicitous for fame" and

"great Ambition unchecked by principle, or the love of Glory, is an un-
ruly Tyrant which never can keep long in a course which good men will
approve." Saying that this letter might be communicated to discreet and
confidential friends, Hamilton stated a question—a question it was enough
to state, to indicate the answer, "if reason not passion presides in the decision": "Can there be any serious question between the policy of leaving the
Antifoederalists to be answerable for the elevation of an exceptionable, &
that of adopting ourselves & becoming answerable for a man who . . . is . . .
a complete *Cataline* in his practice and principles?"[19]

vii   Hamilton had left the Treasury after some five years in office; seven
years after that, he was still defending his conduct at that Convention in which he had taken part some decade and a half before. A newspaper
charged, in general terms, that Hamilton held an opinion in favor of monarchy and had proposed a monarchy to the Convention. Upon being denied,
the charge was at length restated in specific terms: Hamilton had proposed
a system in which a Senate and Governor should be elected by the people
to hold office during good behavior. Now that the specific terms of the
proposed plan have been reported in the charge, responds Hamilton in an
editorial which he did not sign, the charge admits of a decisive answer.
However, before it can be decided whether this system would be a *monarchy* or a *republic,* it seems necessary to settle the meaning of those terms—
for, as yet, no exact definitions have settled what is or is not a republican
government, in contradistinction to one that is monarchical.

On the one hand, consider how narrowly some men would use the term
republic. Men like one of Jefferson's ministers (alluding to Gallatin, who was
Jefferson's Secretary of the Treasury, as Hamilton had been Washington's),
men madly attached to the mad theory of democracy, even reject a government as nonrepublican if it is representative. And, as *republic* has been so
narrowly defined by some that the name is withheld from representative
government, so *monarchy* has been so broadly defined by some authors that
the name would have to be applied to the actual government of the United
States and to that of most states. These authors call a government a *monarchy* whenever the executive authority is placed in a single hand—even if
not for life but only for years and even if conferred not by descent but by
election.

On the other hand, consider how broadly the term *republic* has been
applied. Hamilton's editorial is silent about whether the broad use also has
its madmen, but he does say that the term *republic* has been applied with

as little precision as has the term *monarchy*. Even to England's government, with a powerful hereditary king, the name *republic* was applied, constantly; and to Poland's government before the state's dissolution, with an executive for life, the name *republic* was applied, always. From this it would seem that every government has been deemed a republic if a large portion of sovereignty was vested in a considerable portion of (or, a fortiori, in the whole of) the people, and that no government has been deemed a monarchy, as contrasted with the republican standard, if a hereditary chief magistrate was lacking.

A correct definition of *republican government* would be neither too narrow nor too broad. If this editorial writer were to attempt a correct definition of *republican government* (he is silent about attempting a correct definition of *monarchical government*), he would say this: a government is republican if both the executive and legislative organs are appointed by a popular election and hold their offices upon a tenure that is responsible and defeasible.

He attempts to confirm the definition by exhibiting the unacceptable consequences of denying it: if it is not correct, then the tenure of good behavior for the judicial department is antirepublican, and the government of this state of New York is not a republic. (If tenure during good behavior is inconsistent with a republican executive or legislature, then, apparently, it must also be inconsistent with a republican *judicial* department, even though Hamilton elsewhere suggests that the executive and legislative are each *like* the other in an important respect in which they are both *un*like the judicial department.)

If the definition is correct, then its consequence would be to admit, as republican, governments that would be rejected by those who use the term narrowly: a government would not cease to be republican because a branch of the legislature, or even the executive, held their offices during good behavior, for in this case the two essential criteria would still concur—the creation of the officer by a popular election and the possibility of his removal in the course of law by accusation before and conviction by a competent tribunal.

The editorial writer says that he will not say how far it may be expedient to go, within the bounds of this theory, in framing a constitution. If the definition he asserts be correct in principle, that is enough for its purpose— for, even if Hamilton went further than it was expedient to go, nonetheless, upon the statement of the charge itself, Hamilton never proposed a monarchy.

But he says he will add that whether or not Hamilton made the proposition ascribed to him, it is certain that Hamilton's more deliberate and final opinion adopted a moderate term of years for the duration of the President. This truth, which is not to be doubted, is also made apparent by a plan of a Constitution, drawn up by Hamilton in detail, which, to use the words of the charge, is "in writing now in this city."

It is not certain—rather the editorial says it would be difficult to say—whether Hamilton gave a decided preference to the first system he presented. Thus, if he did make the proposition ascribed to him, it was nevertheless within the bounds of republicanism, and, later on but still at the time of the Convention, he adopted and proposed a second plan, which may not have been second-best for him. Maybe his opinion was nearly balanced between the two, or maybe he even preferred the one last proposed, having brought the former forward only to have it discussed and to see what would be the opinions of different gentlemen on so momentous a subject. In this respect the former proposition would have been like many other propositions brought forward at the Convention.

Hamilton would also have been not at all alone in going so far to provide governmental energy, for, it is now repeated with confidence, the delegation from Virginia, including Madison, voted for the most energetic form of government. This is mentioned, the editorial writer desires it distinctly understood, without the intention to impeach Madison's motives: a man who arraigns the morals of another man for entertaining a speculative opinion on government different from his own is himself worse than arrogant; he must himself entertain notions in ethics extremely crude and certainly unfavorable to virtue.[20]

viii A year and a half later, Hamilton, after some delay for which he said he could offer no apology satisfactory to himself, answered an inquiry from Timothy Pickering. Hamilton reported that the highest-toned propositions which he had made in the Convention were for a President, Senate, and Judges during good behavior, with a House of Representatives for three years—and though he would have enlarged the legislative power of the general government, yet he never contemplated the abolition of the state governments, but on the contrary, they were, in some particulars, constituent parts of his plan.

This report about his position on the federal question is stated defensively: "though I would have . . . yet I never . . . but on the contrary. . . ." So is the report about his position on the more central question: "the highest-toned propositions which I made"—that is, he went no higher. But perhaps that was still too high; he went on to argue that it was not. The essential criteria of republican government were satisfied by his plan: the principal organs of the executive and legislative departments were to be elected by the people and were to hold their offices by a *responsible* and *temporary* or defeasible tenure.

Not only did he think it conformable with the strict theory of a government purely republican, but the leaders of jealous republicanism must have voted for that part of it which would be most questionable to a jealous republican. In the vote taken on the proposition respecting the executive, he said, five states were in favor, among these Virginia; individuals were not distinguished in the voting, which was by delegations, but it was "morally certain," from the known situation of the Virginia members (six in number, two of them, Mason and Randolph, professing popular doctrines), that Madison must have concurred in the vote of Virginia—"thus if I sinned against *republicanism,* Mr. Madison was not less guilty."

After thus reporting on what he had in fact proposed that went furthest toward what he was accused of proposing, and after thus showing that what he had in fact proposed did not go too far, he asserted that he might truly say that he never proposed either a President or Senate for life and that he neither recommended nor meditated the annihilation of the state governments.

And he went on to report that he had even receded from the furthest position to which he had gone on the central question, for the deliberations were like an investigation, in which speeches were experiments:

> in the course of the discussions in the convention, neither the propositions thrown out for debate, nor even those voted in the earlier stages of the deliberation, were considered as evidences of a definitive opinion in the proposer or voter. It appeared to me to be in some sort understood that, with a view to free investigation, experimental propositions might be made, which were to be received merely as suggestions for consideration.

Accordingly, it was a fact that his final opinion was against an executive during good behavior. His opinion that the executive might be elected for an unlimited term, removable only for bad behavior, gave way to the argument that writers had made against elective monarchy: with stakes so high, elections could not be tranquil; the public safety would be endangered by every succession. The changed opinion was embodied in his draft plan of a constitution: "In the plan of a constitution which I drew up while the convention was sitting, and which I communicated to Mr. Madison about the close of it, perhaps a day or two after, the office of President has no greater duration than for three years," he said.

"This plan was predicated upon these bases," which "were the genuine sentiments of my heart, and upon them I acted":

1. That the political principles of the people of this country would endure nothing but republican government.
2. That in the actual situation of the country, it was in itself right and proper that the republican theory should have a fair and full trial.
3. That to such a trial it was essential that the government should be so constructed as to give all the energy and stability reconcilable with the principles of that theory.

Emphasis on the last idea was his last word on the subject: "I sincerely hope, that it may not hereafter be discovered that, through want of sufficient attention to the last idea, the experiment of republican government, even in this country, has not been as complete, as satisfactory, and as decisive as could be wished."[21]

On one point of fact, Hamilton's statement is not correct: he did not incorporate in the draft the change in presidential tenure of office to a duration no greater than three years. According to Madison, this statement that he did do so was not a deliberate lie but a mistake owing to fallible memory. Writing of Hamilton in a letter to J. K. Paulding, ten years after Hamilton's letter to Pinckney, Madison discussed some evidence that Hamilton erred in his attribution of the numbers of *The Federalist* and went on to cite this other error:

As proof of the fallibility to which the memory of Mr. Hamilton was occasionally subject, a case may be referred to so decisive as to dispense with every other. In the year—Mr. Hamilton, in a letter answering an inquiry of Col. Pickering concerning the plan of Government which he had espoused in the Convention of 1787, states, that at the close of the Convention he put into my hands a draught of a Constitution; and in that draught he had proposed a "President for three years." Now the fact is, that in that plan, the original of which I ascertained several years ago to be among his papers, the *tenure* of office for the President is not *three years, but during good behavior.*

Paulding had requested Madison's help in a project of writing a number of biographies of men who took the lead in the first generation of American independence, and Madison made these remarks in response, preceding them by some general remarks on Hamilton:

> That he possessed intellectual powers of the first order, and the moral qualifications of integrity and honor in a captivating degree, has been decreed to him by a suffrage now universal. If his theory of Government deviated from the Republican standard, he had the candor to avow it, and the greater merit of co-operating faithfully in maturing and supporting a system which was not his choice. The criticism to which his share in the administration of it was most liable was, that it had the aspect of an effort to give to the instrument a constructive and practical bearing not warranted by its true and intended character.

Although Madison concluded, concerning the error in Hamilton's letter to Pickering, that "I should do injustice . . . if I did not express my perfect confidence that the misstatement was involuntary, and that he was incapable of anything that was not so," he nonetheless commented, before concluding, that "The error is the more remarkable, as the letter apologizes, according to my recollection, for its not being a prompt one; and it is so much at variance with the known cast of Mr. Hamilton's political tenets, that it must have astonished his political, and, most of all, his intimate friends."[22]

ix   A most intimate friend of Hamilton was Gouverneur Morris. The day before Morris was to deliver the eulogy for his slain friend, he confided in his diary the reasons why "this subject is difficult"; among them were the unpopular political opinions that Hamilton displayed without reserve: "He was in principle opposed to republican and attached to monarchical government, and then his opinions were generally known and have been long and loudly proclaimed. His share in forming our Constitution must be mentioned, and his unfavorable opinion cannot therefore be concealed."[23] The next year Morris was writing to a friend that

> Our poor friend Hamilton bestrode his hobby, to the great annoyance of his friends and not without injury to himself. More a theoretic than a practical man, he was not sufficiently convinced that a system may be good in itself and bad in relation to particular circumstances. He well knew that his favorite form was inadmissible, unless as the result of civil war, and I suspect that his belief in that which he called an approaching crisis arose from a conviction that the kind of govern-

ment most suitable, in his opinion, to this extensive country, could be established in no other way.

Morris commented that "When our population shall have reached a certain extent his system may be proper, and the people may then be disposed to adopt it; but under present circumstances they will not, neither would it answer any valuable purpose."

Morris himself thought, as he said in this same letter, that the Constitution "received, through the judiciary, a mortal wound, and has declined more rapidly than was apprehended by the most fearful." Whatever would happen, "One thing is certain, democracy cannot last. It is not so much a government as the dissolution of government, being, indeed, the natural death of republics; so that, in reality, there are but two forms, monarchy and aristocracy."

It is, however, "next to impossible," Morris said, "that either should exist unmixed" for "the despot must employ many, who will both check and direct his power," and "the most cunning senate cannot avoid giving to individuals a considerable share of authority"; moreover, "be the complexion of a government monarchic or aristocratic, it can do little when unsupported by popular sentiment." Considering "the general question . . . as to the best form of government," Morris said that a government is "if unable to preserve itself, good for nothing; wherefore permanency is an essential object to which minor advantage must be sacrificed. But an absolute, that is, an unmixed monarchy, would hardly last three lives."

So, it seemed to Morris, the best form of government is aristocratic: "Perhaps, on impartial inquiry, it may appear that a country is best governed (taking for a standard any long period, such as half a century) when the principal authority is vested in a permanent senate."

But there seems little probability that such a body should be established here. Let it be proposed by the best men among us, and it would be considered as a plan for aggrandizing themselves. Experience alone can incline the people to such an institution. That a man should be born a legislator is now among unfledged witlings the frequent subject of ridicule. But experience, that wrinkled matron which genius contemns and youth abhors—experience, the mother of wisdom—will tell us that the man destined from the cradle to act an important part will not, in general, be so unfit as those who are objects of popular choice. But hereditary senators could not long preserve their power. In order to strengthen the body it might be needful to weaken the members,

and, fixing the office for life, fill up the vacancies from (but not by) the
people.

Some sort of senatorial predominance seemed to Morris the only alternative to a republican slide from corrupt democracy through anarchy into
monarchy.

Morris did not expect the worst to happen in America. It was true,
he thought, that "thanks to the present administration, we have travelled
farther in the road to corruption during three years than England did in half
a century":

British corruption has, indeed, been greatly exaggerated. It is far from
general, either in the House of Commons or in the election of members
to that house. A choice in the counties being made . . . by free-holders,
is, generally speaking, out of the reach of corrupt influence, and . . . the
ministers always, on important questions, consult the wishes of county
members; so that a measure is abandoned if disagreeable to them. With
us corruption begins where, by the analogies of England, it should have
ended. Our people are deeply corrupted by that licentious spirit which
seeks emolument in the prostration of authority. The outwork of respect has long since been carried, and every new election presents a
more hideous picture of the public mind; so that, if the character of the
people is to be estimated by the objects of their choice, we shall find it
difficult to support a claim to wisdom or virtue.

"No parallel can perhaps be found to such morbid affection, unless among
the Athenians, and even the mob government of that extravagant tribe was
in some respects preferable to representative democracy": "A mob is, indeed, a whimsical legislature and a wild tribunal, but it has, in the midst
of its madness, some sense of national honor and some regard for justice. A
body of representatives, when influenced by Faction, will do acts of cruelty
and baseness which the most profligate among them would, in his personal
character, be ashamed to avow."

Nonetheless, said Morris, "Our population is sparse," and "It is probable that the relaxation of morals will operate chiefly on the judicial department, be more characterized by fraud than violence, and terminate rather
in baseness than tyranny." And, moreover,

there is . . . a point of depression from which things return in a contrary
course. There are also chances which may befall us before we reach that
ultimate point. Being in the great family of nations, our family cannot
be ignorant of our condition. They must perceive that, without force

to protect a territory and commerce widely extended, without wisdom or vigor in our councils, we present a fair object to their cupidity. . . . Nations, like individuals, are not to be reasoned out of vice much less out of folly, but learn wisdom in the school of affliction. . . . America, my good friend, will at length learn some of those things which an attentive study of the ancients long since taught you.

Eventually, Morris thought, "When a general abuse of the right of election shall have robbed our government of respect, and its imbecility have involved it in difficulties, the people will feel what your friend once said, that they want something to protect them against themselves."[24]

Earlier, after dining "in trio" at King's, Morris had compared his own fears with those of his host and Hamilton:

They are both alarmed at the conduct of our rulers, and think the Constitution is about to be overturned; I think it is already overturned. They apprehend a bloody anarchy; I apprehend an anarchy in which property, not lives, will be sacrificed. That it is the intention of those gentlemen who have engaged themselves in the notable business of pulling down the Constitution to rear a monarchy on its ruins, I do not believe; that such is the natural effect of their measures, I am perfectly convinced.[25]

Years after Hamilton's death, Morris, speaking of the Embargo that was imposed when Jefferson was President, contrasted his own hopes with Hamilton's despair. Hamilton, he said, despaired of a form of government whose inevitable evil he foresaw: "It is an evil inseparable from democracy that the leaders of that faction which includes the lower class of citizens may commit the greatest excesses with impunity. This my friend Hamilton distinctly foresaw, and would, were he now alive, reproach his intimate friends for their attachment to a government so liable to abuse." "The reproach, however, would be ineffectual," for Hamilton's intimate friends thought they looked further ahead. Morris as their spokesman said: "They would defend themselves by observing that the great body of American free-holders have such direct interest in the preservation of law and order that they will stand forth to secure their rights when the necessity for it shall appear." And those intimate friends of Hamilton for whom Morris spoke saw distinctly that for the present and for the future immediately before them, there was only patience and fortitude—that is, "They say further that such necessity cannot be shown by a political ratiocination":

Luckily, or, to speak with a reverence proper to the occasion, providentially, mankind are not disposed to embark the blessings they enjoy on a voyage of syllogistic adventure to obtain something more beautiful in exchange. They must feel before they will act. This is proved not only by the history of other nations but by our own. When misfortunes press hard, and not before, the people will look for that wisdom and virtue in which formerly they found safety. They will then listen to the voice which, in the wantonness of prosperity, they despised. Then, and not until then, can the true patriot be of any use.

While the people suffer what they must, from their own base folly, Morris said, their true leaders must firmly and with confidence await their eventual call.

"Those who formed our Constitution," said Morris, "were not blind to its defects." They did prefer a republic to a monarchy, for "They believed a monarchical form to be neither solid nor durable. They conceived it to be vigorous or feeble, active or slothful, wise or foolish, mild or cruel, just or unjust, according to the personal character of the prince." But "fond, however, as the framers of our National Constitution were of republican government, they were not so much blinded by their attachment as not to discern the difficulty, perhaps impracticability, of raising a durable edifice from crumbling materials. History, the parent of political science, had told them that it was almost as vain to expect permanency from democracy as to construct a palace on the surface of the sea. But it would have been foolish to fold their arms and sink into despondence because they could neither form nor establish the best of all systems." The framers' solution, such as it was, was the United States Senate.

Morris had been asked "How far has the Senate answered the end of its creation?"; his reply was this: "further than was expected, but by no means so far as was wished."

To obtain anything like a check on the rashness of democracy, it was necessary not only to organize the Legislature into different bodies (for that alone is a poor expedient) but to endeavor that these bodies should be animated by a different spirit. To this end the States, in their corporate capacity, were made electors of the Senate, and so long as the State governments had considerable influence and the consciousness of dignity which that influence imparts, the Senate felt some of the desired sentiment, and answered in some degree the end of its institution. But that day is past.

The framers had faced a dilemma: "If the State influence should continue, the Union could not last; and if it did not, the utility of the Senate would cease." They did what had to be done: "In the option between two evils, that which appeared to be the least was preferred, and the power of the Union provided for." But their solution to the more urgent problem undermined their solution to the more fundamental problem: "At present, the influence of the General Government has so thoroughly pervaded every State that all the little wheels are obliged to turn according to the great one"—so that the Senate, in the opinion of Morris, "is little, if any check, either on the President or the House of Representatives."

> It has not the disposition. The members of both Houses are creatures which, though differently born, are begotten in the same way and by the same sire. They have, of course, the same temper, but their opposition, were they disposed to make any, would be feeble; they would easily be borne down by the other House, in which the power resides. The President can, indeed, do what he pleases, provided it shall always please him to place those who lead a majority of the Representatives. This matter is understood among the parties concerned. The Representatives, however, do not yet know that their power has no bound except their own discretion; but a pleasant lesson is easily learned, and the more they feel their power the less will be their discretion. Authority so placed is liable as well to excess as to abuse, and this country . . . will experience not a little of both.

Although the present state of things followed rapidly upon the work of the framers, they are not blameworthy, said Morris:

> It is not easy to be wise for all times, not even for the present—much less for the future; and those who judge of the past must recollect that, when it was present, the present was future. Supposing, however, that one or two solitary individuals blessed with an unusual portion of the divine afflatus, could determine what will fit futurity, they would find it no easy task to prevail so far with the present generation as to induce their adoption of a plan at variance with their feelings. As in war so in politics, much must be left to chance; or, in other words, to combinations of which we are ignorant. It was therefore pardonable to suppose that what would in one day, be neither advisable nor practicable, might, in another day, be safe and easy.

"Perhaps there is still in my old bosom too much of youthful ardor and hope," said Morris, "but I do not despair of our country":

True it is, that the present state of things has approached with un-looked-for rapidity; but in that very circumstance there is a source of comfort. In spite of the power of corruption, there is still, perhaps, enough of public sentiment left to sanctify the approaching misfor-tunes. Let not good men despair because the people were not awakened by what has passed. It would be considered that, in proportion to the size and strength of the patient and the dulness of his organs, the dose must be large to operate with effect.

Hamilton, in any case, had provided no practicable alternative. Accord-ing to Morris,

General Hamilton . . . had little share in forming the Constitution. He disliked it, believing all republican government to be radically de-fective. He admired, nevertheless, the British constitution, which I consider as an aristocracy in fact, though a monarchy in name. Gen-eral Hamilton hated republican government, because he confounded it with democratical government; and he detested the latter, because he believed it must end in despotism, and, be in the mean time, de-structive to public morality. He believed that our administration would be enfeebled progressively at every new election, and become at last contemptible. He apprehended that the minions of faction would sell themselves and their country as soon as foreign powers should think it worth while to make the purchase. In short, his study of ancient history impressed on his mind a conviction that democracy, ending in tyranny, is, while it lasts, a cruel and oppressing domination.

According to Morris, Hamilton was confused: misled by a name, he mis-takenly distinguished limited monarchy from aristocracy; and, mistakenly not distinguishing republican from democratical government, he hated the former because the latter was a corrupt transition to despotism. Had Hamil-ton seen that what was in name a limited monarchy was in fact an aristo-cratic republic, he might have acted better.

Not that Hamilton behaved dishonorably, said Morris—his was rather another fault: "General Hamilton was of that kind of man which may most safely be trusted; for he was more covetous of glory than of wealth or power. But he was of all men the most indiscreet." Morris called Hamilton most indiscreet because he spoke too freely: Hamilton would not be restrained in what he said by what he knew.

He knew that a limited monarchy, even if established, could not pre-serve itself in this country. He knew, also, that it could not be estab-

lished, because there is not the regular gradation of ranks among our
citizens which is essential to that species of government, and he very
well knew that no monarchy whatever could be established but by the
mob. When a multitude of indigent, profligate people can be collected
and organized, their envy of wealth, talents, and reputation will induce
them to give themselves a master, provided that, in so doing, they can
mortify and humble their superiors. But there is no instance to prove,
and it is, indeed, flatly absurd to suppose, that the upper ranks of society will, by setting up a king, put down themselves. Fortunately for us,
no such mass of people can be collected in America. None such exists.

Morris found his friend blameworthy: Hamilton meant very well and knew
very much what could not be done:

But although General Hamilton knew these things, from the study of
history, he never failed, on every occasion, to advocate the excellence
of and avow his attachment to monarchical government. By this course
he not only cut himself off from all chance of rising into office, but sin-
gularly promoted the views of his opponents, who, with the fondness
for wealth and power which he had not, affected a love for the people
which he had and they had not. Thus, meaning very well, he acted very
ill, and approached the evils he apprehended by his very solicitude to
keep them at a distance.[26]

Morris's words in criticism of his friend Hamilton are confusing to
read beside the words Hamilton himself committed to paper, which were
those of an energetic well-wisher to republican government. Immediately
after Morris says that Hamilton, admiring the British monarchical constitution, hated republican government as indistinguishable from the democratic state transitional to despotism, Morris then says that "One marked
trait of the General's character was the pertinacious adherence to opinions
he had once formed." Morris makes no mention here of a letter he had received from Hamilton early in the Revolutionary War, in reply to his own
letter to Hamilton that had spoken of defects in the new constitution of the
State of New York.

In this letter, disagreeing with Morris on the central point, Hamilton tells Morris that "the fluctuation of governments in which the popular
principle has borne a considerable sway" has proceeded not from its inherent nature but from other causes. On the one hand, "from its being
compounded with other principles": "compound governments, though they
may be harmonious in the beginning, will introduce distinct interests;

and these interests will clash, throw the state into convulsions & produce change or dissolution." And, on the other hand, "from its being made to operate in an improper channel": when the exercise of governmental powers is "vested wholly or partly in the collective body of the people," then "you must expect error, confusion, or instability." The form of government "most likely to be happy, regular, and durable," is, "in my opinion," says Hamilton, "representative democracy," in which "the exercise of the legislative, executive, and judiciary authorities, is vested in select persons," these persons being "chosen *really* and not *nominally* by the people" and with the right of election being "well secured and regulated." Hamilton's conclusion in this reply to Morris is that "On the whole, though I think there are the defects intimated, I think your Government far the best that we have yet seen, and capable of giving long and substantial happiness to the people. Objections to it should be suggested with great caution and reserve."

This term "representative democracy" was thus applied by Hamilton with approbation to the constitution of the State of New York in this letter that he wrote to a close friend while serving the cause of American liberty as General Washington's aid early in the Revolutionary War.[27]

This term "representative democracy" was later applied by Hamilton to the Constitution of the United States, in notes he made for a speech in the New York Ratifying Convention while serving as the indispensable champion of the proposal made by the Federal Convention. The portion of these notes that is relevant here contains three parts.

In the *first* part Hamilton discusses the meanings of words used for forms of government. The first section under this part shows how *republic* is a word used in various senses, having been applied to aristocracies and monarchies: to Rome under the kings, to Sparta and to Carthage although each had a senate for life, to the United Netherlands despite the stadtholder and hereditary nobles, to Poland despite aristocracy and monarchy, and to Great Britain despite monarchy "etc." The second section shows how there is again great confusion in the use of the words *democracy, aristocracy,* and *monarchy.* The term *democracy* has been defined by some (Rousseau, "etc.") as a government exercised by the collective body of the people—delegation of their power being made the criterion of aristocracy. The term *aristocracy* has been used not only to designate governments in which an independent few possess sovereignty, but also those in which the representatives of the people possess it. And *monarchy* has designated governments in which there is sovereignty in the hands of a single man—the general idea being that he is independent in his situation, for in any other sense it would apply to the State of New York. The third section shows how the terms are used "in my sense." There is *democracy* where the whole power of the government is in the people—whether exercised by themselves or by their representatives, these representatives being chosen by them either mediately or immediately and legally accountable to them. There is *aristocracy* where the whole sovereignty is permanently in the hands of a few for life or hereditarily. There is *monarchy* where the whole sovereignty is in the hands of one man for life or hereditarily. There is *mixed government* when these principles unite. Thus, having given his own definition of every equivocal term he has mentioned but *republic,* Hamilton concludes the first part.

In the *central* part he gives as the consequence of his first part that the proposed government is a *representative democracy*. And he itemizes why: the House of Representatives is directly chosen by the people for two years, the Senate is indirectly chosen by them for six years, and the President is indirectly chosen by them for four years—thus the legislative and executive are representatives of the people; the judicial power also is representative of the people, being indirectly chosen to hold office during good behavior— hence all the officers are at least the indirect choice of the people. Moreover, the constitution of the government is revocable and alterable by the people.

In the *final* part Hamilton writes of how "This representative democracy as far as is consistent with its genius has all the features of good government." He itemizes these features: "an immediate and operative representation of the people which is found in the House of Representatives"; "stability and wisdom which is found in the Senate"; "a vigorous executive which is found in the President"; "an independent judicial, which is found in the Supreme Court, etc."—and then, noting separation of the essential powers of government and saying that the sense of the maxim is to be ascertained, he continues: first, one department must not wholly possess the powers of another (Montesquieu and the British government are mentioned), and second, departments must be separated, yet so as to check each other; and, itemizing the kinds of checks (legislative, legislative-executive, judicial-legislative, and legislative-judicial), Hamilton concludes that all this is done in the proposed Constitution, mentioning that the legislative is in the Congress yet is checked by the executive through the negative, that the executive is in the President yet is checked by the Congress through impeachment, that there is a judicial check upon the legislative through the interpretation of laws, and that the judicial is checked by the legislative through impeachment. Thus Hamilton—as a friend of "representative democracy" in America.[28]

Immediately after Morris presents his criticism of Hamilton, he presents in the same letter his version of America's prospects as seen by

Hamilton. "From his situation in early life, it was not to be expected that he should have a fellow-feeling with those who idly supposed themselves to be the natural aristocracy of this country," and "in maturer age, his observation and good sense demonstrated that the materials for aristocracy do not exist in America"; hence

> taking the people as a mass in which there was nothing of family, wealth, prejudice, or habit to raise a permanent mound of distinction— in which, moreover the torrent of opinion had already washed away every mole-hill of respect raised by the industry of individual pride, he considered the fate of Rome in her meridian splendor, and that of Athens from the dawn to the sunset of her glory, as the portraits of our future fortune.

And, "Moreover, the extent of the United States led him to fear a defect of national sentiment," for even "that which, at the time our constitution was formed, had been generated by friendship in the Revolutionary War, was sinking"—"under the pressure of State interest, commercial rivalry, the pursuit of wealth, and those thousand giddy projects" which had been engendered by "the intoxication of independence, an extravagant idea of our own importance, a profound ignorance of other nations, the prostration of public credit, and paucity of our resources."

Morris then presented the course taken by Hamilton. Despite Hamilton's views, "He heartily assented, nevertheless, to the Constitution, because he considered it as a band which might hold us together for some time, and he knew that national sentiment is the offspring of national existence." National sentiment was sinking, but national sentiment might be kept from extinction if a national government could keep the Union from dissolution—and "He trusted, moreover, that in the chances and changes of time we should be involved in some war which might strengthen our union and nerve the Executive." But this is to say that Hamilton hoped, albeit not very hopefully, that suitable circumstances might prove that republican government might consist with energy in the executive.

Proclaiming long and loudly the merits of the British constitution, Hamilton tried to teach emphatically what he thought Americans needed most to learn—that government cannot be good unless it joins to private safety public strength. In rejecting the hereditary principle in government, a British inheritance from less enlightened times, Americans had not cast off their unenlightened parochial prejudice against executive energy. But the necessity of executive energy was rooted in the nature of things: in some way or other it would return; and if refused a stately republican admission, it would break violently through the front door—or enter by stealth through the back.

Immediately after mentioning Hamilton's hope that war might eventually unite the dissolving union and nerve its feeble executive, Morris reports:

> He was not (as some have supposed) so blind as not to see that the President could purchase power, and shelter himself from responsibility by sacrificing the rights and duties of his office at the shrine of influence; but he was too proud, and let me add, too virtuous to recommend or tolerate measures eventually fatal to liberty and honor.
>
> It was not, then, because he thought the Executive Magistrate too feeble to carry on the business of the State that he wished him to possess more authority; but because he thought there was not sufficient power to carry on the business honestly. He apprehended a corrupt understanding between the Executive and a dominating party in the Legislature which would destroy the President's responsibility, and he was not to be taught (what everyone knows) that where responsibility ends, fraud, injustice, tyranny, and treachery begin.[29]

In some way or other, Hamilton thought, the public business would go forward, or the republic would cease to be. His wish was that the public business might go forward in a way not fatal to liberty and to honor. Monarchy under the free British constitution produced a good administration, but the independent Americans did not have the materials for a constitution of the British sort: their failure to solve the republican problem would produce a tyrant or a boss.

x In his last word on the subject, Hamilton said that he hoped for "the experiment of republican government" to be "as complete, as satisfactory, and as decisive as could be wished"; "I sincerely hope, that it may not hereafter be discovered," he said, that the experiment has been inadequate "even in this country."

Until this American attempt, republican government was a failure; in the full knowledge of previous failure, Americans made another attempt. We find it hard to keep in mind how hard it must have been to take a leading part in this attempt. The act appears less questionable in comfortable retrospect. We must make an effort to see it as it would be seen by a good man considering with care the prospects then.

To such a man there might at times have come such thoughts as these:

As the failure of previous attempts did not deter the American attempt, so, since hope springs eternal in the human breast, the failure of the American attempt will not deter subsequent attempts, but repetition of the attempts will only multiply human misery, for republican government cannot succeed. However, the only way to prove this, and thus to deter subsequent attempts, is by an experiment in which trial is made of a government that is republican but is so constructed as to have all the energy and stability reconcilable with the principles of the republican theory. Patriotism would recoil from making such an experiment if it could be avoided, but Americans will "endure nothing but a republican government," so a senseless repetition of previous experience is the only alternative to the experiment. Hence, philanthropy supplies inducements to what patriotism does not forbid—a true test of the republican theory. If republican government fails despite its being so constructed, succeeding generations of mankind will be spared the miserable consequences of attempts at republican government.

But this is not a line of thought to lift the spirit; there is a more encouraging point of view, from which we can imagine that the man we are considering had thoughts much more like these: While the failure of the American attempt may not deter some thoughtless subsequent attempts, the effect of which can only be to multiply republican failures, thus further confirming the bad reputation of republican government, it is likely that subsequent attempts will rarely if ever be made, for the failure of the American attempt will be taken as proof that republican government must be a failure. But the experiment might prove no more than what previous experience had already shown about the republican theory—that republican government fails when it is not "so constructed as to have all the energy and stability reconcilable with the principles of that theory." Now republican government might succeed if so constructed, and not only will Americans endure nothing but a republican government, but "in the actual situation of the country" it is "in itself right and proper that the republican theory should have a fair and full trial." Hence the inducements of philanthropy will join those of patriotism to make all considerate and good Americans wish for a true test of the republican theory in America, and therefore advocate republican institutions of the greatest possible energy and stability.[30]

xi   Some fifteen years after the Federal Convention, some two years before his death, Hamilton wrote in gloom to the man from whose felicitous pen had come the final wording of the Constitution of the United States—Gouverneur Morris. Of his friend Hamilton said: "You, friend

Morris, are by *birth* a native of this Country but by *genius* an exotic. You mistake if you fancy that you are more a favorite than myself or that you are in any sort upon a theatre suited to you." While of himself he said:

> Mine is an odd destiny. Perhaps no man in the United States has sacri-ficed more or done more for the present Constitution than myself—and contrary to all my anticipations of its fate, as you know from the very beginning I am still labouring to prop the frail and worthless fabric. Yet I have the murmurs of its friends no less than the curses of its foes for my reward. What can I do better than withdraw from the Scene? Every day proves to me more and more that this American world was not made for me.[31]

These words were written by Hamilton about midway between his own death and the earlier death of Washington. It was when Washington died that Hamilton wrote: "he was an Aegis very essential to me." Shortly be-fore Hamilton left his administration, Washington wrote about the opposi-tion organizing against the administration: "the *self-created societies* which have spread themselves over this country," he said, "have been laboring incessantly to sow the seeds of distrust, jealousy, and of course discon-tent, thereby hoping to effect some *revolution* in the government." Only a few years later, Washington received a letter which said, of the opposition: "regular plans are formed, and correspondences . . . commenced against the unsuspecting and unmarshalled friends of government"—"The oppo-sition to the government is here 'systematized.' " Hamilton left office about midway between his own letter reporting to Carrington the origins of oppo-sition, and this letter reporting to Washington that the opposition had been "systematized." A while after the letter to Carrington, Hamilton wrote that "The spirit of party has grown to maturity sooner in this country than perhaps was to have been counted upon."[32]

A while after leaving office, in a letter containing "a brief sketch of my political career," which explained his motives for withdrawing from the office of Secretary of the Treasury as soon as his plan "had attained a certain maturity," Hamilton wrote:

> In that office, I met with many intrinsic difficulties, and many artificial ones proceeding from passions, not very worthy, common to human nature, and which act with peculiar force in republics. The object, how-ever, was effected, of establishing public credit and introducing order into the finances. Public office in this Country has few attractions. The pecuniary emolument is so inconsiderable as to amount to a sacrifice

to any man who can employ his time with advantage in any liberal profession. The opportunity of doing good, from the jealousy of power and the spirit of faction, is too small in any station to warrant a long continuation of private sacrifices. The enterprises of party had so far succeeded as materially to weaken the necessary influence and energy of the Executive Authority, and so far diminished the power of doing good in that department as greatly to take the motives which a virtuous man might have for making sacrifices. The prospect was even bad for gratifying in future the love of Fame, if that passion was to be the spring of action.[33]

Out of office, Hamilton devised plans to counteract opposition to government by employing the power of government. To the Speaker of the House of Representatives, he wrote that

An accurate view of the internal situation of the United States presents many discouraging reflections to the enlightened friends of our Government and country. Notwithstanding the unexampled success of our public measures at home and abroad—notwithstanding the instructive comments afforded by the disastrous and disgusting scenes of the French Revolution, public opinion has not been ameliorated—sentiments dangerous to social happiness have not been diminished—on the contrary, there are symptoms which warrant the apprehension that among the most numerous class of citizens errors of a very pernicious tendency have not only preserved but have extended their empire. Though some thing may have been gained on the side of men of information and property, more has probably been lost on that of persons of a different description.

There had been moreover not only an extension of error but also a development of political opposition: "opposition to the government has acquired more system than formerly—is bolder in the avowal of its designs—less solicitous than it was to discriminate between the Constitution and the Administration—more open and enterprising in its projects"—and it is said

that the opposition-Party in Virginia, the head Quarters of the Faction, have followed up the hostile declarations which are to be found in the resolutions of their General Assembly by an actual preparation of the means of supporting them by force . . . they have taken measures to put their militia on a more efficient footing—are preparing considerable arsenals and magazines and (which is an unequivocal proof how much they are in earnest) have gone so far as to lay new taxes on their citizens.

Hamilton's conclusion was that "Amidst such serious indications of hostility, the safety and the duty of the supporters of the government call upon them to adopt vigorous measures of counteraction."

Hamilton proposed such measures. In the *first* place he proposed "Establishments which will extend the influence and promote the popularity of the Government." The judiciary system was to be extended by subdividing each state into small districts, each with a judge, and by appointing in each county a justice of the peace with only ministerial nonjudicial functions and with no compensation but fees for the services he might perform; both sorts of persons were "essential as well to the energetic execution of the laws as to the purposes of salutary patronage." The great communications were to be improved by turnpike roads, in the interior as well as along the coast; no measure could be more "universally popular." A society was to be instituted with funds to be employed in premiums for new inventions, discoveries, and improvements in agriculture and the arts; this encouragement of agriculture and the arts, "besides being productive of general advantage, will speak powerfully to the feelings and interests of those classes of men to whom the benefits derived from the Government have been heretofore the least manifest."

In the *second* place he proposed "provisions for augmenting the means and consolidating the strength of the Government"—revenues, ships, troops, officers, and supplies. In the *third* place he proposed "arrangements for confirming and enlarging the legal Powers of the Government." Certain temporary laws were to be rendered permanent, particularly that law which authorized calling out the militia to suppress unlawful combinations and insurrections. An amendment to the Constitution was to be proposed for empowering Congress to open canals through territory extending beyond one state; this would help to improve the naturally prodigious facilities for inland navigation, would assist commerce and agriculture, would connect distant portions of the Union, and would "be a useful source of influence to the Government." And "happy would it be" if another amendment could be proposed, which, because it would be inexpedient and even dangerous to propose at this time, was merely thrown out as a suggestion for consideration—an amendment for enabling Congress to subdivide a state when a considerable portion of it made application requesting to be erected into a separate state; this would secure the general government against the machinations of its rivals, "and small States are doubtless best adapted to the purposes of local regulation and to the preservation of the republican spirit."

In the *fourth* place he proposed "laws for restraining and punishing incendiary and seditious practices." The courts of the United States must be the guardians of the reputations of the officers of the general government. Unless their reputations are preserved from malicious and unfounded slander, there will not be the confidence in them essential to enable them to fulfill the ends of their appointment. Therefore it would be constitutional as well as politic to declare that libels at common law, if leveled against an officer of the United States, shall be cognizable in the courts of the United States.[34]

Hamilton also continued his efforts, by writing in the newspapers, to impress upon public opinion the necessity of governmental energy. He well knew that he was dealing with "a people, who descrying Tyranny at a distance and guided only by the light of just principles, before they had yet felt the scourge of oppression, could nobly hazard all in defence of their rights." He well knew that a people who descry tyranny at a distance easily fall prey to false alarms. Earlier, "It was a thing hardly to be expected, that in a popular revolution the minds of men should stop at that happy mean, which marks the salutary boundary between POWER and PRIVILEGE, and combines the energy of government with the security of private rights."[35]

Since then, opposition to government had systematically organized outside government to work upon the minds of men. How long, he asked, could support of government neglect to do the same?

Shortly after Hamilton's gloomy letter to Morris, he was devising a plan for the purpose and promoting it along with plans for meeting the deficiencies of the provision for electing the President. Writing to Bayard again, after the House of Representatives had made Jefferson the President and Burr the Vice President, Hamilton praised the brilliant efforts of the sound part of the community to resist the follies of an infatuated administration, but he urged that they must not be content with a temporary effort to oppose the approach of evil. He feared Burr's intrigues with the Federalists in Washington. Hamilton favored two constitutional amendments before the House, in favor of which New Yorkers of both parties had united.

The *first* of those amendments would distinguish, in the voting, between candidates for the presidency and for the vice presidency. Unless they were distinguished, men would acquire the first place in the government of the nation not by earning the confidence of others but by intrigue and accident, and "our adversaries," he said, have "the advantage in the game" of cabal—"by greater zeal, activity, and subtlety, and especially by an abandonment of principle." The *second* of the amendments would have the electors for President and Vice President chosen by the people in districts under the direction of Congress, rather than chosen in each state in whatever manner the state legislature might direct. This would "let the Foederal Government rest as much as possible on the shoulders of the people, and as little as possible on those of the State Legislatures"—and "is further recommended by its tendency to exclude *combination* which I am persuaded in the general & permanent course of things will operate more against, than for us." These amendments would without doubt be resisted by Burr, whose elevation to the chief magistracy of the United States by Federalist means would be the worst kind of "political suicide."

Bayard replied that no eagerness to recover lost power would betray the Federalists in Washington into doctrines or compromises repugnant or dangerous to their former principles. "We shall probably pay more attention to public opinion than we have heretofore done, and take more pains not merely to do right things, but to do them in an acceptable manner." He went on to agree with Hamilton about the proposed amendments. And he spoke about the judiciary bill before Congress, concluding with a request for Hamilton's opinions about what the Federalists should do.[36]

Hamilton replied that it was well for the truly sound part of the Federalist party to understand that there existed intrigues in good earnest, between several important Federalists and Burr, bottomed upon motives and views not good for the country. The year before, Hamilton had written Bayard "I am glad to find that" Bayard had not gone with the current of Federalist support for Burr. Now he said: "I am glad to find that it is in contemplation to adopt a plan of conduct. It is very necessary; & to be useful it must be efficient & comprehensive in the means which it embraces, at the same time that it must meditate none which are not really constitutional & patriotic. I will comply with your invitation by submitting some ideas which from time to time have passed through my mind."

Hamilton first gave "general views of the subject." By them, he said, "have my reflections been guided."

It is wrong to "expect to produce any valuable or permanent results, in political projects, by relying merely on the reason of men." Indeed, "Nothing is more fallacious" than that, for it ignores this truth about human nature: "Men are rather reasoning than reasonable animals"; they are "for the most part governed by the impulse of passion."

This is "a truth well understood by our adversaries, who have practiced upon it with no small benefit to their cause"—as is shown by the fact that "at the very moment they are eulogizing the reason of men & professing to appeal only to that faculty, they are courting the strongest and most active passion of the human heart—VANITY!"

There is another truth which is "no less true" than that general truth which is understood by the Federalists' adversaries and on which is founded the fact of their practice. This other, particular, truth is that "the Federalists seem not to have attended to the fact sufficiently" and "have erred in relying so much on the rectitude & utility of their measures, as to have neglected the cultivation of popular favor by fair & justifiable expedients."

Hamilton in particular, however, has been attentive to the Federalists' inattention: "The observation has been repeatedly made by me to individuals with whom I particularly conversed." And, far from neglecting what would be expedient, he has "suggested" various "expedients . . . for gaining good will." These, however, "were never adopted."

Hamilton is aware that the situation is not promising. "Unluckily . . . for us," he says, "in the competition for the passions of the people our opponents have great advantages over us." The reason for this is "plain": the passions that are "vicious" are "far more active than the good passions," and "to win . . . to our side" the passions that are vicious, "we must renounce our principles & our objects, & unite in corrupting public opinion till it becomes fit for nothing but mischief."

"Yet . . . we shall in vain calculate upon any substantial or durable results," he warns, "unless we can contrive to take hold of, and carry along with us some strong feeling of the mind." On "the truth of this proposition," he insists, "must be founded" any "plan we may adopt"—if it is "to be successful."

Hamilton grants the problematic character of seeking success by a project founded upon that proposition: "perhaps it is not easy for us to give it full effect"—"especially not without some deviations from what on other occasions we have maintained to be right." Nonetheless, "in determining upon the propriety of the deviations, we must consider whether it be possible for us to succeed without in some degree employing the weapons which have been employed against us." And—since it might be thought better to fail honorably than to succeed by employing the weapons of wrong, even if only "in some degree"—it must also be considered "whether the actual state & future prospect of things be not such as to justify the reciprocal use of them."

There seems to be a need to give some reassurance, for he immediately says: "I need not tell you that I do not mean to countenance the imitation of things intrinsically unworthy, but only of such as may be denominated irregular, such as in a sound & stable order of things ought not to exist."

Moreover, since men of honor who refuse to stoop may seek instead to conquer and transform, some further reassurance is necessary: "Neither are you to infer that any revolutionary result is contemplated. In my opinion the present Constitution is the standard to which we are to cling. Under its banners, *bona fide* must we combat our political foes—rejecting all changes but through the channel [which the Constitution] itself provides for amendments."

Hamilton then gave "the outline of the plan" which his general views of the subject "have suggested." "The principal Engine," Hamilton said, was to be an "Association" formed with two objects: "the support of the Christian religion" and "the support of the Constitution of the United States." This association, to be named the "Christian Constitutional Society," was to be an organization with a national directing council, a subdirecting council in each state, and as many societies in each state as local circumstances might permit.

Its means were to be three: it was chiefly to diffuse information in newspapers and pamphlets; it was also to use all lawful means in concert to promote the election of fit men; and it was to promote institutions of a charitable and useful nature under the management of Federalists—such as emigrant relief societies and academies for instructing mechanics in the principles of mechanics and the elements of chemistry—especially in the populous cities, which "the Jacobins" have employed to give an impulse to the country. (It is reported, Hamilton mentions, that while the question of presidential election was pending in the House of Representatives, parties were organizing in the cities to cut off the leading Federalists and seize the government in the event of there being no election.)

After sketching this plan for the principal engine (the Christian Constitutional Society), Hamilton turned to what Bayard seems to have had in mind in requesting advice: how to meet the menace of the judiciary bill. "In addition" to the organization of the society, Hamilton's advice was this: as soon as possible, bring the repeal of the judiciary law before the Supreme Court; afterward, if not before, prevail upon as many state legislatures as possible to instruct their senators to endeavor to procure a repeal of the repealing law; in Congress propose little but agree to all good measures and resist and expose all bad.[37]

Bayard in reply told Hamilton what he thought of "the project recommended in your last letter of connected associations in the different States for the support of our Constitution & religion": "The plan is marked with great ingenuity, but . . . not . . . applicable to the state of things in this Country. Such an association must be bottomed upon a stronger & more active principle than reason or even a sense of common interest to render it successful. There is more material for such an association upon the other side than upon ours. We have the greater number of political Calculators & they of political fanaticks." Bayard also said that a Federalist attempt at associations organized into clubs would revive jealousies and suspicions now beginning to slumber. Let us not be too impatient, he exhorted: our adversaries will soon show the soundness of our doctrines and the imbecility and folly of their own; in a few years without any exertion by us they will render every honest man our proselyte. He explained that "A degree of agitation and vibration of opinion must forever prevail under a government so free as that of the United States. Under such a government in the nature of things it is impossible to fix public opinion." However, "it is still left to the exertions of good men to prevent infinite evils to which the country is exposed from the selfish and ambitious intrigues of Demagogues."[38]

Hamilton then let his plan fall. His supporters would not support his plan. Bayard, Hamilton's devoted follower and the man who broke the deadlock in the presidential election of 1800, had told him that the government of the United States was too free for any fixing of public opinion: the exertions of good men would be wasted if they made the attempt systematically to form the minds of the citizens, a task impossible to perform, but the exertions of good men would not be wasted if they performed the task of preventing the infinite evils to which the country was exposed by the selfish and ambitious intrigues of demagogues. Hamilton, feeling a religious duty to oppose the career of Aaron Burr, had not yet been obliged to consider himself as a man isolated by Federalist adoption of Burr for their official chief—but the selfish and ambitious demagogue had not ceased his intrigues to be elevated with Federalist help to the first office in the nation, where he then might destroy the republic and establish his despotic empire.

It would be political suicide for the Federalists to help to elevate Burr to the presidency: for Burr to be raised up politically by the Federalists' hands would be for the Federalists to be struck down politically by the Federalists' own hands. For the leader of the Federalists to be struck down bodily by Burr's hand, however, was for Burr to be struck down politically by Burr's own hand: to slay Hamilton would be political suicide for Burr. To be slain by Burr was the greatest deed within the power of Hamilton: it would prevent the infinite evils to which the country was exposed from a career the end of which might be the coronation of Emperor Aaron Burr. Hamilton fell, his life destroyed by Burr; Burr fell, his career checked by the death of Hamilton.

A few months after Hamilton's death, a future President of the United

States (the only President to descend from that high preeminence and sit thereafter as a member of the House of Representatives) received a letter reporting, about the opponents of the Federalists, that "a degree of organization has been effected in the opposite party unexampled, I suspect, in this country, since the revolutionary committees of 1775."[39]

Part Three
Constitutional Integrity

XI

Independent Judgment

We have considered why the republic requires not only popular representation but also the unity and duration of effective administration. We have considered the need to embody those different ingredients of good government in a complex structure of differentiated parts. Now we must consider what makes for the wholeness of that structure of parts. We must consider yet another part of government—one which has particularly to do with the enduring wholeness of the body politic.

In notes for a speech in the New York Ratifying Convention, Hamilton asserts that the "representative democracy" of the new Constitution has ("as far as is consistent with its genius") "all the features of good government," which he lists, identifying the organ in which each of these four features is located: "an immediate and operative representation of the people which is found in the house of representatives," "stability and wisdom which is found in the Senate," "a vigorous executive which is found in the president," and "an independent judicial, which is found in the Supreme Court &c."

In every government there will be a place for some kind of executive activity and judicial activity. In a good government there will be a place for popular representation, and this must be immediate (not virtual) and operative (not merely for show). But immediate popular representation (like immediate popularity), when operative alone, issues in that mutability which is tantamount to folly; a good government will therefore also have a place for that stability in policy which is tantamount to wisdom. Moreover, a servant who is both faithful and steady will nonetheless do little service if he is inactive; a guarantor of fidelity and a repository of stability do not constitute good government if there is not a place for executive vigor as well. The final item in this sketch of a good government is a judicial part with independence.

Each of the other features of good government is found in one place— in the House of Representatives or in the Senate or in the President. The judicial power of the United States, however, is found in the Supreme Court "&c.": only the judicial power of the United States is found not in one place alone, but in one place supremely and in many places additionally. The independent judicial is not localized at a single center but pervades a collection of circuits. The many courts of the United States cannot, however, form one judiciary for the Union if there is not one court of supreme and final jurisdiction.

There ought to be one court of supreme and final jurisdiction—this is a proposition which Hamilton in *The Federalist* says is not likely to be contested. The only question that seems to have been raised concerning it is whether it ought to be a distinct body or a branch of the legislature. But if good government requires a judicial part with independence, then that court which is supreme cannot be located in the legislature. Ultimately, the case for judicial independence is the case against locating the supreme court in the legislature.[1]

The judicial department is discussed in *The Federalist* near the end. We need not here concern ourselves with the federal aspects of *The Federalist*'s treatment of the judiciary, but we should consider what *The Federalist* tells us about how men are to be set apart as judges and about how the judiciary is to be set apart from the other departments of government. Numbers 78 and 79 discuss how men are to become judges and how long they are to continue being judges; Number 81 begins with a discussion of why the highest court ought to be distinct from the legislature.

ii   The central object in considering the manner of constituting the judiciary is the tenure by which the judges are to hold their places. This chiefly concerns their duration in office, the provisions for their support, and the precautions for their responsibility.

In point of duration, Hamilton says, it would doubtlessly be wise to copy from the models of those constitutions which have established good behavior as the tenure of judicial offices. Those who doubt that the Convention acted wisely in including this feature only show their own lack of wisdom. Not only does Hamilton deny that the plan is blamable on this account; he says that the plan would have been inexcusably defective if it had lacked this important feature of good government. The experience of Great Britain affords an illustrious comment on the excellence of the institution.[2]

Among the reasons for the permanence of the judicial offices is a weighty one deducible from the nature of the qualifications they require: primarily this means being learned. Judges apply laws, and a voluminous code of laws is one of the inconveniences necessarily connected with the advantages of a free government. Courts determine particular cases and controversies, and because they should not do so with an arbitrary discretion, they must be bound by strict rules and precedents that define and indicate their duty in every particular case. But, from the variety of controversies which grow out of the folly and wickedness of mankind, the records of those precedents must unavoidably swell to a very considerable bulk, and so it must demand long and laborious study to acquire a competent knowledge of them. Few men in the society, therefore, can have sufficient skill in the laws to qualify them for the station of a judge. But knowledge alone does not suffice to make a character fit for that station. Moral virtue is requisite as well, and, making the proper deductions for the ordinary depravity of human nature, still fewer will be those who unite the requisite integrity with the requisite knowledge.

Consequently, the government can have no great option between fit characters and so cannot afford to discourage fit characters from public service. But a temporary duration in office would naturally discourage such characters from quitting a lucrative line of practice to accept a seat on the bench. It would thus have a tendency to throw the administration of justice into hands less able—and less qualified to conduct it with utility and dignity. Not splendor but dignity is what fits capable men for judgeships. The moral virtue involved is that integrity which raises a man above depravity. We must not reckon upon so much devotion to the republic as to expect many men who are capable of building up a lucrative legal practice to leave it in order to administer justice temporarily.

In the present circumstances of this country, Hamilton says, and also for a long time to come, the available number of fit characters is likely to be small in relation to the need, but the disadvantages deriving from the scarcity of men with the qualifications that would fit them to be judges are far inferior to those which present themselves under the other aspects of the subject. Those other aspects of disadvantage have to do with the inability of judges who are temporary to be independent.[3]

The scarcity of qualified men makes permanent tenure desirable as an inducement for them to accept appointment as judges. This scarcity may

not itself be permanent—but the need for judges to be men with a previously acquired store of knowledge *is* permanent and shows itself in the
mode by which judges are to be appointed.

The subject of the mode of appointing the judges is brought up only
to be treated by a brief sentence directing us back to the discussion of the
executive's power of appointing the officers of the Union in general. If their
mode of appointment is considered by itself, those engaged in "the administration of justice" would seem no different from those officers, appointed by
the chief executive, who engage in "the administration of government . . .
in its most usual and perhaps in its most precise signification," and who are
subordinate to the chief executive.

Late in the discussion of the judiciary, however, Hamilton speaks of
judges in contrast to legislators as men selected for their knowledge of the
laws, acquired by long and laborious study: the members of the legislature
will rarely be chosen with a view to those qualifications which fit men for
the station of judges, he says, and on this account there will be great reason
to apprehend all the ill consequences of defective information. Only with
respect to the members of the judicial department does Hamilton emphasize previous training or knowledge as a qualification for office. In the case
of senators and presidents, though he speaks of his hope that arrangements
will permit and even induce sufficiently wise men to serve, he places emphasis on how a properly established office will elicit beneficial behavior
from the officer who holds it, rather than on how a proper previous training
will fit a man for office. For these nonjudicial officials, talents need only be
sufficiently respectable, and experience and information will be acquired on
the job—if the job is properly established.

But even in the case of the judiciary, where previous training is necessary, the need for learned men is not the chief concern. The chief difficulty
is not to secure a judiciary that is learned; it is to secure a judiciary that is
independent. Hamilton says that the disadvantages of discouraging learned
men are far inferior to other disadvantages of short duration in office, and
the context for his contrast between the qualifications of legislators and
those of judges is his argument for establishing the seat of supreme judicial
power as a distinct branch of government. Learning characterizes a good
judiciary, but its peculiar independence is what distinguishes it.[4]

iii Judicial independence is first discussed in *The Federalist* in connec-
     tion with the tenure by which the judges are to hold their places.
Apart from the precautions for their responsibility, their tenure chiefly
concerns their duration in office and the provision for their support. The

propriety of providing for the judges to hold their offices during good behavior lies in the fact that periodical appointments, however regulated or by
whomsoever made, would in some way or other be fatal to their necessary
independence. The provision conforms to the most approved of the state
constitutions, among them that of New York. But next to what contributes
most to the independence of the judges—permanence in office—nothing
else can contribute more than can a fixed provision for their support. As
experience with some state constitutions has shown, there is need to be
precise and explicit. A mere declaration that permanent salaries should be
established for the judges is not sufficiently definite to preclude legislative
evasions. Hence, the judges of the United States are *at stated times* to receive
for their services a compensation, and also this is *not to be diminished* during their continuance in office. This provision for the support of the judges,
together with the permanent tenure of their offices, affords a better prospect of their independence than is to be found in the constitutions of any of
the states.

An independent judiciary is not an ancient institution. What chiefly
contributes to it is a modern improvement. Indeed, the standard of good
behavior for the continuance in office of the judicial magistracy is certainly
one of the most valuable of the modern improvements in the practice of
government.

The value of this improvement is not confined to any particular sort of
government: it is the best expedient which can be devised in any government, to secure a steady, upright, and impartial administration of the laws.
In any government, expedients for preventing unsteadiness or partiality in
the administration of the laws are valuable. But there is a difference in the
low-down propensities of different forms of government. In a monarchy
the standard of good behavior for the continuance in office of the judicial
magistracy is an excellent barrier to the despotism of the prince; in a republic it is a no less excellent barrier to the encroachments and oppressions
of the representative body. Among the forms of government, monarchy and
republic are the great alternatives that are set in opposition. In whatever
manner the bad propensities of each of these two opposites may differ from
those of the other, the improvement that chiefly contributes to judicial independence is a barrier equally excellent in both constitutions. It seems to
be manifest that this barrier is excellent for keeping a prince in a monarchy
from despotism; it needs to be pointed out that this barrier is no less excellent for keeping a representative body in a republic from encroachments
and oppressions. Despotism is the worst thing politically. But even in that
extreme despotism where the merely willful command of one man is law,

that one man needs servants to execute his commands. A standing apparatus for execution can introduce an element of what is not mere willfulness into the commands of the sovereign power. In a republic all power is not concentrated in the hands of one man. In an improved modern republic all power is not even concentrated in the hands of a single body of men; yet even so, the legislature tends to predominance or even hegemony.

Permanence in office does not suffice for judicial independence. The remark made in relation to the President applies equally to the judiciary: in the general course of human nature, a power over a man's subsistence amounts to a power over his will. We can never hope to see realized in practice the complete separation of the judicial from the legislative power in any system which leaves the judges dependent for pecuniary resources on the occasional grants of the legislators.

Still, it is permanence in office that is the first element in judicial independence. What is indispensable in the courts of justice is an inflexible and uniform adherence to the rights of the constitution and of individuals, and behavior so independent can certainly not be expected from judges who hold their offices by temporary commission deriving from periodical appointments. If there were periodical appointment by one or both of the other two branches of government (the executive and the legislative), then the judges would improperly seek to please, or at least not displease, those who appoint. And if there were periodical appointment by the people, mediately or immediately, then those seeking reappointment would be disposed to consult popularity. But a judge should consult nothing but the constitution and the laws.[5]

The judges are not only to consult the laws; they are also to consult the constitution. If they were obliged to consult only the laws, it might be argued that they ought to be very complaisant to those who make the laws, but the judges ought *not* to be very complaisant to those who make the laws, because those who make the laws are made by the constitution. A limited constitution is one which contains certain specified exceptions to the legislative authority, such as that it shall pass no bills of attainder or ex post facto laws. Thus, the constitution which constitutes the legislative authority also limits it, and limitations of this kind can in practice become effective in no other way than by the refusal of the courts of justice to give effect to acts of the legislative authority that are contrary to the manifest tenor of the constitution. Without this medium of the courts of justice, all the reservations of particular rights or privileges would amount to nothing. Constitutional limitations on legislative authority would in effect be void—were it not for the right, indeed the duty, of the courts to pronounce legislative acts void because contrary to the constitution.

Because this doctrine is of great importance in all the American constitutions, says Hamilton, it is important to understand the grounds on which it rests. There is a pressing reason for Hamilton to present at least a brief discussion of this: some perplexity has arisen from imagining that the doctrine would imply a superiority of the judiciary to the legislative power. It has been urged that an authority which can declare another authority's acts to be void must necessarily be superior to the one whose acts may be declared void.

Hamilton argues first that no legislative act contrary to the constitution can be valid. This is inferred from the proposition that if an act of delegated authority is contrary to the tenor of the commission under which it is exercised, then it is void. No proposition depends on clearer principles than does this. A denial of what is inferred from it implies an affirmation that men acting by virtue of powers may do not only what their powers do not authorize, but even what they forbid. Such a denial, which would set the deputy above his principal or the servant above his master, would imply that the representatives of the people are superior to the people themselves.

Hamilton then answers those who, though conceding that legislative acts are invalid if contrary to the constitution, would argue nonetheless that the constitutional powers of the legislative body are to be judged by the legislative body itself and that its construction of the constitution in respect to its own powers is conclusive upon the other departments. This argument that the legislators are to be the constitutional judges of their own powers supposes that the constitution could intend to enable the representatives of the people to substitute their own will for that of their constituents. This cannot be the natural presumption without some particular provisions in the constitution. In the absence of such particular provisions, it is far more rational to suppose that the courts were designed to be an intermediate body between the people and the legislature, in order, among other things, to keep the legislature within the limits assigned to its authority.

But, it might be asked, why not suppose that the *legislature* was designed to be an intermediate body between the people and the courts, in order, among other things, to keep the *courts* within the limits assigned to their authority? One might reply to this question by asking: among *what* other things? To regard courts as intermediate in controlling the legislature is natural because courts are intermediate in controlling the people. The legislature is the source of the laws, which, through the medium of

the courts, control the people. The people is the source of the constitution—so it might seem natural to complete the symmetry by adding the
words: *which, through the medium of the courts, controls the legislature.* The
intermediacy of the courts is not, however, completely symmetrical: courts
contribute to controlling the *people* by *giving effect* to laws that would control the people, but courts contribute to controlling the *legislature* by *not*
giving effect to laws that would control the people.

The proper and peculiar function of the courts is intermediary: judicial
work is not legislative or executive, but interpretive. Saying what the laws
mean in trying to apply them is the proper and peculiar province of the
courts. It is part of the interpretation of the laws to determine whether laws
conflict and, if laws conflict, what is *the* law. This exercise of judicial discretion in determining between two contradictory laws is exemplified when,
as is not uncommon, two statutes exist at one time, clashing in whole or in
part with each other, but neither contains any repealing words.

Reason and law conspire to dictate that the statutes should be recon-
ciled to each other so far as this can be done by any fair construction; but
where this is impracticable, it becomes a matter of necessity to give effect to
one in exclusion of the other, and the rule which has obtained in the courts
for determining their relative validity is to prefer the later to the earlier. This
mere rule of construction is not itself derived from any positive law; rather
than being a product of legislation, this rule emerged from a process of independent judgment by the courts. Without being legislatively enjoined,
the rule was adopted judicially. It was adopted judiciously, from the nature
and reason of the thing, as consonant with truth and propriety. The courts
as interpreters of the law, when it was a matter of necessity to choose to
which of two conflicting laws to give effect, adopted a rule because they
thought it reasonable. The courts thought it reasonable, for the direction of
their conduct as interpreters of the law, that between the interfering acts of
an equal authority the last indication of its will should have the preference.

When, however, the interfering acts are those of a superior and subordinate authority, of an original and derivative power, then the nature and
reason of the thing teach the converse of that rule as proper: the prior act
of a superior ought to be preferred to the subsequent act of an inferior and
subordinate authority. Accordingly, whenever a particular statute contra-
venes the constitution, the judges ought to adhere to the constitution and
disregard the statute. A constitution is law; it is the law of laws, the law
which makes lawmaking; it is fundamental law. So it is in fact, and so it
must be regarded by the judges. To them, therefore, it belongs to ascertain
the meaning of the constitution as well as the meaning of any particular act

proceeding from the legislative body. The fundamental law is the highest law. The obligation and validity of the constitution is, of course, superior to that of a statute which is irreconcilably at variance with it. The constitution governs the exercise of governmental power. The people enact the law which governs what laws their agents may enact thereafter. The people declare in the constitution their will or intention that the legislature within certain limits has the power to declare its own will or intention in statutes. As interpreters of the law, the judges must not suppress their judgment that a statute is irreconcilably at variance with the constitution, and they must in such a case prefer the law emanating from the original power possessed of superior authority.

Not by any means does this conclusion suppose that the judicial power is superior to the legislative power. It supposes only that the power of the people is superior to both, and that where the will of the legislature as declared in its statutes stands in opposition to that of the people as declared in the constitution, the judges ought to be governed by the latter rather than the former. The judges ought to regulate their decisions by the fundamental law. It need not be supposed that the supreme court is the supreme power for there to be a judicial right and duty of refusing to give effect to acts of legislative power regarded judicially as unconstitutional; it need only be supposed that judgment must intervene between will and execution. An independent seat of judgment must be expected to judge independently.

There is no weight in saying that the courts may, on the pretense of a repugnancy, substitute their own pleasure for the constitutional intentions of the legislature. This might as well happen in the case of two contradictory statutes or in any adjudication upon a single statute; in such a case or adjudication, the courts must declare the sense of the law, and if they should exercise will instead of judgment, they would equally be substituting their pleasure for that of the legislative body. Hence, if the observation proved anything, it would prove that there ought to be *no* judges distinct from the legislative body. But the courts of justice are the bulwarks of a limited constitution against legislative encroachments. What is essential to the faithful performance of so arduous a duty is an independent spirit in the judges, and nothing contributes more to this than does the permanent tenure of judicial offices.[6]

Independent judges, as the bulwarks of a limited constitution against legislative encroachments, thus protect the people from betrayal by the people's agents. The judges ought not to be complaisant to those who make the laws, for those who make the laws are made by the constitution. But those who make the laws are named by the people, and the constitution which makes the lawmakers is made by the people, so it might be thought that the judges should be complaisant to the lawmakers whenever the lawmakers themselves are complaisant to the people, who are the source of legitimate authority. This would, however, be improper. Not only must the intent of the people, as expressed in the constitution, be distinguished from the intent of the people's agents, as expressed in legislative acts; another distinction must also be kept in mind: a momentary inclination of the people is not a solemn authorization by the people.

A fundamental principle of republican government admits the people's right to alter or abolish the established constitution whenever they find it inconsistent with their happiness. But this doctrine does not imply that the people's representatives, whenever a majority of their constituents may be seized by a momentary inclination incompatible with the provisions in the existing constitution, are on that account justified in violating those provisions—or that the courts are more obliged to connive at infractions in this shape than when they proceed wholly from the cabals of the representative body. Rather, until the people have by some solemn and authoritative act annulled or changed the established form, it is binding upon themselves collectively, as well as individually, and no presumption or even knowledge of their sentiments can warrant their representatives in departing from it prior to such an act. But it would require an uncommon portion of fortitude in the judges to do their duty as faithful guardians of the constitution where legislative invasions of it had been instigated by the major voice of the community. The complete independence of the courts of justice is peculiarly essential in a limited constitution: it guards the constitution against legislative infractions of the constitution not only when the encroachments are unpopular but especially when they are popular.[7]

The independence of the judges is also a safeguard against the effects of occasional ill humors that do not encroach upon the constitution but extend no further than to the injury of the private rights of particular classes of citizens by unjust and partial laws. The firmness of the judicial magistracy, by mitigating the severity and confining the operation of such laws, moderates the immediate mischiefs of those which may have been passed. It also operates as a check upon the legislative body in passing them: the legislative body, expecting from the scruples of the courts obstacles to the success of their iniquitous intention, are somehow compelled by the very motives of the injustice which they meditate to qualify their attempts.[8]

The independence of the judges will tend to beget or fortify in the courts a certain temper of integrity and moderation. Its benefits, says Hamilton, have already been felt in more states than one, displeasing those whose sinister expectations they may have disappointed, while commanding the esteem and applause of all the virtuous and disinterested. Considerate men of every description ought to prize whatever will have that tendency to beget or fortify the integrity and moderation of the judiciary, as no man can be sure that he may not be tomorrow the victim of a spirit of injustice by which he may be a gainer today; and every man must now feel that the inevitable tendency of such a spirit of injustice is to sap the foundations of public and private confidence and to introduce instead universal distrust and distress. Not every man is to be found in the class of the virtuous and disinterested or in the class of the considerate men of every description. What is the temper of the multitude of men? Most men, even if under the influence of good humors most of the time, may at times be affected by those ill humors which the arts of designing men or the influence of particular conjunctures sometimes disseminate among the people and which, though they speedily give place to better information and more deliberate reflection, have a tendency in the meantime to occasion dangerous innovations in the government and serious oppressions of the minor part in the community. To be guarded from the effects of those ill humors, both the constitution and the rights of individuals equally require the independence of the judges.[9]

iv   Discussing the standard of good behavior for continuing judges in office, Hamilton contrasts the different departments of power in a government which separates them from each other. The respect in which he contrasts the legislative, the executive, and the judicial departments is power and the lack of it.

Of the three the weakest beyond comparison is the judiciary. (The celebrated Montesquieu, it is noteworthy, even says in the *Spirit of the Laws* that of the three the judiciary is "next to nothing.") The judiciary can never successfully attack either of the other two; indeed, merely to enable it to defend itself requires no less than all possible care. As a lone defender against aggression from another department, the judiciary is doomed to fail unless carefully strengthened; a fortiori, it is simply doomed to failure as a lone aggressor against another department.

After Hamilton considers the judiciary with respect to the capacity of the departments of government for mutual aggression among themselves, he then considers the judiciary with respect to governmental aggression against the people. As the courts of justice can never menace another department, so, he says, though they may now and then oppress an innocent individual, they can never endanger the general liberty of the people. But this last point needs qualification: I mean, says Hamilton, so long as the judiciary remains truly distinct from both the legislative and the executive. He agrees with Montesquieu that "there is no liberty, if the power of judging be not separated from the legislative and executive powers." By emphasizing his agreement with this maxim of the celebrated Montesquieu, Hamilton makes clear what he means by his emphatic statement of the weakness of the judiciary: although special care must be taken to protect the judiciary, the judiciary nonetheless should not be entered into partnership to gain protection. Such an unholy alliance would make the courts a menace to liberty. The judiciary, menaced by the coordinate branches, is not itself a menace to the other branches, nor is it a menace to the people; but it would become a menace to the people if it met the menace from the other branches by alliance with one of them.

Since the courts must be given additional defensive strength, but must not be joined in alliance with a stronger power, it follows that the courts must be fortified. To establish justice, a stronghold is required. The citadel of the public justice and the public security is, in great measure, the judiciary's permanence in office. It is a fortress for the temple of justice.

This quality of permanence in office is an indispensable ingredient in the constitution of the judiciary. Nothing else can contribute so much to the judiciary's firmness and independence. Liberty can have nothing to fear from the judiciary alone, but would have everything to fear from its union with either of the other departments, and all the effects of such a union must ensue from a dependence of the judiciary on another department, notwithstanding a nominal and apparent separation. The natural feebleness of the judiciary places it in continual danger of being overpowered, awed, or influenced by its coordinate branches.[10]

A simple view of the matter proves incontestibly, says Hamilton, that the judiciary is weak and is harmless to the general liberty of the people. Considering attentively the different departments of governmental power when these are separated from each other, one must perceive that from the very nature of its functions the judiciary will always be the department least dangerous to the political rights of the constitution because it will be least in a capacity to annoy or injure them.

Why are judicial functions by nature such that if those who perform them are set apart from those who perform the other governmental functions, then the judiciary must be the department of power least capable of disturbing the constitutional apportionment of power?

Government functions by willing, judging, and enforcing. Will is exerted by the legislature, which prescribes the rules that regulate every citizen's rights and duties. The legislature commands the purse especially; it directs the society's wealth. But the society's strength, for reasons considered earlier, is not well directed by a legislature. Force is exerted by the executive: the hand which holds the community's sword must apply concentrated force amid swiftly changing circumstances. That same executive hand dispenses the honors of the community: the legislature, which subordinates all to general rules, is, for reasons considered earlier, not well suited for elevating particular citizens to participation in ruling. The concerns which are characteristically legislative are economic affairs of property and payment; the concerns which are characteristically executive are polemic affairs of defense and dominance. The judiciary, by contrast, has no influence over either the sword or the purse, no direction either of the strength or of the wealth of the society; it has neither force nor will, but merely judgment. And even for the efficacy of its judgments it must ultimately depend upon the aid of the executive arm.

Is it not, however, also true that the legislature depends upon the judiciary, and ultimately upon the executive, for the efficacy of *its* will? Yes— but the judiciary alone among the departments can take no active resolution whatever.

Still, even if the judges may decide only what others ask them to decide, could not the judges actively invite what they should passively await, and actively incite what they should impassively compare? Yes—but the legislature has, among those active resolutions which are available to it, an ultimate power to hold the members of other departments responsible: improperly obstreperous judges may be made by the legislature to cease being judges. Judicial magistrates are liable, as are other officers, to impeachment, dismissal from office, and disqualification from holding any other office. There is no need to fear that judicial independence will make the supreme court the supreme power.

Judgment is but a part of government. The seat of judgment, if independent, can be a protective citadel for the citizenry; but one cannot be seated there while *actively* dealing in death or taxes, *actively* elevating some to honors or *actively* subordinating all to rules. The will that regulates the complex of appetite, the force that resolves the clash of spirit—these are the means of aggression; the judiciary has at its disposal at most the means of defense. The independence of the judiciary is usually in danger; only its dependence is dangerous.[11]

This danger of dependence is discussed when *The Federalist* speaks of the President's qualified negative upon the acts or resolutions of the two houses of the legislature. The Convention proposed to place in the executive alone the power of returning all bills with objections, with the effect of preventing their becoming laws unless afterward ratified by two-thirds of each component of the legislative body. A qualified negative upon acts of the legislature was also provided earlier in New York's state constitution, but this power was vested in a council consisting of the governor together with the chancellor and the judges of the state supreme court, or any two of them. Departing from the model of the state constitution of New York, the federal plan favored that of Massachusetts. One strong reason for this, says Hamilton, is that the judges, who are to be interpreters of the law, might receive an improper bias from having given a previous opinion in their revisionary capacities; it is impossible to keep the judges too distinct from every other avocation than that of expounding the laws. But the other reason is that the judges, by being often associated with the executive, might be induced to embark too far in the political views of that magistrate, and thus a dangerous combination might be gradually cemented between the executive and judiciary departments. It is peculiarly dangerous to place the judges in a situation to be either corrupted or influenced by the executive.

From the discussion of the standard of good behavior for the continuance in office of the judicial magistracy, it seems that the steady, upright, and impartial administration of the laws in its most usual and perhaps most precise signification is peculiarly the work of the judicial magistracy—even though in its largest sense it also comprehends some of the operations of the executive magistracy. The administration of justice falls peculiarly within the province of the judicial department—whereas the administration of government in its most usual and perhaps in its most precise signification falls peculiarly within the province of the executive department and is committed to persons who ought to be considered as the assistants or deputies of the chief magistrate. The President is constitutionally designated the commander-in-chief of the armed forces and ought to be considered as well the chief executive, but the chief magistrate is not the chief judicial magistrate. Modern men have learned too much from improvements in government even to raise the question whether the chief executive ought to be Chief Justice. The Chief Justice is, rather, the chief among the Justices of the Supreme Court.[12]

v   But concerning that one court of supreme and final jurisdiction, the question seems to have been raised whether it ought to be a branch of the legislature rather than a distinct body. By the plan of the Convention, the judicial power of the United States is vested in one supreme court and in such inferior courts as the Congress may from time to time establish. Upon examination of the arguments, or rather suggestions, which make this provision a charge against the plan proposed, Hamilton finds them to be made up altogether of false reasoning upon misconceived fact. The examination is divided by Hamilton into three parts. In the *first* place he considers the misconceived fact and the false reasoning upon it, which make up the description of the authority of the proposed Supreme Court. In the *second* place he considers the misconceived fact involved in the suggestion that what is proposed is unprecedented. In the *last* place he considers the false reasoning involved in the suggestion that what is proposed is dangerous.[13]

In the *first* place Hamilton examines what the enemies of the plan suggest about the potentiality inherent in the power proposed for the Supreme Court. That court, they say, is to be a separate and independent body whose authority will be superior to that of the legislature; its power to construe the laws according to the spirit of the constitution will enable that court to mold them into whatever shape it may think proper—especially as its decisions will not be in any manner subject to the revision or correction of the legislative body.[14]

Hamilton points out the misconception of fact. This proposed constitution does not directly empower the national or federal courts to construe the laws according to the spirit of the constitution. But any limited constitution—that is, any constitution that attempts to limit the legislative discretion—must by its general theory oblige the courts to take the constitution as the standard of construction for the laws and to make the laws give place to the constitution whenever there is an evident opposition. The state constitutions, being limited constitutions, do not differ in this respect from the proposed federal constitution. When the court believes it finds the legislative product in evident opposition to the constitution, the legislature may believe it finds the judicial product an evident imposition on the constitution. This difference of opinion will arise not because the court appeals to the spirit of the constitution, but because the constitution attempts to set bounds to the legislative discretion and attempts to give effect to these limitations by establishing interpreters of that constitution who are independent of the legislature. There is no force in the objection that this constitution empowers the Supreme Court to reconstruct the constitution by construing it according to its spirit. Whatever force there is in the objection that the Supreme Court will improperly mold the laws into any shape it may think proper must lie in the particular organization of the Supreme Court, that is, in its being composed of a body of magistrates distinct from the legislature—instead of its being one of the branches of the legislature, as in the government of Great Britain and in that of the state of New York.[15]

A supreme court outside the legislature, it is suggested, will be a superlegislature: for the legislature to be truly the legislature—that is, for the legislature to be without a legislative superior—it must have within it the court that is supreme. To point out the false reasoning that leads to this conclusion, Hamilton presents some considerations that will teach us to applaud the wisdom of those who have committed the judicial power in the last resort, not to a part of the legislature, but to a distinct and independent body of men.[16]

The first consideration has to do with the usefulness of separate depositories of power. If one body passes laws and another body applies them, then we might expect the effects of bad laws to be less bad, owing to a disposition to temper and moderate them in the application; we might also expect judges to repair breaches in a constitution infringed by legislators. But if the laws are interpreted by the same body of men (in the character of judges) who made or had even a partial agency in making them (in the character of legislators), then the spirit apt to operate in interpreting them will be the same as that which had operated in making them. Application by such a body would rarely confine the bad effects of bad laws and even less would it refuse to give any effect to unconstitutional laws.[17]

Laws are general; they need to be applied to particulars; this requires interpretation. Thus the functional difference between legislation and interpretation provides an opportunity for bringing into action the maxim that power apportioned is less dangerous than power concentrated. This is one consideration teaching the wisdom of having the supreme court independent of the legislature.[18]

But this is not all. Every reason which recommends the tenure of good behavior for judicial offices, militates against placing the ultimate judiciary power in a body composed of men chosen for a limited period. Besides those reasons which militate generally against placing judicial power in men chosen for a limited period, are there perhaps other reasons which militate in particular against giving permanent standing to the body of men that exercises the judicial power in the last resort? Even if there were, it seems, it would be absurd for these latter reasons to outweigh the former. It might be pernicious but it would not be absurd if no judges had permanent standing, but it would seem to be absurd to permit the final determination of causes by temporary judges while insisting on the initial determination of causes by permanent judges. Whatever this absurdity might be, there is a still greater absurdity in subjecting the decisions of men selected for their knowledge of the laws, acquired by long and laborious study, to the revision and control of men who for lack of the same advantage must be deficient in that knowledge. Because the members of the legislature will rarely be chosen with a view to those qualifications which fit men for the station of judges, there will on this account be great reason to apprehend all the ill consequences of defective information.

But there is no less reason to fear ill consequences *beyond* the likelihood that those chosen to be members of the legislature will not have acquired that legal learning which renders men fit for judicature at the subordinate level; the legislature is also rendered unfit for judicature by the natural propensity of such a body. Legislative bodies have a natural propensity to party divisions. Because of this the pestilential breath of faction may poison the fountains of justice, for the habit of being continually marshaled on opposite sides will be too apt to stifle the voice both of law and equity. The independence of the supreme court is thus not simply a matter of avoiding the subordination of the learned to the ignorant; there is a more manifestly political consideration. Courts of justice composed of men set apart for judicial work are more likely to be impartial than are legislatures, which are naturally full of factious partisans. The place devoted to that impartial judgment by which general laws are applied to particular cases must be insulated from the partisan oppositions habitual in legislatures.

The independence of the judiciary is a safeguard against the natural propensity of bodies of men exuberantly free and equal. The elimination of partisan opposition from a legislature would be not the elimination of party but rather the establishment of dominion by one party—which would itself become either an arena for the opposition of intraparty faction or the instrument of a chief exercising dominion over and by means of party. Without destroying freedom, partisan division and opposition cannot be eliminated from the legislature. The best that can be done is to establish an impartial seat of judgment, as independent of those who may willfully dispose of the purse as it is of those who may forcefully wield the sword.[19]

Contrary to the suggestion, it is not novel and unprecedented for the judiciary to be supremely independent. Not only does the theory of all limited constitutions oblige the judges in deciding cases to make those laws which are opposed to the constitution give way to the constitution, but the practice of particular American constitutions provides the precedent: nine of the state constitutions commit judicial power in the last resort not to a part of the legislature but to bodies of men that are distinct and independent. New York, the state of Hamilton's immediate audience, is in this respect not like her republican sister states; she is like the monarchical mother country.[20]

When charging that the Supreme Court will be able to mold the laws into whatever shape it may think proper, the suggestion called it unprecedented that the Supreme Court's decisions will not in any manner be subject to the revision or correction of the legislative body. It is true, as claimed, that Britain's judicial power in the last resort resides in the House of Lords, which is a branch of the legislature, and that this part of the British government has been imitated in the constitutions of some American states. It is also claimed, however, that the parliament of Great Britain and the legislatures of the several states can at any time rectify by law the exceptionable decisions of their courts. So in the *second* place Hamilton points out the misconceived fact involved in the suggestion about the lack of precedent.

It is true that nothing in the proposed constitution authorizes legislative acts to revise judicial sentences. In this, however, contrary to the suggestion, the proposed constitution is like the constitutions both of the American states and of Great Britain. And it also, like them, does not forbid the practice. In none of the constitutions is positive law, either by its lacking an authorization or by its containing a prohibition, the obstacle to the practice. Rather, the sole obstacle is the impropriety of the thing on the general principles of law and reason. Among these is the principle that a legislature, without exceeding its province, cannot reverse a determination once made in a particular case, though it may prescribe a new rule for future cases. To deny this principle would be to abolish the rationale for the existence of distinct bodies which apply to particular cases the general rules enacted by the legislature. Judges would be mere clerks of the legislature if they were not to exercise judgment independent of the legislature.[21]

In the *last* place Hamilton considers the false reasoning involved in the charge that the allegedly unprecedented lack of legislative means for rectifying exceptionable court decisions is dangerous because there will be no control or remedy for the errors and usurpations of the Supreme Court of the United States. Judicial encroachments on the legislative authority may seem to be a danger, says Hamilton, but they are in reality only a phantom. This may be seen by considering the general nature of the judicial power, the objects to which it relates, the manner in which it is exercised, its comparative weakness, and its total incapacity to support its usurpations by force. From these considerations it may be inferred with certainty that although particular misconstructions and contraventions of the will of the legislature may happen now and then, they nonetheless can never be so extensive as to amount to an inconvenience or to affect perceptibly the order of the political system.[22]

The inference is greatly fortified, moreover, by another consideration. The power of instituting impeachments in one part of the legislative body, and of determining upon them in the other part, would give to that body an important constitutional check upon the members of the judicial department. Precautions for the responsibility of the judiciary are an ingredient in a good constitution of the judiciary, and such precautions are found in the proposed constitution: judges who have been impeached for malconduct by the House of Representatives and tried by the Senate are, if convicted, to be dismissed from office and disqualified from holding any other office. The supreme law would thus provide a safeguard against betrayal of the law by the supreme guardians of the law. But safety against betrayal by the supreme guardians is not the only ingredient in a good constitution of the judiciary; another ingredient is safety against betrayal of superior law by the makers of subordinate law, and this ingredient requires judges who are independent. To provide a safeguard against betrayal by the supreme guardians of the law, the supreme law gives to the ordinary lawmakers the authority to remove false guardians of the law: this is the only provision consistent with the necessary independence of the judicial character, and it is the only one in the state constitution of New York, says Hamilton. The legislative power to remove the judges by impeachment and trial is by itself a complete security against the judges: there can never be a danger that the judges, by a series of deliberate usurpations invading the authority of the legislature, would hazard the united resentment of this body while it had the power to punish their presumption by degrading them from their stations.[23]

This consideration, which ought to remove all apprehensions on the subject, affords at the same time a cogent argument for constituting the Senate as a court for the trial of impeachments. If the court for the trial of impeachments were the Supreme Court, then the judges would be *too* independent to be held responsible for the conduct of *their own* offices.

In our previous examination of the arguments for constituting the Senate as the court for the trial of impeachments, we saw that if the court for the trial of impeachments were the Supreme Court, then the judges would be *insufficiently* independent to judge properly the official conduct of *others*. Impeachment is a political proceeding: prosecution will involve partisanship and partiality, and trial cannot be strictly bound by the prior rules that in common cases limit the discretion of courts in favor of personal security. In cases of impeachment the Supreme Court would not have sufficient dignity and independence to preserve impartiality between an accused individual and his accusers, the people's representatives. Even if, despite a lack of confidence in their own situation, the judges nevertheless summoned up enough fortitude to find the accused innocent and thus to save the honor of a distinguished man, the public tranquility would still be endangered by their lack of sufficient credit and authority to reconcile the people to a decision which clashed with an accusation brought by the people's immediate representatives.

These considerations seem alone sufficient for concluding that the Supreme Court would have been an improper substitute for the Senate as a court of impeachments, but this conclusion will be strengthened not a little by a further consideration. An offender convicted upon impeachment, after having been sentenced to perpetual ostracism from the esteem and confidence and honors and emoluments of his country, will still be liable to prosecution and punishment in the ordinary course of law; and it would not be proper that the persons who had disposed of his fame and his most valuable rights as a citizen in one trial should, in another trial for the same offense, dispose also of his life and his fortune. Those who know anything of human nature will perceive that those who might happen to be the objects of prosecution would lose much of the double security intended them by a double trial. The loss of life and estate would often be virtually included in a sentence the import of whose terms was nothing more than dismissal from a present office and disqualification from a future one.

It might be said, however, that the intervention of a jury, in the second instance, would obviate the dangers. Juries, however, are frequently influenced by judges and are sometimes induced to find special verdicts which refer the main question to the decision of the court.

But if the plan, in constituting the court of impeachments, would have been made worse by substituting the Supreme Court for the Senate, would it have been made better by uniting the Supreme Court with the Senate? Although this union would certainly have had several advantages, these would have been outweighed by the signal disadvantages arising from the agency of the same judges in the double prosecution to which the offender would be liable. The plan of the Convention was therefore perhaps the prudent mean: by making the Chief Justice of the Supreme Court the president of the court of impeachments for an impeached President of the United States, the advantages will be to some extent obtained, while the disadvantages will be substantially avoided. Hamilton concludes by saying that he will forebear to remark upon the additional pretext for clamor against the judiciary that would have been afforded by so considerable an augmentation of its authority.[24]

XII

Partisanship, Partiality, and Parts of Government

After the "Revolution of 1800," Hamilton did not forebear to remark upon the Jeffersonian clamor against the judiciary. In the fifth number of his extensive and minute examination of Jefferson's Message to Congress of 7 December 1801, Hamilton noted that

> we are told that the States individually have "*principal* care of our persons, our property, and our reputations, constituting the great field of human concerns; and that, therefore, *we may well doubt whether our organization is not too complicated, too expensive;* whether offices and officers have not been multiplied unnecessarily, and sometimes injuriously to the service they were meant to promote"; afterwards it is observed that "the judiciary system will, *of course,* present itself to the contemplation of Congress"; and pains had been taken to form and communicate a numerical list of all the causes decided since the first establishment of the courts, in order that Congress might be able to judge of the proportion which the institution bears to the business.

Hamilton commented scornfully about Jefferson's thinking that the work of the federal judiciary was little because the number of cases decided by them had been few: this was itself a sign that Jefferson's capacity for thinking about government was little. The comparatively small difference of expense between an enlarged and a contracted plan for the administration of the judicial power was a secondary consideration, a matter of trivial moment. It weighed inconsiderably against the primary consideration, which was to give the greatest efficacy to this essential part of the system. This was a most momentous matter, the importance of which could be judged only by a test that went beyond a crude count of the number of causes tried, for the mere existence of the courts had had a powerful and salutary effect. Instead of merely counting the number of causes tried in the federal courts, it would have been better to consider the objects which the constitutional arrangement of judicial power was designed to accomplish.

Hamilton lists the objects of the federal judiciary. Its first object has to do with the fact that laws are not self-executing; if the laws of the United States are to have living spirit, rather than being a dead letter, there must be an organ for carrying them into execution, an organ both faithful and effective. In the next place, though there are courts in the state governments, no state government has responsibility for the United States in relations with foreign nations; but this nation's treaties with foreign nations, being part of the supreme law of the land, need, like the ordinary laws of the United States, to be interpreted and executed—and have a special need to be interpreted and executed fairly. The citizens of foreign nations, moreover, need, and believe they need, courts of justice under the authority of the government which has the immediate charge of external relations, including the care of national peace; and this general government might more tenaciously administer justice so as to guard the rights and conciliate the confidence of citizens of other countries. Even in their treatment of Americans who are citizens of another state within the Union, the individual states, being governments over parts of the United States, have a tendency or at least a susceptibility to being partial to themselves in controversies, as well as partial to their own in legislation and adjudication, especially in the pressing matter of real estate; coping with this comprises several of the objects of the judiciary of the United States. Indeed, the central object on the list is this: to guard generally against invasions of right, and especially of property, by fraudulent and oppressive laws of particular states, enforced by their own tribunals.

To show why the judiciary was designed by the Constitution to accomplish all seven of these objects, Hamilton takes a look back at the state courts after independence but before the Constitution was established. To those courts he assigns responsibility for serious mischiefs that were felt then. But a rapid and salutary renovation of our affairs succeeded; and, little less than to any other provision in the Constitution, Hamilton ascribes it to the institution of a competent judiciary.[1]

ii   The series of articles continued, minutely examining every obscure suggestion in the Presidential Message, not only those raising the question of the judiciary. But within a couple of months of Hamilton's remarks on the question of the judiciary, something had happened that "rendered the question far more serious than it was while it rested merely on the obscure suggestion in the Presidential Message." This was, Hamilton says, the progress of a bill lately brought into the Senate for repealing the law of the previous session, entitled "an act to provide for the more convenient organization of the courts of the United States," with the avowed design of superseding the judges who were appointed under it.

That this should happen was hardly to have been imagined before-hand—that a majority of either House of Congress, whether from design or error, would have lent its sanction to a glaring violation of our national compact in that article which, of all the others, is the most essential to the efficacy and stability of the government, to the security of property and to the safety and liberty of person. It was not perfectly unimaginable: the progress of the bill, said Hamilton, was only a step in a larger work in progress promoted by those mountebank politicians who have been too successful in perverting public opinion, who are advancing with rapid strides in the work of "disorganization"—the sure forerunner of tyranny—and who, if not arrested in their mad career, will ere long precipitate our nation into all the horrors of anarchy.

The progress of the bill, though only a step in the work of disorganization, was a tremendous step, for its implications were immense. The bill might seem to be a mere undoing of what was done: a law had been passed, and then the legislature, thinking better of the matter, intended to repeal it. However, as applied to a legislative body, it is true generally but not universally that a power to do includes, virtually, a power to undo; all vested rights form an exception to the rule. In strict theory there is no lawful or moral power to divest by a subsequent statute a right vested in an individual by a prior statute, and accordingly the repeal of a law does not always work the revocation or divestiture of such rights. A reply to this might be that though a legislature might act immorally and wickedly in abrogating a vested right, yet the legal validity of its act for such a purpose is indisputable. But this position, which is odious in any application of it, is questionable in every limited constitution (that is, in every constitution the theory of which does not suppose the whole power of the nation to be lodged in the legislative body). And it is certainly false, in its application to a legislature whose authorities are defined by a positive written constitution, as to everything contrary to the actual provisions of that constitution. To deny this is to affirm that the delegated is paramount to the constituent power. It is, in fact, to affirm that there are no constitutional limits to the legislative authority.

Hence, since the passage of the bill is probable, "probably before these remarks shall be read," Hamilton exclaims, "that Constitution will be no more: It will be numbered among the numerous victims of Democratic frenzy; and will have given another and an awful lesson to mankind." And perhaps this lesson will be but the prelude of calamities to this country at the contemplation of which the imagination shudders. Passage of the bill is a decisive step; the question whether Congress may abolish judges is "the great question which seems destined to decide the fate of our government."[2]

iii   The question was whether the Constitution permits Congress to abolish judges, not whether it permits Congress to abolish courts. Congress may abolish the courts, but the judges shall retain their offices with the appurtenant emoluments, according to Hamilton's construction of the document.

But, he asks, will this construction secure the benefits intended by the Constitution to be derived from the independent tenure of judicial office? He answers that substantially it will: the main object is to preserve the judges from being influenced by an apprehension of the loss of the advantages of office, and if this loss could not be incurred, that influence would not exist—their firmness could not be assailed by the danger of being superseded and perhaps consigned to want. On Hamilton's construction those who would assail the firmness of judges would lose the means of doing so; they would not be able to influence the judges through the judges' fear of losing their status and their income.

An added point is that those whom factious motives might induce to abolish a court would be under great restraint from doing so if they were unable, by doing so, to abolish the judges as well: courts would be much less likely to be abolished unless for genuine reasons of public utility, and judiciary establishments would of course have a much better prospect of stability.[3]

Suppose it is objected that judges who retained their offices after their courts had been abolished would receive compensation without any service in return. Hamilton agrees that, without doubt, the Constitution does contemplate service as the ground of compensation, but, he replies, the Constitution likewise takes it for granted that the legislature will be circumspect in the institution of offices and especially that it will be careful to establish none of a permanent nature which will not be permanently useful.

Suppose it is then replied that even if Hamilton is right—that is, even if it is true that with this general presumption the Constitution anticipates no material inconveniences from the permanence of judicial offices connected with permanent emoluments—nonetheless it should have been foreseen that cases might happen in which service was not needed. Hamilton argues that, even so, there is no difficulty in supposing the willingness of the Constitution to encounter the trivial contingent evil of having to maintain a few superfluous officers in order to obtain the immense good of establishing and securing the independence of the courts of justice. And, as a matter of fact, when compensation is continued without the rendering of service, there *is* a consideration given: the readiness of the officer to render service at the will of the government. But even so the essential inducement is the independence of the judicial character.

Suppose it is objected that Hamilton's construction makes possible an evil that is not trivial: an enormous abuse of power by creating a long list of sinecures and a numerous host of pensioners. Hamilton argues that whenever such a thing shall happen, it will be one of those extreme cases which, on the principle of necessity, may authorize extraconstitutional remedies; but these are cases which can never be appealed to for the interpretation of the Constitution, which, in meting out the powers of the government, must be supposed to adjust them on the presumption of a fair execution.[4]

iv   The stability and hence also the impartiality of the judiciary as an independent department of power were terribly threatened. The threat was posed by the argument that liberty is terribly threatened by the existence of a judicial department in which judges hold their offices by a title absolutely independent of the legislative will. It had been argued that the judicial department if so constituted becomes a colossal and overbearing power, capable of degenerating into a permanent tyranny—at liberty, if audacious and corrupt enough, to render the authority of the legislature nugatory by expounding away the laws and thus to assume a despotic control over the rights of person and property.

Hamilton answers that though the judges hold their offices by a title independent of the legislative will, their continuance in office is not absolutely independent of the legislature. The argument supposes the case of a palpable abuse of power, for which the Constitution has provided a complete safeguard in the authority of the House of Representatives to impeach, of the Senate to condemn. On Hamilton's construction of the Constitution, there is a security *against* as well as *for* the judicial department; but if it be conceded that the legislature has a legal discretion to abolish the judges, then there is absolutely no security for the judicial department.

Yet the republic has peculiar need of security *for* the judicial department. The stability of the judiciary is the surest security for person and property against the factious flux of party: "This most valuable member of the government, when rightly constituted the surest guardian of person and property, of which stability is a prime characteristic, losing at once its most essential attributes, and doomed to fluctuate with the variable tide of faction, degenerates into a disgusting mirror of all the various malignant and turbulent humors of party spirit." The degeneration of the judiciary that really threatens is not its degeneration into a permanent tyranny menacing to person and to property, but rather its degeneration into a fluctuating partisanship incompatible with its being the surest guardian of person and of property. The real danger is on the side of the doctrine opposed by Hamilton. Hamilton is defending the citadel of the temple of justice against

> that foul and fatal doctrine, which emboldens its votaries, with daring front and unhallowed step, to enter the holy temple of justice and pluck from their seats the venerable personages, who, under the solemn sanction of the Constitution, are commissioned to officiate there—to guard that sacred compact with jealous vigilance—to dispense the laws with a steady and impartial hand—unmoved by the storms of faction, unawed by its powers, unseduced by its favors—shielding right and innocence from every attack—resisting and repressing violence from every quarter.

Thus " 'Tis from the triumph of that execrable doctrine that we may have to date the downfall of our government, and, with it, of the whole fabric of republican liberty." The fabric of republican liberty is a complex organization of power designed to safeguard the citizens against the factious partiality engendered by liberty, while empowering their government to withstand the confused vibrations endemic to the republican spirit.

To defend republican liberty one must attack the disorganization of governmental power, for the definition of despotism is the concentration of all the powers of government in one person or in one body. Now the right of the legislature to abolish the judges at pleasure destroys the independence of the judicial department and swallows it up in the impetuous vortex of legislative influence. The executive, moreover, deprived of so powerful an auxiliary, will not long survive. Thus the boundaries between departments will thenceforth be merely nominal, and there will no longer be more than one active and effective department.[5]

V   In the formation of our Constitution, there were certain governing principles, says Hamilton in the fourteenth number of his examination, where he expounds those formative principles governing our form of government.

In the *first* place it is a fundamental maxim of free government, he says, that the three great departments of power—legislative, executive, and judiciary—shall be essentially distinct and independent of one another. In most of our state constitutions, this principle has been very influential, but in the Constitution of the United States it has been particularly attended to. The Constitution of the United States, in order to give effect to it, has adopted a precaution peculiar to itself, in the provisions that forbid the legislature to vary in any way the compensation of the President or to diminish that of a judge.

Hamilton thus begins by stating a maxim fundamental in any government that is free, and pointing out that in the particular form of free government adopted for the United States particular attention was given to the maxim, and a peculiar precaution was provided in order to give it effect. In any free government, power must be departmentalized; in most of the states it has been; particularly in the United States has it been done most peculiarly by fortifying two of the departments against the assaults of the third.

In the *next* place Hamilton explains at length how the source of danger to liberty differs in two different forms of government, princely and popular. In a free form of government the chief source of danger to freedom is the chief department of power. The most powerful part of a free government is the part against which there is most need for precautions to safeguard freedom. But this is to restate Hamilton's point too generally; his emphasis is on how the difference between forms of government is relevant to the peculiar danger in that particular form of government under which Americans live. He calls it a principle equally sound (as sound as the fundamental maxim of free government first cited) that though in a government like that of Great Britain, having an hereditary chief with vast prerogatives, the danger to liberty, by the predominance of one department over the other, is on the side of the executive—yet in popular forms of government, this danger is chiefly to be apprehended from the legislative branch.

He depicts the potency of the legislative power. The power of legislation considered in its own nature, regardless of the form of the government, is the most comprehensive and potent of the three great subdivisions of sovereignty, for it is the will of the government: it prescribes universally the rule of action and the sanctions which are to enforce it—and it creates and regulates the public force and commands the public purse. Consider it if deposited in an elected representative of the people, as it must be in a free form of government. In every such government it is an organ of immense strength, for it has, in most cases, the body of the nation for its auxiliary and generally acts with all the momentum of popular favor. But even so, in some free governments, that is, when there is an hereditary chief magistrate clothed with dazzling prerogatives and great patronage, there is a powerful counterpoise. This counterpoise is in most cases only sufficient to preserve the equilibrium of the government, but in some cases it is sufficient to incline the scale too much to its own side. By contrast, in the other species of free government, that is, in governments wholly popular or representative, there is no adequate counterpoise. This results from the spirit of every such government; what forms that spirit is confidence in the most numerous or legislative department and jealousy of the executive chief. Operating in the constitution of the executive, that jealousy causes this organ to be intrinsically feeble; and, withholding in the course of administration accessory means of force and influence, the jealousy is for the most part vigilant to continue the executive in a state of impotence. Thus, the result is that the legislative body in this species of government possesses additional resources of power and weight, while the executive is rendered much too weak for competition—almost too weak for self-defense.

Thus Hamilton begins by briefly pointing out that in a free government it is a fundamental maxim to departmentalize power—to render the legislative, executive, and judicial departments of power distinct and independent of each other. He says that in the United States Constitution particular attention was given to supporting this departmentalization by means of peculiar props for the two departments other than the legislative. He then explains at length that in the two different species of free government the requisite departmentalization is differently threatened, in the one case by the predominance of the executive, but in the other case, which is that of the United States, by the predominance of the legislature.

The dangers to equilibrium, which might seem at first glance to be evenly balanced, are not so—even apart from the particular relevance of one case to the problem in the United States. The legislative power in itself or by its nature is the power most comprehensive and potent. In a free government, at least a share in the legislative power must belong to a popular representative body: even in the species of free government in which it is not the institution characteristic of the government (characteristic though it may be of the freedom that pervades the country), it is mostly as potent as the executive; and in the species of free government in which it *is* the institution characteristic of the government, it is always at least as strong as and is sometimes even stronger than the executive. In a free government it takes powerful props for the other departments to resist the predominating power of the legislature. It might even seem that the only adequate counterweight is an hereditary chief magistrate clothed with dazzling prerogatives and great patronage—even though this might threaten sometimes to be excessive.

But there is, *finally,* a third principle, not less well founded than the other two, which may give some solid foundation for those who hope to secure durable liberty through governments wholly popular or representative. It is no accident that the chief contending species of government are two, namely monarchical and republican. The practical alternatives are, on the one hand, the dangerous predominance of the princely executive power or, on the other hand, the dangerous predominance of the popular legislative power—for the last of the powers is the least: the judicial, that is, cannot predominate. The third principle is that the judiciary is naturally the weakest of the three departments.

A free government is a departmentalized government; it tends to be menaced by legislative predominance, and it may be menaced by executive predominance, but it cannot be menaced by judicial predominance. Let a government be laid down on departmentalized lines, then regardless of what further specifications differentiate its form from another form, its judiciary will be its weakest department—by nature. By nature the legislative is strongest. The sources of strength to the legislative branches have been briefly delineated, Hamilton reminds his reader. This brief delineation conceded that positive arrangements in some cases may counteract the natural primacy of the legislative department, but when the natural primacy of the legislative is overcome by positive arrangements, it is only to give positive primacy to the department that is second in strength by nature. The executive is evidently the second in strength. The legislative is the will of the government and prescribes universally the rule of action and the sanctions to enforce the rule, while the executive has several active powers, but the judiciary can ordain nothing. The legislative commands the public purse and creates and regulates the public force, while the executive directs the public force and dispenses honors and emoluments. The judiciary, by contrast, commands neither the purse nor the sword and has scarcely any patronage; its functions are not active; its main province is to declare the meaning of the laws. Laws are ordinarily made by the legislature, and even the extraordinary making of law is not the province of the judiciary. Moreover, even for the execution of its decisions the judiciary in extraordinary cases must look to the executive for aid.

The judiciary is an intermediary in its function, an extreme in its lack of strength. Its chief strength is in the veneration which it is able to inspire by the wisdom and rectitude of its judgments. Its chief strength is inseparable from its characteristic lack of strength: whatever strength it has, it derives from the veneration it inspires; if only from ambition, it must display wisdom and rectitude in its judgments. In the weakest department of power, interest most coincides with duty. The characteristic goodness of the judiciary is the patient exercise of wisdom and rectitude in judgment. This character of the judiciary clearly indicates that it is not only the weakest of the three departments of power, but also, as regards the security and preservation of civil liberty, by far the safest.

The weakest department is the safest; it is least dangerous both to the others and to the citizens. In a conflict with the other departments, it will be happy if it can defend itself—to annoy them is beyond its power. And in vain would it singly attempt enterprises against the rights of the citizen—the other departments could quickly arrest its arm and punish its temerity. Acting alone it is no danger; it could be a danger only by acting in subservience to one of the more active and powerful organs of government. The true and best guard against the judiciary's becoming an effectual instrument of oppression in the only way it can, in combination with one of the more active and powerful organs, is a complete independence from each and both of them. Its dependence on either will imply and involve a subservience to the views of the department on which it shall depend; its independence of both will render it a powerful check upon the others and a precious shield to the rights of person and property. Safety and liberty are therefore inseparably connected with the real and substantial independence of the courts and judges.

These were the governing principles in the formation of our Constitution, Hamilton concludes. They suggest the highest motives of constitutional policy against the construction which places the existence of the judges at the mercy of the legislature, for they instruct us that to prevent a concentration of powers, which is the essence of despotism, it is essential that the departments among which they shall be distributed should be effectually independent of each other—but it is impossible to reconcile this independence with a right in any one or two of them to annihilate at discretion the organs of the other. It would require a more express provision, susceptible of no other interpretation, to confer on one branch of the government an authority so dangerous to the others, in opposition to the strong presumptions which arise from the care taken in the Constitution, in conformity with the fundamental maxims of free governments, to establish and preserve the reciprocal and complete independence of the respective branches, first by a separate organization of the departments, next by a precise definition of the powers of each, and lastly by precautions to secure to each a permanent support.[6]

An express provision would be required to counteract the strong
presumptions that arise from interpreting the Constitution in conformity with the fundamental maxims of free government. As evidence that
he is not imposing something on the Constitution but only giving an exposition of the principles which inform the document, Hamilton in the next
number of the series goes on to consider *The Federalist*, in particular the
general discussion of the separation of powers (Numbers 47 through 51)
and the discussion of the judicial part of the proposed government (Numbers 78 through 82). Quoting extensively from *The Federalist*, Hamilton
paraphrases and summarizes the passages he quotes.[7]

This number of Hamilton's examination as "Lucius Crassus," calling in
the testimony of *The Federalist*, begins with these words:

> It is generally understood that the Essays under the title of the Feder-
> alist, which were published in New York, while the plan of our present
> Federal Constitution was under the consideration of the people, were
> principally written by two persons who had been members of the con-
> vention which devised that plan, and whose names are subscribed to
> the instrument containing it. [A note identifies the two persons alluded
> to: "James Madison, now Secretary of State. Alexander Hamilton, for-
> merly Secretary of the Treasury."] In these essays the principles ad-
> vanced in the last number of this examination are particularly stated
> and strongly relied upon, in defence of the proposed Constitution; from
> which it is a natural inference that they had influenced the views with
> which the plan was digested. The full force of this observation will be
> best perceived by a recurrence to the work itself; but it will appear
> clearly enough from the following detached passages.

And it ends with these:

> whatever motives may have subsequently occurred to bias the impres-
> sions of the one or the other of the persons alluded to, the situation
> in which they wrote exempts both from the suspicion of an intention
> to misrepresent in this particular. Indeed a course of argument more
> accommodating to the objections of the adversaries of the Constitu-
> tion would probably have been preferred as most politic, if the truth,
> as conceived at the time, would have permitted a modification. More
> trouble would have been avoided by saying: "The Legislature will have
> a complete control over the judges, by the discretionary power of re-
> ducing the number of those of the supreme court, and of abolishing
> the existing judges of the inferior courts, by the abolition of the courts

themselves." But this pretension is a novelty reserved for the crooked ingenuity of after discoveries.[8]

Having so dealt with Madison, he turns within a fortnight to Jefferson. The next number of Hamilton's examination of Jefferson's same Message to Congress exhibits a passage from Jefferson's own *Notes on Virginia* which "fully recognizes these several important truths": "that the tendency of our governments is towards a CONCENTRATION of the POWERS of the different departments in the LEGISLATIVE BODY; that such a CONCENTRATION is precisely the DEFINITION of DESPOTISM, and that an effectual *barrier* ought to exist . . . that officers during *good behavior* are independent of their Legislatures for their continuance in office." Jefferson, it seems, makes innovations on his own doctrines as well as on our Constitution. A free form of government requires that power be departmentalized. Formal provision in the constitution that there be departmentalization of power is of itself ineffectual for preserving departmental independence. The form of government may be subverted and converted into tyranny if one department in effect even though not in form concentrates all powers in itself. To prevent this there must be formal provision of barriers that can make departmental independence effectual. But even such barriers may be made mere ineffectual forms unless they are interpreted in accordance with the truths effectual for durable liberty, which are sometimes impolitic to emphasize. Among such, is the truth that the rule of law must be given effect by placing the interpretation of law in men whose occupancy of their office endures even though their interpretations antagonize the popular representatives. Under the Constitution judges are responsible to other men for their execution of the law, for they may be removed from office by the men elected to the legislature, but this is permitted only in accordance with the solemn procedure of impeachment provided by the fundamental law.[9]

vii   In the next number of his examination of the President's message, Hamilton continued his discussion of the judiciary department. He did so because of a speech in the House of Representatives (by William B. Giles) which not only repeated the old arguments but made a new one. The new position is this: every office is holden of the President, that is, every officer is removable at the pleasure of the President unless the tenure of his office is particularly excepted—and this is the reason for the clause of the Constitution enabling the judges to hold their offices during good behavior; the clause therefore restricts only the executive, while the legislature is left entirely free to remove any officers by abolishing their offices.

Earlier in the course of this debate, the advocates of the repealing law had denied the right of the courts to keep the legislature within its constitutional bounds by pronouncing laws which transgress them inoperative, and now by the new position the advocates of the repealing law furnish this debate with a second example of a doctrine contrary to every republican idea. First a seat of constitutional judgment independent of the legislature was to be swept away, and now the independence of the judiciary is to be entirely subverted by a dangerous foreign position on executive power. Violation of the Constitution thus is boldly justified by those who, having noisily promulgated popular tenets, are moving to concentrate the powers of the several departments of government. Had the sentiment of Giles been uttered by a Federalist, says Hamilton, the cry of monarchy would have resounded: loudly would it have been proclaimed that the mask was thrown aside in a glaring attempt to transform the servants of the people into the supple tools of presidential ambition. But now, to serve a party purpose, the dangerous position is avowed without a scruple by the party of popularity.[10]

The position is not correct, and by its nature it demands the indignant reprobation of every real republican. In the theory of all the American constitutions, offices are holden of the government—in other words, of the people through the government. Officers are not the chief executive's officers merely because he appoints them, even when he may remove them. Both these acts suppose merely an instrumentality of the organ, from the necessity or expediency of the people's acting in such case by an agent; they do not suppose the substitution of the agent for the people as the object of the fealty or allegiance of the officer.

An indication of this is the constitutional designation of, and oath for, officers. The Constitution everywhere uses the language "Officers of the United States"—as if to denote the relation between the officer and the sovereignty, as if to exclude the dangerous pretension that he is the mere creature of the executive. Accordingly he is to take an oath to support "the Constitution"—that is, he takes an oath of fidelity to the government but no oath of any kind to the President. The American theory of government is popular, not princely like the British; American officers are public servants, not a king's ministers; American sovereignty is vested in the government collectively, not in a monarch in whom the majesty of the nation is understood to reside, and who is emphatically the fountain of honor, and to whom allegiance is due. In our Constitution the President is not the sovereign, but it is of the sovereignty, strictly and technically speaking, that a public officer holds his office.

Hence the basis of the argument fails in point of fact; and its principle suggests the opposite conclusion—that the condition of good behavior is obligatory on the whole government and ought to operate as a barrier against *any* authority by which the displacement may be directly or indirectly effected. The claim that all offices are holden of the President, which might otherwise appear to be a war cry for monarchy, is in these circumstances a mask for party, a means by which those who dominate the legislature may justify their incursions upon the independence of the judiciary, and thus effect a displacement of the judges indirectly.[11]

The partisans in the legislature operate not only by aggressive indirect executive action; they also operate by making a defensive claim: they allege that the doctrine which would restrain the legislature from abolishing judicial offices, held during good behavior, would equally restrain the legislature from abolishing offices held during pleasure. But this is not true, says Hamilton, who explains why the two things stand on different ground.

As to offices held *during pleasure,* Hamilton makes three points. Because an officer during pleasure is a tenant at the will of the government, his right is not infringed when his tenure of office is discontinued by the government—either by the executive organ's removing him from office or by the legislative organ's abolishing his office. Furthermore, because the executive has a qualified negative on the enactment of legislation, his unwillingness to exercise his prerogative to remove officers is, as a general rule, not overcome by the legislature's willingness to do so by abolishing an office. And finally, because the executive is subordinate to the law in all cases which are not particularly excepted, the legislature has authority to remove an officer during pleasure by abolishing his office. These three different considerations reconcile the *legislative* authority to *abolish* with the prerogative of the *chief executive* to *remove* and with the temporary right of *individuals* to *hold.* And therefore there is no reason against the exercise of such an authority, nothing to form an exception to the general competence of the legislative power to provide for the public welfare.

As to the *judges,* however, the case is very different. For various and weighty reasons, no inference will apply to judicial officers that is drawn from the power of the legislature as to other officers. In the *first* place the most persuasive motives of public policy, the safety of liberty itself, require that in order to maintain effectually the separation between the several departments, the judges shall be independent of the legislative body. But there is *also* a clear constitutional indication of intent to guard their independence against the legislature: the provision that their compensation shall not be diminished. Indeed, there is more than an indication: there is an express declaration that they shall hold their offices during good behavior—

hold them, that is, upon a condition dependent on themselves; and this is repugnant to the hypothesis that they shall hold at the mere pleasure of others. *Moreover,* provisions which profess to confer rights on individuals are always entitled to a liberal interpretation in support of the rights and ought not, without necessity, to receive an interpretation subversive of them. *Finally,* provisions respecting the organization of a coordinate branch of the government ought to be construed so as to render it stable and effective—rather than weak, precarious, and dependent.[12]

In America there is a *special* need for construing the provisions of our Constitution respecting governmental organization so as to render the judiciary stable and effective, rather than weak, precarious, and dependent. The framers of that Constitution intended to prop the independence of our judges beyond the precautions which have been adopted in England with respect to judges. This is plain from the provisions respecting compensation, and the intention apparent in this particular is an argument that the same spirit may have governed other provisions.

Hamilton looks at the British statute of the 13th of William III (1700), which is alleged to be the model from which the framers of our Constitution copied the provisions for the independence of our judiciary. Now it is certainly true that from this source is borrowed the idea of the tenure of office during good behavior which is found in several of our American constitutions. The framers of our federal system did not, however, mean to confine themselves to their source. The framers looked to the British statute to be sure—but not *only* to the British statute. The British statute was not so much a model, to be viewed and copied, as it was a source of materials from which to make more effective machinery for American use. Hence the United States Constitution contains a provision for the restraint of the legislative discretion as to judicial compensation, whereas the British constitution lacks this provision. And hence also the British constitution contains a provision which, although imitated in some of the state governments, was omitted from the United States Constitution: the provision for the removal of the judges by the executive, on the application of the two branches of the legislature. Hamilton fortifies his construction of the Constitution by a double interpretation of this provision respecting removal of judges—arguing on the grounds both of its omission from the United States Constitution and of its insertion in the British statute.

The difference in the legal provisions with respect to the tenure of judges is suggestive of the difference in the theory of the two governments. And however it may seem in theory, in fact the difference in the spirit of the two governments would tend to render the independence of the judges more secure under the British statute than it would be in this country upon the construction which allows to Congress the right to abolish. Hamilton explains why the British, while they have need to prop the independence of the judges against the executive, have much less need than do the Americans to prop the independence of the judges against the legislative department. In the British system, because there are more powerful motives for jealousy of executive influence, the legislative department is less likely to enter into improper combination with the executive to invade the judiciary; and because there are more powerful means for executive resistance to legislative control, the executive department is less likely to concur in legislative measures hostile to the independence of the judges. In America the legislative department has weaker motives for jealousy of executive influence, while the executive department has weaker means of resistance to legislative control; and therefore the legislative department is likelier to enter into improper combination with the executive to invade the judiciary, and the executive department is likelier to concur in legislative measures hostile to the independence of the judges. Americans need, as Britons do not, props for securing the independence of the judges against the legislative as well as against the executive power.[13]

XIII
Partisanship, Partiality, and Popular Liberty

The courts are supposed to be the impartial part of government. We have just examined Hamilton's discussion of how legislative partisanship can endanger that independence which makes it possible for the judicial part of government to exercise its powers properly. Now we shall examine Hamilton's discussion of how executive partisanship can employ the powers of the courts as a means of endangering the people's liberties.

That the courts would be intimidated by the legislature was not the only danger in America. There was also a danger that courts would be subservient to the executive. Energy in the executive is not the only characteristic in the definition of good government. Hamilton spoke to this point before the New York State Supreme Court in February 1804 in the case of *The People vs. Croswell*.

The case arose as follows: By means of "a few wholesome prosecutions," the triumphant followers of Jefferson sought to silence vehement attacks upon them in the press. Harry Croswell, editor of *The Wasp*, a small newspaper in upstate New York, attacked Jefferson for having paid a pamphleteer named Callender "for calling Washington a traitor, a robber, and a perjurer—for calling Adams a hoary headed incendiary; and for most grossly slandering the private characters of men who, he well knew, were virtuous." Jefferson had in fact supported Callender's pen, but the Jeffersonian attorney general of New York brought proceedings against Croswell for seditious libel. Croswell was convicted. He appealed his conviction, with Hamilton as his counsel in the argument before the Supreme Court of the state. (It should be added that the court, being divided, did not in the end reverse the verdict, but members of the state legislature had come to hear the argument of Hamilton, and Hamilton's position in the case was very soon enacted into law by them.)

One of the judges in the *Croswell* case, James Kent, later said of Hamilton's oral argument on this occasion that "a more able and eloquent argument was perhaps never heard in any court." Three documents give some indication of what Hamilton said: there is a report printed in a pamphlet by G. and R. Waite, a review of which complained not only of its incompleteness but of its exhibiting Hamilton to the world as a man "speaking neither sense nor grammar"; there is a set of notes taken by James Kent; and there is the text of fifteen propositions on the law of libel read by Hamilton in summation at the close of argument, a copy of which he gave to Kent. As we attempt to understand what Hamilton was arguing, it may be best not to ignore which source we are relying on for the various statements attributed him.[1]

The two great points, according to Kent's notes on Hamilton's argument, are these: can the truth be given in evidence, and are the jury to judge of the intent and the law. "The first point is more embarrassed, the last clear."[2]

Hamilton's own text starts from the proposition that the liberty of the press consists in the right to publish with impunity truth with good motives for justifiable ends, even though it reflect on governmental magistracy or individuals.

On behalf of this definition, he argues, in Waite's version, that unless it be allowed, the privilege of canvassing men, and our rulers, is excluded—even though it is impossible to canvass measures without the right of looking to men. It is essential not only to say that a measure is bad, but to hold up the author to the people, so that he may be removed from the seat of power in this our free and elective government. If this is not to be done, then in vain will the voice of the people be raised against the inroads of tyranny—for if a party but get into power, they may go on from step to step and fix themselves firmly in their seats despite the canvassing of their measures. But if the power be allowed, under the qualifications which have been mentioned, then the liberty for which Hamilton contends will operate as a salutary check.

In Kent's version Hamilton says that it is impracticable to discuss measures and not men. Why examine measures, but to show them to be bad and to show the authors, so that the people may correct turpitude by removing men. There is no other way to preserve liberty and to bring down a tyrannical faction. If measures alone might be discussed, and not also men, then good men would be silent; corruption and tyranny would go step by step in usurpation until nothing is left worth speaking or writing or acting for.

Hamilton's text sums up this part of his argument in its second proposition: the allowance of this right is essential to the preservation of free government; the disallowance of it is fatal.

Waite reports Hamilton's arguing further: it is said that, as no man rises at once into high office, every opportunity of canvassing his qualities and qualifications is afforded without recourse to the press—that his first election ought to stamp the seal of merit on his name. But to say this is to forget how often the hypocrite goes from stage to stage of public fame, under false array, and how often when men obtain the last object of their wishes, they change from what they seemed to be. Men most zealous of the people's rights have become their most deadly oppressors when placed on the highest seat of power, so it becomes necessary to observe the actual conduct of those who have been thus raised up. And Kent notes his saying that men are not to be trusted implicitly in elevated stations, for the humble lovers of the people, full of hypocrisy and cant, very often change when they arrive at power and become deadly enemies and persecutors of the people.

Hamilton conceded in his argument that the right might be abused and that its exercise was subject to control by the tribunals of justice. Waite reports his saying that he does not say there ought to be an unbridled license or that the characters of men who are good will naturally tend eternally to support themselves. He alludes to Washington and says that to put the best and the worst on the same level is something that cannot be endured. He says that the liberty of publishing truth for which he contends—truth published with good motives and for justifiable ends, even though it reflect on government, magistrates, or private persons—is liberty under the restraint of our tribunals: when this liberty is exceeded, let the courts interpose and punish.

And Kent notes his saying that while he contends for the right of publishing truth with good motive, though the censure light on government or individuals, nonetheless he reprobates the novel, the visionary, the pestilential doctrine of an unchecked press. If the doctrine of an unchecked press prevails, this will be an ill-fated country, for such a press is the pestilence of our country. Even the best man on earth, who is now removed from the reach of calumny, felt it. Single drops of water will wear out even adamant. Hamilton does not maintain or contend for this terrible liberty of an unchecked press.

Hamilton's summary propositions assert that truth should not be excluded from evidence in deciding whether the press has committed libel, but his ninth proposition concedes that the truth should not be decisive of itself. Those with bad intent might commit libel by means of printing truth. While the truth or falsehood is in the nature of things a material ingredient in determining the character of libel, it may not always be decisive because truth may be abused. Assertions that are true may still admit of a malicious and mischievous intent, which may constitute a libel.[3]

ii After asserting in the second proposition that free government requires the liberty of the press for which he contends, Hamilton goes on in his third proposition to assert that its abuse is to be guarded against by subjecting the exercise of it to the animadversion and control of the tribunals of justice, but that this control cannot safely be entrusted to a permanent body of magistracy and requires the effectual cooperation of court and jury.

Waite reports his questioning whether it is right that a permanent body of men, appointed by the executive and in some degree always connected with it, should exclusively have the power of deciding on what shall constitute a libel on our rulers. It cannot be denied that every permanent body of men is more or less liable to be influenced by the spirit of the existing administration. Such a body may be liable to corruption and may be inclined to lean over toward party modes. Though our judges as individuals may be interested in the general welfare, yet if they enter into the views of the government, their power may be converted into the engine of oppression. Hence, it must be with the jury to decide on the intent—they must in certain cases be permitted to judge of the law and pronounce on the combined matter of law and of fact.

And Kent notes that Hamilton is for having the check on the press deposited not in a permanent body of magistrates, the court, but in an occasional and fluctuating body, the jury chosen by lot. Judges might enter into the views and spirit of government or may extend the construction and law of libels, and so the jury ought to judge on a combined view of both law and fact. He says that he is no strenuous advocate for the trial by jury in civil cases, but in criminal cases it is the palladium of our rights.

The lessons of English experience are doubly instructive. In the first place, as Waite reports, the trial by jury in the system of English jurisprudence has been considered as the palladium of public and private liberty and in all the political disputes of that country has been deemed the barrier to secure the subjects from oppression. And as Kent notes, the trial by jury in England is cherished as a bulwark against the tyranny and oppression of government, but the jury could not be this security if they didn't have the right to judge of both intent and law.

In the second place, as Waite reports, to mingle this power is still more necessary here than in England. The person who appoints in England is hereditary and cannot alone attack the judiciary but must be united with the two houses of Lords and of Commons in assailing the judges. With us, however, there is a vibration of party, and as one side or the other prevails, so the judges whom they nominate will be of their class and temperament. If you ask any man, however ignorant of the principles of government, who are those who constitute the judiciary, he will tell you that they are the favorites of those at the head of affairs. Thus the independence of judges according to the theory of this our free government is not so well secured as it is in England. We have reasons for apprehension which do not apply to them; and on whatever side a man may be, it is in his interest to have the question settled so as to uphold the power of the jury—consistently with liberty, however, and also with legal and judicial principles, fairly and rightly understood. And, as Kent notes Hamilton's arguing, in the theory of our government the executive and the legislative are one by means of election—how then are our judges to be independent? Here they are not so independent of the legislative and executive as they are in England, and we therefore have more necessity to cling to the right of trial by jury as our greatest safety. The very reasons for the participation of the jury at all require that the jury's part not be confined to determining whether the defendant in fact has published what he has been accused of publishing.

Hence, after Hamilton's third proposition asserts the need for the tribunals of justice to contain participants who are not permanent magistrates, the fourth proposition goes on to assert that confining the jury to the mere question of publication and to the application of terms—leaving them without the right of inquiry into the intent or tendency and thus reserving to the court (that is, the judge) the exclusive right of pronouncing upon the construction, tendency, and intent of the alleged libel—is calculated to render nugatory the function of the jury, thus enabling the court to make a libel of any writing, however innocent or commendable.

It is from the point of view of the common law that Hamilton considers the powers of the jury in such cases of alleged libel. He goes on in subsequent propositions to assert (fifth) that by the general rule of criminal law the intent constitutes the crime and is an inference of fact to be drawn by the jury, and (sixth) that if there are exceptions to this rule, they are confined to cases where not only the principal fact but also its circumstances can be and are specifically defined by statute or judicial precedents. He says

(thirteenth) that in the general distribution of powers in our system of jurisprudence, the cognizance of law belongs to the court, of fact to the jury;
and when, as is always true in civil cases, law and fact are not blended, the
power of the court is absolute and exclusive—but in criminal cases, since
law and fact are there always blended, the power of deciding both of them
is entrusted to the jury. This is for reasons of a political and peculiar nature;
it is for the security of life and liberty.[4]

iii   There is a kind of return to first principles when Hamilton makes
his argument on behalf of adhering to common-law principles, contending that the general rule of the common law is that the jury has the
right to judge intent in the blend of fact and law which is always present in a
criminal case, and contending that truth, though not by itself decisive, is an
ingredient in determining the character of a libel. He asserts that the contrary doctrine is inconsistent with the original principles of the common
law as enforced by statutory provisions and by some leading precedents.

   Some English precedent is found by Hamilton's opponents to adduce
to the contrary. In particular the attorney general of New York cites Lord
Mansfield. Waite reports Hamilton's comment. Hamilton confesses himself
happy to hear that the freedom of the English is allowed—that a nation
with king, lords, and commons, can be free. He does not mean, however, to
enter into a comparison between the freedom of the two countries, having
mentioned the matter only because the attorney general has taken vast pains
to celebrate Lord Mansfield's character. Hamilton does not mean to detract
from the exalted fame of that truly great man, Lord Mansfield—if he had
his faults, he had his virtues. But Mansfield's sentiments were not those fit
for a republic. Never until now has Hamilton heard that Mansfield's reputation was high in republican estimation; never until now has Hamilton
considered him a model whom republicans would imitate. Lord Mansfield
does indeed seem to have been the parent of the doctrines on the other side,
but it was with some self-contradiction that Mansfield contended for those
doctrines, and he might have had some biases not extremely favorable to
liberty. Hamilton therefore says he trusts that those doctrines of the other
side for which Lord Mansfield contended will be proved to be the doctrines
neither of the common law nor of this country. Lord Mansfield's departure from common-law principles is a menace to liberty generally, and it is
especially a menace to the republican species of liberty.

   Kent reports Hamilton's thus defining liberty: that country is free where
the people have a representation in the government, so that no law can pass

without their consent, and where they have a trial by jury. Immediately before mentioning Lord Mansfield, according to Kent, Hamilton compliments the other party especially on their strange and unexpected compliments on the freedom of the English nation—Hamilton agrees with them that the English are a free, a gloriously free people; and, after speaking of Lord Mansfield, Hamilton remarks that we have gone further than the English into the popular principle, and he joins his prayers with the opposite counsel (if indeed, he says, they do pray) that the experiment with us may be successful. But if we depart from common-law principles, he warns, we degenerate into anarchy, and the transition from anarchy is to despotism—to an armed master.

Common-law principles, like principles of representation, support English liberty by limiting monarchy. Departure from common-law principles threatens the English with imminent despotism. Common-law principles, like principles of representation, support American liberty by preventing anarchy. Departure from common-law principles threatens the Americans with eventual despotism. What, then, is this danger to republican liberty? [5]

Hamilton points out, in Waite's report, that the Sedition Act made truth admissible in evidence. He suggests, in Kent's notes, that it ought to be distinctly known whether or not Jefferson is guilty of so foul an act as the one alleged of him, and immediately after this he speaks of Washington. A character so bright and pure as General Washington's, he says, is not only a source of honor to our nation, giving glory to it; it is most useful also as a pattern of virtue to us and our posterity, serving as a model to be imitated. Washington headed our armies with perseverance and success, and he administered our civil government unmoved by calumny and faction. A popular spirit of inquiry only revealed the splendor of his character; to spread the truth about his character was only to increase its utility as a model for imitation. Washington, unmoved by calumny, was unmoved as well by faction; he was thereby himself an impediment to the baneful influence of the specific evil of republican government. [6]

Liberty, a means to security, is also a menace to security and thus tends to its own destruction. Liberty needs to be secured against itself. To speak of "durable liberty" is to name a problem. The character of Washington, the glory of the nation, was most useful to the nation as a pattern of virtue to us and our posterity. In order to secure the blessings of liberty to ourselves and our posterity, we ordained and established the Constitution, says its Preamble, which, presenting the several intentions that informed the ordaining and establishment of the Constitution, mentions ourselves together with our posterity only in connection with the intention to secure the blessings of liberty. The character of Washington helped to ordain and establish, and properly set in motion, that fundamental law which was designed to mitigate the calamitous effects of a republican tendency toward what poisons the blessings of liberty itself.[7]

Immediately after the praise of Washington, Kent notes, Hamilton called the tendency to faction "the Evil Genius of Republics . . . the Poison—the Pestilence that destroys them." (At this point in his notes Kent remarks: "This argument and Speech of General H. was a master Piece of Pathetic, impassioned & sublime Eloquence—It was probably *never surpassed* and made the deepest Impression—I never heard him so great.")

Waite reports Hamilton's saying that all great men have considered a spirit of faction to be the natural disease of our form of government; therefore we ought to be careful to restrain that spirit, and, indeed, we have been careful that when one party comes in, it shall not be able to break down and bear away the others. But if this be not so, in vain have we made constitutions, and we must go into anarchy and from thence to despotism and to a master. Never, he says, can tyranny be introduced into this country by arms. These can never get rid of a popular spirit of inquiry. The only way to crush it down is by a servile tribunal. An army never can do it because the spirit of the country, with arms in hand and disciplined as a militia, would render it impossible. No, it is not thus that the liberty of this country is to be destroyed. It is to be subverted only by a pretense of adhering to all the forms of law, while breaking down the substance of our liberties.

Kent notes that in arguing for the applicability of the common law to the United States, Hamilton digressed into an impassioned, eloquent address on the danger to our liberties—not from a few provisional armies, but from dependent judges, from selected juries, from stifling the press and the voice of leaders and patriots. We ought, says Hamilton, to "*resist—resist—resist*" till we hurl the demagogues and tyrants from their imagined thrones. The most dangerous instrument for destroying American liberty is not anything like murderous Hessian soldiers sent by a Hanoverian monarch; it is rather courts of justice perverted by partisan control. Murder rouses to vengeance—it awakens sympathy and it spreads alarm; but the most dangerous and destructive tyranny is one that sacrifices and crushes individuals by the perverted forms and mask of law. A corrupt court—dependent judges and a packed jury—is the way to cut off and to silence the leaders and real friends of the people. The common law must inform the interpretation of the Constitution, which would otherwise be deformed by faction. Unless the words "crimes and misdemeanors" in the Constitution of the United

States are defined by common law, a faction may make any political tenet or any indiscretion a crime or pretext to impeach, convict, and drive from office the judges of the federal courts. The Constitution uses many words and ideas having reference to the common law—such as "*habeas corpus*"—so that if the common law were not applicable to it, then the Constitution of the United States would be melted away or borne down by faction.[8]

XIV
Return to First Principles

Faction—or, more politically, partisanship—is what makes it necessary for the courts to be independent. The judicial department of the government is distinctive as a seat of independent judgment. The men who officiate there, set apart to be above partiality or partisanship, must in some cases work in cooperation with jurors, who are not representatives but rather are representative members of the people, directly participating in government; and the rule under which these men operate must not suppress critical truths about their rulers, arising from the people.

The argument in the Lucius Crassus papers on behalf of the permanent tenure of judges and the argument in the Croswell case on behalf of the active cooperation of nonpermanent juries were both campaigns in Hamilton's struggle to preserve the courts of justice from what he saw as a party of subversion.

The leader of that party, Jefferson, in his second inaugural address as President, identified the great weapon of the party struggle: "The artillery of the press has been levelled against us," said Jefferson. Hamilton's political career began with a recurrence to first principles, in which he took first to the press and then to the field. Using "the artillery of liberty," and then forming a company of field artillery under his command, he fought against despotic departure from a principle of liberty—the principle of popular participation in the legislature through the institution of representation. Hamilton's career concluded with another recurrence to first principles: he fought against partisan attempts to demolish the citadel of liberty, to silence the artillery of liberty, and to employ the judiciary as an engine of despotism. Defending the press against this assault, Hamilton urged Americans not to stray from another principle of liberty—the principle of popular participation in the judiciary through the institution of the jury. Between that beginning and conclusion, each a fight by Hamilton on behalf of institutional safeguards against abuse of governmental power, he labored to ensure that governmental power would be institutionally available for swift and steady use. Thus the central work of his career, the struggle on behalf of institutions that would secure effective power for governmental use, was surrounded by his struggles on behalf of institutions to secure the safety of the people against abuse of governmental power.

ii   Part of the struggle was the writing of *The Federalist*. In *The Federalist* the review of the constitution concludes with a consideration of the several parts of the government; this concludes with a consideration of the judiciary, and this in turn concludes with a consideration of trial by jury; to this, Number 83 is entirely devoted.[1]

The discussion of trial by jury in *The Federalist* takes the form of a reply to an objection, the objection most successful in the state of *The Federalist's* immediate audience and perhaps in several others. This objection is that the proposed Constitution does not provide for trial by jury in civil cases. A jury is required to condemn a man to loss of his life or of his personal liberty, but not of his property. Hamilton explains the reason why it is, that though criminal cases must be tried by juries, civil cases may be tried by juries or may not be.[2]

For his own part, Hamilton says, the more he has seen of the operation of the institution of trial by jury the more reason he has found to esteem it highly. It is in most cases, under proper regulations, an excellent method of determining questions of property, so that on this account alone it would be entitled to a constitutional provision in its favor—if it were possible to determine limits for it. But there would be great difficulty in framing well a constitutional requirement of trial by jury in civil cases.

The great difficulty arises partly from the very great diversity among the states with respect to their use of trial by jury, and Hamilton says much about this; but even if the differences among the states could easily be harmonized, there would still be difficulties because there are many cases best *not* tried by jury.

This is particularly so in cases which concern the public peace with foreign nations, that is, in most cases where the question turns wholly on the laws of nations. Of this nature are all prize causes, and there are others. From lack of knowledge juries will be incompetent to investigate, and from their susceptibility to impressions of a certain undescribed sort, they will not have regard to what is politic. The effect of an improper commitment to juries of cases turning on the laws of nations would, therefore, be a diminution in national safety.

There are also cases completely domestic that are best not tried by jury. Improper commitment to juries of cases of equity would diminish the generality of law, making law less different from decree and thus less of a safeguard against oppression. It would also require juries to handle long and complex investigations to which by their very spirit they are incompetent, thus diminishing the efficacy of trials. Thus it would also in the end undermine the institution of jury trial itself.[3]

A constitutional provision for jury trial in civil cases, had it been included in the plan, would have expressed either too little or too much. Suppose that jury trial in civil cases could be constitutionally provided in a manner suitable for the present. All reasonable men concede that it ought not to obtain in all cases. Suppose that the practice in New York State could be established for the United States. Even in this state, Hamilton for his own part is convinced, it might be advantageously extended to some cases to which it does not apply at present and might as advantageously be abridged in others. The practice that has seemed suitable to others in the past does not seem suitable to Hamilton in the present. Suppose, however, that this state's practice of jury trial in civil cases were perfectly suitable for the present: even so, with the relentless passing of time, the changes which are continually happening in the affairs of society may in the future render a different mode of determining questions of property preferable in many cases which are tried by jury now—as is suggested by the fact that there are examples of innovations which contract its ancient limits, in these states as well as in Great Britain. Thus, Hamilton suspects it to be in the nature of the thing impossible to fix the salutary point at which the operation of the institution ought to stop, and this strongly argues for leaving the matter to the discretion of the legislature.

The need for flexibility in this matter is now clearly understood in Great Britain, Hamilton says, and also in the state of Connecticut. As for the state of New York, he says, more encroachments have been made upon the trial by jury in this state since the revolution, despite a positive provision in the state constitution, than have happened in the same time either in Connecticut or Great Britain.[4]

Despite the great difficulty in making a constitutional provision for it, trial by jury in civil cases does have its excellence as a method for determining questions of property. This excellence is not, however, its alleged excellence as a safeguard against an oppressive exercise of the power of taxation.

In one respect trial by jury for this purpose in taxation is *useless*. It cannot influence the legislature in laying down the amount of the taxes to be paid or the objects upon which they are to be imposed or the rule by which they are to be apportioned. Furthermore, in respect to the mode of collection, trial by jury is *harmful*. It is an ineffective way for the government to meet the public exigencies; and it is also an inconvenience for individual citizens. This is because the course of a trial to recover taxes imposed on individuals is dilatory and often occasions an accumulation of costs more burdensome than the original sum of the tax to be levied. For this reason trial by jury is mostly out of use as a mode of collecting taxes under the state constitution of New York, being usually replaced by the more summary proceeding of distress and sale, as in cases of rent. Finally, in respect to the conduct of the officers who execute the revenue laws, trial by jury is *superfluous*. Security as to the conduct of the revenue officers will be afforded by the provision for trial by jury in criminal cases. This is because those who oppress the subject by willful abuse of public authority, and those officials who engage in extortion, commit offenses against the government for which they may be indicted and punished.

Trial by jury in civil cases is thus *not* excellent as a safeguard against oppression in the laying and collecting of *taxes*. Rather, the strongest argument in its favor is that it is a security against *corruption,* since one may suppose that there is always more time and better opportunity to tamper with a standing body of magistrates than with a jury summoned for the occasion.

The force of this consideration, it is true, is diminished by others. The sheriffs who summon ordinary juries and the clerks of courts who nominate special juries are themselves standing officers, who, acting individually, are more accessible to the touch of corruption than is the collective body of the judges; and it would be in the power of those sheriffs and clerks to select jurors who would serve the purpose as well as would a corrupted bench. Moreover, it would be easier to gain some of the jurors taken promiscuously from the public mass than to gain men who had been chosen by the government for their probity and good character.

But, nonetheless, making every deduction for these considerations, the trial by jury must still be a valuable check upon corruption, since it gives a double security: it makes it necessary to corrupt both court and jury. Where the jury have gone evidently wrong, the court will generally grant a new trial, and so it would rarely be of any use to practice upon the jury unless the court could be gained as well. And where the judges cannot by themselves alone determine causes, but must have the cooperation of a jury, there the judges will have fewer temptations to surmount in order to keep themselves from prostituting their office. Thus, by increasing the obstacles to success, this complicated agency discourages attempts to seduce the integrity of either the court or the jury.

However, even this admitted excellence of trial by jury in civil cases— its providing, that is, a security against corruption—does not outweigh the difficulty of framing a suitable constitutional provision for it.[5]

A constitutional provision for trial by jury *is* required, however, as a safeguard of *liberty*. But the excellence of trial by jury in *civil* cases appears to depend on circumstances foreign to the preservation of liberty. Hamilton doubts that trial by jury in civil cases is essential to liberty. Yet, although he cannot readily discern any inseparable connection between the existence of liberty and the trial by jury in civil cases, nonetheless he has always seen a connection between the existence of liberty and the trial by jury in *criminal* cases.

Arbitrary impeachments, arbitrary methods of prosecuting pretended offenses, and arbitrary punishments upon arbitrary convictions—these are the great engines of judicial despotism, and they all relate to criminal proceedings. The trial by jury in criminal cases, aided by habeas corpus, seems therefore to be alone concerned in the question. And the plan of the Convention provides for both of these most amply. It is in criminal cases alone that the trial by jury is constitutionally required to safeguard liberty.[6]

Hamilton mentions that one might examine to what extent jury trial in criminal cases deserves to be esteemed useful or essential in a representative republic, or how much more merit it may be entitled to as a defense against the oppressions of a hereditary monarch than as a barrier to the tyranny of popular magistrates in a popular government. But he mentions discussions of this kind only to say that they would be altogether superfluous or more curious than beneficial—since all are satisfied that the institution is useful and friendly to liberty. What he suggests is that though he highly esteems the institution of trial by jury, it *may* be less useful or essential as a safeguard to liberty in a government which is popular than in one which is princely. And he does say later on that particular constitutional provisions for safeguarding rights are, though useful, not as reliable for permanent effects as is the general "genius" of a government, its native spirit. Hamilton condemns as unreliable what is commonly affirmed about the efficacy of provisions for safety. In the next breath he condemns as well what is denied about the safety of provisions for efficacy: it is grating to hear, he says, that there is no security for liberty in a constitution which expressly establishes the trial by jury in criminal cases because it does not also do it in civil cases—when Connecticut, which has always been regarded as the Union's most popular state, has no constitutional provisional for either.[7]

iii   After concluding in Number 83 his review of the Constitution in *The Federalist*, Hamilton replies in Number 84 to miscellaneous objections which earlier did not fit in or were forgotten. He calls the first of these objections the most considerable, and to it he devotes as much of the paper as he gives to all the others put together: it is the objection that the plan contains no bill of rights. He introduces his discussion by pointing out that a bill of rights is absent from the constitutions of many of the states, among them New York, the state which provides his immediate audience and the constitution of which is praised by opponents of the proposed Constitution. After a few more remarks, Hamilton explains why it is good that a bill of rights was not added to the constitution proposed for the United States.[8]

The constitutions of the several states would seem to be in greater need of bills of rights than would the Constitution of the United States. But even the states, which have the regulation of every species of personal and private concerns, have no more need to attach to their constitutions a minute detail of particular rights reserved from government than does the Union, which is intended to regulate the merely general political interests of the nation. The truth is that both of them contain all that it is reasonable to desire in relation to their objects. A minute detail of particular rights, if applicable to either, would certainly apply far less to the merely general government than to state governments in a compound system; but in truth it does not apply at all to a popular system. When nothing is surrendered, nothing need be reserved; the people do not surrender their rights in a popular government as they do in a monarchy; in governments that are popular, therefore, bills of rights have no use like that for which they originated—as stipulations between kings and their subjects, abridgments of prerogative in favor of privilege, reservations of rights not surrendered to the prince. They do not apply to constitutions professedly founded upon the power of the people and executed by the people's immediate representatives and servants: here the people retain everything. No great benefit is lost by the absence of a bill of rights in America; in popular government a bill of rights is unnecessary.[9]

To add to the Constitution of the United States a bill of rights, in the sense and to the extent contended for, is not only unnecessary but would even be dangerous: its presence could do little good but might do much harm—by providing a pretext for claiming powers not granted. Indulgence of an injudicious zeal for bills of rights would give numerous handles to the doctrine of constructive powers.

Hamilton provides a specimen. Why, for instance, should it be said that the liberty of the press shall not be restrained—when no power is given by which such restrictions may be imposed? Such a provision would not confer a regulating power, but it would furnish, to men disposed to usurp, a plausible pretense for claiming such a power. They might say that the constitution ought not to be charged with the absurdity of providing against the abuse of an authority which was not given and that the provision against restricting the liberty of the press implies an intention to vest in the national government a power to prescribe proper regulations concerning it.[10]

A power to prescribe proper regulations concerning the press, if not vested in the national government, is, however, vested in the several state governments; should, then, the state governments be restrained by the state constitutions from restraining the liberty of the press? On the subject of the liberty of the press, much has been said, says Hamilton, but there is not a syllable concerning it in the state constitution of New York; this, however, does not make New York a poor sister in the family of states, for whatever has been said about it in the constitution of any other state amounts to nothing. And there is nothing to be said that amounts to anything: what does it signify to declare that "the liberty of the press shall be inviolably preserved," Hamilton asks; what *is* the liberty of the press—who can give it any definition which would not leave the utmost latitude for evasion? Hamilton says that he holds it to be impracticable, and he draws an inference from this impracticability of giving a tight definition of the liberty of the press: no solid basis for our rights is to be found in fine declarations about liberty inserted in a constitution; the only reliable security is public opinion and the general spirit of the people and of the government.[11]

The opponents of the proposed Constitution do not agree that an additional security is unnecessary. The opponents are somehow aware that the power to tax may be the power to destroy: it is said that duties may be laid upon publications so high as to amount to a prohibition. But the state legislatures cannot be utterly prohibited from taxing publications; and liberty is compatible with taxation of publications to some degree—newspapers are taxed in Great Britain, and yet the press nowhere enjoys greater liberty than in that country. The question of degree must depend on legislative discretion, which cannot be regulated by general declarations respecting the liberty of the press but can only be regulated by public opinion.

However fine the sound of the declaration, it would be quite as significant to declare that the government ought to be free, that taxes ought not to be excessive, and so on, as to declare that the liberty of the press ought not to be restrained. Those aphorisms which make the principal figure in several of our state bills of rights would sound much better in a treatise of ethics than in a constitution of government. And a better recognition of popular rights than volumes of those aphorisms is the statement in the Preamble to the United States Constitution that we the people of the United States, to secure the blessings of liberty to ourselves and our posterity, do ordain and establish this constitution for the United States of America. The Constitution of the United States is professedly founded upon the power of the people and is executed by the people's immediate representatives and servants. In the constitutional articulation of the fundamental structure and operation of governmental power, a preface professing that the people is the original and continuing source of governmental authority is a better recognition of popular rights than would be an addendum declaring fine aphorisms of ethics.[12]

But, the truth is, the Constitution is itself, in every rational sense and to every rational purpose, a bill of rights: the mode observed as to the order of declaring the rights of the citizens does not matter, if they are to be found in any part of the instrument which establishes the government. One object of a bill of rights is to declare and specify the political privileges of the citizens in the structure and administration of the government, thus comprehending various precautions for the public security; and another object of a bill of rights is to define certain immunities and modes of proceeding, relative to personal and private concerns. In the substantial meaning of a bill of rights, therefore, it is absurd to allege that it is not to be found in the work of the Convention. It may be said that it does not go far enough, though this would be hard to show, but it cannot properly be said that there is no such thing.

At the beginning of his reply to the objection that the proposed Constitution for the United States has no bill of rights, Hamilton first replied that the state constitution of New York has no bill of rights, and then he replied to rejoinders to this reply. One such rejoinder to which he replied was that the state constitution of New York, although it has no bill of rights prefixed to it, does contain in the body of it various provisions in favor of particular privileges and rights which in substance amount to the same thing. Hamilton's reply to this is that the body of the proposed Constitution for the United States also contains a number of such provisions. Independent of those which relate to the structure of the government, there are provisions regarding the following: judgment in cases of impeachment, habeas corpus, bills of attainder, ex post facto laws, titles of nobility, gifts from foreign rulers to officers, criminal trials, and treason.[13]

Hamilton, it seems, is not opposed to all particular provisions that protect against governmental power; some such provisions might provide the judiciary with handles by which to oppose men disposed to abuse or usurp power. One might go further than he for reasons he himself gives. Unless what might be called fine declarations are inserted into a constitution, perhaps it would be more difficult to make, or to make acceptable, authoritative pronouncements that form or confirm salutary public opinion and a sound general spirit in the people. Or would such words only provide the judiciary with handles that might serve as pretexts for judges who are disposed to usurp power by opposing men who are properly exercising power? On the other hand, would it be useless or dangerous for a constitution which has the regulation of every species of personal and private concerns to incorporate the definition of the liberty of the press given in the Croswell case by Hamilton? If it is to public opinion and the general spirit of the people and of the government that we must look for the only solid basis of all our rights, to what must we look for a solid basis of that opinion and of that spirit?

iv   Hamilton worked to effect a proper relation of part and whole in the government of America: he sought to solve the problem of contriving a suitable structure of external relations among men so that power partitioned might also somehow be consolidated, and power departmentalized might properly be concentrated and constant in its exercise. Our consideration of that problem brought us to a consideration of that part of government which is most essentially impartial or nonpartisan, which acts independently in the work of maintaining national integrity, in more ways than one. Enthusiastic republicanism, Hamilton taught, must be superseded by enlightened republicanism, and this means republicanism properly organized for administration; but though the right machinery be made and set in motion, this does not suffice for making operational an enlightened republicanism, since the apparatus may be taken over by artful operators without integrity who may make it over by operating it without regard to its integrity. We must reconsider the relation of part and whole in the political thought of Hamilton.

Faction being the disease or pestilence or poison of the republic, we must attend not only to the energy of the governmental machinery but also to the health of the body politic. We must attend not only to the art embodied in institutions but also to the nature of citizenship and leadership. In considering political virtue in its twofold aspect of citizenship and leadership, we must see the republic as being a whole among other political wholes, in addition to seeing it as being a whole in which parties arise laying claims to act for the whole. Our consideration of the constitution of government leads us to consider assertiveness by government that culminates in war and assertiveness toward government that culminates, through subversion, in despotism or rebellion. We must see political virtue, or citizenship and leadership, as being surrounded by war and by rebellion.

However great were Hamilton's other achievements as a political leader, his great official achievement was to ensure that the infant American republic would be able to obtain financial sustenance from the chief sources of support. Money, he said during the labor that produced the government, is with propriety considered as the vital principle of the body politic, as that which sustains its life and motion and enables it to perform its most essential functions. But when he asked what are the chief sources of expense in every government, he said that the answer plainly was: the support of those institutions which are necessary to guard the body politic against these two most mortal diseases of society—wars and rebellions. The sustenance that vitalizes the body politic expends itself not only in animating the enterprises of appetite, but also and even especially in feeding the exertions of spirit.[14]

The great exertions of government, according to Hamilton, are those which preserve the community's integrity against both foreign enmity and domestic subversion; and to sustain a republic amid the inevitable wars and revolutions that will threaten it, there is need for civic spirit. A wholesome body politic is more than machinery that apportions power for efficacy as well as safety. An enlightened populace must be willing to be led by men of honor. To provide for machinery of government while leaving public opinion to chance is to neglect the foundation of efficacy. In a republic whose machinery is well formed for administration, the administration of government may contribute much to the formation of public opinion, but it cannot contribute all that is necessary. As Hamilton saw, the operations of government are in need of steady and single-minded extragovernmental operations. Somehow or other, it seems that we must return to first principles.

Conclusion

Let us conclude by summing up and then by situating what has been presented here of Hamilton's teaching to his countrymen.

American politics is somehow ruled by its beginnings. This book began by showing reasons to believe that Hamilton's part in those beginnings was ruled by thoughtfully articulated principles which informed his handling of particulars. Consideration of those principles in the subsequent chapters was divided into three parts. The first part treated popular representation, as the distinctive foundation of government based on enlightened modern principles. The central part treated efficacious administration, as an unpopular but necessary completion for the principles that require popular representation as the foundation of good government. And the final part treated constitutional integrity, as the wholeness served particularly by one part of a properly partitioned polity.

Chapter II, the first chapter of the first part, related Hamilton's view of the end of civil society (the securing of safety and prosperity for the populace) to his view of civil liberty. Liberty is a means for protecting the populace against oppression from their government, rather than being a stage or an arena for popular participation in public display. The chapter then related these views to Hamilton's contrast between ancient and modern society. War was the principal activity of men in the ancient body politic, and valor was their virtue; but their valiant displays were vicious. The outcome of their excellence was dearth and danger. The spirit of modern society, by contrast, is commercial; modern society is progressively more productive. The chapter then presented Hamilton's view of the historical source of enlightened modern principles of government. The warlike spirit of antiquity, delighting in domination and supported by plunder, was softened by the spirit of Christianity, but the excesses of zealotry led politic men to promote liberal government whose business would be dealing in the basic not the lofty goods; this-worldly cooperation in production and exchange was thus to replace intolerant strife about other-worldly opinions. The dangerous and distracting spirit born from the meeting of the spirit of spiritedness and the spirit of spirituality was to give way before the spirit of enlightened humanity.

Chapter III presented Hamilton's view of the natural source of rightful government: human equality in natural right, deriving from divinely established natural law. The chapter then presented this view as a source both of rightful revolution against government and of rightful vindication of governmental authority against sedition and insurrection. This led to the question of what arrangements will best embody enlightened principles in government.

Chapter IV presented the structural foundation of good government: popular representation. Popular representation frees the populace from continual contention and for productive industry, while safeguarding them against their governors.

Chapter V discussed an auxiliary means of safeguarding the people against their governors: the apportionment of power among several depositories. This device for preventing dangerous government was of special added interest to Hamilton as a device for promoting effective government. Power merely divided into parts tends either to degenerate into an anarchy among the parts or to collapse into the autocracy of one part. Partition must be differentiation. Government by a structure of differentiated parts, while founded upon popular representation, nonetheless can have what government by a popular representative assembly cannot have: efficacy.

Chapter VI, the first chapter of the second part of the book, suggested that an emphasis on efficacy is implicit in the popular principles of modernity. The chapter also presented unity and duration as the ingredients of efficacy and therewith as the two aspects of the problem for Hamilton. In a government amply arranged for safety against government, adequately arranging for efficacy of government is a twofold problem: to concentrate power sufficiently to cause many wills to act as one at one time, and to stabilize power sufficiently for many actions to be in concert for constant purposes during a long time. Unless the powers of government are apportioned to promote administrative efficacy, those who take part in the affairs of the multitudes of men massed in political society will be both uncooperative and improvident. For different sorts of governmental work, the number of officers and their duration in office must be different. The popular representatives in the most usual sense must be many in number and frequently elected, but popular representation in the most usual sense is not the whole of good government. Popular representation is of little avail without effective administration. Although the beginning and the end of good government is the people, between the source and the outcome of good government there operates that organization of means which is administration.

Acknowledging that the first problem of efficacy for the newly independent Americans was the federal problem summed up in the motto *E pluribus unum*, Chapter VII suggested that though federal union was the most urgent problem of unity for Hamilton, his attempt at its solution was not only or even chiefly what caused his enemies to call him "monocrat." The central problem of unity was the establishment of an energetic republican executive. According to Hamilton, the republican fear of monarchical power blinds Americans to the necessities of government: the executive power has an inherent nature, which, human nature being what it is, requires the concentration of power in single men. The circumstances of government require that government be able to act more quickly than is possible if many must agree, and the minds of governors require as inducement the honor that attaches to outstanding individuals who act well. The discussion of unity concentrated mostly on the President, but it led to a discussion of the Senate, a body which not only checks but also cooperates with the chief who is the incarnation of unity.

Chapter VIII moved on to discuss the second ingredient of efficacy: duration. This discussion began by relating mere complexity of governmental structure to duration as an ingredient of efficacy, and it went on to show the contribution made to this ingredient by a properly constituted executive.

Chapter IX concluded this discussion by considering the problem of establishing a senate—an institution feared as the return of aristocratic power, but needed as the embodiment of duration.

Chapter X, the last chapter of the second part of the book, presented Hamilton's presentation of himself as the great friend of republican government, seeking, by the establishment of properly differentiated parts within machinery founded upon popular representation, to give to the republic an efficacy without which it would be destroyed and its principle discredited.

Finally, after the two parts of the book on, respectively, popular representation and efficacious administration, came a third part, on constitutional integrity. This was needed for a full consideration of what makes the parts of the polity a whole and of how its end relates to its beginning.

Chapter XI discussed the distinctiveness of the judicial department of government as a seat of independent judgment.

Chapter XII presented Hamilton's argument in defense of preserving popular liberty by preserving that sharing of power in which those who officiate on the judgment seat are set apart to be above partiality or partisanship.

Chapter XIII presented Hamilton's argument in defense of preserving popular liberty by preserving that sharing of power in which those who officiate on the judgment seat must, in some cases, work in cooperation with other men (jurors) who are not representatives but rather are representative members of the people, directly participating in rule.

Chapter XIV turned toward some aspects of Hamilton's thought which point beyond the parts of government. To preserve the republic's integrity amid the foreign enmity and domestic subversion that inevitably will threaten it, there is need for civic spirit and attachment to the principles of good government. A wholesome body politic is more than governmental machinery which is partitioned for efficacy as well as for safety. To provide for machinery of government while leaving public opinion to chance is to neglect the foundation of efficacy. In a republic whose machinery is well formed for administration, the administration of government may contribute much to the formation of public opinion, but it cannot contribute all that is necessary. As Hamilton saw, the operations of government are in need of steady and single-minded extragovernmental operations.

Among such operations we may count the study of those principles which informed the various political operations of Alexander Hamilton.

In the course of his various operations, Hamilton produced an immense body of deliberative and explanatory words which treated passing particulars. But from the study of his treatment of those passing particulars, we can improve our understanding of the permanent principles of republican government.

There may be readers who believe that Hamilton's lessons have all been learned already, but evidence suggests that Hamilton's teaching has hardly become prevailing doctrine. From my own experience I offer two examples.

As a panelist reviewing applications for grants under a Bicentennial program of the National Endowment for the Humanities, I read a stack of proposals whose unstated premise was that *the* purpose of the Constitution is to protect the citizens against the government. The dominant theme of these proposals was the restraint imposed upon the power of the United

States either by the Bill of Rights or by the existence of the several states.

Later, as a visitor to the hall in Philadelphia where the Constitution was framed, I listened to a guide who spoke repeatedly of the intention of the founders to protect the citizens against their government by establishing a system of checks and balances: not once did he even hint that the framers sought to *energize* government even while they sought safeguards for the citizenry against abuses in the exercise of that great power which they thought they needed to establish.

But even if the arguments of Hamilton are not entirely novel for many readers, the value of considering them with care is suggested by the following words which introduced an exposition of the Constitution in the matter of the tenure of those officials to whom most properly belongs the exposition of the Constitution: "It would be vanity to expect to throw much additional light upon a subject which has already exhausted the logic and eloquence of some of the ablest men of our country; yet it often happens that the same arguments placed in a new attitude and accompanied with illustrations, which may have escaped the ardor of a first research, serve both to fortify and extend conviction," said Hamilton in justification of his teaching.[1]

To take him as our teacher does not mean, however, enlisting ourselves as partisans in a movement now defunct. Readers of this book, having gone so far in letting Hamilton be their teacher for a while, in the end might well look back upon Hamilton's own appraisal of the failings of the movement that he led. Reflection on his diagnosis and prescription (presented above in the concluding section of chapter X) might suggest a way to go further, and deeper, in continuing to think about republican effectiveness. While those who wish to govern a republic must remember that flattering the people is not the same as serving them, they must remember also that they will be refused the opportunity to serve a people whom they do not somehow gratify.

Also pertinent to this would be reflection on the notes in which this book presents Hamilton's Roman counterpoint to the commercial theme of the text in the book's first part. The modern commercial republic is understood in contrast to the military ancient one, but these regimes are both republics, and a people without spirit cannot keep a republic, whether ancient or modern. We must not forget that in the pay book of the artillery company raised and led by the young Alexander Hamilton we find, together, notes on Postlethwayt's *Universal Dictionary of Trade and Commerce* and notes on Plutarch's *Lives*.[2]

Also pertinent would be reflection on those places where this book

presents Hamilton's animadversions upon Jefferson and Burr. These are included not to add a narrative diversion but rather to provide some indication how Hamilton's political science of administration requires us to think
about men's souls. Hamilton condemns a covert ambition which, timorously
avoiding public confrontation, denigrates ambition; he opposes also an unprincipled ambition which exhibits an insolent unwillingness to stop at
anything in the attempt to be supreme.

By suggesting that we benefit from studying the principles which Hamilton set out, I do not mean to suggest that principles all by themselves
suffice for judging particulars of policy. Sound principles, while necessary
to guide policy, cannot determine it: principles need to be applied with
prudence—and prudence considers circumstances.

All good men must rejoice if the outcome of the American experiment
at Philadelphia proves that the republican theory need not fail in practice,
said Hamilton, and he did all that he could to make it succeed; but he did
not regard republican government as something for immediate export to all
mankind. Writing to the same man whom he told of his hopes for an adequate experiment of republican government in this country, Hamilton on
another occasion said: "No regular system of Liberty will at present suit St.
Domingo. The Government if independent must be military—partaking of
the feodal system."[3]

Moreover, of the country by which Santo Domingo had been dominated, Hamilton wrote a month earlier to another correspondent: "The suspension of the King and the massacre of September . . . cured me of my
good will for the French Revolution. I have never been able to believe that
France can make a republic and I believe the attempt while it continues can
only produce misfortunes"—"I hold with *Montesquieu*," he said, "that a government must be fitted to a nation as much as a Coat to the Individual, and
consequently that what may be good at Philadelphia may be bad at Paris and
ridiculous at Petersburgh."[4]

Sound principles, moreover, guide judgment not as isolated propositions, but rather as constituents in a comprehensive view.

Hamilton resisted efforts at Philadelphia, capital of the government of
the young American nation of that day, to hurry through a redefinition of
treason which would punish American partisans of the menacing disorder
that had its capital at Paris: "Let us not establish a tyranny," he said; "Energy
is a very different thing from violence."[5] As this remark suggests, we must
bear in mind Hamilton's constitutional purpose when we read his administrative arguments, such as the argument on behalf of executive energy
which goes like this: "A feeble executive implies a feeble execution of the

government. A feeble execution is but another phrase for a bad execution: And a government ill executed, whatever it may be in theory, must be in practice a bad government."[6] While Hamilton here denies that a government can be good if its executive is feeble, elsewhere he asserts that a government can be bad even if its executive is strong. We might add that when circumstances necessitate putting up with despotism, ill executed despotism or despotism tempered by anarchy may not be as bad as efficacious despotism or despotism well executed. In Hamilton's day a writer from a distant land remarked about his country that its good fortune was in the bad execution of its bad laws. The government of which that writer spoke had its capital at Petersburgh.

Notes

Introduction

1 Hamilton's writings will be cited as follows: "P 2:3" indicates the second volume, at page 3, of *The Papers of Alexander Hamilton*, ed. Harold C. Syrett (New York, 1961–1979). "L 2:3" indicates the second volume, at page 3, of *The Works of Alexander Hamilton*, ed. Henry Cabot Lodge (New York, 1885). (Lodge's edition is superseded in every respect by Syrett's excellent work, most of which unfortunately had not yet appeared during my research.) "F1, p. 3" indicates the first number of *The Federalist*, at page 3, in the edition by Jacob E. Cooke (Cleveland and New York, 1961). In quoting from these editions, I have occasionally modernized or corrected spelling and punctuation. The best one-volume collection of Hamilton's work is *Selected Writings and Speeches of Alexander Hamilton*, ed. Morton J. Frisch (Washington, D.C.: American Enterprise Institute for Public Policy Research, 1985).

   The quotations in this paragraph are from: To Tobias Lear (2 January 1800) P 24:155; F9, p. 51; Montesquieu, *Considérations sur les Causes de la Grandeur des Romains et de leur Décadence* (Amsterdam, 1734), chap. 1.

I Principles

1 F15, pp. 93, 98; F16, p. 101.
2 William Pierce, in Max Farrand, ed., *Records of the Federal Convention of 1787* (New Haven and London, 1966), 3: 89. Bower Aly, *The Rhetoric of Alexander Hamilton* (New York, 1941), pp. 62, 189.
3 Jefferson to Madison (21 September 1795). See also Jefferson's earlier letter of 7 July 1793, urging Madison to "take up your pen . . . and cut him to pieces"; Madison, reluctantly acceding to this appeal, answered Hamilton's "Pacificus" defense of President Washington's Proclamation of Neutrality. See also the later letter of 5 April 1798 from Jefferson to Madison.
4 In *Life, Letters, and Journals of George Ticknor* (Boston, 1876), 1:261, the journal reports (for 10 December 1818 to 12 January 1819) a conversation in which, speaking of Hamilton "with great admiration," Talleyrand "said that he had known during his life, many of the more marked men of his time, but that he had never, on the whole, known one equal to

Hamilton. I was much surprised, as well as gratified by the remark; but still feeling that, as an American, I was, in some sort, a party concerned by patriotism in the compliment, I answered,—with a little reserve, perhaps with a little modesty,—that the great military commanders and the great statesmen of Europe had dealt with larger masses of men, and much wider interests than Hamilton ever had. 'Mais, monsieur,' the Prince instantly replied, 'Hamilton avait deviné l'Europe.' "

5   To Rufus King (2 October 1798) L 8:511.

6   To Lafayette (6 January 1799) P 22:404, saying that this was a consequence of what "I hold with *Montesquieu*"—"that a government must be fitted to a nation as much as a Coat to an Individual." How far Hamilton went with this tenet may be seen in his response to Timothy Pickering (21 February 1799) L 8:528, sketching, as requested, a plan of government suitable for an independent Santo Domingo, which "at present" could not be a "regular system of liberty" but "must be military—partaking of the feodal system."

7   Defense of the Funding System (July 1795) L 7:462–463. Philo Camillus no. 4 (19 August 1795) P 19:159, 162.

8   To Timothy Pickering (15 March 1800) L 8:546. Consider also Hamilton's seconding of the venerable Franklin's motion that the executive not be paid for his service—Constitutional Convention (2 June 1787) P 4:176–177.

9   Questions Proposed to be Submitted to the Judges of the Supreme Court of the U.S. (July 1793) L 4:193–197, for example, was drafted for the man whom Hamilton called "an Aegis very essential to me"—To Tobias Lear (2 January 1800) P 24:155.

10 To Washington (15 September 1790) P 7:36.

11 To Oliver Wolcott (17 February 1797) L 8:450, for example.

12 He went on to argue that "in an affair of such vast magnitude" as the tenure of the judiciary, "it is all important to survey with the utmost caution the ground to be taken, and then to take and maintain it with inflexible fortitude and perseverance. Truth will be most likely to prevail, when the arguments which support it stop at a temperate mean, consistent with practical convenience. Excess is always error. There is hardly any theoretic hypothesis which, carried to a certain extreme, does not become practically false. In construing a Constitution, it is wise, as far as possible, to pursue a course, which will reconcile essential principles with convenient modifications." Lucius Crassus (Examination of Jefferson's Message to Congress of 7 December 1801), no. 16 (19 March 1802) L 7:297, 300–301.

13 To — (21 September 1792) L 8:283–284; To — (26 September 1792) L 8:285; To Gen. C. C. Pinckney (10 October 1792) L 8:286–287. To James A. Bayard (16 January 1801) L 8:584–585.

14 F1, pp. 3, 6.

15 There are twenty-six volumes of Hamilton's *Papers*, and, in addition, there are several volumes of documents, independently edited, for *The Law Practice of Alexander Hamilton*. The quotation about Hamilton's writings is taken from "A Sketch of the Character of Alexander Hamilton," in *Works of Fisher Ames*, ed. Seth Ames (Boston, 1854), 2:261.

16 John C. Hamilton, ed., *The Federalist* (New York, 1864), 1:xcii, ciii. Madison was indignant at Hamilton's thus making use of *The Federalist* (in the writing of which Madison had, at Hamilton's request, collaborated) to support *Pacificus* (which Madison had, at Jefferson's request, opposed in print)—*Letters of Madison*, 3:58.

17 William Kent, *Memoirs and Letters of James Kent* (Boston, 1898), pp. 327–328. This, together with Hamilton's letters of 21 and 26 September 1792 (see above), ought to

be kept in mind in interpreting the story about Hamilton, Bacon, and Caesar told by Jefferson in his letter to Dr. Benjamin Rush (16 January 1811). It would have been more Caesar-like to write books of the sort that Caesar wrote. After becoming General Washington's aide-de-camp, Hamilton received letters from the West Indian clergyman who had sent him to America, congratulating him on his advancement and urging him to "take Minutes and keep a Journal" to become "the Historiographer of the American War": "few men will be as well qualified to write the History of the present Glorious Struggle" (Hugh Knox (31 April 1777) P 1:244–245). Hamilton did not respond to repeated urgings— (10 December 1777) P 2:365–366 and (27 October 1783) P 3:474. Years later Hamilton's son recalled him reading aloud: "With what emphasis and fervor did he read of battles! When translating the commentaries of Caesar, it would seem as though Caesar were present; for as much as any man that ever lived he had the soldier's temperament." And the son reported: "It was his delight in his hours of relaxation to return to scenes and incidents of his early life, when fighting for his country" (John C. Hamilton, *Life of Alexander Hamilton* [Boston, 1879], 7:792–793).

II   The Characteristic Spirit of Society

1   The Farmer Refuted (23 February 1775) P 1:95, 126; Draft of President's Speech to Senate and House of Representatives (6 November 1793) L 7:68; Resolution intended to be submitted to Congress . . . but abandoned for want of support (July 1783) P 3:425; Conjectures about the New Constitution (September 1787) P 4:275; F85, p. 589.

As might be expected of a busy political man, there is in Hamilton's terminology some variation without significance. For safety and *happiness,* see F15, p. 89. For safety and *welfare:* Resolution . . . (July 1783) P 3:426 (also p. 425, for common welfare and defense and for happiness and security). For *security* and prosperity: To Count Latour Dupin Gouvernet (3 October 1798) L 8:512–513.

2   Lucius Crassus no. 6 (January 1802) L 7:326. See also F84, p. 583.

3   Farmer Refuted (23 February 1775) P 1:125.

4   A Full Vindication of the Measures of Congress (15 December 1774) P 1:66; Farmer Refuted (23 February 1775) P 1:100.

5   F8, p. 45.

6   F1, p. 6; F15, p. 92; F22, p. 144; F30, p. 191. Report Relative to a Provision for the Support of Public Credit (9 January 1790) P 6:101, 105. To George Clinton (13 February 1778) P 1:425–426.

7   Consider Camillus no. 18 (1795) L 5:63–64, on the dishonor of seeking security by swindling rather than fighting—or consider these two quotations: "our countrymen have all the folly of the ass and all the passiveness of the sheep. . . . If we are saved France and Spain must save us. . . . I almost wish to hide my disgrace in universal ruin." (To John Laurens [30 June 1780] P 2:347–348). "Every moment's reflection increases my chagrin and disgust at the failure of the propositions concerning the unsubscribed debt. I am tortured by the idea that the country should be so completely and unnecessarily dishonored" (To Theodore Sedgwick [18 February 1795] L 8:337).

8   Continentalist no. 6 (4 July 1782) P 3:106.

9   Defense of the Funding System (July 1795) P 19:66, 69–70. Consider Adam Smith, *The Theory of Moral Sentiments* (New Rochelle, New York, 1969), pt. 4, chap. 1 ("Of the Beauty which the Appearance of Utility Bestows upon all the Productions of Art, and of

the Extensive Influence of this Species of Beauty"), especially pp. 257–258 and 265–268, containing a suggestion of the greatest utility in civic pedagogy.

10 Continentalist no. 6 (1782) P 3:102–103. Consider Blackstone, *Commentaries on the Laws of England*, bk. 1, chap. 8: "as the true idea of government and magistracy will be found to consist in this, that some few men are deputed by many others to preside over public affairs, so that individuals may the better be enabled to attend their private concerns; it is necessary that those individuals should be bound to contribute a portion of their private gains, in order to support that government, and reward that magistracy, which protects them in the enjoyment of their respective properties." See also Montesquieu, *De l'Esprit des Lois* (Pléiade, Oeuvres Complètes, II), livre 11, chap. 6, pp. 397, 399–400.

11 New York Assembly: Remarks on an act acknowledging independence of Vermont (28 March 1787) P 4:140.

12 Consider this letter to his friend, a lieutenant colonel in the army fighting for American independence: "Peace made . . . a new scene opens. The object will be to make our independence a blessing. To do this we must secure our *union* on solid foundations; an herculean task and to effect which mountains of prejudice must be levelled! It requires all the virtue and all the abilities of the Country. Quit your sword my friend, put on the *toga,* come to Congress. . . . We have fought side by side to make America free, let us hand in hand struggle to make her happy" (To John Laurens [15 August 1782] P 3:145). Within two weeks Laurens was killed, "a sacrifice to his ardor in a trifling skirmish in South Carolina . . . how I truly loved him" (To Marquis de Lafayette [3 November 1782] P 3:193). A while before, when another officer had written to ask his "widow" whether he should quit the service to return to her, Hamilton wrote of her to the woman he himself was soon to marry: "You see what a fine opportunity she has to be enrolled in the catalogue of heroines. . . . [S]he will set you an example of fortitude and patriotism. I know that you have too much of the Portia in you . . . that if you saw me inclined to quit the service of your country, you would dissuade me from it. I have promised you . . . to conform to your wishes. . . . It remains with you to show whether you are a Roman or an American wife" (To Elizabeth Schuyler [August 1780] P 2:397). Later, writing as "Tully," he defended suppressing the insurrection against the excise tax on whiskey: "Those who . . . dissuade you from exertions adequate to the occasion . . . treat you as fools or cowards, too weak to perceive your interest or your duty, or too dastardly to pursue them. . . . To the plausible but hollow harangue of such conspirators you cannot fail to reply, How long, ye Catalines, will ye abuse our patience?" (Tully no. 3 [28 August 1794] L 6:26).

13 F8, p. 47; F24, p. 156; F29, pp. 183–184. Defense of the Funding System (July 1795) P 19:53.

The qualities that make for heroism somehow manifest themselves though an age be unsuited to unprofitable display. There are "the adventurous stratagems of avarice," as smuggling is referred to in F12, p. 76. More respectably, F11, p. 66, speaks of "the adventurous spirit, which distinguishes the commercial character of America." And consider Adam Smith, *The Wealth of Nations* (New York, 1937), bk. 4, chap. 7, pt. 3, pp. 586–588, on the political psychology of the fight over taxation without representation.

Hamilton began his civic career in that fight and rose to prominence in the war that arose from that fight. Hamilton's earliest extant piece of writing is a letter written a few years before, to his boyhood friend, then in New York City to attend college, when Hamilton himself was a poor orphan in his early teens working in a West Indian countinghouse:

"my Ambition is prevalent that I contemn the grov'ling and condition of a Clerk or the like, to which my Fortune &c. condemns me and would willingly risk my life tho' not my Character to exalt my Station. . . . I mean to prepare the way for futurity. I'm no Philosopher you see and may be justly said to Build Castles in the Air . . . yet . . . we have seen such Schemes successful when the Projector is Constant I shall conclude saying I wish there was a War" (To Edward Stevens [11 November 1769] P 1:4). According to his son, Hamilton's favorite books when he came to America were Alexander Pope's poems and Plutarch's *Lives*. The reading notes he kept in the pay book of the State Company of Artillery, which he commanded during the war (before becoming aide-de-camp to the commander in chief) begin with items of commercial geography, mostly taken from Postlethwayt's *Universal Dictionary of Trade and Commerce* and amounting to somewhat more than seventeen pages in print, and conclude with a few pages more on vital statistics and on interest, taxes, and money. In between are very brief extracts from Demosthenes, comparing political leadership to generalship, and some seventeen printed pages on Plutarch; between these two is a very brief couple of items on American matters of state "to be attended to" (Pay Book . . . [*ca.* 1777] P 1:373–411).

Later, defending the reeligibility of the chief magistrate, Hamilton spoke of ambition in relation to private interest and public benefit. Exclusion from reeligibility, he said, would diminish the inducements to good behavior: "the best security for the fidelity of mankind is to make their interest coincide with their duty"; "even the love of fame, the ruling passion of the noblest minds, which would prompt a man to plan and undertake extensive and arduous enterprises for the public benefit, requiring considerable time to mature and perfect them, if he could flatter himself with the prospect of being allowed to finish what he had begun, would on the contrary deter him from the undertaking, when he foresaw that he must quit the scene before he could accomplish the work, and must commit that, together with his reputation, to hands which might be unequal or unfriendly to the task" (F72, p. 488). (He went on to speak of avarice as well as ambition. For an earlier version of the premise, see the quotation from Hume in The Farmer Refuted [1775] P 1:94–95; but note the qualification in F76, pp. 513–514.)

Speaking of the French Directory, Hamilton referred to "the most imperious passions": "the strongest passions of bad hearts—inordinate ambition—the love of domination, that prime characteristic of the despots of France . . . the fanatical egoism of obliging the rest of the world to adapt their political system to the French standard of perfection" (Titus Manlius [The Stand] no. 6 [19 April 1798] P 21:435). Ambition may be "inordinate:" it is first on the list of "motives not more laudable than these"—followed by "avarice, personal animosity, party opposition" (F1, p. 5). It would seem that the ruling passion of the noblest minds is ruled by something higher, which distinguishes fame from infamy. Consider: Statement by Hamilton as to his motives in meeting Burr (10 July 1804) L 8:626–628; To Mrs. Hamilton (10 July 1804) L 8:628–630. See note 18 to chap. X, below.

14 To Washington (14 April 1794) L 4:429. Camillus no. 20 (1795) L 5:78–79, 83, 85–87. Report on Public Credit (16 January 1795) L 3:35.

15 Report on Public Credit (16 January 1795) L 3:36, 38–40. F30, pp. 192–193. Camillus no. 21 (1795) L 5:107.

16 Report on Public Credit (16 January 1795) L 3:38. F30, p. 192; F6, p. 32; F34, p. 211.

17 To Washington (15 September 1790) P 7:50. (In this letter Hamilton spoke without disapproval of this general disinclination to war, although a few lines later he spoke dif-

ferently of some other particular attitudes against risking war with Britain in her conflict with Spain: there were, he said, persons of Dutch descent who would be prejudiced in favor of Britain if she were joined by the Dutch, and there were persons unfriendly to the American Revolution and even friends of the Revolution "who retain prepossessions in favour of Englishmen and against Spaniards"—"In a popular government especially, however prejudices like this may be regretted, they are not excluded from political calculations.") Camillus no. 10 (1795) L 4:469–471.

18   F11, p. 71. Address of the Annapolis Convention (14 September 1786) P 3:688. To Robert Morris (30 April 1781) P 2:620. F12, pp. 73–74; F30, p. 188.

19   F12, p. 74. Continentalist no. 6 (1782) P 3:101–102.

20   Hobbes, *Leviathan*, chap. 30. Locke, *Second Treatise of Government*, sec. 42.

21   Defense of the Funding System (1795) P 19:62.

22   To Rufus King (3 June 1802) P 19:62.

23   Thomas Jefferson, *Notes on Virginia* (1782), Query 19.

24   First draft of Washington's speech to Congress (7 December 1796) L7:177. See also, P 6:209–210, n. 3: Washington to Congress (8 January 1790); House of Representatives (15 January 1790).

25   Report on Manufactures (5 December 1791) L 3:295–298, 300–302, 306, 310–314, 316–317. Additional Supplies for 1792: Secretary of the Treasury to the House of Representatives (16 March 1792) L 2:224. Adam Smith, *The Wealth of Nations* (New York, 1937), bk. 1, chaps. 1–2, pp. 3–16; bk. 5, chap. 1, pt. 3, art. 2, pp. 734–740.

26   To Washington: Objections and Answers respecting the Administration of the Government, Objection 11 (18 August 1792) P 12:247–248.

Report on Public Credit (16 January 1795) L 3:14–15, 41–42. Defense of the Funding System (July 1795) P 19:51–53, 55, 57, 59–60. For an early treatment of the theme, in relation to public banks, see: to Robert Morris (30 April 1781) P 2:617–619. Rousseau, *Les Confessions* (Pléiade, Oeuvres Complètes, I), livre 12, p. 630. Compare Madison's Notes for 20 August in Farrand, ed., *Records of the Federal Convention of 1787*, II, 344. Rousseau, *Discours sur les Sciences et les Arts* (Pléiade, Oeuvres Complètes, III), Seconde Partie, pp. 19–20, 22. Rousseau, *Emile* (Paris, 1964), livre 2, p. 82 (Garnier).

And, on seeking "to promote his action by the byass of his nature," see F72, pp. 488–489; and consider "the degree of authority required to direct the passions of so large a society to the public good," F13, p. 80. Also: there is a "favorite dogma" that "Industry will succeed and prosper in proportion as it is left to the exertions of individual enterprise"—this, "when taken as a general rule, is true; but as an exclusive one, it is false, and leads to error in the administration of public affairs." It is "doubtless" true that "human enterprise" should "in matters of industry" be "left free in the main, not fettered by too much regulation"; but it is known to "practical politicians" that human enterprise in matters of industry "may be beneficially stimulated by prudent aids and encouragements on the part of the Government." The numerous examples proving this will be "neglected only by indolent and temporizing rulers, who love to loll in the lap of epicurean ease, and seem to imagine that to govern well is to amuse the wondering multitude with sagacious aphorisms and oracular sayings" (Lucius Crassus no. 3 [24 December 1801] P 25:467). And what he is reported to have said in the New York Ratifying Convention: "Experience has by no means justified us in the supposition, that there is more virtue in one class of men than in another. Look through the rich and poor of the community; the learned and the ignorant. Where does virtue predominate? The difference indeed consists, not in the quantity but kind of vices, which are incident to the various classes; and here the advantage of character belongs to the wealthy. Their vices are probably more favorable to the prosperity of the state, than those of the indigent; and partake less of moral depravity" ([21 June 1788] P 5:43).

27 Pay book (1777) P 1:400. Here he seems to echo Hume (though without citation).

Hume, discussing in his *Essays* (in "Of the Populousness of Ancient Nations") the "method" by which "the ancients" avoided being "overburdened with too numerous a family," says that "this practice . . . is not spoken of by any author of those times with the horror it deserves, or scarcely with disapprobation"; Hume then remarks that "It was Solon, the most celebrated of the sages of Greece, that gave parents permission by law to kill their children," and he mentions that an instance of the practice is mentioned as a merit by "Plutarch, the humane good-natured Plutarch."

In this essay Hume also discusses why "the ancient republics were almost in perpetual war": this was "a natural effect of their martial spirit, their love of liberty, their mutual emulation, and that hatred which generally prevails among nations that live in close neighborhood." According to Hume, "the maxims of ancient war were more destructive than those of modern, chiefly by that distribution of plunder, in which the soldiers were indulged"; and "the battles of antiquity . . . were wrought up to a degree of fury quite unknown to later ages," for "Nothing could then engage the combatants to give quarter, but the hopes of profit, by making slaves of their prisoners. . . . How inveterate the rage where the maxims of war were, in every respect, so bloody and severe." The battles so destructive and so bloody were, moreover, supplemented by wars "carried on entirely by inroads, and robberies, and piracies . . . a method of war . . . more destructive in small states, than the bloodiest battles and sieges." In either method—battle or piracies—"war in a small state is much more destructive than in a great one" because in a small state "all the inhabitants . . . must serve in the armies" and the territory is "all exposed to the inroads of the enemy." The whole territory is exposed because in a small state "the whole state is frontier"; and if the whole state is frontier, there must be more of "that hatred which generally prevails among nations that live in close neighborhood."

And "not only in times of war, but also in those of peace," it appears that "ancient manners were more unfavorable than the modern . . . in every respect, except the love of civil liberty and of equality," but though "these people were extremely fond of liberty," they "seem not to have understood it very well"; "A fourth, a third, perhaps near half a city was slaughtered, or expelled, every revolution . . . and as these were frequent in such violent governments, the disorder, diffidence, jealousy, enmity, which must prevail, are not easy for us to imagine in this age of the world." Now, "To exclude faction from a free government, is very difficult, if not altogether impracticable; but such inveterate rage between the factions, and such bloody maxims are found, in modern times, amongst religious parties alone."

In modern times, however, one might find another element besides the bloody maxims of parties in their rage: Hume, in another essay, "Of the Balance of Power," contrasted "the ancient Greek spirit of jealous emulation" with "the prudent spirit of modern politics."

28 Camillus no. 20 (1795) L 5:78–79. Compare the combination of humane feeling and hard cool prudence in the letter to Major General Henry Knox (7 June 1782) P 3:91–92.

29 Camillus no. 19 (1795) L 5:70, 74–75.

30 Pay Book (1777) P 1:400.

31 The War in Europe (1799) L 5:462–463.

32   F1, p. 5. Second Letter from Phocion (April 1784) P 3:553–554. Concerning Americans
      loyal to Britain during the struggle for independence, Hamilton wrote: "It is an axiom
      that governments form manners, as well as manners form governments. The body of the
      people of this state are too firmly attached to the democracy, to permit the principles
      of a small number to give a different tone to that spirit. The present law of inheritance
      making an equal division among the children, of the parents' property, will soon melt
      down those great estates, which if they continued, might favour the power of the *few*.
      The number of the disaffected, who are so, from speculative notions of government, is
      small: The great majority of those, who took part against us, did it from accident, from
      the dread of British power, and from the influence of others to whom they had been
      accustomed to look up. Most of the men, who had that kind of influence are already
      gone: The residue and their adherents must be carried along by the torrent . . . if the
      government is mild and just" (P 3:553).

33   Remarks on the Quebec Bill (15 June 1775) P 1:166, 168; pt. 2 (22 June 1775) P 1:171,
      174–175.
         And ten years after the Letter from Phocion cited in the last note, Hamilton wrote:
      "The world has been scourged with many fanatical sects in religion—who inflamed by a
      sincere but mistaken zeal have perpetrated under the idea of serving God the most atro-
      cious crimes. If we were to call the cause of such men the cause of religion, would not
      every one agree, that it was an abuse of terms?" Now "the ruling party in France is actu-
      ated by a zeal similar in its nature (though different in its object) to that which influences
      religious fanatics. Can this political phrenzy be dignified with the honorable appelation
      of the cause of Liberty with any greater propriety than the other kind of phrenzy would
      be denominated the cause of religion?" The Cause of France (1794) P 17:585.
         Three years after this, Napoleon, in a speech to the French Directory, said that "La
      religion, la féodalité et le royalisme, ont successivement, depuis vingt siècles, gouverné
      l'Europe; mais de la paix que vous venez de conclure, date l'ère des gouvernements
      représentatifs" (P 21:404, n. 7); but the abuse of terms in this address was criticized by
      Hamilton, in the third number of his Titus Manlius series: "The late address of *Buona-
      parte* to the Directory," he said, "prophanely unites Religion (not superstition)" with
      royalty and the feudal system as "the scourges of Europe for centuries past" ([7 April
      1798] P 21:403–404).

34   New York Assembly: Remarks on an act for regulating elections (24 January 1787)
      P 4:22ff.; (29 January 1787) P 4:30ff.

35   Camillus no. 22 (1795) L 5:113–114.

36   Hamilton, according to Robert Troup (recalling Hamilton as his college roommate) "had
      read most of the polemical writers on religious subjects; and he was a zealous believer
      in the fundamental doctrines of Christianity; and, I confess, that the arguments with
      which he was accustomed to justify his belief, have tended, in no small degree, to con-
      firm my own faith in revealed religion" (Nathan Schachner, ed., "Alexander Hamilton
      Viewed by His Friends: The Narratives of Robert Troup and Hercules Mulligan," *William
      and Mary quarterly*, 3d ser., 4 [1947]:213). Hamilton made Troup the executor of his will
      (To Robert Troup [25 July 1795] L 8:351). See also: John C. Hamilton, *Life of Alexander
      Hamilton* (Boston, 1879), 7:790. And consider: Statement by Hamilton as to his motives
      in meeting Burr (10 July 1804) L 8:626–628; To Mrs. Hamilton (10 July 1804) L 8:628–
      630. This is not the place to consider what additional remarks would have to be made in
      the light of, for example, the letter to James A. Bayard (April 1802) L 8:596–599.

III *The Natural Rights of Mankind*

1   Farmer Refuted (23 February 1775) P 1:86–88.

2   Full Vindication of the Measures of Congress (15 December 1774) P 1:51. Hamilton said this in defense of the American refusal to trade with fellow subjects of the British king— the manufacturers of Great Britain and Ireland and the inhabitants of the West Indies, who, "though . . . not chargeable with any actual crime towards America, . . . may, in a political view, be esteemed criminal," for if one part of a civil society "endeavors to violate the rights of another, the rest ought to assist in preventing the injury: When they do not, but remain neutral, they are deficient in their duty, and may be regarded, in some measure, as accomplices . . . one part cannot encroach upon another, without becoming a common enemy" (ibid., pp. 51–52).

3   Vindication of the Funding System no. 3 (1791?) L 2:295–299; Camillus no. 19 (1795) L 5:69, 73; Report on Public Credit (16 June 1795) L 3:34; F84, p. 583.

4   Farmer Refuted (23 February 1775) P 1:104.

5   Hamilton first wrote the word "perhaps"; he then crossed it out and wrote the word "probably."

6   To John Jay (14 March 1779) P 2:17–19. Later in the year he wrote to Laurens himself: "I think your black scheme would be the best resource the situation of your country will admit. I wish its success, but my hopes are very feeble. Prejudice and private interest will be antagonists too powerful for public spirit and public good. . . . Even the animated and persuasive eloquence of my young Demosthenes will not be able to rouse his country-men from the lethargy of voluptuous indolence, or dissolve . . . self-interest, to inspire them with the . . . wisdom of legislators and . . . enthusiasm of republicans! . . . an idle dream. . . . [T]here is no virtue in America—that commerce which presided over the birth and education of these states has fitted their inhabitants for the chain, and . . . the only condition they sincerely desire is that it may be a golden one" (To John Laurens [11 September 1779] P 2:166–167).

7   P 3 (4 February 1785) 597, (13 March 1786) 654. Camillus (The Defense) no. 3 (29 July 1795) P 18:517–520; Philo Camillus no. 2 (7 August 1795) P 19:101–102; To Washington (9 July 1794) L 4:329.

8   F15, p. 96. A Full Vindication of the Measures of Congress (15 December 1774) P 1:47–48, 51–52; Farmer Refuted (23 February 1775) P 1:88–89, 96, 104, 136.

9   To John Jay (26 November 1775) P 1:176–178. First Letter from Phocion (1–27 January 1784) P 3:484–487, 494. Second Letter from Phocion (April 1784) P 3:549–51, 556. F78, pp. 527–28. Camillus no. 36 (1796) L 5:296–98.

10 F28, pp. 176–77. To Washington (14 April 1794) L 4:289.

11 New York Assembly: Remarks on . . . Vermont (28 March 1787) P 4:126–127, 131–132.

12 To John Dickinson (25–30 September 1783) P 3:449–453. See also: Tully no. 1 (23 August 1794) L 6:19–22; no. 2 (26 August 1794) L 6:22–26; no. 3 (28 August 1794) L 6:26–32.

13 Farmer Refuted (23 February 1775) P 1:104, 121–122, 164–165.

14 Lucius Crassus no. 17 (20 March 1802) L 7:312–313.

15 Second Letter from Phocion (April 1784) P 3:557. See also F1, p. 3.

16 To Robert Morris (30 April 1781) P 2:610. Compare Constitutional Convention, Notes (1 June 1787) P 4:163: the reason for preferring a free government to an absolute monar-chy is "the tendency of the Free government to interest the passions of the community in its favour, beget public spirit and public confidence." Also: "where the public good is

evidently the object more may be effected in governments like ours than in any other"—
"free countries have ever paid the heaviest taxes. The obedience of a free people to general laws however hard they bear is ever more perfect than that of slaves to the arbitrary
will of a prince" (To James Duane [3 September 1780] P 2:413).

The behavior of some of his compatriots during the struggle for independence led him
to write to his beloved comrade: "in perfect confidence I whisper a word in your ear. I
hate money making men" (To John Laurens [22 May 1779] P 2:53).

Hamilton's first "Publius" letters were an attack on Samuel Chase of Maryland, who,
knowing as a delegate to the Continental Congress of its secret plan to get flour to supply
the French fleet, had relayed the information to associates in a plan to profit by cornering
the supply of flour and raising its price. Referring to those "who, taking advantage of the
times, have carried the spirit of monopoly and extortion, to an excess, which scarcely
admits of a parallel," Hamilton wrote: "When avarice takes the lead in a State, it is commonly the forerunner of its fall. . . . There are men in all countries, the business of whose
lives it is, to raise themselves above indigence, by every little art in their power. When
these men are . . . influenced by the spirit I have mentioned, it . . . might be expected,
and can only excite contempt. When others, who have characters to support, and credit
enough in the world to satisfy a moderate appetite for wealth, in an honorable way, are
found to be actuated by the same spirit, our contempt is mixed with indignation. But
when a man, appointed to be the guardian of the State, and the depository of the happiness and morals of the people—forgetful of the solemn relation, in which he stands—
descends to the dishonest artifices of a mercantile projector, and sacrifices his conscience
and his trust to pecuniary motives; there is no strain of abhorrence . . . nor punishment . . . which may not be applied to him, with justice" (Publius Letter, I [16 October
1778] P 1:562–563).

In the last letter of the series, Hamilton characterized a very different sort of man:
"The station of a member of Congress, is the most illustrious and important of any I am
able to conceive. He is to be regarded not only as a legislator, but as the founder of an
empire. A man of virtue and ability, dignified with so precious a trust, would rejoice that
fortune had given him birth at a time, and placed him in circumstances so favourable for
promoting human happiness. He would esteem it not more the duty, than the privilege
and ornament of his office, to do good to mankind; from this commanding eminence, he
would look down with contempt upon every mean or interested pursuit. To form useful
alliances abroad—to establish a wise government at home—to improve the internal resources, and finances of the nation would be the generous objects of his care. He would
not allow his attention to be diverted from these to intrigue for personal connections, to
confirm his own influence; nor would he be able to reconcile it, either to the delicacy
of his honour, or to the dignity of his pride, to confound in the same person the representative of the Commonwealth, and the little member of a trading company." A man in
the illustrious station of which Hamilton conceived would be "anxious for the permanent
power and prosperity of the State," rather than for his own personal influence and profit
(Publius Letter, III [16 November 1778] P 1:580–581).

17 To Marquis de Lafayette (6 October 1789) P 5:425. Six months later Lafayette sent to
    George Washington "a picture of the Bastille just as it looked a few days after I ordered
    its demolition, with the main key of that fortress of despotism." This was, he wrote, "a
    tribute which I owe as a son to my adoptive father, as an aid de camp to my General,
    as a Missionary of Liberty to its Patriarch" (Lafayette to Washington [17 March 1790],

Letters of Lafayette to Washington, 1777–1799 ed. Louis R. Gottschalk [New York, 1944], p. 348). This key was transmitted from Lafayette to Washington by Thomas Paine, who called it not only "this early trophy of the Spoils of despotism," but also "the first ripe fruits of American principles translated into Europe." Since it is "not to be doubted" that "the principles of America opened the Bastille," he wrote, "therefore the Key comes to its right place" (Thomas Paine to Washington [1 May 1790], Mancur D. Conway, *The Life of Thomas Paine* [New York, 1892], 1:273). Lafayette himself said, in his own letter sent to Washington with the key to the Bastille: "we have made an admirable, and almost incredible destruction of all abuses, prejudices, etc."; "every thing not directly useful to, or coming from the people has been levelled"; "we have made more changes in ten months than the most sanguine patriot could have imagined"; "this Revolution, in which nothing will be wanting but energy of government just as it was in America, will propagate [and] implant liberty and make it flourish throughout the world, while we must wait for a Convention in a few years to mend some defects which are not now perceived by men just escaped from aristocracy and despotism" (Lafayette to Washington [ed. Gottschalk], p. 347), also from the letter of the 17th.

Hamilton, in Americanus no. 2 (7 February 1794) P 16, reports (at p. 14) that "The combined powers, it is said, will never forgive in us the origination of those principles which were the germs of the French Revolution. They will endeavour to eradicate them from the world"; and then (on pp. 18–19) Hamilton endeavors to refute those who say this—by indicating the difference between the American Revolution and the French Revolution. For this difference, see the very strong statement To — (18 May 1797) P 14:475–476. Consider also Address to the Electors of the State of New York (21 March 1801) P 25, part of which is presented below, toward the end of chap. VI, sec. iii; consider also in that address at P 25:354: "Surely ye will applaud neither the wisdom nor the patriotism of men, who wish you to exchange the fair fabric of Republicanism which you now enjoy, modelled and decorated by the hand of federalism, for that tremendous Form of Despotism, which has sprung up amidst the volcanic eruptions of *principles at war* with all past and present experience, at war with the nature of man." On this, consider note 14 to chap. X, below.

IV   The Structural Foundation of Government

1   F9, p. 52; F13, pp. 80–81; F23, pp. 150–151; F26, p. 169; F28, p. 177; F85, p. 593. In defending the constitutional proposal against the charge that the Convention had gone to an extreme, Hamilton thus showed it to be rather in the middle between two extremes. In the Convention itself, Hamilton had acted similarly: when the New Jersey Plan was brought forward as a supposedly moderate alternative to the supposedly extremist Virginia Plan, Hamilton brought forward a plan at the other extreme from the New Jersey Plan; he thus produced a situation in which the previously extreme Virginia Plan became the middle road. See Herbert J. Storing, "The Constitutional Convention: Toward a More Perfect Union" (University of Chicago: Works of the Mind Lecture, April 1961).

2   Hamilton did not utterly lack an appreciation of the small republic's charm. As a young officer fighting for American liberty, he wrote to his future wife: "If America were lost we should be happy in some other clime more favourable to human rights. What think you of Geneva as a retreat? 'Tis a charming place; where nature and society are in their greatest perfection" (To Elizabeth Schuyler [6 September 1780] P 2:422–423). But America

was won: a retreat was not needed; it was necessary to go forward. When "the despots of France" invaded "the Swiss Cantons—the boast of Republicans—the model to which they have been glad to appeal in proof, that a republican government may consist with the order and happiness of society," this was an outrage—Titus Manlius (The Stand) no. 3 (7 April 1798) P 21:407—but the Swiss Cantons were not a model to be imitated.

3 F8, p. 47, F76, p. 510, Draft of President's Eighth Annual Address to Congress (10 November 1796) P 20:386–387.

4 F11, p. 72.

5 Rousseau, *Du Contrat Social*, livre 1, chap. 6, note; livre 3, chap. 15. Although Rousseau attacked representation he favored magistracy: *Discours sur l'Origine . . . de l'Inégalité . . .* (Pléiade, Oeuvres Complètes, III), Dédicace, pp. 113–115; but one must ask whether Rousseau's attack on representation is a solid foundation for a safe and effective magistracy in a popular government framed for durable liberty.

6 F8, p. 45.

7 F9, p. 53; F27, p. 172; F68, pp. 460–461. Also: the continent-wide Congress "will be in general better composed for abilities, and as well for integrity as any assembly on the continent" (Continentalist no. 5 [18 April 1782] P 3:79).

8 Continentalist no. 1 (12 July 1781) P 2:651; F9, pp. 50–51; F18 (a paper written with Madison), pp. 111–113; F28, p. 177. New York Ratifying Convention (21 June 1788) P 5:38–39. And consider F73, p. 493: "this stern virtue is the growth of few soils."

9 Continentalist no. 1 (1781) P 2:651–652. F9, pp. 51–55; F27, p. 172 (as emended); F60, pp. 404–406; F61, p. 413. New York Ratifying Convention (27 June 1788) P 5:99–100.

10 F26, p. 169; F28, pp. 178–180.

11 Farmer Refuted (23 February 1775) P 1:92, 97, 100, 105–106. The House of Commons is called "the democratical part" of the British government at p. 92 as well as at p. 105.

12 Full Vindication of the Measures of Congress (15 December 1774) P 1:53, 66. Farmer Refuted (23 February 1775) P 1:88, 92–93, 97, 100–101, 104–105, 107, 126. The quotation is from Hume's *Essays* ("That Politics May be Reduced to a Science").

13 Full Vindication of the Measures of Congress (15 December 1774) P 1:48. Farmer Refuted (23 February 1775) P 1:91–92, 115, 164–165. Even without a plan by turbulent men to erect a republic, the commotions for liberty in America became a war for independence from Britain, and the love of liberty then required prudent and moderate men to make republican plans; but an enlightened well-wisher to republican government had then to become a warm advocate for executive energy.

14 New York Assembly: Remarks on an act granting to Congress certain imposts and duties (15 February 1787) P 4:73.

15 Opinion as to the Constitutionality of the Bank of the United States (23 February 1791) L 3:183.

16 F22, pp. 139, 145–146.

17 F28, p. 178.

18 Gouverneur Morris to Hamilton (May 1777) P 1:253–254; To Gouverneur Morris (19 May 1777) P 1:255. For a fuller account, see chap. X, sec. ix, below.

19 New York Ratifying Convention: Notes for speech (12 July 1788) P 5:149–152. For a fuller account, see chap. X, sec. ix, below.

20 Montesquieu, "Preface" to *De l'Esprit des Lois*; Hume, "Of Essay Writing" (at beginning) in *Essays*.

In a letter to Montesquieu (10 April 1749), Hume writes of "mes reflexions que j'ai faites en lisant votre ouvrage [*L'Esprit des Lois*], dont la plupart servent à confirmer plus en plus les principes sur lesquelles votre système est fondé" (*Letters of David Hume*, J.Y.T. Greig, ed. [Oxford, 1932], 1:133ff).

21 Rousseau, *Discours sur l'Origine . . . de l'Inégalité* (Pléiade, III), Première Partie, pp. 141–142, 169–172. *Du Contrat Social* (Pléiade, III), livre 1, chap. 6, pp. 360–362; chap. 8, pp. 364–365; livre 2, chap. 7, pp. 381–384; livre 4, chap. 8, pp. 465–467.

22 Hume, *Essays*, "Idea of a Perfect Commonwealth."

23 Rousseau, *Les Confessions* (Pléiade, I), livre 12, p. 630.

24 Many places in his writings show Hamilton's reading of Hume. In Hamilton's first public controversy, during the conflict between the American colonies and Great Britain, his follow-up pamphlet quoted Hume twice: once from the essay "Of the Independency of Parliament," on the fundamental psychological maxim of politics, and once from the essay "That Politics may be Reduced to a Science," on the greater oppressiveness toward their provinces of governments that are free. During the Constitutional Convention, he referred to Hume on corruption and the British constitution. And the last paragraph of the series of papers on behalf of the proposed U.S. Constitution quoted the essay "Of the Rise and Progress of the Arts and Sciences," calling Hume "a writer, equally solid and ingenious." Farmer Refuted (23 February 1775) P 1:94–95, 100; Constitutional Convention (22 June 1787) P 4:216–217 (Madison and Yates differ in their versions of the import of Hamilton's remark); F85, p. 594.

Hamilton studied not only the political but also the commercial essays of Hume. In a private letter advising the Superintendent of Finance on principles and measures of administration under the weak government of the Confederation Congress, Hamilton referred to the essay "Of the Balance of Trade." In his first series of papers urging new foundations to strengthen the government of the Union, he spoke about misunderstandings of the essay "Of the Jealousy of Trade," calling Hume a "very ingenious and sensible writer." And in the retrospective defense of his program as first minister in the government formed for a more perfect Union, he spoke about the essay "Of Public Credit," calling Hume "profound and ingenious." To Robert Morris (30 April 1781) P 2:608; Continentalist no. 5 (13 April 1782) P 3:77; Defense of the Funding System (July 1795) P 19:67. Hamilton cited Hume's *History* in some notes he made on history as a young lawyer ([December 1786] P 3:705). According to Adam Smith, writing of Europe after the fall of the Roman Empire: "commerce and manufactures gradually introduced order and good government, and with them, the liberty and security of individuals, among the inhabitants of the country, who had before lived almost in a continual state of war with their neighbors, and of servile dependency upon their superiors. This, though it has been the least observed, is by far the most important of all their effects. Mr. Hume is the only writer who, so far as I know, has hitherto taken notice of it" (*The Wealth of Nations*, bk. 3, chap. 4, p. 385). Hume took such notice in his essays "Of Commerce" and (variously titled) "Of Luxury" or "Of Refinement in the Arts." There is an echo of the point made by Hume and Smith in Hamilton's Report on Manufactures: manufactures and commerce tend to establish and confirm substantial and permanent public order ([5 December 1791] P 10:294).

In many other places Hamilton seems to echo a passage in Hume without naming him. In a letter attributing "want of discipline and their defects" in the American army during the War for Independence "as much to the skeleton state of our regiments as to any other cause," Hamilton explains that the same number of men in an army fight less

well, from lack of confidence, if there is not a full complement of men in their corps;
and he observes: "opinion, whether well or ill founded, is the governing principle of
human affairs" (To William Duer [18 June 1778] P 1:499–500). He makes a similar point
about opinion in discussing finance: see To — (December 1779) P 2:242, or To Robert
Morris (30 April 1781) P 2:624. In human affairs generally, and in the governing affairs
of purse and sword, opinion governs. Compare Hume, *Essays*, "Whether the British Government Inclines more to Absolute Monarchy or to a Republic": "though men be much
governed by interest, yet even interest itself, and all human affairs, are entirely governed
by *opinion*." There is also in Hume, *Essays*, "Of the First Principles of Government," a
related remark: "It is . . . on opinion only that government is founded; and this maxim
extends to the most despotic and most military governments." Hamilton seems to echo:
"All governments, even the most despotic, depend in a great degree, on opinion" (New
York Ratifying Convention [21 June 1788] P 5:37).

    Also, see above, note 27, chap. II.

25   F33, p. 205. New York Assembly: Remarks on an act for regulating elections (27 Janu-
    ary 1787) P 4:29. New York Ratifying Convention (21 June 1788) P 5:37, 41–42. F35,
    pp. 215–222; F36, pp. 222–224, 228–229. In his Report on Manufactures (5 December
    1791), Hamilton wrote that he objected, except in cases of "distressing emergency," to
    poll or capitation taxes according to a fixed rate, "which operate unequally and injuri-
    ously to the industrious poor." L 3:381.

    Hamilton did insist on the need for the representative body to be numerous enough
for safety (see, below, chap. X, sec. i).

V   *The Partition of Power*

1   Continentalist no. 1 (12 July 1781) P 2:652.
2   Titus Manlius (The Stand) no. 1 (10 March 1798) L 5:396. F76, p. 510. To the Electors of
    the State of New York (7 April 1789) P 5:322–324. F84, p. 584. Constitutional Conven-
    tion (8 September 1787) P 4:244. New York Ratifying Convention (21 June 1788) P 5:38;
    (27 June 1788) P 5:96–97.
3   F26, pp. 168–169. F28, pp. 178–180. F60, p. 404. F61, pp. 412–413. F82, pp. 555–556.
    F84, pp. 581–583. New York Ratifying Convention (21 June 1788) P 5:38, 43–44. New
    York Assembly (15 February 1787) P 4:81–82.
4   F71, p. 483. New York Ratifying Convention (20 June 1788) P 5:20, 43; (27 June 1788)
    P 5:94–97, 104. Remarks on the Quebec Bill: Part One (15 June 1775) P 1:166–169. Un-
    submitted Resolution (July 1783) P 3:420–421. F84, p. 584. F73, p. 498. F78, pp. 528,
    530. To Robert Livingston (25 April 1785) P 3:609.
5   New York Ratifying Convention (21 June 1788) P 5:38. F70, p. 472. F71, pp. 481–483.
    F74, p. 501. F65, pp. 440–441. F60, pp. 404–405.
6   F71, pp. 483–486. New York Ratifying Convention (21 June 1788) P 5:54–55. F73, pp.
    493–498. To Washington (5 May 1789) P 5:335. Constitutional Convention (12 Septem-
    ber 1787) P 4:248. F65, pp. 439–444. F66, pp. 445–447. F75, p. 504.
7   Compare Mr. Justice Brandeis, dissenting, in Myers v. United States, 272 U.S. 52 (1926),
    at 293: "The doctrine of the separation of powers was adopted by the Convention of 1787,
    not to promote efficiency but to preclude the exercise of arbitrary power. The purpose
    was, not to avoid friction, but, by means of the inevitable friction incident to the distri-

bution of the governmental powers among three departments, to save the people from autocracy."

But consider, for example, F75, p. 507, where Hamilton presents an argument against admitting the House of Representatives to a share in the formation of treaties: he mentions objections having to do with the spirit presiding over a body so variable and so numerous and then says that the very complication of the business, by introducing a necessity of the concurrence of so many different bodies, would of itself afford a solid objection.

Separation of powers understood simply as a device to prevent autocracy can degenerate into paralysis or into institutionalized civil strife eventuating in autocracy.

VI Administrative Efficacy

1   Aristotle, *Politics, passim* on "politeia." Thucydides, II.64–65 and II.22. Aristotle, *Rhetoric*, 1354b17 and 26; 1356a11. Liddell and Scott, *A Greek-English Lexicon*, 9th ed. (Oxford, 1940), p. 1785. Nietzsche, *Goetzen-Daemmerung*, "Was ich den Alten verdanke," 3.

2   Machiavelli, *Il Principe*, XV, XVIII; *Discorsi*, I.9, III.35, I.16.

3   Bacon, *Novum Organum*, Aph. LXXI.

4   Descartes, *Regulae ad Directionem Ingenii; Discours de la Methode; La Geometrie.*

5   Hobbes, *The Elements of Law*, ed. Tonnies (New York, 1969), pt. 2, chap. 2, para. 5, pp. 120–121; *The Citizen*, X, 9–15 and 19.

6   Montesquieu, *De l'Esprit des Lois*, XI.6 (Pléiade ed.: Oeuvres), 2:397, 399, 400.

7   Adam Smith, *The Wealth of Nations* (New York, 1965), bk. 4, chap. 7, pt. 3, pp. 586–588. Hume, *Essays*, "Of the Balance of Power."

8   To James Duane (6 September 1780) P 2:420–421; cf. The Farmer Refuted (February 1775) P 1:158. F25, p. 162. To McHenry (23 November 1799) L 6:265–266.

9   To Jay (19 November 1798) L 6:94. To Washington (18 August 1792) L 2:267; F36, pp. 224–226; To Oliver Wolcott (3 October 1795) L 8:357.

10 To Washington (2 December 1794) L 8:329–331; To McHenry (19 August 1799) L 6:196–197.

11 To McHenry (21 January 1799) L 6:148.

12 To McHenry (30 July 1798) L: 6:91, and (19 August 1799) L 6:195.

13 The Public Conduct and Character of John Adams, Esq., President of the United States (1800) L 6:419–420. To Tobias Lear (2 January 1800) P 24:155. To Rufus King (2 October 1798) L 8:511; cf. To Gouverneur Morris (27 February 1802) L 8:591–592. King was then U.S. Minister Plenipotentiary to Great Britain; and Morris, though superseded in 1794 as U.S. Minister Plenipotentiary to France, remained in Europe for four more years. On the presidential power of removal, see also, in chap. VIII, below, section vi and the beginning of section vii.

14 Continentalist no. 1 (12 July 1781) P 2:649–650.

15 To Washington (3 May 1799) L 6:167. F70, p. 472. The Farmer Refuted (23 February 1775) P 1:155–156. To Washington (15 September 1790) P 7:51. Continentalist no. 1 (12 July 1781) P 2:649–650, 661–662; no. 3 (9 August 1781) P 2:663. To Robert Morris (28 September 1782) P 3:170; (30 April 1781) P 2:621. F26, p. 164. F1, p. 5. Unsubmitted Resolution (July 1783) P 3:425–426. To Washington (17 March 1783) P 3:292; (18 August 1792) L 2:267–271. New York Ratifying Convention (21 June 1788) P 5:44–

45. Catullus to Aristides no. 3 (29 September 1792) L 6:355. One might expect the Americans to be a people more likely to fall prey to false alarms of tyranny than to submit with ease to a tyrant's depradations—they were, after all, described by Hamilton as a people who "descrying Tyranny at a distance, and guided only by the light of just principles before they had yet felt the scourge of oppression, could nobly hazard all in defence of their rights" (Lucius Crassus no. 17 [20 March 1802] P 25:576).

16   Lansing or Burr (1804) L 7:325. To Theodore Sedgwick (10 July 1804) L 8:616. New York Ratifying Convention (21 June 1788) P 5:39–40; (27 June 1788) P 5:94. Defence of the Funding System (July 1795) P 19:36. The Continentalist no. 6 (4 July 1782) P 3:102–104; New York Assembly (19 January 1787) P 4:11–12; (17 February 1787) P 4:94–96. To Robert Morris (13 August 1782) P 3:135–137. From Robert Morris (28 August 1782) P 3:154. To John Jay (25 July 1783) P 3:416–417. F1, pp. 5–6. To Rufus King (5 January 1800) L 8:540. Lucius Crassus no. 18 (8 April 1802) L 7:322. To Richard Harrison (5 January 1793) L 8:292. Camillus no. 5 (1795) L4:414–415. Constitutional Convention (17 September 1787) P 4:253. Defence of the Funding System L 7:416–417 and 420. To George Clinton (24 February 1783) P 3:272–273. To Washington (3 July 1787) P 4:223–225. Lucius Crassus no. 1 (17 December 1801) L7:200–201; no. 9 (18 January 1802) L 7:244–246; no. 18 (8 April 1802) L 7:314, 322. To Rufus King (5 January 1800) L 8:540; (3 January 1802) L 8:600, 602. To Gen. C. C. Pinckney (29 December 1802) L 8:605–606. To Washington (25 March 1783) P 3:306. F6, pp. 34–35. F12, pp. 75–77. F30, p. 193. F36, pp. 229–230. To Col. Edward Carrington (26 May 1792) L 8:248, 262. Jefferson to Madison (20 December 1787). Jefferson to William B. Giles (31 December 1795). Address to the Electors of the State of New York (21 March 1801) P 25:353, 357, 370–371. Jefferson to Spencer Roane (6 September 1819).

17   Madison, quoted in Memoranda by N. P. Trist (27 September 1834), reprinted in Max Farrand, *Records of the Federal Convention of 1787*, 1937 rev. ed. (New Haven, 1966), 3:534.

VII Unity

1   France (1796) L 5:343. The Continentalist no. 6 (4 July 1782) P 2:106.

2   Constitutional Convention (29 June 1787) P 4:221. F85, pp. 590–594. In 1780 Hamilton wrote, to a delegate to Congress, "agreeably to your request and my promise," his "ideas of the defects of the present system and the changes necessary to save us from ruin"; "the fundamental defect" was "a want of power in Congress" (that is, the imperfection of the Union) and "the first step must be to give Congress powers competent to the public exigencies"; of the two modes of doing this, the one to which Hamilton saw no objection "that has any weight in competition with the reasons for it" was calling "a convention of all the states with full authority to conclude finally upon a general confederation"; To James Duane (3 September 1780) P 2:400–401, 407–408 (aspects of this letter other than the federal are discussed below—see chap. VII, sec. iii, and chap. VIII, sec. ii).

An eminent historian of the Continental Congress writes that it was not a new idea to have the states send delegates to a constitutional convention to overhaul the entire system, but "the form, the manner, and the situation in which the idea was now presented . . . lent to it a weight and a substance that it had not hitherto exhibited"; "it would seem to have been directly, perhaps chiefly, from this implantation by Hamilton [in the letter to Duane of 3 September 1780] that the Federal Convention of 1787 eventually grew" (Edmund C. Burnett, *The Continental Congress* (New York, 1964), p. 487).

3   The Continentalist no. 3 (9 August 1781) P 2:661; no. 5 (18 April 1782) P 3:78. Unsubmitted Resolution (July 1783) P 3:425. To Washington (24 March 1783) P 3:304. F11, p. 72. F15, pp. 93–94, 96–98. F16, pp. 99–104. F20 (with Madison), pp. 128–129. F23, pp. 147–150. F80, pp. 534–535, 537. F82, pp. 555–556. To the National Advertiser (21 July 1787) P 4:230. First Letter from Phocion (January 1784) P 3:489. Defence of the Funding System (July 1795) P 19:27–28.

4   F22, pp. 140–142. F70, pp. 474–478.

5   To James Duane (3 September 1780) P 2:400–401, 404–406, 408–409. Cf. Unsubmitted Resolution (July 1783) P 3:420–421. See also: To — (December 1779 to March 1780) P 2:246–247. To Isaac Sears (12 October 1780) P 2:472.

Some months before the letter to Duane of September 1780 (as well as Hamilton's editors can determine, it was between December of 1779 and March of 1780), Hamilton wrote a letter to an unknown addressee about credit and the need to establish a Bank of the United States under the inspection of the Board of Trade. In the letter the following paragraph appears as a footnote.

"This Board [of Trade] ought immediately to be established at all events. The Royal Council of Commerce in France and the subordinate chambers in each province form an excellent institution and may in many respects serve as a model. Congress have too long neglected to organize a good scheme of administration and throw public business into proper executive departments. For commerce I prefer a Board, but for most other things single men. We want a Minister of War, a Minister for Foreign Affairs, a Minister of Finance, and a Minister of Marine. There is always more decision, more dispatch, more secrecy, more responsibility where single men, than when bodies are concerned. By a plan of this kind, we should blend the advantages of a Monarchy and of a republic in a happy and beneficial Union. Men will only devote their lives and attentions to the mastering a profession on which they can build reputation and consequence which they do not share with others." P 2:246–247.

This footnote is of interest as Hamilton's first brief step into administrative science; Hamilton extended it in the more important, slightly later letter discussed above, which he wrote to Duane. It should be noted that the letter to Duane does not mention among the advantages of administration by single men one important item that is mentioned in this earlier letter: more secrecy.

It should also be noted that this letter contains, so far as I can tell, Hamilton's first use of the term "responsibility" in the full sense in which it came to be used in the study of public administration. (For Hamilton's use of the term in the letter to Duane of 3 September 1780, see P 2:405 and 406. So far as I can tell, his first use of the term in print is in Continentalist no. 3, on 9 August 1781, P 2:663, where he argues that Congress has responsibility without means.) Compare Douglas Adair (in "The Federalist Papers, a Review Article," *William and Mary Quarterly*, 3rd ser., vol. 22 [1965]), on "responsibility."

Adair reports: "According to the *Oxford English Dictionary on Historical Principles*, the word itself is an American invention, and its first appearance in the language is credited by the OED to the long discussion of Senatorial 'responsibility' in Madison's *Federalist* no. 63. There the word appears four times in two paragraphs (the first English occurrence is credited by the OED to Burke in 1792). There is an equally long discussion of Executive 'responsibility' in Hamilton's no. 70 (the word appears three times) and no. 77 (two times)" (p. 137). Adair goes on to say: "The word 'responsibility' is apparently a coinage of James Madison; its first obscure appearance (that I have found) is in Madison's committee report to the Continental Congress on the Quartermaster Department [July 22, 1780] in William T. Hutchinson and William M. E. Rachal, eds., *The Papers of James Madison* (Chicago, 1962), 2:44–45. There is some evidence that it was used with some frequency by Madison and some of his colleagues in the Federal Convention. At any rate, James Wilson on December 4, 1787, in the Pennsylvania Ratifying Convention is talking about presidential responsibility without any self-consciousness (Jonathan Elliot, *The Debates in the Several State Conventions on the Adoption of the Federal Convention . . .* [Philadelphia, 1863], 2:480); and by the close of that convention (December 11, 1787) both Federalists and Antifederalists seem to be making use of the term (ibid., 2:530, 532). It appears unobtrusively in Madison's Federalist no. 48 (February 1, 1788) and no. 57 (February 19, 1788), and in Hamilton's no. 23 (December 18, 1787) prior to the eye-catching and extended use in no. 63 (March 1, 1788) and no. 70 (March 15, 1788). Jay also uses it in no. 64 (March 5, 1788). And so Publius in March 1788 definitely fixes this word in the language once and for all" (pp. 137–138, n. 8).

If Adair has indeed found Madison's first use, then Hamilton would seem to have priority over Madison in this use of the term "responsibility"—and would also seem to be its inventor.

6 F70, p. 472; F72, p. 486.

As early as 1777, Hamilton said he was not enamored of plurality in the executive. Recording, in his notes on Plutarch, that "the having two Kings, the senate and the Ephori" were considered in antiquity to be "the causes of the duration of the Spartan government," Hamilton observes (in one of his rare judgments upon what he records in those notes): "the first circumstance would be in modern times a source of endless confusion and distraction" (Pay Book of the State Company of Artillery [1777] P 1:397).

But it was after American independence was achieved, and there remained the work of rendering that independence a blessing by perfecting the American union, that Hamilton carried further his argument for executive unity. Continuing to reflect on antiquity, he wrote that as far as the experience of other nations teaches anything about the matter, "it teaches us not to be inamored of plurality in the executive." He gives as instances the experience of the Achaeans with two praetors and of the Romans with the consuls and military tribunes. But "the experience of other nations will afford little instruction on this head," so, "quitting the dim light of historical research," Hamilton calls for "attaching ourselves purely to the dictates of reason and good sense" (F70, pp. 473–474).

7 F72, p. 486. Hamilton's Plan: P 4:208. Madison: Speech on the location of the capital (18 September 1789) in *Writings* (Hunt, ed.), 5:423 (I am obliged to Murray Dry for drawing my attention to this remark by Madison).

8 F72, pp. 486–487. Cf. New York Assembly (15 February 1787) P 4:75.

9 Finance: To Robert Morris (30 April 1781) P 2:604–606. To Washington (18 August 1792) P 12:236. Defense of the Funding System (July 1795) P 19:3–6, 41–42 (cf. Robert Morris, *Papers*, ed. Ferguson et al., 1:287). The Continentalist no. 4 (30 August 1781) P 2:673.

10 Spending: Explanation (11 November 1795) L 7:81, 87, 110. To McHenry (12 November 1799) L 6:257–259; (21 March 1800) L 6:288–291; (5 May 1800) L 6:293–294. To Caleb Swann (26 May 1800) L 6:302–304. Lucius Crassus no. 11 (3 February 1802) L 7:256–262.

Note that among the "measures to be taken without delay," in the list of "Measures of Defence" compiled by Hamilton in 1799 during the crisis with France, is this item VII: "It is essential that the Executive should have half a million of secret-service money. If the measure cannot be carried without it, the expenditure may be with the approbation of three members of each House of Congress" (L 6:139).

11   What is central is somehow one with what is first and last. A month after Robert Morris was named Superintendent of Finance during the War for Independence, Hamilton wrote to him: "I was among the first who were convinced that an administration by single men was essential to the proper management of the affairs of this country. I am persuaded now it is the only resource we have to extricate ourselves from the distresses, which threaten the subversion of our cause." Hamilton noted that "the people have lost all confidence in our public councils" ("there is . . . so universal and rooted a diffidence of the government, that if we could be assured the future measures of Congress would be dictated by the most perfect wisdom and public spirit there would still be a necessity for a change in the forms of our administration to give a new spring and current to the passions and hopes of the people") and "our friends in Europe are in the same disposition" ("the Court of France will never give half the succours to this Country while Congress holds the reins of administration in their own hands, which they would grant, if these were intrusted to individuals of established reputation and conspicuous for probity, abilities and fortune"). Men would not lend money to those who showed by their arrangements that they did not mean business. Money was the means to American independence, and a good administration was the means of obtaining that means: "an executive ministry composed of men with the qualifications I have described would speedily restore the credit of government abroad and at home, would induce our allies to greater exertions in our behalf, would inspire confidence in monied men in Europe as well as in America to lend us [those] sums of which it may be demonstrated we [stand] in need from the disproportion of our national wealth to the expences of the War." Hamilton told Morris: "I heard [with] the greatest satisfaction of your nomination [to] the department of finance. In a letter of mine last summer to Mr. Duane, urging among other things the plan of an executive ministry, I mentioned you as the person who ought to fill that department"— "an office by which you may render America and the world no less a service than the establishment of American independence! Tis by introducing order into our finances— by restoring public credit—not by gaining battles, that we are finally to gain our object. Tis by putting ourselves in a condition to continue the war not by temporary, violent and unnatural efforts to bring it to a decisive issue, that we shall in reality bring it to a speedy and successful one . . . you are the Man best capable of performing this great work." Hamilton then went on to discuss finance, especially a plan for a bank. To Robert Morris (30 April 1781) P 2:604–606. (Morris had been named Superintendent of Finance on 20 February 1781.) The government that presides at the center over the well-being of the country needs to be able to dispose of vast quantities of the medium of exchange. A center to preside over that government is also needed, for one-man administration is needed for credit, and credit is essential in the ultimate fact of government: even modern commercial nations, and especially modern commercial nations, must be equipped for war (F6, pp. 31–32; F24, p. 157; F34, p. 211), and in the wars of a modern commercial nation, finance is of the essence.

12   Foreign relations: F75, pp. 504–509. F64 (Jay, referred to in F75 at p. 505), pp. 434–436. F69, pp. 467–468. F84, pp. 585–586. F22, pp. 139–143. To Washington (7 March 1796)

F20, pp. 68–69; (24 March 1796) P 20:82–85; (29 March 1796) P 20:85–102; (2 April 1796) P 20:106–107. To William Loughton Smith (10 March 1796) P 20:72–73. To Rufus King (16 March 1796) P 20:76–77.

13   War: Continentalist no. 3 (9 August 1781) P 2:663. F74, p. 500. F70, p. 476. F6, p. 46. F69, p. 465. Pay Book of the State Company of Artillery (1777) P 1:390. F25, p. 161. To George Clinton (1 June 1783) P 3:368–369. To Rufus King (15 February 1797) L 8:448. To Oliver Wolcott (17 February 1797) L 8:448–449. To Timothy Pickering (22 March 1797) L 8:454. Titus Manlius (The Stand) no. 6 (19 April 1798) L 5:437, 439; no. 4 (12 April 1798) L 5:421; no. 1 (10 March 1798): 5:399–400. To McHenry (3 May 1799) L 6:168–169; (17 May 1798) L 8:481; (27 June 1799) L 6:185–186. To Oliver Wolcott (30 March 1797) L 8:455–456. To Rufus King (8 April 1797) L 8:461. To Gen. C. C. Pinckney (29 December 1802) L 8:606. To Oliver Wolcott, Jr. (5 June 1798) P 21:487.

The energy that is wisdom has, however, a variety of aspects; compare To the New York Committee of Correspondence (22 March 1777) P 1:212 and To Robert R. Livingston (28 June 1777) P 5:275–277: a lethargic management of affairs that is kept in action only by the fear of immediate danger must be distinguished from a politic exertion of courage and strength that may to the less discerning be indistinguishable from cowardice and weakness; Fabian conduct is a most active policy; the feelings of a soldier may be wounded when he sees an enemy parading before him and daring him to a fight which he is obliged to decline—nonetheless, a part must be sacrificed to the whole, and passion must give way to reason, which attends to what is effectual.

14   Pacificus no. 1 (29 June 1793) P 15:33–43. At F69, p. 468, referring to the exclusive possession by the Union of that part of the sovereign power which relates to treaties, Hamilton delicately raises the question whether, if the confederacy were to be dissolved, that delicate and important prerogative of the British sovereign would not vest *solely in the executives* of the several states.

15   F70, pp. 471–472. F85, p. 90. The enlightened well wishers to the republican species of government must at least hope, Hamilton says, that there is no foundation to the supposition that a vigorous executive is inconsistent with the genius of republican government—for they can never admit its truth without at the same time admitting the condemnation of their own principles.

16   Pay Book of the State Company of Artillery (1777) P 1:396. Notes in Fed. Conv. (1 June 1787) P 4:163. To James Duane (3 September 1780) P 2:413. The Continentalist no. 3 (9 August 1781) P 2:663.

According to Blackstone, "the executive part of government . . . is wisely placed in a single hand by the British constitution, for the sake of unanimity, strength, and dispatch. Were it placed in many hands, it would be subject to many wills: many wills, if disunited and drawing different ways, create weakness in a government; and to unite those several wills, and reduce them to one, is a work of more time and delay than the exigencies of state will afford. The king of England is therefore not only the chief, but properly the sole, magistrate of the nation; all others acting by commission from, and in due subordination to him: in like manner as, upon the great revolution in the Roman state, all the powers of the ancient magistracy of the commonwealth were concentered in the new emperor." Blackstone, *Commentaries on the Laws of England* (12th ed.), bk. 1 (Of the Rights of Persons), chap. 7 (Of the King's Prerogative).

Blackstone thinks it clear that "Upon the whole . . . whatever may have become of the *nominal,* the *real* power of the crown has not been too far weakened by any transactions in the last century. Much is indeed given up; but much is also acquired. The stern commands of prerogative have yielded to the milder voice of influence: the slavish and exploded doctrine of non-resistance has given way to a military establishment by law; and to the disuse of parliaments has succeeded a parliamentary trust of an immense perpetual revenue." He looks forward to a time when "this adventitious power of the crown will slowly and imperceptibly diminish, as it slowly and imperceptibly rose," when the sinking fund will lessen national debts, when the posture of foreign affairs and the introduction of a real national militia will allow the formidable army to be thinned and regulated, and when, in consequence of all, the taxes will be reduced. But till then, he says, it will be the duty of Englishmen, while reverencing the crown, to guard their freedom, and to hope that they may long, very long, continue to be governed by a sovereign who has manifested the highest reverence for the free constitution of Britain. Bk. 1 (Of the Rights of Persons), chap. 8 (Of the King's Revenue).

Even in a monarchy there is something grating in the assertion of monarchical will against the inclinations of the many men who are governed; see Blackstone on "Le roy s'avisera" (bk. 1, chap. 2).

Great Britain is a limited monarchy; it does not look like or have the form of a republic. Writing in an absolute monarchy, or at least one not much limited, Montesquieu asked his readers to look at a certain nation, left unnamed though he clearly means Great Britain, where the republic hides under the form of monarchy, or there is the form of an absolute government on the foundation of a free government; it differs from the extremes that are productive of evil, the extremely absolute monarchies and the states that are extremely free. Montesquieu, *De l'Esprit de Lois*, V. 19, p. 304; XIX.27, pp. 580 and 583.

17 F67, pp. 452–457. Compare F67 with F52 (House of Representatives), with F62 (Senate), and with F78 (Judiciary).

18 The power of filling casual vacancies in the Senate, ascribed by the outrageous opposition to the President of the United States, is in fact expressly allotted to the executives of the individual states.

19 F68, pp. 457–462. It should be noted that the sense of the people could be expected to operate even though the Constitution did not require the electors to be chosen by popular vote. The Constitution empowered the several states to decide how the electors would be chosen, and it came as no great shock when the states then decided for popular vote. It should also be noted that "moral certainty" is not "absolute certainty," "seldom" is not "never," and "probably" is not "certainly": Hamilton finds in the mode of electing the President "no inconsiderable recommendation of the constitution"; he does not say that the mode of election is such a guarantee of ability and virtue in the President as to render checks on him dispensable.

The poet is quoted at F68, p. 461. The pronouncement is repeated at F76, p. 509. The poet was Alexander Hamilton's early favorite, Alexander Pope; the lines are from *An Essay on Man* (3:303–304). Pope's literary executor, William Warburton, in his 1751 edition of Pope's *Works*, notes: "The reader will not be displeased to see the Poet's own apology, as I find it written in the year 1740, in his own hand, in the margin of a book, where he found these two celebrated lines misapplied. 'The author of these lines was far from meaning that no one form of Government is, in itself, better than another . . . but that no form . . . in itself, can be sufficient to make a people happy, unless it be administered with integrity.'" William K. Wimsatt, Jr., ed., *Alexander Pope: Selected Poetry and Prose* (New York, 1964), p. 155, n. 15. The questioning of these lines from Pope is the point of departure for Hume's essay "That Politics May Be Reduced to a Science."

20 Having devoted the first of the papers on the executive to a most blamable misrepresentation of the plan by the opposition, and the second of the papers to a most praiseworthy
feature of the plan acceptable to the opposition, Hamilton traces the real characteristics
of the proposed executive in the third paper, number 69, in order to place in a strong
light the unfairness of the representations which have been made in regard to it.

21 F70, pp. 471–480.

22 All that remains to the discussion of executive power after this is the discussion of those
remaining powers of the executive to which no objection has been made—except some
cavils not worth discussing.

23 See F65–F66; then see F64, pp. 432–438, and F65, p. 439. F76, pp. 509–513. F77, pp.
516–519. F66, pp. 448–450. F69, pp. 468–469. F77, pp. 519–520. It would be impracticable for the people at large ordinarily to exercise the power of appointment; this, says
Hamilton, will be readily admitted by all—if only because it would leave the people at
large little time to do anything else.

24 F70, p. 478. F77, p. 519. F74, pp. 500–503. F69, p. 466.

VIII Unity and Duration

1 New York Assembly: First Speech (19 January 1787) P 4:12; Second Speech (19 January
1787) R 4:16. To Rufus King (3 June 1802) L 8:601. To James Duane (3 September 1780)
P 2:404–405, 409–411. Continentalist no. 6 (4 July 1782) P 3:103.

2 To James Duane (3 September 1780) P 2:401, 404–406, 409–411.

3 Continentalist no. 6 (4 July 1782) P 3:103.

4 Continentalist no. 4 (30 August 1781) P 2:669–671.

5 Second Report on the Further Provision Necessary for Establishing Public Credit (Report
on a National Bank) (13 December 1790) P 7:333, 326–327.

6 Report on a Plan for the Further Support of Public Credit (16 January 1795) P 18:102–
104. Madison called Hamilton's report of 16 January 1795 his "Valedictory Report"; James
Madison to Thomas Jefferson (26 January 1795 and again 15 February 1795). Hamilton's
editor points out that this was not Hamilton's last report (there was a later "Report on the
Improvement and Better Management of the Revenue of the United States" on 31 January
1795), but it was nonetheless Hamilton's last major report, for it "contains both a summary of where the Treasury Department has been under his direction and his views on
where it should go after he had left the Government." "Introductory Note," P 18:47, with
n. 2. The editor also notes that the report, which emphasizes "plans for extinguishing
the current debt with existing sources of revenue," has not been reprinted in important
collections of Hamilton's reports and papers on public credit, commerce, and finance.
Madison called the report "arrogant" (To Jefferson [15 February 1795]); but the French
Minister to the United States wrote that "Cet ouvrage est sans doute écrit avec la pro-
fondeur et la sagesse qu'il possède au suprème dégré dans les matières de finances et de
calcul." Fauchet to Commissioner of Foreign Relations (31 January 1795), "Introductory
Note," P 18:46–47, with n. 1 and n. 2.

7 Report on a Plan for the Further Support of Public Credit (16 January 1795) P 18:127–
128. To Washington (1 June 1796) L 8:402.

8 To William Short (1 September 1790) P 7:11 (copy enclosed in Report on Foreign Loans,
13 February 1793). Address to the Public Creditors (1 September 1790) P 7:2.

9 Report on a Plan for the Further Support of Public Credit (16 January 1795) P 18:94–95.

10 Defence of the Funding System (July 1795) P 19:61.

11 F6, p. 31; F73, pp. 495–497.

12 F71, p. 484. F72, pp. 487–488, 491.

13 F72, pp. 491–492, 488–489.

14 F72, p. 491.

15 F71, pp. 481–483. F72, pp. 487, 492. Cf. F71, p. 482, and F72, p. 492: those who regard the executive's best recommendation as a servile pliancy to a prevailing current in the legislature, or even in the community at large, entertain notions that are "very crude"; there is "an excess of refinement" in the idea of disabling the people to continue in office men who have in the people's opinion entitled themselves to the people's approbation and confidence. (Although the term "leadership" did often have pejorative connotations in Hamilton's time, it is used positively here and elsewhere in this book, being the term that has come into usage to signify the notion that Hamilton was seeking to make respectable among republicans. See chap. XIII, below, for a situation in which Hamilton spoke of "Leaders & *real* Friends of the People," and of "Leaders & Patriots" as opposed to "Demogogues & Tyrants" [LPI, 840, 838].)

16 F71, pp. 481–482, 484–485.

17 F71, pp. 482–483. "Ruling passion" was a phrase used by Alexander Pope.

F17, pp. 105–106 (giving Hamilton's reply to that objection which urged, against the principle of legislating for the individual citizens of America, that it would enable the government of the Union to absorb "those residuary authorities, which it might be judged proper to leave with the States for local purposes"), says: "The administration of private justice between citizens of the same State, the supervision of agriculture and of other concerns of a similar nature, all those things in short which are proper to be provided for by local legislation, can never be desirable cares of a general jurisdiction. . . . [T]he attempt to exercise those powers would be as troublesome as nugatory; and the possession of them, for that reason, would contribute nothing to the importance, or to the splendour of the national government." . . . "I am at a loss to discover what temptation the persons entrusted with the administration of the general government could ever feel to divest the States of the authorities of that description. The regulation of the mere domestic police of a State appears to me to hold out slender allurements to ambition. Commerce, finance, negotiation, and war seem to comprehend all the objects, which have charms for minds governed by that passion"—"and all the powers necessary to these objects ought in the first instance to be lodged in the national depository."

Recommending Hamilton for high military position (25 September 1798), Washington wrote to President Adams about "the abilities and integrity of this man who had been the principal and most confidential aid of the Commander in Chief": "By some he is considered an ambitious man, and therefore a dangerous one. That he is ambitious I shall readily grant, but it is of that laudable kind which prompts a man to excel in whatever he takes in hand."

See To William Hamilton (2 May 1797) P 21:78—quoted in chap. X, below; see also note 33 to that section.

18 F72, p. 488.

19 F71, p. 481. F72, pp. 487–488.

20 F72, pp. 486–491.

21 F72, p. 487. F76, pp. 513, 515–516.

22   Pacificus no. 1 (29 June 1793) P 15:39–40. The immediate purpose of *Pacificus* was to
     justify the proclamation of neutrality by the President in 1793. When Hamilton was ap-
     proached by Hopkins, who was to republish *The Federalist* in 1802, Hamilton "hesitated
     his consent to republication," and, when Hamilton did consent, he insisted that the edi-
     tion include the *Pacificus* letters; he gave Hopkins the impression that "he did not regard"
     The Federalist "with much partiality," but he remarked to Hopkins that "some of his
     friends had pronounced" the *Pacificus* letters "to be his best performance." See, above, in
     chap. I, note 16 and the text to which it is attached.
         After Hamilton's statement (F76, p. 515) that "The consent of that body would be nec-
     essary to displace as well as to appoint," editor Cooke notes that at this point Hopkins
     adds the following footnote: "This construction has since been rejected by the legisla-
     ture; and it is now settled in practice, that the power of displacing belongs exclusively
     to the president." Cooke further notes that this is one of the two interpolations in the
     Hopkins edition which related statements in *The Federalist* to events after 1787–1788
     (editor's note on pp. 650–651, Cooke's edition of *The Federalist*). Hamilton, according
     to his son, supervised the Hopkins edition of 1802, though he did not himself make the
     revisions and corrections (pp. xv–xvi of the editor's introduction, Cooke's edition of *The
     Federalist*).
23   Later on Hamilton did take for granted the President's power of removal: alleging that
     President John Adams through vanity refrained from counseling with his constitutional
     advisers, Hamilton said that it must be Adam's own fault if he be not surrounded by men
     who, for ability and integrity, deserve his confidence, as the President not only nominates
     his ministers, but may displace them if he pleases. The Public Conduct and Character of
     John Adams, Esq., President of the United States (1800) L 6:419.
         Edward S. Corwin, in his article of 1927, "Tenure of Office and the Removal Power
     under the Constitution" (*Columbia Law Review*, vol. 27, no. 4), criticizing the opinion of
     the Chief Justice for the Supreme Court in *Myers v. United States* (1926), discusses (pp.
     370–371) the Chief Justice's use of Alexander Hamilton as a witness in his behalf (for
     which, see 272 U.S. 137 *et. seq.*)
         Corwin raises the question whether Hamilton changed his mind between writing Fed-
     eralist number 77 and the "Pacificus" letters in 1793 (which Corwin repeatedly refers
     to as "Letters of Publius"). He argues that Hamilton's position in 1793 was entirely har-
     monious with his position in 1789 (which Corwin mentions as if it were the date of
     Federalist number 77), on the supposition that Hamilton's "Pacificus" regards the power
     of removal as an incident to the power of appointment.
         Corwin draws this conclusion, on this supposition, after quoting against the Chief Jus-
     tice the words of Hamilton quoted by the Chief Justice. The quotation from "Pacificus"
     says that the executive power of the United States is completely lodged in the President
     subject only to the exceptions and qualifications made by the Constitution expressly,
     these exceptions being three, one of them the participation of the Senate in the appoint-
     ment of officers. The Chief Justice quotes this and continues the quotation from Hamilton
     (272 U.S. at 139), but Corwin does not continue; Corwin stops short of the following two
     sentences which complete Hamilton's paragraph and speak of the very matter at issue:
     "This mode of construing the Constitution has indeed been recognized by Congress in
     formal acts upon full consideration and debate. The power of removal from office is an
     important instance."
         The sentences quoted by the Chief Justice but omitted by Corwin in quoting the quo-

tation render Corwin's supposition highly doubtful, to say the least. If the power of removal is held by "Pacificus" to be an incident to the power of appointment, therefore (since "Pacificus" expressly mentions the Senate's participation in appointments as one of the express exceptions to the executive power lodged by the Constitution in the President alone) "Pacificus" must hold that it was wrong for Congress to allow that the President alone might exercise the power to remove. Either "Pacificus" regards Congress as having improperly applied the proper mode of construction when it allowed that the President alone might remove, or "Pacificus" does not regard the power of removal as an incident to the power of appointment—and Corwin's conclusion, that the "alleged change of mind remains highly doubtful, to say the least," though it may be true, is not established by his argument.

Corwin seems to have changed his own mind about whether Hamilton changed his mind: see Corwin's treatise, *The President: Office and Powers*, 4th rev. ed. (New York, 1957), p. 88. The only evidence given in the note in Corwin's treatise (p. 375, n. 66) is a quotation from Madison's letter to Rives (10 January 1829), which reports that an edition of *The Federalist* at New York contains a marginal note to the passage about removal, saying that Hamilton changed his view of the Constitution on that point.

24 F77, pp. 515–516; Catullus no. 4 (17 October 1792) L 6:357.

25 Forrest McDonald, *The Presidency of George Washington* (New York, 1975), pp. 173–174.

P 20:64–68, Introductory Note. To Oliver Wolcott, Jr. (7–10 March 1796) P 20:69. To George Washington (7 March 1796) P 20:68–69. P 20:73, n. 2. To William Loughton Smith (10 March 1796) P 20:72–73. P 20:73–74, n. 3. To Rufus King (16 March 1796) P 20:76–77. To George Washington (24 March 1796) P 20:81–82. To George Washington (26 March 1796) P 20:82–85. To George Washington (29 March 1796) P 20:85–86. P 20:105, n. 3 and n. 4. P 20:85, n. 1. Washington to Hamilton (31 March 1796) P 20:103–105. To George Washington (2 April 1796) P 20:106–107. To Rufus King (2 April 1796) P 20:106. P 20:86, n. 2. To George Washington (8 April 1796) P 20:108. P 20:67, n. 21. P 20:66.

Camillus no. 37 (6 January 1796) P 20:13, 19–20. P 20:73–74. The previous July the newspapers had contained arguments that the provisions of the treaty interfered with such powers of Congress as taxation, regulation of trade, prescription of uniform rules for naturalization, and others as well. Those objections to the treaty which are founded on a claim of interference with congressional powers, Hamilton argues in "Camillus," tend to render the power of making treaties merely nominal. The power to make laws and the power to make treaties are concurrent and coordinate; the power to make treaties and not the power to make laws must act where what is requisite is the cooperation of other nations. For instance, though Congress by the Constitution has the power of laying taxes, nonetheless a treaty may restrain its exercise in particular cases. A nation, like an individual, may abridge its moral power of action by agreement, and the organ charged with the legislative power of a nation may be restrained in its operation by the agreements of the organ of its federative power, that is, of its power to contract. The executive, within its sphere, is no less the organ of the nation's will than is the legislature.

26 James Thomas Flexner, *Washington: The Indispensable Man* (Boston, 1969), pp. 344–347; Forrest McDonald, *The Presidency of George Washington* (New York, 1975), p. 173; Jefferson to Madison (21 September 1795).

Enclosure in Letter to George Washington (29 March 1796) P 20:86–103.

1 Constitutional Convention (21 June 1787) P 4:214. F61, pp. 413–414.

IX　Duration

2　F65, p. 439.

3　F65, p. 439; F77, pp. 515, 519.

4　F65, pp. 439–442.

5　F75, pp. 506–507.

6　F75, pp. 503–504; F64 (Jay), p. 432.

7　F64 (Jay), pp. 432–433, 436.

8　F64 (Jay), pp. 434–435.

9　F84, pp. 585–586; F75, p. 506.

10　F62, pp. 415–417. F63, pp. 428–431. (Both papers were also claimed by Madison—see sec. v, below.)

11　F62, p. 418.

12　F63, pp. 426–428.

13　F62, pp. 418 and 423–424.

14　F62, pp. 418–419 and 422–423.

15　F62, pp. 419–420.

16　F62, pp. 420–421.

17　F63, pp. 424–426.

18　Jacob E. Cooke, ed., *The Federalist* (Cleveland and New York, 1961), "Introduction," pp. xxix–xxx. New York Ratifying Convention (24 June 1788) P 5:65–79; (25 June 1788) P 5:80–89.

19　The fullest version of the speech is that by Francis Childs, but there are sketchier notes by John McKesson and by Melancton Smith. It is tempting to rely simply on Childs: what he reports is fuller and is like a speech rather than a set of notes. The notes of McKesson and of Smith, however, agree in containing items left out by Childs, and their notes usefully confirm or modify our impression from Childs.

20　P 5:67–69 (Childs); P 5:75 (McKesson); P 5:78 (Smith).

21　P 5:69–70 (Childs); P 5:75–76 (McKesson); P 5:78 (Smith).

22　P 5:73–74 (Childs); P 5:77 (McKesson); P 5:79 (Smith).

23　P 5:74 (Childs); P 5:77 (McKesson); P 5:79 (Smith).

24　Only two versions of this speech are reported—one by Francis Childs and another sketchier one by John McKesson.

25　P 5:80–82 (Childs); P 5:86–87, 89 (McKesson).

26　P 5:82–83 (Childs); P 5:87 (McKesson).

27　P 5:83 (Childs); P 5:88 (McKesson).

28　P 5:85–86 (Childs); P 5:88–89 (McKesson).

X　Republican Constitution

1　Constitutional Convention (6 September 1787) P 4:243.

2　Constitutional Convention (8 September 1787) P 4:244. New York Ratifying Convention (27 June 1788) P 5:96–97. F84, p. 584.

3　Constitutional Convention (17 September 1787) P 4:253, 274.

4　Of Hamilton's speech to the Convention on 18 June, Hamilton's editor says: "this speech is perhaps the most important address ever made by Hamilton—if its importance can be measured by its use in subsequent evaluations of Hamilton's political philosophy or by the controversy about it during his lifetime." P 4:178.

In the present work we shall not examine the records of this speech, but only records of the controversy about it during Hamilton's lifetime—in particular, Hamilton's subsequent self-interpretation in response to the fearful or hostile evaluations of him that were generated or confirmed by interpretations of reports of the speech.

The records of the speech cannot be understood without interpretation. There are four sets of notes made by men who were at the Convention listening. Madison, Yates, Lansing, and King all left records; and when these are read together, with close attention, the seemingly slight differences of diction or arrangement, especially at transitions, sometimes give very different impressions of what the original might have been like. In addition, besides Hamilton's text of the "Plan of Government" incorporated in the speech, and the text of his elaboration of the plan (the "Draft of a Constitution" which he gave to Madison at the end of the Convention), there is also a set of notes by Hamilton himself—or, rather, two sets of notes, one for the former part of the speech and another for the latter part.

In considering the latter part of the speech, where Hamilton takes up the question of the form of the general government, we must not neglect to take into consideration the former part of the speech, which treats the question of federal union, the problem of more perfectly uniting states only feebly united in a confederation of great extent. We must not forget the context of the discussion: the speech was not a discourse of political philosophy. The question of republicanism arose in it as part of the attempt to meet the crisis of federalism: the immediate effect of the speech was to make the Virginia plan seem immensely more choiceworthy than the New Jersey plan, by which it had just been challenged.

Thus, to understand Hamilton's speech of 18 June requires a detailed comparison of the various records, and a detailed consideration of the circumstances into which the speech intervened as a deed. Because this interpretation of Hamilton's work of 18 June, and the argument concerning texts and context needed to support it, would require more extensive treatment than would be suitable here, we must here confine ourselves to Hamilton's subsequent statements. We may take some consolation in the fact that the editor calls it merely "perhaps" the most important address made by Hamilton—and then only "if its importance can be measured by" the discussion which it generated subsequently.

5 Farrand, *Records*, I: compare p. 375 and p. 379. Also compare pp. 375–376 with pp. 379 and 381: Madison conflates Gorham's motion and speech; Yates places Gorham's speech later, immediately before Hamilton's. Farrand says of Madison's report of Gorham's speech: "Substance of this taken from Yates, according to whom Gorham made remarks to this effect later in the debate,—in fact they have no point until after the remarks of Butler and Mason." Farrand, *Records*, I, p. 376, n. 12. Generally speaking, the point of a speech may well appear somewhat different if it is seen coming after the speech of a different man. According to Farrand, Madison, in other speeches on this point, long afterward added to his own notes by borrowing from Yates (Farrand, p. 376) as he did elsewhere in his notes (Farrand, p. xviii). Yates reports a speech on this point by Madison, which Madison himself does not report (Farrand, cf. p. 376 and p. 380). Madison places Butler's remarks before King's; Yates places King's before Butler's (Farrand, cf. p. 376 and p. 379).

6 Constitutional Convention (22 June 1787) P 4:216–217; Farrand, *Records*, I, 375–376,

379–381. Hume: *Essays*, "Of the Independency of Parliament." Also Constitutional Convention (23 June 1787) P 4:217; Farrand, *Records*, I, 386–394. Madison's notes on the 23rd say that Madison renewed his motion of the preceding day, but Madison's Memoranda, preserved with his Debates, note that there is no allusion to it in the notes for that or the three days preceding (cf. p. 386 and p. 390 [including n. 16] of Farrand). As Farrand also points out (p. 390, n. 18), Yates on the preceding day reports no formal motion by Madison but does report a speech by Madison to that effect. On the 23rd Yates does not report a speech accompanying the making of the motion by Madison, but Madison does report one (cf. p. 386 and p. 391 of Farrand) and Yates reports a speech by Madison elsewhere, but Madison does not (cf. p. 389 and p. 392 of Farrand).

7 F76, pp. 513–515; F77, pp. 516, 519.

8 To the Supervisors of the City of Albany (18 February 1789) P 5:257–258. To the Electors of the City of New York (7 April 1789) P 5:322–325. See also New York Assembly (19 January 1787) P 4:11–12.

9 See Henry Jones Ford, *The Rise and Growth of American Politics* (New York, 1967; reprint of 1898 edition), chap. 17, p. 215; Frank J. Goodnow, *Politics and Administration* (New York, 1967; first published 1900), chap. 5, pp. 109–110, and chap. 6, pp. 133–134.

10 To Edward Carrington (26 May 1792) P 11:426–429, 442–444.

Jefferson himself reports a conversation with Hamilton in Philadelphia the previous summer. Jefferson notes that he put down in writing, the moment Hamilton left the room, the substance of Hamilton's much longer declaration, which seemed more formal than was usual for a private two-man conversation—as if Hamilton intended to qualify some less guarded expressions dropped on former occasions.

The present occasion was this: Early in the year Paine's *Rights of Man* had been published in England, and Jefferson, reading it in May, had forwarded it for reprinting, with a favorable note which the printer used in the preface. This quoted Jefferson as writing that he was extremely pleased that by the reprinting something would at length be publicly said against "the political heresies which have sprung up among us." These political heresies, Jefferson later made clear, were found in John Adams's *Discourses on Davila*, which Philadelphia newspapers had serialized. In June a Boston newspaper printed a series of letters, signed "Publicola," which attacked Paine's views and supported those of Adams. Although in fact "Publicola" was John *Quincy* Adams, the author was believed to be John Adams by most people, including Jefferson. So it was that on 13 August 1791 Jefferson mentioned to Hamilton a letter from John Adams disavowing "Publicola" and denying ever having entertained a wish to bring this country under a hereditary executive or to introduce a hereditary branch of legislature, etc. It was in response to this that Hamilton made his declaration to Jefferson.

Jefferson reports that Hamilton condemned Adams's writings and most particularly *Davila* as having a tendency to weaken the present government and declared *in substance* as follows: My own opinion, said Hamilton, is that the present government will not answer the ends of society by giving stability and protection to its rights, and it will probably be expedient to go into the British form. I own this to be my own opinion, though I do not publish it in Dan and Beersheba. Since we have undertaken the experiment, I am for giving it a fair course, whatever my expectations may be. Indeed, the success so far is greater than I had expected, and therefore success seems at present more possible than it did before now; and if the present government does not succeed, other and yet other stages of improvement ought to be tried before we give up the republican form altogether—because that mind must be really depraved which would not prefer the equality of political rights which is the foundation of pure republicanism, if it can be obtained consistently with order. Therefore, however pure the intentions (and I am sure, said Hamilton, that the intentions of Adams were pure), nonetheless, whoever by his writings disturbs the present order of things is blamable. Jefferson's notes (13 August 1791) P 9:35–36.

11   Washington to Hamilton (29 July 1792) P 12:129–133. To Washington (18 August 1792) P 12:228–229. To Washington, Enclosure: "Objections and Answers respecting the Administration of the Government" (18 August 1792) P 12:251–254, 258.

12   "An American" no. 1 (4 August 1792) P 12:159–160, 163–164; no. 2 (11 August 1792) P 12:193.

13   P 12:356, n. 1. Amicus (11 September 1792) P 12:354–355. Hamilton's account of the Convention's reasons for secrecy was as authoritative as could be: he had, after all, been one of three men appointed by the Convention to prepare its "standing rules and orders" ([25 May 1787] P 4:159).

Hamilton's editor notes that Hamilton here "may be referring to the vote on the tenure of the presidency. On July 17, 1787, the delegations from New Jersey, Pennsylvania, Delaware, and Virginia voted in favor of amending the clause to change the presidential term of office from seven years to 'during good behavior.' . . . Among the members of the Virginia delegation present on that day were James Madison, George Mason, and Edmund Randolph" (P 12:357, n. 4).

For Madison on the proceedings of the Convention and the publication and interpretation thereof, see, in *Letters and Other Writings of James Madison* (Philadelphia, 1865): To Thomas Ritchie (15 September 1821), 3:228–229; To John G. Jackson (27 December 1821), 3:243–247; To Joseph C. Cabell (2 February 1829), 4:10–11.

14   P 12:379, n. 2; Catullus no. 3 (29 September 1792) P 12:504–506; also see P 12:501–504, which is where Hamilton, referring to Jefferson, speaks of the time "when characters studious of artful disguises are unveiled"; "When the vizor of stoicism is plucked from the brow of the Epicurean; when the plain garb of Quaker simplicity is stripped from the concealed voluptuary."

For Jefferson on Jefferson as an Epicurean, see Thomas Jefferson to William Short (31 October 1819): "I too am an Epicurean. I consider the genuine (not the imputed) doctrines of Epicurus as containing everything rational which Greece and Rome have left us."

In this All Hallow's Eve letter, Jefferson tells us not only what of rational moral philosophy has been left to us by classical antiquity, but also what we owe to Jesus: "a supplement of the duties and charities we owe to others" has been left to us by "Jesus. . . . Abstracting what is really His from the rubbish in which it is buried . . . as separable from that as the diamond from the dunghill."

On Christmas Eve of Jefferson's first year as President, Hamilton came out with the third number of his eighteen-piece critical examination of Jefferson's first annual message to Congress, signed "Lucius Crassus." In this attack on Jefferson, as was shown in note 26 to chap. II, above, the term "epicurean" is again used pejoratively by Hamilton, speaking of rulers who, being "indolent" and "temporizing," convert into an exclusive dogma the beneficial general rule that liberates private enterprise from too much public regulation. This conversion deprives private enterprise of the stimulation of beneficial public enterprise. The exclusive rule of laissez-faire is the rule of rulers who are neither vigorous nor provident, but who play with words to amuse themselves and others when there is work to do. The Epicurean attitude does not stimulate in the man who would be governor the provident energy that good government requires. A man who governs well does not believe the government to be best which governs least. The true ruler's ruling passion cannot be the love of ease.

Compare the quotation from Locke, in chap. II, sec. iv, above, on "the great art of government" and on "that Prince who shall be so wise . . . as by established laws of liberty to secure protection and incouragement to the honest industry of Mankind."

Jefferson, indeed, right after his remarks on Epicurus in the letter cited, says: "Epictetus, indeed, has given us what was good of the Stoics; all beyond, of their dogmas, being hypocrisy and grimace. Their great crime was in their calumnies of Epicurus and misrepresentations of his doctrines." It might be said that Jefferson sides with the Stoic position insofar as it can be combined with that of Epicurus.

At p. 169 of *Natural Right and History* (Chicago: University of Chicago Press, 1953), Leo Strauss writes of the connection between Epicurus and "a doctrine which has revolutionized human life everywhere on a scale never yet approached by any other teaching"; Hobbes is said to be "the creator" of this doctrine, by siding "with Cato against Carneades" while joining "the Epicurean tradition"; this doctrine is said to "belong together" with a certain "distinctly modern phenomenon" and to constitute an "epoch-making change" that was "well understood by Edmund Burke," who speaks in his *Thoughts on French Affairs* of how the modern heirs of Epicurus are "of a character nearly the reverse" of their forbears, who were "unenterprising": "of late they are grown active, designing, turbulent, and seditious."

For Hamilton on Hobbes, see the beginning of chap. III, above. See also note 36 to chapter II, above (which, however, it is best to read together with the paragraphs of text to which notes 33, 34, and 35 of that chapter are attached. For Hamilton on the distinctly modern phenomenon which belongs together with the doctrine of Hobbes the creator and which supports the French "plan to disorganize the human mind itself, as well as to undermine the venerable pillars that support the edifice of civilized society," see Titus Manlius no. 3 (7 April 1798) P 21:402–405; on this, see the present chapter's note 18, below; also see, at pp. 738–741 of P 26, Views on the French Revolution (1794). For Hamilton on the zealotry of those who conduct the modern war against the old-time zeal, see pp. 585–586 of P 17, The Cause of France (1794), quoted in note 33 to chap. I, above. For Hamilton on diverse American views of the French Revolution, see Americanus no. 1 (31 January 1794) P 15:670–671, and Titus Manlius no. 2 (4 April 1798) P 21:390–391. For Hamilton on the change in American attitude, and on the importance of estimating rightly the French Revolution, see The French Revolution (1794), at pp. 586–588 of P 17. See also note 17 to chap. III (with the body of the text to which the note is attached), above; and see, in the Conclusion, below, note 5 and the note before it with the body of the text to which it is attached. Some of these passages are quoted, below, in notes 37 and 38 to the present chapter.

Consider the Address to the Electors of the State of New York (21 March 1801) at P 25:366: "In vain are you told that you owe your prosperity to your own industry and to the blessings of Providence. To the latter doubtless you are primarily indebted. You owe to it among other benefits the constitution you enjoy and the wise administration of it, by virtuous men as its instruments. You are likewise indebted to your own industry. But has not your industry found aliment and incitement in the salutary operation of your government—in the preservation of order at home—in the cultivation of peace abroad—in the invigoration of confidence in pecuniary dealings—in the increased energies of credit and commerce—in the extension of enterprise ever incident to a good government well administered. Remember what your situation was immediately before the establishment of the present constitution. Were you then deficient in industry more than now? If not, why were you not equally prosperous? Plainly because your industry had not at that time the vivifying influences of an efficient, and well conducted government."

15 P 12:252; To — (26 September 1792) P 12:480; To — (21 September 1792) P 12:408. Statement by Hamilton as to his motives in meeting Burr (1804) L 8:626–629; To Mrs. Hamilton (10 July 1804) L 8:629–630. This was Hamilton's last letter to his pious wife, one of whose nicknames had been "The Saint"; in the letter Hamilton says that if he is killed by Burr, it will be because religious scruples keep him from firing at Burr in a duel that political considerations keep him from refusing. There were political considerations that could also keep him from firing, but a wish to give effect to them would keep him from saying a word about them. For earlier statements on dueling, see: Account of a Duel between Major General Charles Lee and Lieutenant Colonel John Laurens (24 December 1778) P 1:602–604; To William Gordon (5 September 1779) P 2:154; To Nathaniel Mitchell (20 July 1787) P 4:226–227; To William Pierce (20–26 July 1787) P 4:228; To Colonel Moore (18 September 1799) L 6:227–228.

16 Tully no. 3 (28 August 1794) P 17:160. To James A. Bayard (26 August 1800) P 25:58.

17 To — (8 November 1796) P 20:376–377; To John Jay (7 May 1800) P 24:464–466.

18 To James A. Bayard (16 January 1801) P 25:323; To Oliver Wolcott, Jr. (December 1800) P 25:287; To Gouverneur Morris (13 January 1801) P 25:315; To James A. Bayard (16 January 1801) P 25:323.

"In reviewing the disgusting spectacle of the French revolution," Hamilton finds it "difficult to avert the eye entirely from those features of it which betray a plan to disorganize the human mind itself, as well as to undermine the venerable pillars that support the edifice of civilized society" (for which, see note 14 to this chapter, above), and he says that though "latterly the indications of this plan are not so frequent as they were," yet "from time to time something still escapes which discovers that it is not renounced"— an example of this being "the late address of *Buonaparte* to the Directory"; he then calls Bonaparte "That unequalled conqueror, from whom it is painful to detract; in whom one would wish to find virtues worthy of his shining talents" (Titus Manlius no. 3 [7 April 1798] P 21:402–404). With this, compare, in chap. I, above, note 4 (taken together with the body of the text to which it is attached). See, below, the present chapter's note 38.

19 To James A. Bayard (16 January 1801) P 25:319–320, 322–324.

20 To The New York Evening Post (24 February 1802) P 25:536–538 and 538, n. 1.

21 To Timothy Pickering (18 September 1803) L 8:607–608.

22 Madison to J. K. Paulding (April 1831), *Letters and Other Writings of James Madison* (Philadelphia, 1865), 4:176–177. The following point should be noted in comparing the Draft of a Constitution with the earlier Plan of Government. In the Draft the ninth section of Article IV concludes with these words about the executive: "He shall hold his office during good behaviour removeable only by conviction upon an impeachment for some crime or misdemeanor" (P 4:262). This was also the arrangement provided earlier in Articles IV and IX of the Plan incorporated by Hamilton into his speech to the Convention (P 4:208 and 209); but in the autograph Draft, the words after "He shall hold his" are inserted in the margin, where they are preceded by the letter "A" (P 4:262, n. 9).

Is this an indication of some thought by Hamilton of modifying the executive sketched in the Plan so that the version in the Draft would incorporate opinions presented in the Convention subsequent to the presentation of the Plan?

The text of the Draft of a Constitution reprinted by Hamilton's editors is the autograph draft in the Manuscript Division of the New York Public Library. Madison made a copy of the Draft of a Constitution; it is in the Madison Papers of the Library of Congress. The Hamilton Papers of the Library of Congress contain another copy of the Draft—this one in an unidentified handwriting. The Hamilton Papers of the Library of Congress also contain a facsimile copy, as does the John C. Hamilton Transcripts collection: these two facsimiles, say the editors, "at first glance appear to be in H's writing" but "close examination . . . reveals minor variations of the sort a copyist might make while attempting an exact duplicate of a draft"—"A plausible reason for the existence of the facsimiles has not been found." P 4:253, n. 1.

23   Gouverneur Morris: Diary entry (13 July 1804), in *The Diary and Letters of Gouverneur Morris*, ed. Anne Cary Morris (New York, 1970), 2:456, chap. 44.

24   Gouverneur Morris to Aaron Ogden (28 December 1805), ibid., 471–475, chap. 45.

25   Gouverneur Morris: Diary entry (18 January 1804), ibid., 454, chap. 44.

26   Gouverneur Morris to Robert Walsh (5 February 1811), ibid., 523–531, chap. 47.

27   Morris to Walsh, ibid., p. 524. Hamilton to Gouverneur Morris (19 May 1777) P 1:255— in reply to: Gouverneur Morris to Hamilton (May 1777) P 1:253–254.

The young Hamilton disagreed with Morris's central point, Hamilton thinking it "very disputable" to say "that instability is inherent in the nature of popular government," even though "unstable democracy" is an epithet "frequently" heard. With reference to the new constitution for the State of New York, Hamilton agreed with Morris's first point: Hamilton agreed "That there is want of vigor in the executive" and commented that "To determine the qualifications proper for the chief executive Magistrate requires the deliberate wisdom of a select assembly, and cannot be safely lodged with the people at large." Hamilton also agreed with Morris's last point: Hamilton agreed "That the complexity of your legislature will occasion delay and dilatoriness," but he differed from Morris in his comment on the point. Morris had said in apology that "a simple legislature soon possesses itself of too much Power for the Safety of its Subjects." Hamilton said that he thought that the delay arising from the complexity of the legislature was not much of an evil, "as expedition is not very material in *making* laws, especially when the government is well digested and matured by time"; but Hamilton also said that he thought that "the danger of an abuse from a simple legislature would not be very great, in a government where the equality and fulness of popular representation is so wisely provided for as in yours," and that the "much greater evil" which he feared might arise from the complexity of the legislature was "that in time, your senate, from the very name and the circumstance of its being a separate member of the legislature, will be liable to degenerate into a body purely aristocratical."

28   New York Ratifying Convention: Notes for speech (12 July 1788) P 5:149–152.

29   Morris to Walsh, *Diary and Letters*, pp. 524–525.

30   To Timothy Pickering (18 September 1803) L 8:607–608. See also F1, p. 3.

31   To Gouverneur Morris (29 February 1802) P 25:544–546. This letter was a reply to the letter from Gouverneur Morris to Hamilton (22 February 1802) P 25:527–529, the context of which was the controversy over repeal of the Judiciary Act—for which, see chap. XII, below. On 11 February 1802 Hamilton at a meeting of the New York City

bar argued against memorializing Congress even though the contemplated repeal of the Judiciary Act was an unequivocal violation of the Constitution in a most vital part—see P 25:520–527 for versions of his remarks. A week and a half later Morris wrote to say that he was sorry that Hamilton had opposed sending the petition. The next day the twelfth number of Hamilton's Lucius Crassus papers was published (for which, see chap. XII, sec. ii, below); a week later Hamilton replied to Morris in the letter quoted above (the letter, dated 27 February 1802 by earlier editors, is, in the definitive edition of Hamilton's *Papers*, dated 29 February 1802). In this letter Hamilton thanks Morris for his frankness and explains why he not only believes he himself was right but would pursue the same course if the matter were to be done over: if the bar memorialized Congress, this would not be useful as a preventive; to express opinion by letter would, for the people, be as good as doing so by a memorial; a letter was best because it "saved our delicacy," and "I am not over fond of the precedent of the bar addressing Congress"; "But I did what I thought likely to do more good—I *induced* the Chamber of Commerce to send a memorial." Hamilton goes on in the letter to speak more generally of his own public position, in the words quoted above, and, praising Morris for speeches in the Senate against repeal of the Judiciary Act, he closes the letter by speaking more generally of his friend's public position, in words also quoted above.

Between these two gloomy assessments of how out of place the two men are, Hamilton wrote the following words, occasioned by the proposal, made in Morris's letter, that a general meeting of the citizens of New York be called to consider constitutional measures to meet the dangers that were threatening. At such a meeting, Morris had said, there might be appointed a large committee composed chiefly of merchants, and such a group of intelligent and moderate men selected from the first by the people might become a Committee of Correspondence that would work with other such Committees to defend the Constitution. Hamilton rejected Morris's plan, counseling his hasty friend as follows: "The suggestions with which you close your letter suppose a much sounder state of the public mind than at present exists. Attempts to make a show of a general *popular* dislike of the pending measures of the Government would only serve to manifest the direct reverse. Impressions are indeed making but as yet within a very narrow sphere. The time may ere long arrive when the minds of men will be prepared to make an offer to *recover* the Constitution, but the many cannot now be brought to make a stand for its preservation. We must wait awhile." Within two months, Hamilton, preparing for the making of an offer of constitutional recovery that the many would not then refuse, was at work on plans to build an engine that might work upon the minds of many men; the many, he had hopes, if properly prepared might yet be brought to make a stand that would preserve their republican constitution. See, in the present chapter, below, the plan outlined to Bayard and its sequel. Compare Morris, quoted above, in the text to which the present chapter's note 26 is attached, beginning with the words "Luckily, or to speak with a reverence proper to the occasion, providentially. . . ."

32 To Tobias Lear (2 January 1800) P 24:155. Washington to John Jay (1 November 1794); Colonel John Nicholas to Washington (22 February 1798). To William Short (5 February 1793) P 14:7.

33 To William Hamilton (2 May 1797) P 21:78. On leaving office, Hamilton drafted a defense of his financial plan, in which, discussing the first part of the plan, the assumption of state debts, he gave the following account (Defence of the Funding System [July 1795] P 19:22–26, 29–30, 40–43):

The theory of our constitution in respect to taxation was an example new in the world: in it there was concurrent and coordinate authority both in one general head and in many distinct members united under that head. Something new in the world had to be done in America because the only alternative to proposing something new in the world was to propose either something intrinsically unwise or something unwise to propose in the existing state of things because unlikely to obtain consent. Under this new arrangement, the objects of the Union could be effected only if the members were under as little necessity as possible of exercising the power of taxation.

On the other hand, if the debt were *left* to the states, then the government in its infancy, before habit and opinion were engaged in its favor, would not be exposed to the clamor and unpopularity of resorting to modes of taxation less agreeable than duties on imposts. Avoiding this inconvenience might have had many benefits for the country, and it surely had many charms for the person who was to propose a plan. But there were decisive considerations that argued *for* assumption.

The *least* of these, however, was the tendency of assumption to strengthen the number of ligaments between the government and the interests of individuals. The great inducements, rather, were chiefly that it would give simplicity and energy to the national finances, would avoid the collisions of multifarious and conflicting systems, would secure to the government for national exigencies the complete command of the national resources, and would consolidate public credit.

Hamilton nonetheless discusses at length the feeblest motive—because of its importance as an objection in the view of those who feared the overbearing power of the general government, and who in declamations represented the assumption as a premeditated plan to overthrow the governments of the states. Assumption would have been an inefficacious means for strengthening the infant government by gaining supporters as suggested—because it imposed upon the government the necessity of resorting early to unpalatable modes of taxation which jeopardized its popularity and gave to its enemies a handle for attacking it. Only the personal popularity of Washington made it feasible to risk the immediate unpopularity of the modes of taxation which assumption made necessary. However, if these revenues had not been introduced at the beginning, the delay would have made it more difficult to introduce them later. The very delay in establishing them might have been construed as an implicit condemnation of them. Thus, assumption was not a device to purchase immediate popularity: it was, among other things, a device for drawing on an extraordinary reserve of popularity to introduce immediately unpopular measures whose long-term efficacy for satisfying popular wants would only eventually increase the popularity of the government of the United States. The first part of Hamilton's plan as Secretary of the Treasury involved an act not so much of cunning as of fortitude.

See, in chap. VIII, above, note 17.

34   To Jonathan Dayton (October–November 1799) P 23:599–604.

35   Lucius Crassus no. 17 (20 March 1802) P 25:576; F26, p. 164.

36   To James A. Bayard (6 April 1802) P 25:587–588; James A. Bayard to Hamilton (12 April 1802) P 25:600–601. We have already considered the earlier letter to Bayard (16 January 1802) in which Hamilton opposed the Federalist inclination to elevate Burr rather than Jefferson.

37   To James A. Bayard (16–21 April 1802) P 25:605–610.

For a long time, for seven years at least, it had been Hamilton's opinion that "If there be any thing solid in virtue—the time must come when it will have been a disgrace to have advocated the Revolution of France in its late stages" (The French Revolution [1794], at p. 588 of P 17). In P 26 (though also dated 1794), at pp. 738–741, may be found the following Views of the French Revolution, scrutinizing the virulent germs that sent out poisonous roots not yet eradicated and sent up shoots from which grew deadly fruits.

Hamilton writes: "the present AERA is among the most extraordinary, which have occurred in the history of human affairs. Opinions, for a long time, have been gradually gaining ground, which threaten the foundations of Religion, Morality and Society. An attack was first made upon the Christian Revelation; for which natural Religion was offered as the substitute. The Gospel was to be discarded as a gross imposture; but the being and attributes of a GOD, the obligations of piety, even the doctrine of a future state of rewards and punishments were to be retained and cherished.

"In proportion as success has appeared to attend the plan, a bolder project has been unfolded. The very existence of a Deity has been questioned, and in some instances denied. The duty of piety has been ridiculed, the perishable nature of man asserted and his hopes bounded to the short span of his earthly state. . . . Irreligion, no longer confined to the closets of concealed sophists, nor to the haunts of wealthy riot, has more or less displayed its hideous front to all classes.

"Wise and good men took a lead in delineating the odious character of Despotism; in exhibiting the advantages of a moderate and well-balanced government, in inviting nations to contend for the enjoyment of rational liberty. Fanatics in political science have since exaggerated and perverted their doctrines. Theories of Government unsuited to the nature of man, miscalculating the force of his passions, disregarding the lessons of experimental wisdom, have been projected and recommended. These have every where attracted sectaries and every where the fabric of Government has been in different degrees undermined.

"A league has at length been cemented between the apostles and disciples of irreligion and of anarchy. Religion and Government have both been stigmatised as abuses; as unwarrantable restraints upon the freedom of man; as causes of the corruption of his nature, intrinsically good; as sources of an artificial and false morality, which tyrannically robs him of the enjoyments for which his passions fit him; and as cloggs upon his progress to the perfection for which he was destined.

"As a corollary from these premises, it is the favourite tenet of the sect that religious opinion of any sort is unnecessary to Society; that the maxims of a genuine morality and the authority of the Magistracy and the laws are a sufficient and ought to be the only security for civil rights and private happiness.

"As another corollary, it is occasionally maintained by the same sect, that but a small portion of power is requisite to Government; that even this portion is only temporarily necessary, in consequence of the bad habits which have been produced by the errors of ancient systems; and that as human nature shall refine and ameliorate by the operation of a more enlightened plan, government itself will become useless, and Society will subsist and flourish free from its shackles.

"If all the votaries of this new philosophy do not go the whole length of its frantic creed; they all go far enough to endanger the full extent of the mischiefs which are inherent in so wild and fatal a scheme; every modification of which aims a mortal blow at the vitals of human happiness.

"The practical development of this pernicious system has been seen in France. It has served as an engine to subvert all her ancient institutions civil and religious, with all the checks that served to mitigate the rigour of authority; it has hurried her headlong through a rapid succession of dreadful revolutions, which have laid waste property, made havoc among the arts, overthrown cities, desolated provinces, unpeopled regions, crimsonned her soil with blood and deluged it in crime, poverty and wretchedness; and all this as yet for no better purpose than to erect on the ruins of former things a despotism unlimited and uncontrouled; leaving to a deluded, an abused, a plundered, a scourged and an oppressed people not even the shadow of liberty, to console them for a long train of substantial misfortunes, of bitter sufferings.

"This horrid system seemed awhile to threaten the subversion of civilized Society and the introduction of general disorder among mankind. And though the frightful evils, which have been its first and only fruits, have given a check to its progress, it is to be feared that the poison has spread too widely and penetrated too deeply, to be as yet eradicated. Its activity has indeed been suspended, but the elements remain concocting for new eruptions as occasion shall permit. It is greatly to be apprehended, that mankind is not near the end of the misfortunes, which it is calculated to produce, and that it still portends a long train of convulsion, Revolution, carnage, devastation, and misery.

"Symptoms of the too great prevalence of this system in the United States are alarmingly visible. It was by its influence, that efforts were made to embark this country in a common cause with France in the early period of the present war. . . . It is by its influence, that every succeeding revolution has been approved or excused . . . —that even the last usurpation, which contradicts all the ostensible principles of the Revolution, has been regarded with complacency; and the despotic constitution engendered by it slyly held up as a model not unworthy of our Imitation.

"In the progress of this system, impiety and infidelity have advanced with gigantic strides. Prodigious crimes heretofore unknown among us are seen. The chief and idol of"—the uncompleted fragment here breaks off. See, below, the present chapter's note 38.

38 James A. Bayard to Hamilton (25 April 1802) P 25:613.

Midway between the time he wrote the essay that presents Views of the French Revolution (left uncompleted) and the time he wrote the letter to Bayard that outlines the plan for a Christian Constitutional Society (rejected as inapplicable), Hamilton wrote a series of papers urging his "countrymen" to make a "stand" in "manful vindication" of their "rights and honor": "The despots of France are waging war against us," he declared; we must "resist," he said—indeed we must "resist with energy" (Titus Manlius no. 1 (30 March 1798) P 21:382, 385–386). In the midst of the series, the third number, turning briefly from the immediate purpose, begins with the remark that "In reviewing the disgusting spectacle of the French Revolution, it is difficult to avert the eyes entirely from those features of it which betray a plan to disorganize the human mind itself, as well as to undermine the venerable pillars that support the edifice of civilized society."

Hamilton then turns his eye to look upon such features. These are of two sorts.

In the *first* place, "The attempt by the rulers of a nation to destroy all religious opinion, and to pervert a whole people to Atheism, is a phenomenon of profligacy reserved to consummate the infamy of the unprincipled reformers of France"; "The proofs of this terrible design," says Hamilton, "are numerous and convincing"; he then presents some of "the dreadful proofs of a conspiracy to establish Atheism on the ruins of Christianity—

to deprive mankind of its best consolations and most animating hopes—and to make a gloomy desert of the universe."

In the *second* place, he says, "Equal pains have been taken to deprave the morals as to extinguish the religion of the country. . . . [A] new law of divorce . . . makes it as easy for a husband to get rid of his wife, and a wife to get rid of her husband, as to discard a worn out habit. To complete the dissolution of those ties, which are the chief links of domestic and ultimately of social attachment, the Journals of the Convention record with guilty applause accusations preferred by children against the lives of their parents."

He then says about all these things that he has mentioned, what almost goes without saying, that "The pious and the moral weep over these scenes as a sepulchre destined to entomb all they revere and esteem." He goes on to speak of a person of another designation: "The politician, who loves liberty, sees them with regret as a gulph that may swallow up the liberty to which he is devoted. He knows that morality overthrown (and morality *must* fall with religion) the terrors of despotism can alone curb the impetuous passions of man, and confine him within the bounds of social duty." "But," he then abruptly says, "let us return to the conduct of revolutionary France towards other nations, as more immediately within our purpose." Titus Manlius (7 April 1798) P 21:402–405.

39 Josiah Quincy to John Quincy Adams (23 November 1840).

XI Independent Judgment

1 New York Ratifying Convention: Notes for Speech (12 July 1788) P 5:151. F81, p. 542.

2 F78, pp. 521–522, 530.

3 F78, pp. 529–530.

4 F78, p. 522, referring to F76–77; cf. F72, p. 486. F81, p. 544.

Consider also Federalist 51 (claimed by both Hamilton and Madison), where the following argument is made: The preservation of liberty requires that power be partitioned, and this requires that each department's members be appointed as independently as possible of every other's. To insist rigorously on the principle of independent appointment might be inexpedient in the constitution of the judiciary department in particular. This principle in full rigor would require the appointments to be simply independent, but the difficulties in this require deviations. The manner of their being chosen distinguishes the judges: they alone of the members of the three departments are chosen by the members of one of the other departments. That seems to be the only way to avoid the difficulties and expense of drawing their appointments from the people somehow, while also ensuring that they have the qualifications which distinguish the judges, for they alone must have acquired special learning by previous training. However, although the primary consideration, the qualifications which distinguish them *before* being appointed, make them, *in* being appointed, dependent on another department, nonetheless, the permanent tenure that distinguishes them *after* being appointed must, soon after that, destroy all sense of dependence on the other department that has appointed them. F51, p. 348.

5 F78, pp. 522, 529; F79, pp. 531–532.

Hamilton observes that the Convention made a difference between the President's compensation and that of the judges: the former can neither be increased nor diminished, the latter can not be diminished (but may be increased); this probably arose from the differences in the duration of the respective offices, he says. From the remark Hamilton then makes, it seems that there is more prudence and efficacy in expecting men to resist the promise of gain than to resist the threat of loss—the former requiring only tolerable, the latter extraordinary, fortitude. F79, pp. 521–532.

6   F78, pp. 524–527.

7   F78, pp. 524, 527–528.

8   Few may be aware, says Hamilton, how much influence this will have upon the character of our governments. On the benefits of institutionalizing the anticipation of some resistance to evil, see also the mention of the forcible though silent and unperceived operation of the executive's power of a qualified negative on legislation (F73, p. 498). And consider the suggestion that the importance of the judiciary is not measured by the number of cases it handles. (Lucius Crassus no. 5 [29 December 1801] L 7:224–228).

9   F78, pp. 527–529.

10 F78, pp. 522–524. Hamilton's quotations from Montesquieu are both from *L'Esprit des Lois* XI.6.

11 F78, pp. 522–524. F79, pp. 532–533.

12 F73, pp. 494, 498–499; F78, pp. 522, 530. The use of the term "the administration of government" in "its largest sense" is distinguished from its use in "its most usual and perhaps . . . its most precise signification" at F72, p. 486; for an instance of use of the term "the administration of justice," see F78, p. 530.

13 F81, pp. 542–543.

14 F81, p. 542.

15 F81, p. 543.

16 F81, p. 544.

17 F81, pp. 543–544.
    In order to insist upon their point, "the authors of the objection must renounce the meaning they have labored to annex to the celebrated maxim requiring a separation of the departments of power. It shall, nevertheless, be conceded to them, agreeably to the interpretation given to that maxim in the course of these papers, that it is not violated by vesting the ultimate power of judging in a *part* of the legislative body. But though this be not an absolute violation of that excellent rule; yet it verges so nearly upon it, as on this account alone to be less eligible than the mode preferred by the convention." F81, p. 543.
    "The same contradiction is observable in regard to this matter, which has been remarked in several other cases. The very men who object to the Senate as a court of impeachments, on the ground of an improper intermixture of powers, advocate, by implication at least, the propriety of vesting the ultimate decision of all causes, in the whole, or in a part of, the legislative body." F81, p. 542.

18 The case against locating the supreme court in the legislature is also the case against the supreme court's acting like a superlegislature.

19 F81, p. 544.

20 F81, pp. 544–545.

21 F81, pp. 542, 545.

22 F81, pp. 542, 545.

23 F81, pp. 545–546; F79, pp. 532–533.

24 F81, p. 546; F65, pp. 439–443.

XII Partisanship, Partiality, and Parts of Government

1 Lucius Crassus no. 5 (29 December 1801) L 7:224–228.
2 Lucius Crassus no. 12 (23 February 1802) L 7:265–266, 271; no. 16 (19 March 1802) L 7:301.
3 Lucius Crassus no. 16 (19 March 1802) L 7:303.
4 Lucius Crassus no. 17 (20 March 1802) L 7:307–308.
5 Lucius Crassus no. 14 (2 March 1802) L 7:283–284.
6 Lucius Crassus no. 14 (2 March 1802) L 7:284–288.
7 Lucius Crassus no. 15 (9 March 1802) L 7:290–295.
8 Lucius Crassus no. 15 (9 March 1802) L 7:288–289, 296–297.
9 Lucius Crassus no. 16 (19 March 1802) L 7:299.

Jefferson, years later, in the letter in which he said that "The Revolution of 1800 was as real a revolution in the principles of our government as that of 1776 was in its form," construed the Constitution on the judiciary thus: the judiciary is only one of three departments, and it is "that one too" which is "unelected by, and independent of the nation"—but "experience has already shown . . . that . . . impeachment . . . is not even a scare-crow," and "whatever power in any government is independent, is absolute also; in theory only, at first, while the spirit of the people is up, but in practice, as fast as that relaxes. Independence can be trusted nowhere but with the people in mass. They are inherently independent of all but moral law." Hence, said Jefferson, "each department is truly independent of the others, and has an equal right to decide for itself what is the meaning of the Constitution in the cases submitted to its action; and especially, where it is to act ultimately and without appeal." Otherwise, the Constitution "is a mere thing of wax in the hands of the judiciary, which they may twist and shape into any form they please." Thomas Jefferson to Spencer Roane (6 September 1819).

10 Lucius Crassus no. 17 (20 March 1802) L 7:304.
11 Lucius Crassus no. 17 (20 March 1802) L 7:304–306.
12 Lucius Crassus no. 17 (20 March 1802) L 7:308–309.
13 Lucius Crassus no. 17 (20 March 1802) L 7:310–312.

XIII Partisanship, Partiality, and Popular Liberty

1 Kent's remark is quoted by Julius Goebel, Jr., ed., *The Law Practice of Alexander Hamilton: Documents and Commentary* (New York and London, 1964), 1:848, n. 130 (hereinafter this work will be cited as LP). Kent made the remark at the convention called in 1821 to amend the New York State Constitution of 1777; Kent later wrote his celebrated *Commentaries on American Law*. The reviewer of Waite's version of Hamilton's oral argument is quoted in LP 1:793, n. 62.
2 Kent, LP 1:833.
3 Fifteen Propositions on the Law of Libel (February 1804) LP 1:840; Waite's version of argument in Croswell case, LP 1:809; Kent's notes on the argument in Croswell case, LP 1:833; Fifteen Props., LP 1:840; Waite, LP 1:811–812; Kent, LP 1:834; Waite, LP 1:810; Kent, LP 1:833; Fifteen Props., LP 1:841.
4 Fifteen Props., LP 1:840; Waite, LP 1:810–811; Kent, LP 1:833–834, 837; Waite, LP 1: 822–823; Kent, LP 1:836; Waite, LP 1:811; Kent, LP 1:834; Fifteen Props., LP 1:840–841.
5 Waite, LP 1:832–833, 815, 833; Kent, LP 1:839.

6 Waite, LP 1:829; Kent, LP 1:839.

7 Consider Hamilton's only quotation of the Preamble in *The Federalist*: "'WE THE PEOPLE of the United States, to secure the blessings of liberty to ourselves and our posterity, do *ordain* and *establish* this constitution of the United States of America'" (F84, p. 578). Compare the quotation with the original.

8 Kent, LP 1:839; Waite, LP 1:830–831; Kent, LP 1:838, 839–840, 839, 838.

XIV   Return to First Principles

1 F47 (Madison), p. 323; F78, p. 521; F83, p. 558; F84, p. 575.

2 F83, p. 562.

3 F83, pp. 562, 564–566, 568–570.

4 F83, pp. 572–574.

5 F83, pp. 563–564.

6 F83, pp. 562–564.

7 F83, pp. 562, 574.

8 F84, p. 575.

9 F84, pp. 578–579.

10 F84, p. 579.

11 F84, p. 580.

12 F84, p. 580 n., pp. 578–579.

13 F84, pp. 581, 575–578.

14 F30, p. 188; F34, p. 212.

Conclusion

1 Lucius Crassus no. 12 (23 February 1801) L7:266.

2 See note 17 to chap. I; notes 7, 12, and 13 to chap. II; and notes 6 and 16 to chap. III. Also in order would be reflection on the places where this book presents Hamilton's religious and anti-Jacobin statements.

3 To Timothy Pickering (21 February 1799) P 22:492–493—in reply to: From Timothy Pickering to Hamilton (6 February 1799) P 22:473–474. Pickering, the Secretary of State, had asked Hamilton to advise him what to advise Toussaint, who would declare Santo Domingo's independence from France if the United States would allow of a free commercial intercourse: Toussaint would listen to a practicable and efficacious plan for administering the government of the island, which could not be a republic, said the Secretary of State. Hamilton sketched for him the features of a plan.

4 In reply to a letter from Lafayette implying that, though Lafayette's engagements did not permit him to follow the fortunes of the republic of France, yet Lafayette's attachments had never been separated from the fortunes of that republic, Hamilton differed from his friend, in the words quoted above. But he assured Lafayette of his own enduring friendship for him, as well of America's; the only thing in which our parties agree, he said, is to love Lafayette. When Lafayette replied with a justification of his political conduct amid revolutions and vicissitudes, Hamilton wrote back that no explanation of Lafayette's political principles was necessary to satisfy Hamilton of the perfect consistency and purity of Lafayette's conduct; it was needless to detail to Lafayette his own political tenets—he would only say that he held with Montesquieu what is quoted above. To Marquis de Lafayette (28 April 1798) P 21:450–451; from Marquis de Lafayette to Hamilton

(12 August 1798) P 22:73–76; to Marquis de Lafayette (6 January 1799) P 22:404. For Montesquieu: *De l'Esprit des Lois*, I.3. See also: The Farmer Refuted (23 February 1775) P 1:104, 121–122, 164–165; Second Letter from Phocion (April 1784) P 3:557. Also see note 17 (with the body of the text to which it is attached) in chap. III, above.

Also see Titus Manlius no. 2 (4 April 1798) P 21:396, 393: "in blowing up the dreadful flame which has overwhelmed Europe in misfortune, France is the party principally culpable"; "the prominent original feature of her revolution is the spirit of proselytism, or the desire of new modelling the political institution of the rest of the world according to her standard"; "The republic of America, no less than the despotism of Turkey, was included in the anathema."

5   To Oliver Wolcott, Jr. (29 June 1798) P 21:522.

Hamilton on the menace with its capital at Paris and on how to deal with it: the French must be supposed, upon the evidence, to have "a plan to acquire an absolute ascendant among nations"; . . . "the supposition does not imply the intention to reduce all other nations formally to the condition of provinces. This was not done by Rome in the zenith of her greatness. She had her provinces and she had her allies. But her allies were in fact her vassals. They obeyed her nod. Their princes were deposed and created at her pleasure. Such is the proud pre-eminence to which the ambition of France aspires." "Revolutionary France has been and continues to be governed by a spirit of proselytism, conquest, domination and rapine." . . . "[W]hat is to be done? Shall we declare war? No—there are still chances for avoiding a general rupture which ought to be taken. Want of future success may bring the present despots to reason. Every day may produce a revolution which may substitute better men in their place and lead to honorable accommodation. Our true policy is, in the attitude of calm defiance, to meet the aggressions upon us by proportionate resistance, and to prepare vigorously for further resistance. This course, it will be objected implies a state of war. Let it be so. But it will be a limited and mitigated state of war, to grow into general war or not at the election of France. What may be that election will probably depend on future and incalculable events. The continuation of success on the part of France would insure war. The want of it might facilitate accommodation. There are examples in which states have been for a long time in a state of partial hostility without proceeding to a general rupture." Titus Manlius no. 4 (12 April 1798) P 21:414–415; no. 6 (19 April 1798) P 21:434, 437–438. See also in chap. II, above, the quotation from "Titus Manlius" given in note 13 and the quotation from "The Cause of France" given in note 33.

For Hamilton on error in opinion about "the Revolution in France in its late stages," see The French Revolution (1794) P 17:588: "The error entertained is not on a mere speculative question. The French Revolution is a political convulsion that in a great or less degree shakes the whole civilized world and it is of real consequence to the principles and of course to the happiness of a Nation to estimate it rightly."

For the continuing importance of estimating rightly the French Revolution in its Jacobin culmination, we have the testimony of no less a figure than the man whose name succeeded that of Peter in the city formerly known as Petersburgh: see the conversations recorded by "Nikolay Valentinov" in the central chapter of his memoirs, *Encounters with Lenin*.

6   F70, pp. 471–472—right after this example from Roman history: "how often that republic was obliged to take refuge in the absolute power of a single man, under the formidable title of dictator."

Index

Harvey Flaumenhaft is tutor at St. John's College in
Annapolis, Maryland.

Library of Congress Cataloging-in-Publication Data
Flaumenhaft, Harvey, 1938–
The effective republic : administration and constitution in
the thought of Alexander Hamilton / Harvey Flaumenhaft.
Includes bibliographical references and index.
ISBN 0-8223-1214-X (cloth)
1. Political science—United States—History.
2. Republicanism—United States—History. 3. Hamilton,
Alexander, 1757–1804—Contributions in political
science. I. Title.
JA84.U5F59 1992
320.473—dc20   91-30952 CIP